Along the Towpath

A Journalist Rediscovers the Ohio & Erie Canal

Al Simpson

Edited by Russ Musarra

University Libraries
Akron, Ohio

Published by The University of Akron Libraries in partnership with the Ohio & Erie
Canal Corridor Coalition and the Ohio & Erie Canal Association.

Edited by Russ Musarra

Illustrated by Chuck Ayers

Cover art by Chuck Ayers

Design and Layout by Stephen Paschen

The University of Akron Libraries
The University of Akron
315 Buchtel Common
Akron, Ohio 44325-1701

Table of Contents

Foreword

A Dream Becomes a Reality

This book represents Al Simpson's nearly six-year effort to generate and sustain public interest in restoration of the Ohio & Erie Canal. His series, "Along the Towpath," appeared in the *Canton Repository* from the fall of 1964 through early 1970 and is republished here with the newspaper's permission.

Ideally, the editors would have presented the series as Simpson wrote it, word for word. There were more than 170 columns, plus other news articles and editorials, which, he noted in a Nov. 11, 2002 letter on the matter, "fanned the flames of public interest in the canal restoration." But such a body of work was far more than could feasibly be included in one volume. So the editors did their work carefully and judiciously, reducing the word count where possible, but always mindful of retaining the author's "voice."

Simpson's writings chronicle the beginning of the grassroots movements to save the state-owned canal lands for public recreational use. As Simpson wrote, Ralph Regula, first as Village Solicitor of Navarre and later as a member of the Ohio Legislature, spoke as an advocate for preserving the lands for public use. Both were leaders in Stark County in what at the national level became a movement that resulted in the National Historic Preservation Act of 1966.

Along the Towpath provides important historic documentation of canal-lands preservation. The columns and articles tell the story of visionaries, of volunteerism, canal-boat builders, trail advocates and canoeists — all interested in maintaining and protecting green space. It is important to recognize the contributions of these articles and the people and activities they describe; this is the origin of the canal renaissance. These individuals and organizations are ultimately the leaders that help make the Heritage Corridor. It took about 20 years for the vision of Al Simpson and Ralph Regula to become institutionalized in the formation of the Ohio & Erie Canal Corridor Coalition and another eight for U.S. Rep. Regula to lead the successful passage of the authorization for 25 National Heritage Corridors, including the Ohio & Erie Canal National Heritage Corridor.

The Simpson and Regula vision is gradually coming to fruition as each new mile of the Towpath Trail is completed between Cleveland and New Philadelphia (about 65 miles of 110 as of January 2003). This book is also part of their vision, to preserve for future generations the story of the beginning of the "ribbon" of recreational space and resources preserved for the benefit of all.

The book is a cooperative effort between the University of Akron and The Ohio & Erie Canal Corridor Coalition. The committee that moved the newspaper version to this book is comprised of Russ Musarra, editor; Delmus Williams, dean of the University of Akron Libraries; Dan Rice, executive director of the Ohio & Erie Canal Corridor Coalition; and Lynn R. Metzger, University of Akron, anthropologist and coordinator of the project.

The committee is grateful to the *Canton Repository* for permission to use the columns, articles and editorials. The originals are on microfiche in the Canton Public Library. The photocopies of those originals and all the materials relating to this book are in the University of Akron Archives. We are also grateful for the assistance of Leslie Baus and Michael Kolsky for their exacting work of photocopying the originals and typing in the computer, and to Kaye Ketcham for formatting and proofreading.

But, we are especially thankful to Al Simpson, who has been confident in the project, answered a "million" questions and generally cheered us on.

We hope you will enjoy your walk *Along The Towpath.*

— Lynn R. Metzger

Prologue

How the Dream Began

The series "Along the Towpath" began as a simple newspaper assignment and grew into a labor of love, which Al Simpson researched and wrote on his own time after the initial story. The author is passionate about preserving the stories for their historical value and says, "Years from now people can look at that and see how the canal came back and how the corridor came to be because of what was done in those early days..."

It all began when the Navarre village solicitor, Ralph Regula, now the U.S. representative for Ohio's 16th congressional district, told *Repository* managing editor Clayton G. Horn he was going to walk the towpath from Canal Fulton to Navarre to assess its development potential for public use. Ohio was divesting itself of these lands, and local governments — county, city, village and township — had first call. If they didn't take them, the lands would be sold to private owners, something Regula didn't want to happen. He suggested a reporter accompany him on the 16-mile hike. Horn said he had just one reporter who could walk that far.

"That was me," Simpson said in a recent interview at his home near Sperryville, Virginia. "I got the assignment, and that's when I met Ralph. We've become good friends since then... So I went on that walk and wrote a big story and that story started the interest in the canal. A lot of people became aware of it. I became aware of it. I didn't realize the potential either until we took that walk."

That initial meeting "resulted in the establishment of a prized and enduring friendship and a collaboration which fueled the launching of the 'Save the Canal' project in Stark County and expanded the vision of a future state or national canal-lands park," Simpson wrote in 1996, in an article for the *Repository* after the creation of the Ohio & Erie Canal Heritage Corridor.

"As early as 1925, a study of Summit County was commissioned to evaluate the potential for public parks, including some of the Ohio & Erie Canal lands," Simpson wrote. "Although the survey foresaw the possibility of a link with the Cleveland Metropolitan Park System, there was little or no follow-through in the ensuing decades. The canal became a breeding place for mosquitoes, a dumping site for trash, and parts of it were illegally filled in and reclaimed by adjoining property owners. It was not until 1964, when the State of Ohio decided to divest itself of the canal lands it owned for more than 100 years that actions were taken, which sparked the genesis of the Ohio & Erie Canal Heritage Corridor."

Simpson likens Regula's vision for the canal lands to that of George Freeman Pollock, who promoted creation of Shenandoah National Park. He speaks from the perspective of friend and former press aide, a post accepted after he retired from the *Repository*.

"Stark County is where it all began," Simpson wrote, "and the man who, like George Pollock in the mountains of Virginia, shepherded his dream from conception to birth is Congressman Ralph Regula... In my first article about the canal, I wrote these words about Ralph: 'He looks beyond the borders of Stark County and envisions a continuous 309-mile hiking trail along a restored towpath from Lake Erie to the Ohio River.' Today, such a trail is well advanced due to the work of volunteers and local governments from north to south."

Regula sponsored legislation to create the corridor in 1993. It was passed by the House but died in the Senate without coming up for a vote. It took nearly three more years, during which time Regula "became the negotiator between Republicans and

Democrats in Congress and the Clinton administration," for the corridor to become a reality as part of an omnibus parks bill affecting 41 states, Simpson wrote.

"Along the Towpath," which began 51 years after floods and their aftermath put the canal out of business, chronicled these grassroots efforts in minute detail, as Simpson took his readers on hikes and towpath cleanups, introduced them to older residents who shared their recollections of the canal days and profiled such committed citizens as the late Ted H. Findley of New Philadelphia, who headed the Canal Society of Ohio and lovingly shared his expertise with all who asked.

The series "became an excellent vehicle, along with other means, for creating lines of communication between groups in adjoining communities and counties that either were or became interested in the canal restoration project," Simpson wrote.

Looking back today, Regula says he had a dream for the canal and that Simpson did a good job of capturing it.

"He told the story that got the public interested," the congressman said.

Simpson tipped his hat to the late Clayton G. Horn, writing in 1996, "without his endorsement I would not have been able to write my columns and articles, and the *Repository* would not have played its major supportive role." When interviewed, he added, "It was sort of a gift to me, I guess because of my interest, that they let me do it... The support was in that they continued to let me do it."

On May 10, 1964, six months before "Along the Towpath" made its first appearance in the *Repository*, Simpson wrote of that first 16-mile hike. The next day the *Repository* published an editorial endorsing the idea of "saving the Ohio & Erie Canal as a strip of park land, perhaps all the way from Lake Erie to the Ohio River..."

The editorial suggested readers "imagine the year is 2000, with our posterity making second guesses about our decisions... The Ohio & Erie Canal is parkland available for the asking. If no one asks, the land will suffer the fate that awaits everything which lacks guardians and friends in our careless society. It will turn into a dumping ground. Its natural beauty will be destroyed. Its possibilities as a place of refuge from noise, clutter, strife and confusion will be wasted. And most assuredly, posterity will survey the drab consequences and curse us for squandering a part of its heritage."

It was a theme Simpson would often revisit as the series unfolded.

Ralph Regula, tireless promoter of the Ohio & Erie Canal, is pictured here on the left with journalist Al Simpson.

Al Simpson

Book One · 1964

May 10, 1964
Let's Save the Old Canal!
Ohio & Erie Restoration Would Provide Scenic Park

Sixteen miles and 16 million raindrops.

Of these ingredients — and more — this tale is woven.

It is a story of a man and an idea to save the Ohio & Erie Canal — to restore it, beautify it, preserve it and pass it on to future generations, a heritage rich in natural beauty, history and recreational potential.

The story will unfold slowly, like the barges that moved along the canal about which it is written.

A similar story was written 10 years ago about another canal, the Chesapeake and Ohio, and another man, William O. Douglas, associate justice of the U.S. Supreme Court.

This one concerns the Ohio & Erie Canal and Ralph Regula, Navarre attorney and member of the Ohio State Board of Education.

The stories of the two canals and the two men are alike in many ways. The canals are similar in that they were constructed for the same purpose, floating tons of grain, coal, lumber and flour across the face of a lusty growing nation.

The men are similar in that they both are lawyers, both love nature in its primitive state and both are vigorous proponents of conservation programs.

In 1954, Justice Douglas focused the nation's attention on the C&O Canal when he led 36 conservationists and newsmen on an eight-day hike along it.

The waterway's scenic and historic values were threatened with destruction as the result of a proposal to construct a motor parkway along the towpath and, in some places, the bed of the canal. In protest, the towpath march was made and the resulting publicity helped defeat the highway proposal. Shortly afterward, the National Park Service recommended that the canal property be preserved as a national park.

Today the vestiges of the Ohio & Erie Canal are in danger of eradication. To avoid that eventuality, Ralph Regula and other interested persons have initiated action to save the canal lands.

To help publicize these efforts and their purpose, Ralph invited conservation-minded Robert Vail Jr. of Canton and this writer to accompany him on a hike down the Ohio & Erie Canal towpath from the center of Canal Fulton to the center of Navarre, in a trek reminiscent of the walk

taken a decade ago by Justice Douglas and his associates.

It was at this point, as we left the railroad station in Canal Fulton and started down the grassy towpath with spring and bounce in our stride, that the first of the 16 million raindrops fell. And they kept on falling throughout the five-hour-and-45-minute, 16-mile "trudge," "slog" or, better yet, "slosh" through the dripping underbrush and "leaking" trees (measured by a pedometer strapped to Ralph's leg).

Without hats and inadequately dressed for rainy weather, we were soon sodden and remained that way. Once we approached a bridge, expecting to find shelter beneath it, only to find that the roadbed was grillwork, which only slightly retarded the pelting raindrops.

As we walked, Ralph talked of the canal, its present status and his hopes for its future. The matter first came to his attention when, as solicitor for the village of Navarre, he learned that the state of Ohio planned to divest itself of the canal lands in the area.

The state has owned the land more than 100 years. It was given authority to appropriate property for canal construction by a law passed on Feb. 4, 1825.

For 50 or more years, since the last barge passed through the locks in Stark County, this section of the canal lands has been largely undisturbed. The towpath and canal bed remain in a remarkable state of preservation and are clearly defined along most of the route. In Massillon, where the canal has disappeared, future hikers of the canal towpath may easily shift to the grass-crowned levee of the Tuscarawas River.

After Navarre, Canal Fulton and Massillon received notification from the state of the availability of the canal lands, the mayors of the three communities met to discuss a course of action. They decided to recommend to the councils of their respective communities that application be made to the state for title to all canal lands between Canal Fulton and Navarre, the lands to be used for public recreation and parks for all of western Stark County.

State law provides that if the Canal Land Authority "finds that any such canal lands are needed or can be used for public recreation, parks, historical sites, drainage courses, roads and highways, or other projects of public nature, the (authority) director shall cooperate with the directors of other departments of the state... to authorize the use of such lands for such purposes."

The mayors decided that, although restoration and development of the canal lands is a long-term project, it was an opportunity of a lifetime and "the potential of such an oasis in a metropolitan county is a stimulus to the imagination and a test of our ability and cooperation."

Navarre Solicitor Regula said, "We can't lose anything by acquiring title to the canal lands. For even if we do not develop them at the present, this land will be there for future generations. The law provides that government subdivisions adjacent to canal lands get the first opportunity to acquire the lands free of charge. It does stipulate, however, that lands granted to government subdivisions must be used for public purposes. Otherwise, it reverts to the state of Ohio."

Under the law, the alternative to acquisition of the canal lands by public subdivisions, such as the three municipalities or Stark County, would be the sale of the canal to adjacent private landowners, some of whom are already using part of the canal lands without authority. Sale of any part of the canal in Stark County would break the continuous trail through the county.

Compromise Reached

After Massillon and Navarre requested title to the canal lands (Canal Fulton decided it preferred to have the county commissioners assume title), Perry Township, through its trustees, requested title to all of the canal within its borders, outside the city of Massillon.

This presented the state with counter claims as Massillon and Navarre had planned to divide between them the land the township was now requesting. Faced with this problem, the state advised the subdivisions to try to reach an agreement with regard to their requests. At this point, the whole idea was withering on the vine.

Then, at the crucial moment, Regula suggested that the Stark County commissioners take over all canal lands available in the county outside of the three communities.

Navarre and Massillon withdrew their requests and, following a meeting of representatives of the various subdivisions, it was agreed that the commissioners would take over all the lands outside the communities, subject to a reservation in favor of Perry Township for the use of the canal lands in the township for a sewage treatment plant if and when the township needed it. County Engineer Joseph A. Sturrett's office is writing a description of lands to be acquired. This will be submitted to the state for approval. After its approval, the governor will issue a deed to Stark County for the land.

Up to this point, Ralph had been maneuvering to get the canal land to preserve it. Now he is hopeful the commissioners will set up a county park authority to develop the lands.

As we walked along through the downpour, Ralph pointed to that possibility and looked far ahead to the year 1980 when Stark County is expected to have 700,000 residents. Observing that Cleveland and Columbus have had to go far outside their municipal limits to purchase property for their park systems because land was not available in the cities, Ralph declared that Stark County is fortunate in this respect.

"People don't know what they have here," he said. "I think, in the years to come, people are going to need places where they can find quiet and seclusion. The canal is one of those things you never pay any attention to. You don't realize what a delightful recreational area it could be. I have lived in this community (Navarre area) all my life and I've driven past the canal hundreds of times. You just don't see the possibilities until you see it through new eyes."

Through those eyes Ralph sees a grassy hikers' path extending from the Summit County line approximately 28 miles to the Tuscarawas County border, through natural wilderness abloom with wild flowers and inhabited by a multitude of birds. The towpath trail could also be used by bicycle riders and equestrians.

"People ought to get out on their feet," Ralph said.

Dodging between the raindrops, briars and water-laden branches, I agreed, adding, "Especially on nice sunny days."

Endorsing everything Ralph said, I held out further for rewatering the canal bed wherever possible. As a canoe enthusiast, I could see a delightful 28-mile canoe trail down the waterway with only a few portages. In the winter, it could become a skater's dream reminiscent of the canals in Holland.

It Will Need Work

As it stands today, the canal is not altogether pretty. In some places, where people have used its banks for a dump, it is downright ugly. But underneath it all, its potential beauty shows through. It needs only restoration to make it a thing of consummate beauty.

As we sloshed along, impressions came thick and fast, nurtured by what we saw: skunk cabbage; old whiskey bottles and detergent bottles floating in the canal; beds of mist-moistened violets; golden patches of wild mustard; wild onions; the Tuscarawas River, always dirty and always to the right of us; campfire ashes left by fishermen; waterfowl flushed from the canal; the delicate white blossoms of the wild plum trees; spring beauties underfoot; beds of Dutchman's-breeches; the songs of many birds singing in the rain.

Despite the dismal conditions under which we were exploring the canal, Ralph remained optimistic. Passing a grove of dead elms, gaunt, gray and grotesque in the early morning mist, Ralph blithely observed: "One good thing about them, the pileated woodpeckers love them."

On several occasions, he declared, "There's no limit to what could be done, absolutely no limit."

He looks beyond the borders of Stark County and envisions a continuous 309-mile hiking trail along a restored towpath from Lake Erie to the Ohio River.

For this to become a reality, each county along the way would have to accept responsibility in a manner similar to that planned in Stark County.

This could, in time, result in a hiking trail comparable to the Appalachian Trail, which extends from Maine to Georgia, and the trail along the Chesapeake and Ohio Canal, which hugs the Potomac River and extends 185 miles from the Alleghenies to tidewater.

But the Ohio & Erie Canal would have its own distinctive Ohio beauty and history.

A decade ago, when Justice Douglas and other conservationists fought to save the "waterway to Washington," many critics scoffed at the government's purchase of the 5,254 acres of C&O canal lands for $2 million. They called it a "century old white elephant." Others, more farsighted, suggested it might turn out to be "the biggest bargain since Alaska."

New life now looms ahead for the derelict C&O Canal and already a 23-mile section from Washington to Seneca has been restored by the government as part of the National Capital Parks System.

Great Falls Tavern, historic hostelry and lockkeeper's home, has been refurbished and made into a museum. Thousands of visitors pass through its doors each year to view exhibits tracing the history of the canal.

Even as the dry bed of the C&O follows the tortuous bends of the Potomac, so, in a remarkable parallel, the bed of the Ohio & Erie follows the sweeping bends of the Tuscarawas.

Civic-minded people of one canal town along the C&O have cleared the canal and the state has stocked it with pan fish. Hundreds of kids drop in their lines during an August fish rodeo. It is the town's big picnic day of the year.

Many Could Assist

Stark County's garden clubs, sportsmen's groups, Boy and Girl Scouts, Audubon Society and numerous other civic and service groups could work wonders in the restoration and beautification of the old Ohio & Erie.

Welfare labor, using materials available to the county, could do much of the necessary cleanup work. Through their efforts, the section of the canal south of Canal Fulton, which is under the jurisdiction of the Ohio Department of Natural Resources, has been vastly improved, and is today the most attractive section of the canal in the county.

A *National Geographic Magazine* article on the C&O Canal several years ago concluded with these words:

"The canal has known and survived countless misfortunes and always its admirers have refused to let it slip into oblivion. Converting the canal into a national historical park would win hundreds of thousands of new friends for the old strip. Tomorrow's generations will never see the barge traffic that once graced the lovely canal, but they may follow the old C&O from beginning to end and relive its days of glory."

The vital days of the Ohio & Erie Canal have long since passed. But it, too, can be saved from oblivion, preserved and restored to become — as Justice Douglas said of the C&O — "a refuge, a place of retreat, a long stretch of quiet and peace... a wilderness area where man can be alone with his thoughts, a sanctuary where he can commune with God and with nature."

Henry David Thoreau, the sage of Walden Pond, wrote: "In wildness is the preservation of the world."

There is a long strip of wildness in western Stark County that could do its share of preserving this tiny part of the world from the erosion of a tranquilizer society. It is available, without cost, to Stark County and three of its municipalities.

Stark County has an opportunity to set an example for other canal counties of the state, to lead the way in accepting responsibility for its section of the old canal and restoring it for the benefit of all Ohioans.

If we fail to expend our energies today, to acquire, use and preserve these lands, we will surely fail to reap the potential benefits inherent in a canal lands park.

In some far distant time then, geologists or archaeologists may stumble on a vestigial trace of the canal and wonder: "What manner of men lived here?"

June 7, 1964

Restored C&O Canal Shows Ohio Potential

FORT FREDERICK, Md. — We slept last night within bow and arrow distance of an American fort, built here in the Maryland hills 20 years before the Declaration of Independence. The walls of the reconstructed fortress, made entirely of rough stone, reach a height of 20 feet and are 4 feet thick at the base. Built during the French and Indian Wars, the fort occupies a dominating position on North Mountain overlooking the broad Potomac River. In later years, the fort, from its impregnable position, commanded the lines of early American communications below — the Potomac River and the Chesapeake and Ohio Canal.

It is because of the old C&O that we are here. Because Ralph Regula, Navarre solicitor, is imbued with the desire to save the Ohio & Erie Canal from piecemeal distribution, in the hope that it ultimately can be made into an historical-recreational park for the benefit of all Americans, and because I share and encourage his vision, we decided to have a firsthand look at the 185-mile Chesapeake and Ohio Canal.

We took our families with us for a four-day look-see, which was highlighted by an interview with United States Supreme Court Justice William O. Douglas and a meeting with officials of the National Park Service in Washington.

It was Justice Douglas who, almost single-handedly, stepped in at the last moment to save the C&O from passing from the American scene.

The old canal, one of the least altered of all of America's canals, was, legislatively speaking, well on its way to becoming a superhighway when Justice Douglas went into action. He invited two editors, who had written editorials lauding the plan to use the canal bed for a highway, to accompany him on a hike along the entire length of the canal's towpath. Other influential people accompanied the three men.

Following the hike, the editors reversed their position and came out editorially in favor of saving and restoring the Chesapeake and Ohio as a national park.

Twenty-three miles of canal, from Georgetown in the nation's capital to Seneca, Md., have been restored and improved recreationally, and the remaining 162 miles are under federal control. The towpath is maintained the entire distance for hiking.

Further restoration and development has been stymied. Although approved by the Senate, the project has been blocked by the House of Representatives' failure to endorse a bill for this purpose, largely as a result of the position taken by a key member of the House from eastern Ohio.

The full potential of a restored Ohio & Erie Canal unfolds like the flowers that bloom along its banks in the spring — after one has explored the C&O.

At Oldtown, Maryland, a 5-mile stretch of the canal, including several locks, has been restored by the village's sportsmen's club and is suitable for hiking, bicycle riding, boating and fishing.

Near Paw Paw, West Virginia, the canal tunnels through a mountain. More than half a mile long, the tunnel still is considered an engineering marvel. Walking through the subterranean chill along its rebuilt towpath in near darkness, the hiker emerges into a picturesque mountain canyon reminiscent of the scenic mountain trails of the West.

When the canal builders reached the Monacacy River in Maryland, they built the largest of the canal's 12 stone aqueducts to carry the water of the canal across the river. Built of stone from nearby Sugar

5

Loaf Mountain, the aqueduct remains in a fine state of preservation. Lack of funds prevents its rewatering as a canoeway.

Stark County also once had an aqueduct to carry the Ohio & Erie Canal across the Tuscarawas River near Bolivar. Its stone piers can still be seen from State Route 212.

In the lovely Potomac plantation country northwest of Washington, Great Falls Tavern, an historic hostelry, has been converted into a museum that annually attracts thousands of visitors. In its canal-bank setting of lock-gate waterfalls, the white colonial museum is one of the most attractive sights along the C&O.

At Seneca, one of the most recreationally developed sites along the canal, bicycles may be rented for cycling up and down the towpath. Many boats are anchored along an inlet of the Potomac River and some may be rented for boating and fishing.

One of the more picturesque stone lock-tender houses, of the many along the C&O, is in danger of toppling. It is being held in position by huge timbers until it can be repaired more permanently.

Near Hancock and Spring Gap, Maryland, the skeletons of two canal boats are rotting at the bottom of the nearly dry canal bed. Inquiry of local residents enabled us to locate them.

In Georgetown, a modern-day "Canal Clipper" plies a section of the canal, passing through restored locks. It is chartered by many groups and organizations. Recently, one of the area schools held its prom on the "Clipper." The students danced during the four-hour, mule-powered cruise.

Can the Ohio & Erie Canal become another Chesapeake and Ohio? It is nearly twice as long. It is scenic. It is historic. And it belongs to Ohio.

Justice Douglas, in telling us of the fight to save the C&O, said, "The dominant opinion in Maryland is now in favor of the restoration of the canal and in making it a hiking path and canoeway."

The old C&O has been saved. It belongs to the United States government and thus to all the people.

But the Ohio & Erie remains to be saved. Some of it is gone forever. But most of it is still the property of the State of Ohio. However, unless it is acquired by other political subdivisions, the state plans to dispose of it. It is to prevent this and to save the canal lands for posterity that Ralph Regula is working.

The Navarre solicitor says there are three kinds of canal fever: the malaria-type, which afflicts the men who build the canals; the get-rich-quick fever, which struck investors who were lured into financing uneconomic canals; and the modern-day canal fever, which infects people with the idea of preserving the big ditches as combination historic-recreational parks.

Ralph has a good case of the latter fever and I'm running a high temperature myself.

Actually, we hope it's catching!

6

State Officials Find Stark Canal Plan Exciting

Canal Offers Opportunity For Splendid Park System

Stark County received encouraging news today pointing to state support of its plan to save the Ohio & Erie Canal lands and make them into a recreational-historical park.

Fred E. Morr, director of the Ohio Department of Natural Resources, after meeting in Columbus with Ralph Regula, Navarre solicitor and State Board of Education member, agreed to assist in the acquisition and development of the canal by the Stark County commissioners. The director termed the proposal to convert the old canal lands into a park system an exciting opportunity for outdoor recreation, of interest not only to the county but to the entire citizenry of Ohio.

"The program of Gov. James A. Rhodes for acceleration of park and recreational developments has gained by the efforts of Mr. Regula and the Stark County commissioners," he declared. "These historically important and beautifully natural sites are rapidly being lost for public use through the increased housing developments, highway and industrial usages following the rapid population growth in our state."

Mr. Regula also met with Alfred C. Gienow, director of the Ohio Department of Public Works; Sherman L. Frost, executive secretary of the Ohio Water Commission, and Ned E. Williams, chief engineer of the Department of Natural Resources.

Following the conference and a brief meeting with Gov. Rhodes, Mr. Regula commented, "I am extremely pleased with the great interest shown by Gov. Rhodes and Fred E. Morr... in the Stark County canal lands."

The final paragraph of the news story from the Nevada Test Site read:

"An Atomic Energy Commission spokesman termed the test a complete success. The reason for the test: to see how atomic energy might some day be applied to canal digging."

The headline was small — for here, in populous Ohio, it seems unlikely that atomic energy will ever be employed to bludgeon out a canalway.

After all — Ohio has an extensive canal system, although it hasn't been used as a canal for half a century. The Ohio & Erie Canal, extending from Cleveland to Portsmouth, and the Miami & Erie, reaching from Toledo to Cincinnati, exist today in varying degrees of preservation.

Still, great changes could be wrought in the state canal lands, albeit without the benefit of atomic energy.

Ohio, using the two canals as a skeleton, could flesh out a recreational-historical-educational park system that would surpass in size, beauty and usefulness any similar park system existing in the nation today.

And Stark County has the opportunity to become the canal lands showplace of the state. It can make of its 20-mile stretch of canal a showpiece of canal restoration, beautification and utilization — an example for other counties to follow.

Most of the Ohio & Erie Canal is in restorable condition. Some of it is gone forever and some sections would be impracticable to reconstruct. But great stretches, covering hundreds of miles, await only the magic touch of restoration to become a statewide asset of significant value.

Stark County could set the pace. To put "flesh" on its part of the state-long park skeleton, Stark County has numerous possibilities for canalside parks.

North of Canal Fulton, near the northern border of the county, Lake Lucern, now privately owned, could become an excellent state park if purchased by the state. The 42-acre lake, with surrounding land, has great potential as a wildlife area, tent and trailer campground, stopover for hikers, launch spot for canoe caravans, and picnic grounds. Its waters, if properly controlled, could be used to rewater the canal north to Summit County.

Canal Fulton Community Park, which adjoins the canal, is already attractive and could be made more so.

South of Canal Fulton, at Lock 4, site of the only restored canal lock in the county, the State Department of Natural Resources has jurisdiction over a small but scenic park, which currently enjoys considerable patronage by picnickers. Here, on a set schedule, the lock could be operated for the benefit of the public.

Just south of Massillon, 760 acres of farmland belonging to Massillon State Hospital lie between the canal and U.S. Route 21. Of the 760 acres, 220 are in pasture, 90 in woodland and 450 under cultivation. There are two cottages and three barns on the farm.

Although the new Route 21 and the proposed U.S. Route 30 by-pass will pass through this tract, it is large enough to provide a great number of tent and trailer sites for towpath hikers, canoeists and vacationing motorists desiring to camp on the high bluff overlooking the canal.

Farther south, the village of Navarre and Bethlehem Township have established a community park with various recreational facilities, which could become the fifth link in Stark County's canal lands parkway.

A sixth park might be created on the slopes surrounding "Wildcat Basin," a widened section of the canal (now dry) in Bethlehem Township, which once served canalmen as a watery "turntable" for their boats.

The terminal park, at the southern border of the county, could be on the Stark County side of the remaining stonework of the old aqueduct that carried the canal across the Tuscarawas River — the border between Stark and Tuscarawas counties at this point. If, at some future time, the aq-ueduct could be rebuilt to serve its original purpose, this park would become a key park in the statewide system.

This is a suggested blueprint for a Stark County canal lands parkway.

Ambitious plan? Perhaps, but not necessarily.

Of the seven parks described, only three would require purchase of land from private owners. If exorbitant prices were demanded for this land, other, less expensive sites, could be selected or, as a last resort, condemnation action could be taken. Arrangement by cooperation among various divisions of the state government, and between the county and other subdivisions, could make the other four sites available, possibly without cost.

Perhaps the state could best achieve a vast canal lands park system by maintaining ownership of all canal lands and granting the canal counties complete jurisdiction to restore and manage the canal within their respective boundaries.

Friendly competition between counties, in their efforts to make their sections of the canal the best in the state, could result in a magnificent park system without equal.

The potential of such a parkway for Stark County and, on a larger scale, for Ohio is difficult to estimate. It could bring national recognition to the state and could be used as a model for the development of other waterway parklands across the nation.

On July 4, 1825, canal construction began in Ohio with great enthusiasm at the Licking summit near Newark. The hundreds of miles of canals constructed in the ensuing years were a great boon to the people of the state until they were superseded by the railroads.

Perhaps today, 139 years later, the canal lands again may become a boon to the residents of Ohio — a recreational, historical and educational bonanza — a heritage from the past.

Naturalists Back Plan
Canal Lands Park Potential Praised

What is the potential of the proposed canal lands park?

Clayton Lakes, fish management supervisor of District 3 of the State Division of Wildlife, says: "I don't know any area that has more potential. The canal is a real family recreation area."

Describing the proposed canal lands park as a backyard vacation spot, he admitted he was "amazed at the quality and quantity of fish" netted and returned to the canal in recent testing operations near Canal Fulton.

Observing that fishing in the canal will fall off as hot weather warms the relatively shallow water (four to five feet), he revealed some of the division's stocking statistics.

Ten thousand fingerling bass and 1,000 northern pike about an inch long were placed in the canal this year, with a total of 3,000 having been stocked in the last three years. Some larger fish found, including walleyes, are believed to have come from Nimisila Reservoir in Summit County.

Ronald C. Miller, district supervisor of District 3, said his Akron district headquarters will "cooperate whenever possible to provide recreation for the people of the State of Ohio. People are beginning to hunt and fish in shifts, particularly fishermen."

A canal lands park would be "great for Boy Scouts qualifying for merit badges," he noted. "With all the trees labeled, the towpath would be an excellent nature trail. It also would be a bird watcher's paradise. It is ready-made for school outings. The buses could drop the kids off at one access place along the canal and pick them up at another access park some distance away. The pupils couldn't get away from the teacher and, like going through a funnel, they would come out at the other end of the towpath, having learned their nature lesson along the way."

Just what is the potential of the canal lands park?

Ralph Regula, Navarre solicitor who sparked the move to save and preserve Stark County's canal lands, says, "Exploration of Stark County's canal lands inspires a vision of a wilderness ribbon joining parks that combine history, education and recreation. These natural areas would provide countless hours of pleasure for residents of our communities for little expenditure of travel time and money."

The potential — if not unlimited — is certainly tremendous.

November 22, 1964

Along the Towpath

There are those who believe — and say — that efforts to restore Stark County's newly acquired section of the Ohio & Erie Canal will falter, diminish in fervor and gradually disappear. The canal, they say, ultimately will dry up completely, fill with weeds and trees, erode and disappear — because no one will care.

There are others who are working steadily, thoughtfully and with a great deal of zeal to recreate the canal, wrest it from its present state of disuse and abandonment and make it into the core of a county or metropolitan park system.

The latter group visualizes a canal parkway extending from the Summit County line just south of Clinton 25 miles to the Tuscarawas County line west of Bolivar, interrupted only by the city of Massillon and the village of Navarre.

This group sees historical and educational values and recreational benefits in large measure to be derived from such a park system.

Its initial efforts to prevent the canal lands from being broken up and sold to private and commercial interests have succeeded in Stark County and the county now has title to the canal lands.

The magnitude and duration of efforts to resurrect the canal will rest with the Stark County commissioners, their canal lands advisory committee and, in the final analysis, with the people of Stark County, who may be called upon to support the development of the canal parkway through passage of a countywide levy.

This column, appearing from time to time, will endeavor to chronicle the progress, report the obstacles and, in general, keep the residents of Stark County informed of developments "Along the Towpath."

Up Canal, Down Canal

Last Sunday's summer-like weather, combined with the announcement in *The Repository* that an additional stretch of the towpath between Crystal Springs and Canal Fulton had been cleared for hiking, brought forth towpath strollers in increasing numbers.

Empty cars, which nearly filled the Lock 4 parking area about 4 p.m., indicated their occupants were somewhere up or down the canal from the tiny park. One family was grouped about a cheery fire enjoying an early evening cookout.

Men, women and children, some of them with "walking sticks" picked up along the way, drifted out of, into and through the park. Some were going "up canal" and others "down canal" but all seemed to be enjoying themselves.

Paul S. Marks, who supervises relief workers improving the towpath, asked one group of women and children how they liked hiking along the canal.

"It's real nice," "fine," were their replies.

"They're going to fix it up more, aren't they?"

Through the Brambles

By automobile, by Jeep, by canoe and, most of all, by shanks' mare, Ralph Regula and I have traveled all but one or two miles of the original 25-mile route of the canal in Stark County. Last Sunday we explored the relatively overgrown section extending north from Canal Fulton to Lock 3 at Clinton in Summit County. We had been invited to look over this stretch of the canal bed and towpath by Paul Marks, who has some exciting ideas for the improvement of this section.

Also accompanying us was Ray Simpson of Canton. Ray, who for 10 years as a member of the Sierra Club of California, has made many distance hikes on the mountain and forest trails of California. He acted as leader many times for Sierra Club river trips in California and Utah.

As a member of the American Youth Hostel, he participated in long-distance bicycle trips through Ohio, Michigan and Wisconsin, staying at youth hostels overnight.

Sizing up the Ohio & Erie Canal and its

towpath from the standpoint of a hiker, canoeist and cyclist, and comparing it with other trails and waterways he had traveled, Ray found it potentially "very good." He also saw the possibility of locating a hostel at one of several attractive sites near the canal.

"The Canal Park, if developed, would fit in well with the objectives of all the conservation groups with which I have been associated," Ray observed. "In California, we had to travel many miles to reach the trails, while here people with varied interests can satisfy their recreational desires much closer at hand."

Nearing the end of our hike, Ralph bent over and picked up a king-size seedpod, one of many covering the towpath at the spot. Paul identified it as the pod of a honey locust tree, which, he said, is comparatively rare in Stark County.

"They seem to like it along the canal," he said. "There are a number of them here."

Just one more asset — along the towpath.

November 29, 1964

How Do You Get There?

I had occasion to telephone a local attorney the other day and, as I was terminating the conversation, he said, "I'm glad you called, Al. I was going to call you today. Where is that parking lot near the canal you mentioned in your column?"

"Oh, you mean at Lock 4," I replied.

"Well, wherever you start out to hike the towpath," he said. "I'm thinking of taking the boys out for a hike along the canal Thanksgiving Day."

I gave him directions to the county's attractive Lock 4 park and then thought perhaps others would like them too. So here they are:

Lock 4 is approximately half a mile south of the Canal Fulton village limits, on the west side of Erie Avenue (old Route 21). For those who do not know their way

around Lawrence Township, the best way to get to the park is through Canal Fulton and south on Erie Avenue.

Those coming from the south may prefer to drive north out of Massillon on Erie Avenue, through Crystal Springs and past Butterbridge Road to Lock 4.

There are other places hikers may get on the cleared section of the towpath — at Crystal Springs and in Canal Fulton particularly. But Lock 4, at the present time, is probably the most popular and certainly the most scenic gateway to the towpath.

Troop Hikes Towpath

"They did a little growling towards the end, when they were getting tired. But they enjoyed it enough that they would hike it again. And they were really fascinated by the lock at Lock 4."

This was William R. Lawrence —Scoutmaster of Boy Scout Troop 11 at Christ Community Methodist Church at 35th Street and Cleveland Avenue N. — telling me of the troop's recent all-day hike down the Ohio & Erie Canal towpath from Canal Fulton to Navarre.

Eighteen boys and three leaders made the 16-mile trek on a beautiful fall day. They camped in the village park at Canal Fulton the previous night and started out after breakfast the next morning. They ate their sack lunches near Crystal Springs and arrived in Navarre about 5 p.m. They pitched their tents overnight in the park at Navarre and held church services there Sunday morning. The Scoutmaster observed that the people in Navarre and Canal Fulton were very friendly and cooperative with the Scouts in arranging the weekend trip.

"It was quite an experience for me," Bill said. "It gave me a lot of pride to walk down the towpath and think of all the early Americans who had trod that path ahead of us. I've already told several other troops about it and they indicated they probably will hike the towpath in the spring."

Bill said he hopes to get an official Boy Scout patch authorized for those who hike a required mileage along the canal. And he also hopes to get the Ohio & Erie Canal towpath listed in the trailbook of the Order of the Arrow, a national service

organization affiliated with the Boy Scouts. Including a map in the trailbook and providing information relative to campsites would bring troops from 100 or more miles away to Stark County to hike the towpath trail, Bill declared.

Stark County troops in the past usually have gone to Mansfield for their day-long hikes, Bill explained. But the 19-mile Johnny Appleseed Trail there is 90 percent along roads with very little cross-country hiking. The towpath trail, on the other hand, is nearly all cross-country.

"Our Scouts were pretty tired but they all were proud of themselves for having hiked it," Bill recalled. "I'd recommend it for anyone to try."

Canal Researcher

Members of the Advanced Topics course in history at Malone College must select a subject of special historical interest to them for their individual seminars.

Guess what Robert L. Witmer of Louis-ville, a junior education-history major, chose? Sure, the Ohio & Erie Canal.

Bob is doing his research now in preparation for writing on "The Effects of the Ohio & Erie Canal on the Stark County Area."

"The canal has always intrigued me," Bob says. "I think Mr. Regula (Ralph S. Regula, newly-elected state representative) is right in saying the canal should be preserved."

The Malone student is getting background material on the canal to better understand the waterway's effect on Stark County. But he says information is hard to come by and he wishes he could find more authentic material.

He recently spent a day with Ted Findley of New Philadelphia, president of the Canal Society of Ohio, and plans to spend more time with him. Bob has walked 75 percent of the canal towpath in Stark County, and inspected the canal from New Philadelphia south to Coshocton with Mr. Findley.

"The highways have hurt the canal a lot in Tuscarawas County," he said, "but there are some very nice sections left which could be saved."

In discussing the heyday of the canal, Bob declared, "We can't imagine what things were like then — no roads, nothing — just a wilderness."

One opinion Bob has formed as a result of his study is that Alliance may well have been a bigger city than Canton or Massillon if it hadn't been for the canal. And he wonders what the status of agriculture would be today in Stark and Wayne counties if it hadn't been for the canal.

December 6, 1964
Snowshoes and Snow-Treads

Snowshoes would have been appropriate for towpath hikers the early part of last week — and bicycles with snow-tread tires. But the work of clearing undergrowth from the path went steadily ahead. Another crew of men was added Wednesday, bringing to 12 the number of relief workers engaged in clearing the towpath and canal bank.

In addition to cutting the undergrowth, the men now have started to burn the piles of brush, which accumulated during the dry season. They continue to work in the area between Crystal Springs and Butter-bridge Road.

Canal Skating Planned

The *National Geographic Magazine*, in its December issue, features an article about our nation's capital. The author, in reminiscing about his boyhood in Washington, tells of "the burnt flavor of potatoes roasted in a bonfire on winter nights when we went skating on the Chesapeake and Ohio Canal." He observes that "on winter nights they still skate on the C&O Canal."

At present, skating is not permitted on the Ohio & Erie Canal in Stark County but plans for this healthful winter sport are being made and soon young couples and entire families may be gliding up and down the canal with steel blades flashing. The initial skating area will be north and south of the county's Lock 4 Park. But until the ice is drilled and tested, safety precautions taken and an announcement made, no skating is permitted.

Tells Canal Story

Ralph Regula, cochairman of the Stark County Canal Lands Development Advisory Committee, has made 27 speeches about the canal to as many organizations during the last seven months. He has talked to Rotarians, Lions, Kiwanis clubs, garden clubs, senior citizens, landscapers, Jaycees and school and churchmen's groups.

Interest in Stark County's development of canal lands has spread into neighboring counties and Ralph has addressed groups in Tuscarawas and Summit counties.

My wife, Marion, and I were privileged recently to attend the annual Ladies Night dinner of the Greensburg Lions Club with Ralph and Mary Regula. Ralph was the speaker and his subject was the canal.

Although we didn't realize it until after we arrived at Young's Restaurant on Nesmith Lake, at the outskirts of Akron, the restaurant was an appropriate place for Ralph's talk. Formerly Young's Hotel, the frame building dates back to the canal days and a number of pictures hanging in the lobby of the restaurant show scenes of canal activity.

It is a matter of record that the first canal boat launched on the Ohio & Erie Canal left Akron, July 4, 1827, for Cleveland, 37 miles away.

The canal today, just across the road from the restaurant, is still filled with water. Standing on the front porch at Young's and stretching the imagination a little, one might half expect to see a mule skinner and his team round the bend in the canal with a passenger-laden canal packet in tow, their destination — Young's.

Engineer Plugs Leak

Tony Sturrett, superintendent of new construction for the Stark County engineer, reports the major leak in the canal wall south of Canal Fulton has been plugged and the bank of the canal repaired.

The Ohio Department of Natural Resources' Division of Wildlife hired the county engineer's office to do the work. Using bulldozers and pans, Mr. Sturrett and his men worked nine days to stop the leak and raise the canal wall 2½ feet in the leaking section. They used the same clay-like material that the canal wall originally was built of and they hauled it from the same site. The canal water is now at the highest point it can reach for the present and awaits only dredging to continue on its way toward Massillon.

December 27, 1964

Canals in the News

Despite wintry blasts, skidding temperatures, floods in the West, the war in Vietnam and all the activities of the Christmas season, canals were back in the news in a big way. President Johnson's go-ahead for a new sea-level waterway method of transportation is economically as important today as it was in the heyday of the Ohio & Erie Canal.

Despite the age of the O&E, there still is a great deal of usefulness left in it, although a different kind. Its educational, historical and recreational values were recognized and publicized this year.

Next year, it is hoped, the continuing development of the canal lands will result in greatly expanded use by all segments of the population.

The Ohio & Erie was also in the news, although in an historical way. The *Massillon Evening Independent* reprinted an item from its files of 100 years ago in which it was reported that the canal was (on December 18, 1864) navigable and had been for some days — for skates.

Sixty years ago, a similar item attested to the progress made in the intervening years. It was noted that navigation (not for skates) on the canal had been made possible "by the use of the ice breaker." A fleet of six craft arrived in Massillon all laden with coal for Russell and Co.

Meanwhile, down Florida way, traffic in "America's Venice" is encountering difficulty. A photograph and accompanying explanation in *The Repository* reveals that boaters in Fort Lauderdale are having difficulty finding their way around the city's winding canals. One solution was to put up canal signs like you would street signs.

There's no danger of anyone confusing Stark County's one and only Ohio & Erie Canal with another canal but maybe some signs indicating points of interest along the towpath would prove useful.

From the Mailbag

I received two interesting picture post cards in the mail recently — pertaining to the canal, of course. One was of Jones Locks at Canal Dover (now Dover) in Tuscarawas County and the other was of the Tuscarawas River at Canal Dover.

The picture of the lock shows it in operation with the water halfway up the gates, the lock tender standing in front of his home, the bypass waterfall, the towpath (in excellent condition) and the unspoiled "countryness" of the wooded hills.

A stamp collector had gotten to the cards and removed the stamps long before I received them, but the Canal Dover postmark on one of the cards was clearly distinguishable — July 5, 1912.

The cards were sent to me by Helen Rosenbluh of Canton, and, with her permission, will be added to the growing collection of canal lore in the Stark County Historical Center. Gervis Brady, director of the center, said the historical society will welcome any useful items relating to canal history and will add them to the permanent canal display at the center. This exhibit includes scale models of a canalboat and locks.

Lots of Help

The Appalachian Trail, a 2,050-mile hiking path extending from Maine to Georgia, lies within half a day's drive of more than half the population of the United States.

Stark County's Towpath Trail along the Ohio & Erie Canal extends roughly 25 miles from Summit County to Tuscarawas County. It lies within half a day's driving distance of several million people.

Some 50 hiking clubs and countless individual nature lovers cooperate with the National Park Service in maintaining the Appalachian Trail. Surely, there are many clubs and individuals in Stark County who would enjoy cooperating with the county commissioners in maintaining and improving our canal towpath trail.

Book Two · 1965

January 17, 1965
What! No War Canoes?

We haven't heard of anyone planning to launch an Indian war canoe on the Ohio & Erie Canal this coming summer but things are looking up for increased use of the waterway by conventional canoes.

Take the Byron D. Keller family for instance. The six members of the Canton family hope to buy their own canoe and use it on the canal. The Kellers rented canoes last summer at Turkeyfoot Lake. They needed two to accommodate their family. Then they read about the canoeing possibilities of the canal and decided they wanted their own canoe.

"The kids (Bill, 15; Anne, 13; Jim, 10, and Pat, 6) are just the right age for this kind of family activity," Mrs. Keller says. "Motorboats are so noisy and canoes are so quiet. Besides you get some physical activity yourself, canoeing."

When the Kellers and others put their canoes in the Ohio & Erie this summer, they can expect to find eight miles of navigable water awaiting them. Plans for the immediate future would put water in the canal from the northern limits of Canal Fulton to just north of Massillon.

When they dip their paddles in the water it will have a special meaning for the Keller family. Mrs. Keller's forebears came to this area by way of the Ohio & Erie. Her ancestors settled originally in the Cleveland area after arriving in this country from Germany. Then they came south by canal boat and settled in the Canal Fulton-Massillon area.

Help Wanted

Paul Marks, the man on the front line of the canal reconstruction, has a need — large timbers — the larger the better to reconstruct the footbridges across the canal spillways, which allow excess water to flow into the Tuscarawas River. The bridges are necessary for an uninterrupted towpath.

Somehow he came up with the diagrams and specifications of the original footbridges.

"We'll do the sawing and we'll build the bridges," Paul says, "but we don't have the timbers."

South on the Canal

A longtime Canton resident stopped in the other day to talk canals and show me an interesting lithograph dating back to the canal days.

William H. Bope came to Canton in 1910 and was superintendent in charge of constructing many Canton buildings, including McKinley High School, in the intervening years. Now retired, he raises big tomatoes, which patrons of Bender's Tavern and the Mergus restaurant have been enjoying for 20 years.

But it was the Ohio & Erie Canal that Mr. Bope wanted to talk about, specifically the canal south of here — down in Fairfield County, where he lived as a boy.

Mr. Bope's grandfather, Col. Jacob Bope (who later became a general), built most of the big mills along the canal from Hebron to just south of Columbus. A contractor, he transported his supplies from Cleveland down the canal to Baltimore in Fairfield County.

Now 79, William Bope recalls riding on the canal boats when he was six years old. He recalls that usually, where there was a lock on the canal there was also a mill. Most of them were four or four and a half stories high.

The lithograph was a canal scene — the Baltimore Mills in Fairfield County at lockside. The drawing shows in considerable detail the activity around the mill where grain was ground into flour and feed.

As for the canal in that area today, Mr. Bope says much of it hasn't been eradicated. He particularly calls attention to a scenic stretch from Buckeye Lake into Millersport.

"Each year the Columbus newspapers come out and take pictures of the canal there in the spring," he said. "If you are down that way, don't miss it."

From Timbers to Lithographs

Two items in last week's column brought gratifying response from readers.

The mention that timbers were needed to reconstruct the footbridges across canal spillways resulted in a number of phone calls from people with timbers to offer. Attorney Ben Sebring of Canton was the first to call. He offered a large timber he had stored in his garage. And then David Klamer of Canton Wood Products called to offer timber.

Paul Marks, who is supervising construction, also received a number of calls, and said, "We are extremely pleased at the public response to our request for timbers. This will enable us to begin the bridge project very shortly."

The second item concerned William H. Bope and his black and white lithograph of an early Ohio & Erie Canal scene.

Early this week, I returned from lunch to find a modern (1965) lithograph on fine parchment on my desk. It was a gift from an old friend, George Karinos of Canton. The attractive watercolor scene was of the canal at New Hope, Pa., in the summertime. To any canal buff it would cry out for a frame.

The caption with the lithograph reads: "For years, mule-drawn barges carried freight along the Delaware River to Philadelphia in the waterway known at various times as the Lehigh Navigation Canal and the Delaware Canal Locks. Today barges still carry sightseers along this picturesque passageway in the vicinity of New Hope."

The artist, Howard N. Watson, has made a barge trip on the Lehigh look very appealing. I, for one, would like to "barge" through New Hope someday.

Thanks, George!

O&E in the News

Our own Ohio & Erie was in the news again last week when it was discussed at the annual meeting of the Stark County Regional Planning Commission. State Rep. Ralph Regula and Robert Teater, assistant director of the Ohio Department of Natural Resources, spoke of Stark County's canal lands, their potential and future plans for their development.

The regional planning commission, in its preliminary general development plan for 1985, shows a developed recreation area along the canal from Canal Fulton to Crystal Springs. The remaining stretches of the canal conceivably could be developed in the same manner after 1985, according to the planners.

Those interested in the canal lands development will be pleased with the regional planning commission's preliminary plan for the canal. But there are some among them who visualize and are working toward development of Stark's entire canal strip long before 1985.

Mr. Teater, in discussing the state's plans for possible development of the Hugle Run lake in Paris Township, said the state might also be able to help in some way with the proposal to acquire Lake Lucern at Canal Fulton for multiple-purpose use in the development of the Ohio & Erie Canal parkway.

Senior Citizen Recalls Canal

Most of us who are interested in Stark County's section of the Ohio & Erie Canal and its development as a recreational-educational-historical parkway have never seen it as anything but a dried up, overgrown big ditch — except in the Canal Fulton area, where the canal today must look much as it did in its "youth."

But there are still a few among us, all senior citizens, who remember the canal as it was when it was an operating avenue of commerce.

One gets a bit of an archaeologist's thrill when he finds and is able to talk with one of these eyewitness residents. I was pleasantly surprised the other day, while talking to a fine friend of long-standing, to learn that he was one of those who, as a lad, had seen the canal "living and breathing."

Adam (Ad) Willaman, who lives in North Canton, is a retired foreman at The Hoover Company. One of his many memories associated with the North Canton-Canal Fulton area is the day his father took him to Canal Fulton and he saw a canal boat "just coming into the village."

Ad recalls his father took him by the hand and they went around a corner of a big building and there it was. "The boat looked just about like the one with your canal column," Ad said, "except there was just one horse."

Ad, who will be 88 on his next birthday and does a lot of walking, confided that he wants to see what improvements have been made along the canal.

"Next summer I'm going to walk south on the towpath from Canal Fulton and see how far I can go," he said with a hearty chuckle.

Canal Magazine

The January issue of the quarterly magazine "Towpaths" came to my desk, compliments of The Canal Society of Ohio, which publishes it. The magazine, beginning its third year, keeps the society's membership informed of news involving canals and provides them with historical information about the canal era.

President Ted H. Findley of New Philadelphia, in his letter to the membership, reported on one bit of philanthropy that should help to swell the growing interest in canal lore.

It seems that some of the society's members are subscribing to the magazine for their local libraries. As the society's membership is statewide, this will bring additional canal information to students throughout Ohio.

Ted also reports that a recommendation, advocating restoration of Lock 2 at Akron and the creation of a park around it, has been made to that city's planning commission.

The route of the canal through the center of the city, including its "stairsteps" of 16 locks, is being covered over and filled in. The recommendation pleads that at least this one lock be maintained as a monument to the "Grand Canawl."

Akron, history books relate, owes its existence directly to the Ohio & Erie Canal.

It is a shame that Akron cannot duplicate Georgetown in our nation's capital, where the Chesapeake and Ohio Canal is stepped down through a series of locks, creating much picturesque scenery and preserving a part of a special era in our nation's history.

February 14, 1965
Feet Itch? Maybe It's Canal Fever

The balmy spring-like weather of the past week was all some of us needed to develop a good case of canal fever. The itch that goes with this malady comes on strong in the spring. It's the itch to get out on the towpath and see what's going on along the canal.

Among those hankering to get out and stretch their legs on the towpath are the members of the senior citizens' historical club at the Downtown YMCA.

Mrs. Blossom Perkins, director of the YMCA Senior Center, reports club members are eager to get out and explore the improved canal towpath and the new trails at the Stark Wilderness Center near Wilmot.

"They love to get out like this," Mrs.

Perkins says, "and we go by the busload."

Because of their interest, the senior citizens invited Ralph Regula of Navarre, cochairman of the Stark County Canal Lands Development Advisory Committee, and Ted Findley of New Philadelphia, president of the Canal Society of Ohio, to speak about the history of the Ohio & Erie Canal and the plans for its redevelopment. Friday, they were to hear Prof. Arnold Fritz, president of Stark Wilderness Center, tell about plans for the nature center.

"They want these things to be preserved and they want to help out," Mrs. Perkins said of the club members. "They want to make a contribution to the wilderness center drive and already one project has netted them $35 for their fund."

Mrs. Annie Meiser is historical club chairman and Homer J. Berger is chairman of the club's wilderness center project.

And then there is the active club member who, according to Mrs. Perkins, was a mule skinner on the Ohio & Erie during his youth. I'm looking forward to meeting him.

Boosts Canal Parks

A very nice letter arrived the other day from Mrs. Robert Cook of Navarre. Mrs. Cook is the mother of four active children and a Cub Scout den mother besides.

"We are always looking for a place for a picnic or a hike," she writes, "and I, for one, am looking forward to celebrating the opening of the canal parks and also the wilderness center."

Her letter aptly noted one of the major values of the canal lands park and wilderness center — proximity to hundreds of thousands of urban dwellers:

"These recreational areas, so near to home, make it possible for the kids and I to commune with nature and yet be home to have supper ready for Dad. Add to this the thought of traveling a part of history and it becomes a little more meaningful to children when they study it."

Canalside Resident

Out near the west edge of town, another resident of Navarre well remembers the canal when it was a busy waterway. Mrs. Helen Edwards lives in a 100-year-old home some 50 feet from the canal.

Her father, Marquis Hoagland, was in charge of the state boat that carried crews doing repair work on the canal between Cleveland and Canal Dover. Three of the lots in her present property were called dock lots because the canal freighters would tie up there to load wheat.

Now 75, Mrs. Edwards clearly recalls the canal boats passing her home when she was a girl and young woman.

Although the canal bed adjoining her property has only spring water in it today, she still finds it interesting and looks forward with pleasure to the time when the village carries out its plan to rewater the canal in that stretch.

In the meantime, she has put out a salt lick in her yard and keeps hay on hand to feed the deer that come to the canal to drink the spring water.

"After a heavy snow or in very hot weather they come as close as 15 feet from the kitchen door for bird feed and straw," she says. "And in the hot summer days they come to cool themselves by standing in the spring water in the canal."

February 21, 1965

Bicycle Enthusiasts Eye Towpath

A pair of newcomers to the Canton area are looking forward to spring and the opportunity to enjoy their hobby along the Ohio & Erie Canal towpath.

Gene and Micki Badal are bicycling enthusiasts. They moved to Canton a little over a year ago from Chicago where they enjoyed bicycling on the paths in the parks near Lake Michigan.

Micki, who says bicycling is very popular in Chicago, would like to see the same interest develop here, and she and her husband hope to organize a bicycle club within the New Neighbors League, of which they are members. She envisions a club of more than 100 members, drawn from the Canton, North Canton, Massillon and the

Louisville area, ranging in age from 18 to 50 plus.

Last week Micki was inquiring about the condition of the towpath and the best areas in which to ride bicycles.

Canal a 'Gold Mine?'

Gov. James A. Rhodes has called Ohio's tourist industry "a billion-dollar business" and has named a committee to look into creation of a travel and tourist council to guide and expand the state's tourist industry. He said the state has lost millions of dollars over the years by not advertising its attractions properly.

The Ohio & Erie Canal and its counterpart canal system in the western part of the state represent state-long veins of pure gold from the tourist standpoint. Covered over and hidden in many parts of the state, this canal "gold vein" is only recognized for its true worth where it is exposed — cleaned up and restored as is being done here in Stark County.

Interest has attracted some tourists from distant places — without state advertising.

Restored and rewatered wherever possible, with a series of parks spaced along its length and with a museum established at an eye-catching site, Stark County's section of the old canal could bring untold numbers of tourists to the county.

If all the canal counties would do the same, Ohio would have a remarkable tourist attraction with tremendous money-making possibilities — which today are being overlooked.

Let's turn prospector — uncover the canal "gold vein" and start a gold rush of tourism.

Eyes Tourist 'Gold'

The day after the preceding item was written, an attractive pamphlet came to my attention. The brochure, prepared for Marsh Industries of Dover by the tourist committee of the Tuscarawas County Chamber of Commerce, extols the many attractions of the county.

With text, photographs and map, it makes a visit to the "Cradle of Ohio History" seem very attractive.

Among the 23 locations highlighted on the map are a number of locks on the Ohio & Erie Canal. And in the historical section of the brochure, a paragraph is devoted to telling of the many remnants of the canal to be seen throughout the county, including many original stone locks and the stone piers of the old canal aqueduct across the Tuscarawas River near Bolivar (visible from Route 212).

Perhaps the State of Ohio hasn't yet caught the gleam of canal "gold" but Tuscarawas County's Chamber of Commerce has spotted it.

Items in the News

Village Council at Navarre has authorized Mayor David Meyer to obtain an estimate from W.V. Ames Excavating of Beach City on the cost of dredging the canal bed from the village waterworks garage to the water treatment plant, a distance of approximately 150 yards.

Mayor Meyer, who is a member of the Stark County Canal Lands Development Advisory Committee, says 8 to 10 inches of gumbo on top of the clay-lined bed of the canal must be removed.

After the stretch of canal is rewatered, the mayor said, it will be stocked with fish for the benefit of anglers, young and old.

This rewatered section of the canal, although small, will be the first in the southern part of the county. Questioned about the possibility of extending the rewatered section, Mayor Meyer said the canal could be rewatered north toward Massillon provided a source of water can be found.

One hundred years ago this month, the residents of Massillon were waiting for iron for a new bridge in the community. It was to come from Cleveland but it could not be sent until the Ohio & Erie Canal thawed enough for the canal boats to get through.

And, according to the newspapers of the day, the canal had "a face of solid ice for some two or three months although the weather of the last few days (about February 8-11) had softened it up a bit."

Hint for Hikers

Go to Bolivar. Take Tuscarawas County

Road 102 south a very short distance to Fort Laurens Park, site of Ohio's first fort. Walk south on the Ohio & Erie Canal towpath past three well-preserved locks.

As of last Sunday, the towpath was in very good condition, with only a few fallen branches to step over. The Tuscarawas River, just below and to the left, although muddy, provides many interesting scenes. Set your own pace.

February 28, 1965

Shades of Rip Van Winkle

On a wall of the lobby of Young's Restaurant on Nesmith Lake, at the outskirts of Akron, are hung a number of pictures showing canal scenes during the heyday of the Ohio & Erie. Among the photographs is one showing a lineup of "Merry Oldsmobiles" with their picnicking drivers and passengers.

Come the last Sunday in April, local shutterbugs should be able to duplicate these pictures or perhaps even combine them. For plans are being made by the Canton chapter of the Antique Automobile Club of America to make its first tour of the season (weather permitting) along the Ohio & Erie Canal.

Ray Dodds of Massillon, chapter president, and Jack Ittner of Canton, assistant tour chairman, said plans call for the members to have lunch at Happy Valley Barn near Stanwood and then begin their tour in northern Tuscarawas County or southern Stark County.

The caravan of 20 to 25 vintage vehicles would move leisurely northward toward Canal Fulton, taking in "the sights" along the way. The historical vehicles would stop at points of interest, and to allow their passengers to walk the towpath where it has been cleared and improved.

If there is a Rip Van Winkle anywhere in the western hills of Stark County, and if he should awaken the last Sunday in April, and if he should just happen to see the club's caravan of vintage cars parked alongside the rewatered Ohio & Erie — he could doze off again without the slightest notion that he had been asleep — not for 20 years but for nearly 60.

To a Wanderland

New Philadelphia Kiwanis Club members got the double-barreled treatment at their dinner meeting last week — from the canal buff's point of view that is.

They were privileged to hear two of the state's best spokesmen for preserving and restoring the Ohio & Erie Canal — State Rep. Ralph Regula of Navarre, who gave the main address, and Ted H. Findley, president of the Canal Society of Ohio, who showed color slides of the canal in Stark and Tuscarawas counties.

Two of Tuscarawas County's commissioners were present and heard Mr. Regula's convincing arguments for obtaining title to the canal lands from the state.

With nearly 40 miles of canal, including a dozen locks and long stretches of picturesque scenery, Tuscarawas County has the potential for an even more beautiful canal parkway than Stark County.

Joined together into a 65-mile wanderland — terrific, just terrific!

19th Century Map

Jack Leggett, a fellow scribe on *The Repository* staff, showed me a nifty little pocket map the other day. Its red hardback folder was trimmed in gold and the map inside was even more colorful.

I carefully unfolded the map and saw that it was published in Philadelphia, Pa., 133 years ago. It was a "Map of the States of Ohio, Indiana & Illinois and part of Michigan Territory compiled from the latest Authorities" — as they existed in 1832.

The population of all the counties in each of the states was listed on the inside of the cover. It was interesting to note that Stark County's population was 27,784, Tuscarawas' was 14,298 and that Cuyahoga, including Cleveland, had only 10,361 residents.

The only communities shown in Stark County were Canton, Kendall (now Massillon), Osnaburg (East Canton) and Hamburg (near present Waynesburg).

But the canal routes were presented

loud and clear.

The explanation at the bottom of the map showed only state capitals, "county towns," "canals existing or in progress" and "proposed canals." The legend said nary a thing about roads or highways.

The Ohio & Erie Canal, shown in red ink, is the most prominent physical feature shown in the interior of the state.

March 7, 1965

Who'll Be First To Build Canal Boat?
Navarre, Fulton or Massillon?

Let's dream a little bit — about the Ohio & Erie Canal and its reconstruction. It's actually happening. The canal is being reconstructed.

Here in Stark County, plans and work are advancing steadily. It has been the hope of those most dedicated to the preservation of the canal that Stark County could make a showpiece of its canal lands, in the belief that the other counties would be stimulated to restore their sections of the canal. "Seeds" were planted — speeches were made, articles were written, key individuals were contacted — and already those seeds are bearing fruit.

From the south (Tuscarawas County) came news last week that the New Philadelphia Kiwanis Club is backing the canal project and has requested the Tuscarawas commissioners to obtain title to the canal lands in that county. Members of the Tuscarawas County Chamber of Commerce's tourism committee have expressed interest in the potential tourist appeal of the canal.

From the north (Summit County) comes news that the Akron Planning Department is studying a proposal to develop a park and historical site along part of its canal lands. Plans call for dredging the canal bed, turning Lock 17 into a working lock, creating a museum for canal history, constructing a typical canal bridge to serve as a footbridge and building a replica of a canal boat.

All of these proposals coincide with plans already programmed by the Stark County Canal Lands Development Committee, which serves the county commissioners.

Stark County's rewatered canal sections will soon provide it with an 8-mile stretch that can be navigated by a canal boat. This county thus has a jump on its neighboring counties to the north and south. But unless a boat is constructed soon, this lead time may quickly disappear.

Tuscarawas or Summit could then be the first to have a canal boat plying the old watercourse.

Surely there must be organizations in Stark County that would enjoy building an authentic canal boat that could be used all summer to transport local residents and tourists from Canal Fulton and Massillon to Crystal Springs.

I can see it now — the canal packet "Massillon" pulling into Crystal Springs and discharging its passengers who then transfer to the "Canal Fulton" for the remainder of the trip to the village for which it was named.

While we are dreaming, let's go a little further. Let's consider rebuilding the old aqueduct, which carried the canal across

the Tuscarawas River at the Stark-Tuscarawas county line. The stone piers still stand today, rising out of the river like remnants of an ancient Roman aqueduct. Visible to motorists from Route 212, they are probably mistaken for piers of an abandoned railroad.

Three alternatives suggest themselves here. First and best would be the complete restoration of the aqueduct so that, once again, the rewatered canal would be carried intact across the river, and canoeists as well as hikers could get across the river without a portage or detour.

The second alternative would be to spill the water of the canal into the river at both ends of the aqueduct and merely maintain a dry bed across the river. This would enable hikers and bicyclists to cross and would be historically authentic.

The third would be to construct a footbridge from pier to pier for hikers only.

If the reconstruction of the aqueduct were to be accomplished through the volunteer efforts of labor unions in the two counties, it would be an outstanding service contribution, not only to their contemporaries but to generations to come.

At Niagara Falls, you can ride a cable car above the whirlpool in the Niagara Gorge. Maybe someday, you can ride a modern-day canal packet across the aqueduct over the Tuscarawas River.

This has been a dream, yes, but it can become reality. It has in our nation's capital. There, on the reconstructed Chesapeake and Ohio Canal, travelers who would like to take a short trip on the canal may do so between May and October.

A mule-drawn sightseeing barge, with a lecturer aboard, leaves Lock 3 in Georgetown and proceeds to Lock 5 in Brookmont, Md., where it stops for 10 minutes before returning.

The four-hour trip, through one lock, enables the visitor to move backward in time to the mid-1800s, back to the days when George Washington walked the route of the canal.

Here in Ohio, a comparable ride would take us back to the Indian days — a real Disneyland ride right here on our own Ohio & Erie.

Why not develop a little canal boat-building competition right here in Stark County among our three canal communities — Canal Fulton, Massillon and Navarre?

If a race develops to be the first to get a canal boat into the water, we are almost sure to beat Tuscarawas and Summit.

Massillon, being by far the biggest, probably has the edge in resources. But Canal Fulton and Navarre can muster up a lot of civic spirit, which is what it takes for volunteer efforts.

Navarre doesn't have much water yet for its boat but it does have enough to float it. And, with a boat to "sail," maybe the canal in that area will be rewatered sooner.

It could be a lot of fun, reminiscent of the gay '90s atmosphere associated with sesquicentennial observances, what with the sounds of hammers and saws coming from the Massillon, Navarre and Canal Fulton "shipyards" on spring weekends.

The race to be first down the ways might well attract national attention.

And then some bright sunshine-filled summer day this could be the picture: A huge crowd gathers at canalside and along the towpath to watch the launching. The high school band, smartly attired in bright colored uniforms, marches up and prepares to board the packet along with local dignitaries. Maybe even the governor would come.

With its mule team out in front, the canal boat glides off up the canal with the band playing *Down by the Old Mill Stream*.

I can't quite see the name on the packet's stern. It could be "Massillon," "Canal Fulton" or "Navarre."

Towpath Restaurant

Well, what do you know? I see where Massillon is going to have a "Towpath Restaurant" with appropriate decor.

According to plans submitted to that city's health department by Ohio China Wholesale Co. of 405 3rd St. NE, Canton, such a restaurant will constitute the major feature of a $100,000 face-lifting at the Massillon Inn at 412 Lincoln Way E.

Straws in the Wind

I had hoped to announce that construction was under way on at least one canal boat this week — in Navarre, Massillon or Canal Fulton. But if any work has started, it is being kept under wraps.

There are straws in the wind, however. Mayor William Keen of Massillon, cochairman of the Canal Lands Development Advisory Committee, did tell me that Massillon had the keel laid on its canal packet. But then he confessed that, regrettably, he was only pulling my leg.

Then I saw the mayor Friday at the canal lands committee meeting. As he left the meeting, he was clutching a pamphlet, in an almost secretive manner, which he had obtained from Ted Findley of New Philadelphia, president of the Canal Society of Ohio.

Interested, I inquired what the book was about.

"Just a book," the mayor replied, a trifle evasively, flipping through the pages so rapidly I couldn't see much. But he had a sort of "cat that swallowed the bird" or "I've got a secret" look as he said it. And I did clearly see two good pictures of a canal packet in the pamphlet. Hmmmmmmmm!

When I arrived at the meeting, Mayor John Cullen of Canal Fulton and his fellow townsman, Clyde Gainey, had their heads together. They didn't tell me but I found out from another source that both an individual and an organization in Canal Fulton have expressed definite interest in building a canal boat. Hmmmmmmmmm!

We don't have a boat under way yet, but here's a twist for you: We already have the prospect of a copper or bronze plaque to be attached to the first canal boat after its construction and dedication.

H. Curtis Miller of North Canton, president of Legalcraft, Inc., called to say that he would like to work toward the donation of a copper nameplate or dedicatory plate for the first canal boat. Expressing his desire to cooperate in working out such a project, he said he would welcome a call from anyone of like mind.

To top it all off, Paul Marks told me at the canal lands committee meeting that he knows of a donor (anonymous for the time being) who will provide the burros to pull the boat!

All we need now is the boat to go with the plaque and team.

News for Fishermen

The canal lands committee meeting Friday included a report of special interest to fishermen. In response to the committee's request, the division of wildlife of the State Department of Natural Resources plans to place 1,000 northern pike and 5,000 bass in the canal this spring.

Pedal-Pushers Plan

Micki Badal and her husband, Gene, who called several weeks ago to inquire about riding bicycles down the towpath, have been pleasantly surprised at their success in forming a cycle group within the New Neighbors League of Canton. Micki reports 17 couples in the Canton and North Canton area have signed up.

"We're just waiting for the weather to break," says Micki.

Canal Students

Interest in the Ohio & Erie Canal is beginning to be expressed by the younger generation. I had just returned from the canal lands committee meeting Friday when I received a call from Lyn Krichbaum, a senior at North Canton Hoover High School. Lyn is doing a term paper in her English class on the "Restoration of the Ohio & Erie Canal."

And over Massillon way, Jane Sandy is writing a research paper on the canal. Jane, who is a seventh grader, wrote to committee member Clyde Gainey for any information he could make available to her.

The developing interest in the canal restoration is, of course, most widespread among adults.

One of those interested in the history of canals is Mrs. Virginia Mayberry of Canton. Mrs. Mayberry went for a drive last fall down in the Sandy and Beaver Canal country, which extends from Bolivar in Tuscarawas County to near East Liverpool. As a result of this and succeeding trips, she would like to obtain a copy of Max Gard's book, *The Sandy and Beaver Canal*, which is out of publication.

"We often travel far from home and don't recognize the history we have close to home," she says with conviction.

March 21, 1965
An Idea From Magnolia

Prospects for a canal boat on the Ohio & Erie are looking brighter although I haven't heard of one actually being started yet. It would seem that one of the country's three canal communities would be the logical builder of such a boat.

But not necessarily so.

In fact, most of the recent expressions of interest in constructing such a craft have come not from Navarre, Massillon or Canal Fulton, but from Canton, North Canton and Magnolia. And perhaps this is the way it should be. After all, the canal now belongs to the county — to all of us Stark residents. So maybe the first boat on the canal should be named "The Stark County."

Charles J. Mills of Magnolia apparently thinks so. And he has a thought-provoking idea. Mr. Mills, who says he is longingly watching the canal boat project, wrote:

"As I am now 73 years old, I can remember as a boy in school at St. John's School in Canton, that when the McKinley Monument was being built all school children were asked to take part in its construction. To raise funds, each child was to donate 25 cents to that fund. We watched the monument gradually rise, atop the distant hill. When it was finished, we all received a certificate for framing and on it was a picture of the monument we helped to build. And were we proud of our part in it!

"It seems to me that children today would perhaps like to take a little part in the building of a canal boat, which would be a future pleasure to them, their families and their future children. The boat would not cost as much as the monument and we oldies could help too. Now is the time, before schools close for the summer. Then we could start our Stark County boat."

Shutters, Yet!

Readers of this column will recall that last week I reported Mayor Keen of Massillon, cochairman of the Stark County Canal Lands Development Advisory Committee, was acting just a bit cagey with a pamphlet that contained some pictures of canal packets. I had the notion that perhaps the mayor was planning to get the jump on the other canal communities in building the first boat.

But this week I, too, have a good picture of a canal packet. Milt Haitema, a fellow newspaperman, was going through *The Repository's* old files when he came on a feature story headlined "Friendly Canal Cradled Veteran 'Skipper'." It was a story written in 1941 about Alfred Leonard of Louisville, then 74, whose cradle was his parents' canal barge, "The Cecilian."

Accompanying the article was a picture of an old packet, complete with shutters on the windows. The caption beneath the photo, which showed more than 20 men and women standing or sitting on the flat top of the packet, read:

"The spot where the picture was taken is not known but it is believed to have been somewhere in Stark County when a group of boatmen were holding a Sunday afternoon picnic."

In one of the direct quotations in the story, the old canal boat skipper said:

"The canal as a method of transportation was indeed slow — the average speed of passenger boats, including stops, was not more than four miles an hour — but it was picturesque and its people were friendly."

To 'Birdify' Canal

Among groups and organizations expressing interest in the restoration of the Ohio & Erie Canal and a desire to help in the project is the Canton Audubon Society.

President Jack Minger has appointed Mrs. Judson Case and Mrs. Arthur Christenson cochairs of a committee to study ways and means of improving a section of the towpath in cooperation with the canal lands development advisory committee. Attention is being given to the Butterbridge Rd. area.

Mr. Minger listed some possible recommendations of the committee as the establishing of trails for sighting birds and wildlife, construction of bird houses in the area so that birds will nest in the vicinity of the canal, and the building and maintaining of feeding stations during the winter.

The Audubon president said these are only a few of the ways in which volunteers from the society can help to make canal "towpathing" more interesting and educational.

March 28, 1965

Indiana Canal Attracts Tourists

Down East the federal government is gradually restoring the old Chesapeake and Ohio Canal, which extends from our nation's capital to Cumberland, Maryland.

Here in Stark County, the county government, through its canal lands development advisory committee, is restoring the Ohio & Erie Canal.

To the west — in Indiana — it's the state government that is restoring and developing a canal — the old Whitewater Canal in the southeastern part of the state.

The exciting news of the Indiana waterway was brought to my attention last week by George Karinos of Canton, who has taken an interest in the local project. George brought me a clipping from the *Chicago Tribune* featuring a story from Metamora, Ind.

The caption under the accompanying picture of an open-sided canal boat on the waters of the tree-lined canal read:

"Southeastern Indiana's Whitewater Canal comes alive with a new kind of traffic — tourist traffic. A new canal boat carries passengers on an hour-long ride through the antique hand-operated locks and past an old mill. The canal, at Metamora, parallels U.S. Highway 52."

The article describes how the jet-powered boat takes tourists from a roadside park (like Lock 4 Park here in Stark County) into an "era of yesterday" during the hour-long ride. The vessel, which is canopied to protect passengers from sun and rain, seats 30.

Last year was the first year the boat was operated for tourists. It was also last year that the canal was reborn due to the efforts of a young Hoosier politician, Rep. Robert Gordon.

Coincidentally, it was last year that Stark County's portion of the Ohio & Erie Canal was saved for posterity by the efforts of a young Buckeye politician, Rep. Ralph Regula of Navarre.

All through the summer, tourists from across the nation stopped to take a look at the Indiana canal and ride the boat.

John C. Moore, superintendent of the project for the state of Indiana, said of the flow of tourists:

"We were just swamped with 'em all summer and we expect even a bigger crowd this summer."

Discussing plans for this summer, Mr. Moore declared: "The first warm day and we'll have the canal boat in operation."

Last summer the boat operated only on Saturday and Sunday, except for reservations made for weekday rides.

The Whitewater Canal, like most of the other waterways in the eastern and midwestern United States was built in the 1830s and carried heavy freight traffic until the beginning of the Civil War and the coming of the railroads.

Just as with the Ohio & Erie, parts of the Whitewater Canal were filled in. But the state became interested in the Metamora portion of the canal in the early 1940s and five years later began restoration. The restoration is continuing and plans call for renovation of an old mill powered by a waterwheel, which had operated until recent years.

The canal has proved fascinating to canoers, who each summer come from many sections of the Midwest to compete in the annual Whitewater canoe races sponsored by the state.

Members of the Stark County canal lands committee have discussed raising or altering some the bridges and culverts of the Ohio & Erie Canal to improve the waterway for boating.

Efforts are under way to do the same sort of thing on the Whitewater. Plans call for the raising of two bridges downstream so the canal boat trips can be extended. One of the present spans may become a drawbridge.

The Hoosier State hopes to continue development of its new tourist attraction. More power to it!

But, in keeping with Governor James A. Rhodes' drive to make Ohio first in many fields, why not restore our Buckeye canal from Lake Erie to the Ohio River and make it the finest canal park system in the nation — a naturally attractive, historically significant part of the "Wonderful World of Ohio?"

April 4, 1965
Canal Boat Would Be Authentic

Apparently no hammer has been lifted and no saw honed to begin work on the construction of a canal boat for Stark County's rewatered section of the Ohio & Erie Canal. But more and more promises of assistance are coming in.

The latest and one of the most impressive comes from the Stark County Historical Center through its director, Gervis Brady, who said last week, "If a boat is built, we would be eager to provide the furnishings and equipment to give the boat an air of authenticity. We have available descriptions and pictures of the canal boats and of the furnishings in their interiors."

Permanently on display at the historical center at McKinley's Monument is a scale-model canal lock built by Stephen Yost of Massillon and an exact replica of a canal freighter, built by William McLaughlin of Canal Fulton.

Canal Boat Fund

One of the most heartening letters to come to my desk came from Mr. and Mrs. Jay C. Foltz of Canton. After writing that they are "quite interested and thrilled" about the canal project, the Foltzes said:

"We, too, would like to see the start of a canal boat. So here is a small contribution to indicate that we really want to see it started. Hope this might be the beginning to get others interested in such a worthy project."

Their unsolicited check has established a canal boat fund.

Boy Scouts To Help

There are others who want to help on the canal project, like Boy Scout Troop 27 at Lake Cable. Scoutmaster Walter Robinson and Asst. Scoutmaster William F. Lawrence report that 25 to 30 scouts have volunteered to spend a day working on the canal project in April or May. Their efforts will be credited toward their Boy Scout conservation project. The type of work they do will be determined by Paul Marks, general foreman of work on reconstruction of the canal.

For Canal Birds Only

Paul Marks, incidentally, can't do enough for the canal project. Not only does he supervise the workers in clearing the towpath and repairing the canal banks, he operates the bulldozer in digging out filled-in sections of the canal, patrols the waterway throughout the county as a deputy and searches out any source of pollution. Now he has offered a number of redwood bird feeders to the Canton Audubon Society.

Paul, who made the feeders himself, attached only two strings to the donation — that the feeders be installed in the vicinity of the canal and that feed be kept in them during the winter. Audubon Society President Jack Minger said he would welcome the feeders and that, beginning in October, a committee of the society would keep them in feed on a scheduled program.

From Massillon

On March 30 the canal in Massillon was in fine navigable condition and the boats were running on regular schedule. That's March 30, 1865, of course, a century ago to the day.

Throughout the month of April, the Massillon Museum will feature as part of its "Canal Days" exhibit a scale-model canal boat made by Clyde Gainey of Canal Fulton. The first-floor display also will include old canal photographs by William L. Bennett of Navarre, taken between 1895 and 1905.

The brochure announcing the museum's exhibits features a cover photograph of the canal in Massillon, looking north from the Tremont St. bridge to Main St. The picture shows Bammerlin's Malt House as it appeared about 1890, two boats and several trees with broken limbs. The photographer always claimed that the branches were broken by the weight of passenger pigeons, now extinct.

She Wouldn't Squeeze

One thing a canal boat doesn't do very well is squeeze. But it's been tried. When the first canal boat built near Hebron, the Lady Jane, was to make its historic initial trip through the Circleville aqueduct, its builders learned they had made a terrible blooper.

The Lady Jane was about a foot too wide to go through the aqueduct or any lock in the Ohio canal system. She never got to Circleville. Actually, she never got out of sight of her "birthplace." The Lady Jane wouldn't squeeze and so suffered her great humiliation.

Progress Note

One night last fall, Ralph Regula, co-chairman of the Stark County Canal Lands Development Advisory Committee, addressed the Greensburg Lions Club in Summit County and told them about Stark County's canal project.

His enthusiasm was catching. Recently he received a letter from the club telling him that, in response to his suggestion, formal requests have been made for transfer of some of the canal lands in Summit from the state to local subdivisions, including the Akron Metropolitan Park District.

April 11, 1965
A Description That Fits

"Where the Historical Past Is Combined With the Opportunity for a Great Future."

Sound like someplace you know? Like maybe the Ohio & Erie Canal in Stark County? I rather like the description — and it certainly could fit our Stark canal communities.

But the words actually describe Brookville, Ind., and Franklin County, "In the Heart of the Beautiful and Historic Whitewater Valley," according to a brochure prepared by the Brookville Chamber of Commerce.

John C. Moore, custodian of the Whitewater Canal State Memorial at Metamora, Ind., sent the pamphlet along with a friendly letter telling me more about the Whitewater Canal and its reconstruction.

The cover drawing of the brochure shows a lock tender swinging open the huge wooden gates of a lock so a canal freighter can enter. The brochure contains a number of photographs, including several of canal scenes near Metamora. One particularly interesting photo showing the restored aqueduct, built in 1843, looks like a covered bridge except that it shelters a canal instead of a road.

Two maps show points of interest such as covered bridges, the Whitewater Canal State Memorial, restored canal locks, the aqueduct, falls, an old mill, which is to become a museum, and a canal basin where canal boats once tied up.

So many similarities exists between the redeveloped Whitewater and the redeveloping Ohio & Erie that comparisons are unavoidable.

The O&E once had an aqueduct across the Tuscarawas River, north of Bolivar, which could be restored. It also had and still has "Wildcat Basin," south of Navarre, where the boats tied up and turned around.

Now overgrown, it has development potential.

Mr. Moore writes that the towpath of the Whitewater is used as a Boy Scout hiking trail and that they also make canoe trips down the canal.

"It attracted hundreds of Scouts from several neighboring states as well as from all over Indiana," Mr. Moore wrote. "They camp at the feeder dam and the next day hike the trail or make the canoe trip."

Here in Stark County, area Scout officials are discussing the possibility of establishing an official Boy Scout hiking trail along the Ohio & Erie towpath. A canoe trail also is a possibility.

Concerning Whitewater's canal boat, Mr. Moore writes, "Last July, the conservation department put a canal boat in operation. It was an immediate hit. In 13 weeks... 4,243 persons rode the boat. We had visitors from Japan, Italy, Denmark, Canada and many, many of our own states. The boat ride takes them through the locks and that is what people enjoy. By the way, the boat was built by local people."

Towpath Bird Walk

As work on the canal towpath progresses, pedestrian traffic is increasing. As the weather continues to improve, more and more residents of the Stark community are expected to go "towpathing." One of the groups looking forward to a trip along the canal is the membership of Canton Garden Center. Come April 21, they plan to hike the towpath for their third bird walk of the year. They will start at Lock 4 Park and hike south. Members will carry Audubon cards to record the birds sighted and they expect to see a number of water birds. The center's bird walks are open to the public.

April 18, 1965

New Beauty for the Towpath

It's too late this year, but come next Easter a section of the Ohio & Erie Canal towpath will be decked out in new spring finery — thanks to the Stark Landscape Association.

Three nurseries, all members of the association, have donated 15 to 20 flowering crab apple trees to beautify a stretch of the canal near the footbridge just north of Crystal Springs. Because the nurseries — Lake Cable Nursery, Vail Nurseries and Easterday's Garden Path — are in Jackson Township, the trees are planted along the small section of the towpath in Jackson Township.

The trees, five to six feet high, may possibly bloom a little this year but next year they should bloom profusely and be a thing of beauty to behold. Their pink buds will open to white blossoms. And in the summer and fall there will be fruit to attract birds. A few years hence, when we walk down the towpath toward Crystal Springs in the spring, we will stroll through a tunnel of lovely blooms made doubly attractive by their reflection in the waters of the canal.

Free Housing

Trees weren't the only additions to the towpath environs last week. A number of birdhouses were put up along sections of the canal lands that have a natural habitat suited for them. A committee of the Canton Audubon Society placed the redwood houses donated by Carlos E. Parks of North Canton. The houses, generally, are of the type suited for wrens, flycatchers, tree swallows, bluebirds, chickadees, downy woodpeckers and tufted titmice.

This fall, redwood bird feeders, donated by Paul Marks of Canton, will be put up by the Audubon group and a committee will keep the feeders supplied with seed.

Jack R. Minger, society president, said many winter migrants will be seen at these feeders as they drift down from the north and friends of the birds will be able to observe them at close range. He stressed that placing the houses and feeders is just a part of the society's long-range program to improve a section of the canal lands. The group also plans to place benches just off the towpath and birdbaths and rubbish containers in an area near the bird feeders. All of this should make strolling along the towpath more interesting, particularly for

those who care for our feathered friends.

The Mayor Recalls

Mayor William Keen of Massillon, co-chairman of the Stark County Canal Lands Development Advisory Committee, recalls another time when trees were planted along the canal.

It was 25 years ago this month when Massillon schoolboys and members of that city's Boy Scout troops helped to plant thousands of trees in the state park along the old canal north of the city. The mayor was one of the assistant Scoutmasters who helped plant the trees.

Stark Interest Noted

It was nice to be mentioned in the president's letter, which accompanied the most recent issue of the Canal Society of Ohio's quarterly magazine.

President Ted H. Findley of New Philadelphia told the society's membership this column "reveals the enthusiasm and interest that the Stark County people are taking in their section of the canal."

The canal society, incidentally, is planning its first tour of the year May 22-23. The picnic event will be held in the Lockington-Piqua area in the western part of the state, where there is much canal history to be seen.

In the meantime, Mr. Findley will be guest speaker Wednesday at 8 p.m. at the Massillon Museum. He will narrate a show-ing of his slides highlighting the Ohio & Erie Canal.

Movie Features Canal

During the weeks of May 2-7 and May 16-21, the Massillon Museum will feature the canal era again — this time through a Technicolor movie *Canals — Towpaths West* — as part of its school tour program. The 17-minute film will be shown through arrangements with Massillon Public Library. It portrays the adventures of a boy mule driver on the Chesapeake and Ohio Canal at the peak of its activity and vividly illustrates the roles canals played in opening the West and providing a roadway to eastern markets.

April 25, 1965
Uncle Sam Circulates Canal Story

I'm sure it is by no means a collector's item — at least not yet — but there is a new envelope in the mails. Originating here in Stark County, it is reaching out across the country, letting others know that there is something going on in the county's canal lands.

The envelope features an artist's improved version of the towpath scene at the top of this column, printed in a golden tan. In the upper left corner, in lettering as deep green as the water of the canal, are the words "Canal Lands Development Committee, Stark County, Ohio."

The letterhead is printed in the same combination of colors and features a canal packet copied from one in the huge mural that adorns a wall of the Coshocton National Bank at Coshocton. Down the side of the letterhead, on top of tiny wildlife, camping, fishing and boating scenes, are words that describe the committee as being "composed of those who are dedicated to the preservation of the Ohio & Erie Canal in Stark County and to the development of a park thereon."

The stationery was printed by Mayor David Meyer of Navarre and presented to the committee of which he is a member. The mayor conceived the idea for the stationery. George Russell of Navarre did the art work.

Maybe some future philatelist will consider these envelopes, associated with the rebirth of a section of the Ohio & Erie Canal, a collector's item.

In the Comics, Yet!

Did you happen to read the "Jackson Twins" on the *Repository's* comic page last week? It seems that two characters in the comic learned their common forefather was an Irishman who came to this country to help build the Erie Canal in New York State. Probably had some kin out here in the Ohio country working on the Ohio & Erie. O'Toole was the name! Patrick, that is!

Towpath Bird Fanciers

Maybe you also noticed in last week's *Repository* that 24 members of Canton Garden Center hiked a section of the canal north of Crystal Springs. The women saw 34 species or subspecies of birds, including a ruby-crowned kinglet, green heron, horned lark, brown thrasher, mallards and many more common birds.

They enjoyed it so much they are planning to go back again. And the next time they intend to hike the canal all the way from Butterbridge Rd. to Crystal Springs — watching for birds along the way. For they know that birds, and all wildlife for that matter, are necessary to healthy land and contribute directly and indirectly to our happiness and standard of living.

Fun Days on Canal

A sprightly octogenarian walked into the newspaper office the other day and asked for the man who writes about the canal. Shown to my desk, he introduced himself as W.J. Lewis of Akron. With a twinkle in his eyes, he told me that he had lived in Clinton, just north of Stark County, between the river and the canal, for many years.

"I had a lot of fun on that old canal," he recalled with a chuckle. "Used to swim in the locks and fish in the canal... Used to jump on the boats at one lock there at Clinton and ride about a mile down the canal to the next lock, where we would jump off. We knew all the gate tenders and boat captains. In the wintertime we would skate from Clinton to Canal Fulton on the canal. And in the spring and summer we often walked down the towpath on Sunday to pick flowers..."

Then came the big flood of 1913, which destroyed the canal as an operating waterway. He remembers it well, as the water reached the second floor of their house before subsiding.

Mr. Lewis would like to see a canal boat on the Ohio & Erie again. In fact, he mistakenly thought there was a full-size boat at the Stark Historical Center and made a trip out to see it, only to find that the canal schooner was just model size.

"I don't suppose I will ever see one again," he said, calling attention to his 82 years.

"You never can tell," I said as he took his hat to leave. "We're sure trying to get one built and operating again."

To See Canal by Bus

When members of the Stark County Regional Planning Commission meet May 12, it will be in the form of a tour of the county's canal lands. James P. Holl, commission director, estimated that 40 persons will make the trip by bus. Members of the Stark County Canal Lands Development Advisory Committee will accompany the commission members. Holl said at least five stops are planned — Canal Fulton, Lock 4 Park, canal's end just north of Massillon, Navarre and the Wildcat Basin or aqueduct areas at the south end of the county.

Fosters Canal Lore

Congratulations to the Canal Society of Ohio and its president, Ted Findley of New Philadelphia! Under Ted's leadership, the society has fostered "public knowledge and appreciation of the canal lore and history of Ohio" so well that it has been presented an achievement award by the Association of Historical Societies of Ohio.

Must Have Been A Beautiful Sight

I have written so much about canals and towpaths in the past year that it is a pleasure to read something about them written by someone else. I particularly enjoyed the recent "Letter to the Editor" from Mrs. Grace Schumacher of Canton. Writing from her memory of happy days spent picnicking on and along the canal, she really made the scene come alive when she wrote how the children ran and shouted when the mules pulling a canal boat were sighted "coming around the bend." And again, when she recalled "how beautiful the big boat looked with its flags and colored ribbons fluttering in the soft summer breeze."

Her recollection of the fun everyone had "going through the locks" served to strengthen my already strong belief that such a ride would be as much fun today — if we had a canal boat.

From the Mailbag

Another heartening letter received last week reminded me that it has been just a year since Ralph Regula, Robert Vail Jr. and I hiked 16 miles along the canal through 16 million raindrops, and a multitude of weeds and brambles.

A lot of water has flowed down the canal since then.

And the canal restoration project is as far along as it is because comparatively few people have done a great deal on a voluntary basis during the last 12 months.

But about the letter. It was from Mrs. John Clayton Carver of Canton. And in it she volunteered to be a volunteer in the canal project. Observing that she has been reading this column "ever since you took the first journey through the weeds and water," Mrs. Carver offered to assist in any way, from serving on a committee to licking postage stamps.

Thank you Mrs. Carver. Of such stuff is the fabric of dreams woven into reality.

Hit Photo Jackpot

Made quite a haul this past week — pic-torially and historically — through the kindness of a fellow *Repository* employee, John Wohlwend of Carrollton. John permitted me to have prints made from his personal collection of canal scene negatives made at the turn of the century. As a re-sult, the old photos will appear from time to time with this column — the first one today.

As a boy, John lived at Lock 17 on the Ohio & Erie Canal in Tuscarawas County. He often worked in the Buckeye Roller Mills there, helping his father, the late Walter Wohlwend, who owned the mill. The mill still is operating today in the village now called simply Seventeen. But electric power is used today instead of water-power and Route 16-36 now passes through the village where the lock used to be.

The accompanying photograph shows the mill, operated today by Eugene Wilson, as it looked in 1900 when flour and feeds were loaded onto railroad cars and canal boats through the covered chute across the canal. Although John loaded grain onto trains, he never helped to load a canal boat. The big flood of 1913 had taken out the canal before John started to work at the mill. But he prizes his photographs of the early boats and would like to see one of the colorful vessels afloat again on the old Ohio & Erie.

Vintage Travel Fun

Hiking the towpath of the Ohio & Erie Canal is fun. Gliding over the surface of the canal in a canoe is, if anything, more exciting. But for a really slick way to see the canal and its towpath — in comfort and in a comparatively short time — it's hard to beat the way my wife and daughter and I saw it last Sunday. We were privileged to be the guests of Jack and Lucille Ittner during the Antique Automobile Club of America's Canton Chapter tour of the canal. Jack was tour leader for the trip, which originated at Lock 4 Park and terminated at Fort Laurens Park at the edge of

Bolivar in Tuscarawas County.

Aboard the Ittners' 1917 Dodge Brothers touring car with top down we purred along at a reasonable 35 mph at the head of a caravan of 14 vehicles dating to the early part of the century. In fact, the nifty right-side drive Overland owned by Ray M. Dodds of Massillon, president of the chapter, was probably driving about the countryside when the great flood of 1913 destroyed the canal as an artery of commerce.

With due respect for its age, Ray occasionally would get out and, with practiced skill, crank it back to life. Other old-timers in the caravan included a venerable Packard, a sporty 1926 Stutz, 1931 Chrysler roadster, impressive Dusenberg, fancy Flint and regal Pierce-Arrow.

Sitting three or four feet higher than in a modern car, on soft leather seats, we were afforded a much better view of the canal lands from the old vehicles than if we had been riding in '65 models. Although there were no shock absorbers in Jack's 1917 Dodge and the tires were high pressure, the hard-surfaced roads made for a smooth ride. And the superb weather made possible a ride back through time that was delightful in every respect.

After a stop at the fountain in old Rochester Square at Navarre for a refreshing drink and a look at the brick home, which had been a canal days boarding house, we continued south to Fort Laurens Park at Bolivar. There, at the site of the first fort in Ohio, the tour left the canal and its associated history and drove back into the traffic noise of 1965. But not before some members discussed making a historical vehicle tour to southern Indiana later in the summer to visit the Whitewater Canal State Memorial at Metamora, where, among other things, they could have the fun of riding through the locks in a canal boat.

Canal Society of Ohio

Another organization concerned with a form of transportation prevalent at the turn of the century and many years before is the Canal Society of Ohio. It, too, holds an annual spring tour. Members of the society, headed by Ted H. Findley of New Philadelphia, are planning to visit places of historical interest on the route of the old Miami and Erie Canal from Lockington to Spencerville in western Ohio.

Headquarters for the tour will be in Piqua. A short tour of historical sites in northern Miami County is planned for the afternoon of May 22, and an informal meeting at 8 that night will feature short talks on local canal history and a slide presentation of canal scenes. The canal tour will begin at Lockington at 9:30 a.m. May 23.

Officers of the society, aware of the developing interest in the Ohio & Erie Canal in Stark County, have extended an invitation to all persons interested to participate.

The Lockington Locks, incidentally, represent the greatest concentration of locks on the Miami and Erie Canal. The Shelby County attraction is listed in the booklet, "The Wonderful World of Ohio," and is pictorially shown on the official map of Ohio. But unlike much of our canal here in Stark County, there is no water at the Lockington Locks.

Throughout the year, Canal Society of Ohio members tell the story of the Ohio canals in schools and at public meetings, frequently illustrating their talks with slides and motion pictures. And when they have their guided tours to various parts of the state, the public always is invited.

May 16, 1965

Buzzing Canal by Bus

There are many ways of traversing Stark County's canal lands from north to south. I have tried many of them but still have a few to attempt — like by helicopter, bicycle, horseback or via the canal in a Japanese-type one-man submarine. I've enjoyed each trip — whether it was on foot, in a canoe, through a carpet of violets, over ice and snow, in a 1917 Dodge touring car or by chartered bus.

After accompanying members of the Stark County Regional Planning Commission on their bus tour of the canal lands Wednesday, I view this form of transportation as ideal for many persons desiring to tour the canal lands who are not physically able to travel the route in a more active way.

The planning commission members were fortunate to have the mayors of Canal Fulton, Massillon and Navarre; Paul Marks, general foreman of work on reconstruction of the canal, and Clyde Gainey of the Stark County Canal Lands Development Advisory Committee along to discuss the canal history and development plans.

But those who have traveled on sightseeing buses know that it would be no problem to train tour guides to lecture on the history of the canal, explain the reconstruction work and discuss points of interest as the bus moves along.

The planning commission tour started at the Harter Estate in Canton at 5:45 p.m. and terminated there about four hours later. The tour included a picnic-box supper at picturesque Lock 4 Park and stops at Canal Fulton, Crystal Springs, Navarre, Bolivar and places of interest in between.

The plan of the tour would lend itself admirably to large sight-seeing groups and would be extremely flexible time-wise.

Senior citizens and groups of handicapped persons could walk the towpath as little or as much as they wished at the various stops. The combination of history, reconstruction and recreational activity to be observed along the canal should prove entertaining for many as it was for the planning commission members. Parks at Canal Fulton, Lock 4 and Navarre are available for picnic meals, a popular part of any such tour.

Last Sunday Ralph Regula, cochairman of the canal lands committee, and I made our first anniversary hike along the towpath. It was just a year ago that we hiked 16 miles through the rain on the overgrown towpath from Canal Fulton to Navarre. This time we hiked only six miles, in the sunshine and on a cleared towpath. Our companion was Ralph's young son, Richard, a second-grade pupil and a promising hiker. We saw sections of the canal that a bus-tour group would not see. Actually, the prettiest sections of the canal, in general, are those most distant from the access points.

It almost seems that these lovely back-in stretches of the canal and towpath are a reward to the hardiest hikers and most persevering canoeists. The landscapes are more scenic, the towpath, at times, is covered with violets and overhung with wild crab apple blossoms. We saw many brightly colored orioles along the towpath.

Two suggestions: Leave one car at one access point and drive the second car to another access point. Thus you only have to walk one way, you see the most attractive sections of the canal and your transportation is waiting for you when you are done "towpathing." And if it is a hot day, a canteen of water comes in handy. We didn't have any.

Scouts Build Canal

One of the most heartening aspects of the canal restoration to those who are giving their time and energy to the project is the interest being shown by the younger generation. Probably the most active and helpful of the youth groups is the Boy Scouts.

One troop showing a great deal of interest in the canal is Troop 27, sponsored by the Lake Cable Recreation Association. The troop invited Mayor William Keen of Massillon, cochairman of the Stark County Canal Lands Development Advisory Committee, to speak about the history of the canal and the plans for its restoration.

Then five Scouts and two adult leaders took a trip up the canal in the patrol boat with Paul Marks, canal lands deputy, to survey possible work projects for the troop. As a result, next Saturday, members of the troop will clean up one of the old dry docks in which the canal boats were repaired.

Further evidence of Troop 27's interest was seen in its display for the recent Scout-O-Rama at Memorial Auditorium. The display was built around a papier-mache and mud model and it featured a lock and bypass, miniature trees and shrubs, water, a boat, an aqueduct and a loading dock.

Scoutmaster W.F.K. (Robbie) Robinson disclaims any credit for the model canal, declaring, "The boys made it all — the whole thing."

If the Boy Scouts of Stark County were older and more experienced, they would be an excellent group to build a full-size canal boat for the canal. And if you saw the Scout-O-Rama, you know they would do it!

May 23, 1965
Believe It or Not — A Canal Steamer

Shades of Mark Twain!

Did you know that a paddle-wheel steamboat once plied its way up and down the Ohio & Erie Canal? And that it was owned and operated by a Massillon resident and docked near his home at the north edge of Massillon?

I didn't. But then the old canal and its history are full of surprises.

A call from Julian Converse of Massillon put me on the track of the old canal steamer, "Arvine," and the man for whom it was named, Arvine Heppert.

Soon I found myself sitting on the porch of the brown-shingled Massillon home in which Mr. Heppert was born, talking with him about the days when he rode aboard his father's coal-fed steamer.

When George Heppert bought the excursion steamer back around 1887, young Arvine was a lad of 7. On the Fourth of July he will be 86 years old but he well remembers steaming through Stark County on the excursion boat "Arvine," which his father named for him.

As Mr. Heppert thought back to his youth, we could look across the Tuscarawas River to where the canal and the steamer used to be.

"It went anywhere on the canal," he declared. "It was the only steamboat on the Ohio & Erie."

Mrs. Clarence Lewis, Mr. Heppert's sister, who lives in the family homestead, brought forth an 1890 photograph of the boat and two clippings to prove the point.

Sure enough, there was young Arvine, all dressed up and sitting atop the boat bearing his name. His father, the captain, was in the stern, near where the funnel reached skyward, and two male passengers were amidships.

The one newspaper clipping, dark brown with age, read:

"The steam yacht 'Arvine' will run to Lock Mill Grove, north of the city, on Sunday, August 19, leaving the Main Street wharf at 9 o'clock. An orchestra will be on board."

The other one, apparently from the *Newcomerstown Visitor* in Tuscarawas County, read:

"It was rather a new and novel sight to see a steamboat make its appearance on the canal in this port last Saturday evening. It was the excursion boat 'Arvine' of Massillon and was on its way to the reservoir at Newark. The captain said the boat made about 10 miles an hour."

Mr. Heppert said the boat would make many trips during a busy day, taking Massillon residents and others from the wharf at the canal bridge on Lincoln Way in Massillon (no longer existing) to the numerous picnic areas along the canal beyond the city.

His sister recalled that her mother told her "all the big class, the rich folks" would charter the boat for excursion. A five or six-piece orchestra aboard the boat would entertain the passengers.

Mr. Heppert and his sister laughed in reminiscence when he told of the time the family's steamer broke a coupling somewhere near Zoar and had to be towed into Massillon, like all the other canal boats of the day, by a team. Oh, the ignominy of it all — the proud stern-wheeler, the speedy steamer "shipwrecked" near Zoar and forced to suffer the humiliation of limping back home to Massillon under horse power.

Mr. Heppert, who now lives in Springfield, was to return there today. It was a pleasure to meet and talk with him and be able to record a small but unique chapter in the history of the Ohio & Erie Canal.

Mystery Hike

The Christian Youth Fellowship of North Canton Community Christian Church was to hold another of its mystery tours today. The tour groups, which usually number 25, travel by car to unannounced locations for recreation, hikes, meetings and picnics. Today, according to Dick Logan of North Canton, adviser of the group, the tour will be a mystery hike along the Ohio & Erie Canal towpath. The group plans to start at Crystal Springs and hike north to Lock 4 Park, where they will have a picnic supper and install new officers. (If any of you mystery hikers got up early and read this before going to church, please keep it a mystery for the others.)

May 30, 1965
Windfall Needed -- A Wooden One

Although progress is being made in the Ohio & Erie Canal restoration and beautifications, the plan to build an authentic canal boat hasn't quite gotten off the ground. The plan, in its present status, is like a kite being held aloft ready to fly, when there is no wind. The wind, in this case, is the lumber needed to build the boat.

There have been many offers of assistance, materials and some money. A team to pull the boat has been promised and furniture to outfit it authentically.

And now comes a generous offer of a building in which to build the boat, just 400 to 500 feet from the canal and roughly 1,000 feet from a launching site at Lock 4 Park south of Canal Fulton. Peter Neidert, who built and then skippered the pontoon boat that proved so popular with visitors to Canal Fulton's sesquicentennial celebration last August, has said he will provide space to build the boat at his farm implement agency south of the village and then help to build it.

A number of other craftsmen also have volunteered to help in the construction and the necessary tools would be available. But the lumber is missing.

Ironically, I am told an offer to supply the wood was made by a resident of North Canton. But somehow contact with him was broken, his identity was lost and no member of the canal lands development advisory committee knows where or how to reach him.

Maybe he'll read this column.

Bicyclist Travels the Towpath

One of the forms of towpath recreation that has a great potential in Stark County but hardly has been attempted yet is bicycling. Widespread enjoyment of this healthful recreation awaits improvement of the towpath.

But an experienced cyclist can get through the entire distance from Canal Fulton to Crystal Springs, as did Kenneth Witmer of Perry Heights. Last Sunday Ken, who is a long-time cycle rider, rode seven miles along the towpath and then retraced his course. The 14-mile ride took about three hours, with a stop or two for a drink of water from his canteen.

Although he didn't see any other bicycle riders, Ken did pass quite a few fishermen. The only time he pushed his bike on the towpath was when he passed several women fishing and he didn't wish to disturb them.

Ken's bicycle was a special model with a spring fork, spring seat and 20-inch wheel. Parts of the trip would have been a little rough for an ordinary bike, he said.

Ken says he would not advise novice bike riders to attempt the towpath from Butterbridge Road south. But from the bridge north into Canal Fulton the towpath is fairly good. There are a few rough stretches and an occasional groundhog hole, which can be avoided, but, with proper care, this part of the towpath should be enjoyable for novice cyclists.

Ken said a towpath bicycle ride should prove very interesting to people who like birds and nature in general. He hadn't seen a wild duck for a long time until he saw a mother duck and four ducklings at the canal's edge during his ride.

When he pedaled into Lock 4 Park Sunday evening, Ken found all the picnic tables filled with people.

Summing up his report on his trip, Ken said, "The towpath should be a swell place for bike riders. I hope it can be developed further."

Canal Is Attraction

The canal is slowly gaining recognition as a Stark County attraction. I noted further evidence of this the other day while looking over an advertising folder for Lake Sherman located southwest of Canton. The folder, which reaches out to campers, swimmers, fishermen and picnickers wherever they may be, lists eight "local area attractions."

One of them is the "Old Ohio Canal."

Something New Added

Paul Marks, general foreman of work on reconstruction of the canal, and his crew have erected a flagpole near the pump shelter at the county's Lock 4 Park. Paul says a planter has been constructed around the base of the pole and flowers have been planted in it. Come the Fourth of July, Old Glory will be waving over restored Lock 4, just 140 years to the day after ground was broken for construction of the Ohio & Erie Canal at Licking Summit.

May Walk in June

On the same day the Explorer Scouts start their canoe trip, some 24 third and fourth grade pupils of Canton Country Day School will take a June "May walk" along the towpath. They will take their lunches with them and eat at Lock 4 Park before setting out down the towpath. They will be accompanied by their teachers, Mrs. Joyce Farrell and Mrs. Annabelle Lurie, and several mothers.

The fourth grade has been studying early Ohio history and should find the trip rewarding from an educational standpoint as well as from the recreational.

A third-grade pupil recently gave a report on a book about the building of the Erie Canal in New York State. His report stirred real interest on the part of his fellow pupils, who then did other projects relating to the canal.

So both classes are looking forward to the trip. Mrs. Farrell said they will combine "a little science observation" with their study of the history of the old waterway.

Have a good time, kids, and remember that a president of the United States once trod that towpath as a barge-team driver. Anything is possible in these wonderful United States.

Barge-Team Driver

An interested reader obligingly called last week to tell me that the May issue of The *National Geographic Magazine* contained a drawing of a canal boat and a reference in the text to the canal era. I found that the article concerned James A. Garfield, 20th president of the United States, who had been a "canal boy" on the Ohio & Erie during his youth.

The artist's sketch from the Library of Congress is strikingly similar to the drawing at the top of this column. However, it shows young Garfield astride a lead horse of a team pulling a barge along the canal.

Fatherless before he was two years old, young James Garfield drove barge teams along the canal at an early age.

Canoe Caravan

Members of Explorer Scout Post 128 of St. Mark's Episcopal Church in Canton plan to use the canal as a springboard for a 50-mile, five-day canoe trip from Canal Fulton to Coshocton starting Friday. Robert Peters, a Scout committeeman, said seven boys accompanied by three men will make the trip in five canoes, camping along the way. Frank Marzick is adviser to the 14-to-16-year-old Explorers.

The canoe fleet will paddle down the canal as far as the water is navigable and then portage the short distance to the Tuscarawas River to continue on to Coshocton.

June 6, 1965

Stark Has Second Canal in Sandy & Beaver

Southeastern Residents Get 'Fever'

Stark County's three major canal communities may become five. Canal-conscious communities that is.

For more than a year, the Ohio & Erie Canal communities of Canal Fulton, Massillon and Navarre frequently have drawn the attention of Stark residents as one development followed another in the program to first save and then restore the old waterway.

Efforts of the Stark County Canal Lands Development Advisory Committee, appointed by the county commissioners to reclaim and improve the canal, its towpath and adjacent lands, have been watched with interest.

Plans to create a county-long ribbon parkway embracing the canal and towpath have captured the fancy of Stark citizens interested in preserving a key part of the county's history and providing, at the same time, a close-at-hand public park for the enjoyment of many varied forms of recreation.

Some of those citizens live in the southeastern section of Stark County — in Magnolia and in Waynesburg. Inspired by what is going on in western Stark County, they took stock of their own canal, the little-known and less-publicized Sandy and Beaver Canal, and said: "It could happen here."

And it could!

The 73-mile-long Sandy and Beaver Canal originally reached from Glascow, Pa., on the Ohio River, to Bolivar on the Ohio & Erie just south of the Stark-Tuscarawas county line.

Today, although in need of considerable clearing and improving, a full-watered, mile-and-a-half stretch of the old canal has the potential to become a lovely strip park, tying together the two Sandy Township communities.

This section is the longest part of the old waterway now in use and a perfect example of the canal as it appeared more than 100 years ago. Clearly discernible at Magnolia is one of the basins where canal boats passed and were stored.

Spatterdock clogs part of the canal now and the towpath is overgrown and threatened in places by erosion. But there is much of beauty along the canal and, once improved, it would be a delightful place to canoe, hike or picnic.

At the Waynesburg end of the canal, one of the old stone locks still stands at the side of a concrete dam in Sandy Creek that replaced the old wooden canal dam. The lock now controls the flow of water from the creek into the canal.

At the Magnolia end of the canal, water is shunted from the canal into the race of what is surely one of the most picturesque original water-powered flouring mills in Ohio.

Built in 1834, the A.R. Elson Co.'s Magnolia Flouring Mills still stands today in an excellent state of preservation. Big and warmly red in the fading afternoon sunlight, it is an artist's delight.

Just beyond the mill is the village park, which could be extended and made the western terminus of a canal parkway.

There are a number of persons in Magnolia who would like to restore, or rather improve, the Stark section of the Sandy and Beaver where feasible. Already they have talked with members of various community organizations concerning the possibility of undertaking a project of this type.

But whereas the Ohio & Erie Canal was owned by the state and subsequently was deeded to the county, the land along the Sandy and Beaver is privately owned or under the jurisdiction of the United States government. Some form of agreement with the owners of the land would have to be achieved before the canal park could become a reality.

Someone always has to start the ball rolling in a project of this type. In Magnolia, it was Glenn Fishel, who has known the canal well ever since he played along it as a boy.

As the result of a call from Glenn, State Rep. Ralph Regula of Navarre, cochairman of the county's canal lands development advisory committee, met with him and several of his fellow townsmen who are enthusiastic about the proposed canal project.

We toured the Sandy and Beaver and came away impressed with its potential as a small, but in some ways superior, counterpart of the Ohio & Erie park project.

Glenn and his friends are hoping to interest enough individuals and organizations in their hometown to set up a planned program of developing a section of the canal lands at a time, provided the right to do so can be obtained from the property owners.

They would gradually work toward Waynesburg. In the meantime, they would hope to interest groups in Waynesburg in doing the same thing.

Projecting the idea a little further, the meeting of cleanup squads midway between the two towns could signal the rebirth of this remnant of the Sandy and Beaver and the establishment of a very attractive two-village canal park.

Why are Glenn Fishel and his fellow townsmen so excited about the Sandy and Beaver canal project? It is probable that they have caught the modern-day canal fever, which is diagnosed as the "reconstruction type."

But there is more to it than that. Glenn, in talking about his family, says, "We like to camp out and travel to different historical sites. As we travel across Ohio and see these places, we find they aren't as nice as some of the things we have right here at home — if we fix them up a little."

June 13, 1965

Historical Booklet Due for Museum
The How-To-Do-It of Canal Building

Suppose you were a budding archaeologist and you unexpectedly came into the possession of the rules and specifications used to build the Pyramids of Egypt. What a thrill! I had a thrill something like that the other day.

Being somewhat of a canal buff for the past year, I have hiked along three canals, read about many others, listened to lectures and viewed films about canals, and studied maps of canal routes.

I have interviewed men who have ridden on canal boats, searched for and found the rotting skeletons of canal barges weed-covered at canal bottom, and written thousands of words about these historical waterways.

And through it all I have marveled at the engineering know-how that went into the construction of the big ditches and wondered how, without modern machinery, the canal builders were able to do such an excellent job 140 years ago.

But about my thrill.

It was in being presented a finely preserved 136-year-old booklet titled *Rules and Specifications, Relating to the Construction of the Ohio Canal, and the Estimating of Work Performed Thereon.* The booklet was printed in Cleaveland (note spelling) in 1829.

The instructions are so detailed and comprehensive that if we had an equally descriptive book on the Pyramids, you and I could supervise the construction of the great tombs.

Subheadings in the canal booklet include: Grubbing and Clearing; Dimensions of the Canal; Mucking and Ditching; Embankment and Excavation; Draining; Locks - Dimensions; Backing; Abutments and Piers of Aqueducts; Puddling; Protecting Banks; Road Bridges.

Ever wonder just how the towpaths were built? Here, from the specifications, is how:

"The towing path bank shall be at least

ten feet broad at the top, and the opposite bank not less than six feet. When either bank is raised above the natural surface of the earth, both the inner and the outer slope thereof shall have a horizontal base of one foot, nine inches for every foot in perpendicular height... The surface of the towing path bank shall be nine inches higher on the side next to the canal than on the other side, and the opposite bank six inches higher on the side next the canal... Both banks shall be so constructed as to remain at least two feet above top water line after they shall have become solid and well settled."

There's more, much more.

And because of the generosity of Mrs. Paul W. Jenkins, who gave me the booklet, this wealth of authentic information will be preserved for future generations. For, with her approval, I plan ultimately to present it to (hopefully) a canalside branch museum or historical center.

And now if only we could locate comparable specifications for a canal boat. Perhaps someone somewhere has or knows where such information may be obtained.

Some information of this type is available to the canal lands committee, but more detailed and exact specifications would help tremendously in constructing a canal boat.

And, as of this week, there is renewed hope that Stark County can be the first canal county to launch an authentic packet since the early days of this century. I can't say more at this time. But a new development has encouraged me greatly. There soon may be exciting news "Along the Towpath."

June 20, 1965
Cleveland-Cincinnati Hikeway

New highways are springing up all over Ohio — Interstate Routes 77, 271, 80 and 71. They are smooth, swift and necessary. They are as modern as today and they help to keep Ohio growing and booming. And everybody knows about them and watches for each new section to be completed.

But there is one interstate route abuilding that comparatively few Ohioans know about. Started back in 1958-59, the route was designed to reach from Conneaut, near the Pennsylvania border, to Cincinnati, near the Indiana line.

Today, some 150 or more miles in six counties have been completed and many more are in the planning stages.

The "highway" is called the Buckeye Trail and it's for hikers. It has been described as penetrating "some of the most rewarding and historic land in this section of America — the foothills of the Appalachian highlands."

Those who are working to complete the trail believe that we must have places where we can get away from the encroaching industrialization and urbanization, and escape the noxious gases of automobiles — places where we can walk alone or in groups in the midst of nature.

But what does this have to do with the Ohio & Erie Canal towpath in Stark County?

There is a good possibility the towpath may become a part of the Buckeye Trail.

If it does, it can be attributed, in large measure, to the vision of State Rep. Ralph Regula of Navarre who, upon first learning of the Buckeye Trail, conceived the idea of substituting the canal towpath through Stark, Summit, Cuyahoga and Tuscarawas counties for the northern section of the trail originally planned farther east.

With Cleveland serving as the northern terminus, the millions in populous northeastern Ohio would have a close-at-hand entrance, via the towpath trail, to southern Ohio's beautiful state parks and camping areas. The walkway passes through heavily forested hills and through the cave area.

The open trail extends from Ash Cave to Old Man's Cave to Lake Logan to Enterprise to Greendale to Murray City to Burr Oak Lake to Johnson Summit (Morgan County) to Stockport to Brown's Knob (Noble County) to Caldwell and presently terminates north of Seneca Lake in Guernsey County at Salt Fork Lake.

Rep. Regula has presented his idea to officials of the Buckeye Trail Association who are enthusiastic about its potential.

With the canal reconstruction development under way in Stark and Summit counties and the beautifully preserved canal in Cuyahoga County, plus the overall historical features of the canal, the idea seems a natural.

The Buckeye Trail Association hopes eventually to build shelters every 8 to 15 miles, depending on the terrain, so hikers can hike for several days in a row through much of the state's finest scenery, without leaving the trail.

The association, which is a nonprofit organization, has relied on voluntary labor for scouting and clearing the trail, just as most of the development of the canal project in Stark County has been accomplished by volunteers, with the approval of the county commissioners who are without funds for the work.

According to an article about the trail in the June 1964 issue of *Ohio Conservation Bulletin*, forerunner of the new magazine, *The Wonderful World of Ohio*, the procedure for building the Buckeye Trail is this:

"Enlistment of local residents interested in the trail; rough scouting to check a route featuring historic scenic landmarks; checking the route against topographical and aerial maps, land records, etc.; obtaining permission to cross lands, both public and private; scouting; tying rags and/or plastic tape to trees and bushes where the route might go; calling in other officers of the organization to assure uniform standards of trail layout, and finally holding an all-state meeting for the final clearing and marking of the trail."

By using the canal towpath in the three or four northern counties, most of these steps could be eliminated. The trail would be ready-made. And final completion of the trail could conceivably be advanced by years.

Buckeye Trail officers and others interested in its development look into the future and see the trail tying into a regional network of trails through Indiana, Michigan, West Virginia and Kentucky, and eventually connecting with the Maine-to-Georgia Appalachian Trail, somewhere in the Blue Ridge mountains of Virginia.

So someday, perhaps, if you don't feel like venturing forth onto the ever-growing network of superhighways for your vacation, you can lace on your hiking shoes, shoulder your pack and set off down the towpath of the Ohio & Erie Canal for the sand dunes of Michigan, the cave country of Kentucky, the pine forests of Maine, the red earth of Georgia or the apple-candy country of the Shenandoah Valley.

June 27, 1965
How About A 'Towpath Tramp'?

Do people hike anymore? Walk for extended distances, that is? Maybe carry a light pack? Or just a walking stick?

Or, with the ever-increasing dependence on wheels, is hiking a lost pastime?

Last week this column was devoted to the possibility that the Ohio & Erie Canal towpath through Stark County might become a part of the state-long Buckeye Trail.

A check this week failed to turn up a single hiking club in the county. The last club of this type, sponsored by the Canton YMCA, apparently walked itself out some years ago.

Maybe now is the time for a rebirth of this healthful recreation, which can be enjoyed by persons of all ages. With the clearing of the canal towpath and restoration of the towpath bridges, an ideal hikers trail is available.

Young and old can set their own pace, walk in safety away from vehicular traffic, breathe fresh air and look on woods and water pleasing to the eye — meanwhile improving muscle tone and stimulating the circulation.

I have an idea about towpath tramping that may or may not catch on. But here it is, for what it is worth:

How about an annual Towpath Tramp — sponsored by one or more organizations such as service clubs, volunteer fire departments, YMCAs and YWCAs, chambers or junior chambers of commerce?

One and all would start hiking at Canal Fulton — with their feet pointed south.

Each and every one would walk as far as he could or thought he should.

Each hiker that walked at least as far as Lock 4 Park, 1¼ miles south of Canal Fulton, would receive a polished native wood walking stick or cane with a band of color around it. The color of the lacquered band would designate how far the hiker had tramped along the towpath.

For example, a blue band could be for the 1¼-mile hiker, a green band for those who made it to Crystal Springs, a red one for all who trudged into Massillon, a black band cane for the sturdy sloggers who made it to Navarre and a gold band walking stick for the stalwarts who tramped the more than 20 miles to the old aqueduct foundations in the Tuscarawas River at the Stark-Tuscarawas county line.

Members of the sponsoring organizations would have to station checkers along the way to verify the hikers' mileage cards and hand out canes at towpath exit points.

Last September (an excellent month in which to have a Towpath Tramp) the Akron Metropolitan Park District promised a staff to anyone from 8 to 80 who walked seven prescribed trails in six different parks. The response was far beyond expectations. Nearly 1,000 persons turned in records verified by park rangers' signatures and nearly 4,000 blanks were issued to prospective hikers.

The oldest hiker to complete the seven-trail stint was 81 years old and there were many under 8 years of age. Many entire families turned in records and one mother told park authorities she carried her 7-week-old daughter every step of the way on the seven hikes.

Akron, of course, is a larger metropolitan area than Stark County's five cities lumped together. Perhaps that is why the residents there seem to use their park trails more.

Akron Park Director Arthur T. Wilcox, commenting at the time of the hiking program, said, "There have never been so many people hiking the trails."

Stark County residents don't have to wait until our population approaches that of Akron to begin enjoying our newly restored hiking path along the Ohio & Erie Canal.

We can start right now getting in condition. And, if some physical fitness-minded organization likes the idea of a Towpath Tramp, maybe it will become more than just an idea by the time the leaves don their fall colors and drift down to float along on the slow-moving waters of the canal.

Having hiked enough of the towpath to earn a gold band walking stick, I can assure you that tramping the towpath can be tougher than you might think. But it also can be more fun than you think.

If anyone likes the Towpath Tramp idea enough to do something about it, let me hear from you!

July 4, 1965
January in July Along the Canal

Here it is, July already — one of the two hottest months of the year. With the temperature already having reached the high 80s and into the 90s, it seems a good time to look at the Ohio & Erie Canal in the winter.

This cooling thought came to me while I was looking through a historical book entitled *Our Home Town Memories.* The book, loaned to me by Mrs. Raymond Henson of Lake Cable, is a pictorial memory-book of the city of Newark, Ohio, the scenic and historic "Moundbuilders City," through the heart of which flowed the Ohio & Erie Canal.

Numerous pictures of canal boats and canal scenes are scattered throughout the book. The coolest picture of all, of course, was captioned "When Canal Supplied Ice."

Here is what it says beneath the picture:

"This old print of the John Simpson West End Ice Houses was when the ice was cut from the frozen canal. In the background may be seen the large ice houses along the Ohio Canal. The covered ice wagon bears the sign 'Simpson's West End ICE' — the last word in large caps. The ice wagon is drawn by a team of small mules — one brown and the other gray. The other two-horse spring wagon was also used for delivering ice."

(No, this writer is not related to the Newark ice merchants. The identical last names constitute a pure coincidence.)

Another real cool picture in the book shows the aqueduct, which carried the canal across the north fork of the Licking River at Newark. Hanging down from the abandoned aqueduct are masses of heavy ice including stalactites, which appear to be 25 to 30 feet long, reaching from the bottom of the aqueduct to the river surface below. The picture of the frame aqueduct, built in 1828, was taken before the raging floodwaters of the river swept it away.

Beneath a picture of a canal boat tied up beside a large warehouse, the author of the book philosophizes a bit about right of way and makes a comparison between the early canalers' insistence on having the right of way and the same insistence on the part of today's motorists. He recalls that old-timers told yarns about fistfights among the canalers who demanded the right of way getting in and out of the locks.

Right of way claims also precipitate hot arguments and often result in the tragic accidents today because the same "demon desire" for pushing the other fellow around causes highway mayhem. At least, in the canal days, a good dunking in the canal usually would cool off the disputants. Today, if they are lucky enough to get off uninjured, they frequently are cooled off in the local "jug."

Still another photo, made in 1898, shows the stone-wall remains of the old canal towpath at the Licking River Narrows, known as the "Black Hand Gorge." In early canal days, travelers are said to have acclaimed the Black Hand Gorge as the most beautiful site along the Ohio & Erie Canal.

Included in a group of "yesterday" and "today" pictures of the canal and its locks is a picture of a stone monument bearing a bronze tablet. Erected in 1925, the monument marks the spot where Gov. DeWitt Clinton of New York State turned the first spadeful of earth for the Ohio & Erie Canal July 4, 1825, at Licking Summit south of Newark.

The monument, which was paid for by the citizens of Licking County, can be reached by walking through a field. The governor, incidentally, arrived at Cleveland by steamer and then went by stagecoach to Newark.

One of the final pictures in the book is another winter scene. It shows many ice skaters on the canal at Fifth Street in Newark enjoying the winter sport — a real cool view for July.

Fish for the Canal

Did you notice the picture in the sports section of *The Repository* last Tuesday — the one showing two men placing fish in the canal? Approximately 300 northern pike, ranging in size from 7 to 10 inches, were placed individually in the canal by the division of wildlife of the State Department of Natural Resources. Spokesmen for the division have said that a large number of largemouth bass, averaging about 3 inches in length, will be stocked in the canal next.

Scouts Enjoy Rodeo

About the time the canal was being stocked with fish, some 52 Boy Scouts of the St. Joan of Arc parish troop were trying to take fish out of the canal. William George, scoutmaster, said members of the troop enjoyed a fishing rodeo while they were camped at Lock 4 Park.

Shooting Banned

One hundred signs soon will be posted along the canal banks stating that there positively will be no shooting on county grounds, by order of the Stark County commissioners.

Weed Cutter Working

Paul Marks, general foreman of work on reconstruction of the canal, reports his crews are still cutting vegetation in the canal. They have finished cutting between Crystal Springs and Butterbridge Rd. and Monday they will move north of Butterbridge. Paul also reports that fishing activity along the canal is increasing.

July 11, 1965

Battle Cry for Canal Fans

"Keep your concrete-pouring hands off the Potomac River!"

How do you like that for a conservationist's battle slogan?

I think it is great and would like to suggest another:

"Keep your concrete-pouring hands off the Ohio & Erie Canal!"

The original slogan was suggested by Thomas L. Kimball, executive director of the National Wildlife Federation, as the battle cry for the C&O Canal Association in its crusade to have the 185-mile C&O Canal declared a national historic park and its effort to prevent the construction of 16 major dams proposed by the Army Corps of Engineers.

Based on the same conservation-oriented thinking, the second slogan would be directed toward preventing Ohio's road builders from continuing to eradicate one section after another of the historic Ohio & Erie Canal.

In the case of the Potomac River, there are ways to solve the main problem of flushing pollution other than to build the 16 deep-drawndown reservoirs, which would inundate much of the Chesapeake and Ohio Canal. The canal association and its coalition of farm, labor, conservation and citizens organizations suggested the pollution should be prevented at its source and not flushed afterwards.

In the case of the Ohio & Erie Canal, there is plenty of other land, perhaps somewhat more expensive, which could be used for new highways. It would seldom be necessary to eliminate the state's historic canal. Often the road could be moved 50 to 100 feet away and provide tourists and Ohio travelers a scenic look at our historic waterway.

This is particularly true in Coshocton County, where one of the loveliest sections of the canal is doomed to become just another concrete highway in the near future unless a change of thinking in high places occurs. The stretch from the inter-section of Routes 93 and 16 east to Newcomerstown is in a good state of preservation, although unwatered. It is made doubly attractive in many places by its close proximity to the Tuscarawas River, which is quite scenic in this area.

Supreme Court Justice William Douglas, when he took "friendly exception" to an editorial in the *Washington Post* that supported a proposal to build a highway on the remaining canal right of way of the Chesapeake and Ohio, said the entire 185 miles of the canal from Washington to Cumberland, Maryland, should stay as it is: "A long stretch of quiet and peace... a place not yet marred by the roar of wheels and the sound of horns."

Why doesn't this apply as well to the Ohio & Erie?

Last April, on the occasion of the eleventh annual reunion hike of the C&O Canal Association led by Justice Douglas and Department of the Interior Secretary Stewart Udall, the justice said, "We need federal appropriations to get the canal locks repaired and restored, not for the purpose of operation, but to make it possible to rewater the entire distance of the canal. We ought to have a canoeway 180 miles long with portages around the locks. It would make a wonderful canoeway."

Why doesn't this apply, at least to a great extent, to the Ohio & Erie?

In fact, in May of 1964, I wrote to this effect: "I was convinced the old waterway, if rewatered, could become a delightful canoe trail, possibly extending, once again, from Lake Erie to the Ohio River, with necessary portages."

The justice also told the association members, "We should have campsites all along the way, with fresh water piped in so people could have picnics or camp overnight. And some kind of shelter so that hikers will have a place to put down their sleeping bags during inclement weather — and fireplaces with available wood."

Why doesn't this apply to the Ohio & Erie Canal? In fact, here in Stark County, a program to achieve these objectives is under way on a limited scale.

The justice added, "To tell the truth, I always call the C&O Canal the poor man's national park; it has more appeal to the average man than any park that I know of because it is so close to the large population centers of the East."

This positively does apply to the Ohio & Erie Canal.

For more than a year now I have heard State Rep. Ralph Regula, the Justice Douglas of the Ohio & Erie, tell many audiences that he considered the Ohio & Erie the poor man's park system, a parkway with much to offer right in our backyard, not in some far-removed section of the state.

Sen. David B. Brewster of Maryland, who joined the Eleventh Reunion hikers, declared, "I am convinced that we should preserve the Potomac River Valley. And one way that we should do it is to expand the C&O Canal and the park area that is involved."

Among the significant statements made during the hike was Secretary Udall's comment that, "The wisdom of Justice Douglas and those who made the original hike over a decade ago has certainly been proven now by President Johnson's program to preserve the Potomac and make it a model for the country. Certainly, if a highway had pre-empted the canal, this would not be possible. And so we have this as a foundation on which to plan what we hope will be one of the finest river preservation programs in the country.

"Fortunately, the American people are rediscovering their rivers. We've abused them, misused them, used them as sewers and worse... It's a fortunate thing that people in this section of the country began to rediscover the Potomac about 10 years ago — before it was too late. The C&O Canal is really the centerpiece of the whole thing because here is something we already have and own as a foundation on which we can build."

And, mindful of efforts here in Stark County to build an authentic canal boat, listen to this!

Director Kimball expressed his hope that one result of the current intensive study of the Potomac will be to again fill the entire 185 miles of the canal, making possible canal barge trips between Washington and Cumberland.

Here in Ohio, Gov. James A. Rhodes and his administration are doing much to improve our state and make it, in truth, the "Wonderful World of Ohio."

What if a coalition of historical, conservation, recreational, educational and other organizations would submit a formal resolution to the governor suggesting that:

No part of the Ohio & Erie Canal be altered by highway construction in the future.

All present plans to alter the canal by highway construction be reconsidered and abandoned if at all possible.

State support be given, as it is being given in Stark County, to all county and municipal efforts to save and reconstruct the canal.

Wouldn't such a resolution, if acted upon favorably, help make the "Wonderful World of Ohio" more wonderful?

The Quotations

Most of the quotations in this column were from an article by Colin Ritter, one of nine men including Justice Douglas, who walked every foot of the 185-mile hike along the Chesapeake and Ohio Canal in 1954. The article appeared in the June issue of the magazine *American Forests*. I am indebted to Leslie Deibel of Canton for calling it to my attention.

July 18, 1965
Canada Saves Village, Canal Boat

Caught up in the activities associated with restoring Stark County's section of the Ohio & Erie Canal, it is easy to begin to believe that our local project is the only one of its kind. But such is not the case. Not only are there other similar restorations in the United States but now I find that Canada, too, has restored and is preserving a part of its history, which includes a canal boat, dock and warehouse.

In looking through a recent issue of *The East Canton News*, I became interested in an article by publisher George H. France, who had just returned from a 12-day tour of Ontario with a group of 26 editors and publishers from as many American states. The article describes Upper Canada Village, between Toronto and Ottawa on the St. Lawrence Seaway, where life as it was lived a century ago is depicted in the restored village.

Whereas here in Ohio we have neglected and chopped up and eradicated parts of the Ohio & Erie Canal and its history, the Canadians restored some 40 structures in their village, all 100 years old and some more than 200 years old.

They brought the buildings in, brick by brick and piece by piece, from an area that would have been flooded by the vast seaway project. They also dug a circular canal 2,000 feet long and built one bank higher than the other as a towpath. The canal boat, which carried freight, has been altered to seat 20 persons. It is pulled by mules or oxen on its excursion trips.

Mr. France says the boat is narrower and more pointed than any canal boat or picture of one he ever has seen. It also has a mast. His logical supposition is that the Canadian canal boats frequently crossed large lakes and thus needed a sail to get from one section of a canal to another.

Surreys with fringe on top pass slowly by restored inns, homes, churches and canal landings in the village, providing visitors with a retrospective look at an operating water-driven sawmill, wool carding and spinning plant, bakery, cheese house and other nostalgic reminders of slower and quieter days.

Canal Boat Paintings

The Towpath Restaurant and Lounge, which opened last month in Massillon, is proving popular with local and out of town diners, many of whom express interest in the city and its canal heritage. Two murals point out this area's historic ties to the canal. Both were done from photographs taken while the Ohio & Erie Canal was in full operation before the flood of 1913. The artist is Dominic Tomei of Akron, an amateur painter who is a professional machinist in Cuyahoga Falls.

The painting in the lounge is from a photograph loaned by George Snyder of Massillon, who obtained the photograph from his grandmother, who found it in her attic. It is supposedly a scene photographed south of Navarre around 1890. The dining room mural features a canal boat being towed by a team on the towpath. It was taken from a photograph borrowed from the Massillon Museum.

State Group Meets

Barring inclement weather, members of the Canal Society of Ohio should be enjoying Stark County's hospitality and its restored sections of the Ohio & Erie Canal today. The statewide group was to hold its annual meeting today in Fulton Grange Hall at Canal Fulton.

Ted H. Findley of New Philadelphia, president of the society, described Canal Fulton as an ideal place for canal buffs to visit. He observed that, with water in the canal from above the village to well below Lock 4, the canal looks much as it did a century ago.

As a special feature of the day, Peter Neidert of Canal Fulton has agreed to put his pontoon boat on the canal and take the society members for rides down the canal. The members will eat at Lock 4 Park, where they can see the restored operating lock.

Although one might expect a canal organization to visit Canal Fulton, the event is indicative of the tourism benefits that can be derived by the village through an influx of individuals and organizations interested in the restored waterway, lock and someday, perhaps, an authentic canal boat.

This column would like to add another welcome to all the members of the Canal Society of Ohio. Good canawling!

July 25, 1965
Ohio Canal Buffs Visit Stark

Canal Fulton was the mecca of Ohio canal buffs last Sunday when more than half the membership of the Canal Society of Ohio rallied in the village for their fourth annual meeting. The village was chosen for the get-together this year because of the on-going program of preservation and restoration of the Ohio & Erie Canal in Stark County.

The operable lock at Lock 4 Park near the village, the attractive little park, the miles of rewatered canal and barbered towpath all pleased the visiting canal enthusiasts.

But the ride on Peter Neidert's pontoon "packet" climaxed the canal buffs' day. Held down to the 3-miles-per-hour speed of the original canal boats, the tiny excursion craft made seven leisurely trips up and down the canal, from Canal Fulton to Lock 4 Park, with 15 passengers aboard each trip.

"Everybody surely got a bang out of that ride," said Ted H. Findley of New Philadelphia, president of the canal society. "It was the frosting on the cake. I was sorry there wasn't time enough to permit the public to take a free ride. We could have had more public than members riding. But we had leased the boat so as to provide free rides for the members who had come from Columbus, Cleveland, Warren, Akron and all over the state, and we wanted to make sure they got a ride. We just ran out of time."

Mr. Findley and the other officers of the society were unanimously voted back into office at the meeting held at Fulton Grange Hall. The president reported that the society experienced a big swell in membership during the past year and that, without the benefit of a membership drive, there now are more than 200 members across the state.

"It has just been a healthy growth from interested people," he explained.

Included in those "interested people" is State Rep. Ralph Regula of Navarre, co-chairman, with Mayor William Keen of Massillon, of the Stark County Canal Lands Development Advisory Committee. Rep. Regula spoke briefly on the canal development in Stark County and of canal legislation he has introduced in the General Assembly to facilitate further utilization of canal lands in other counties.

The other officers of the society are L.W. Richardson of Cleveland, vice president; Harry R. Valley of Lakewood, secretary-treasurer; Herbert W. Dosey of Cleveland Heights, corresponding secretary; and

Harriet W. Leaf of Akron, historian. Carry-over directors are Ted Dettling, Charles A. Pfahl and Leonard B. Hiebel, all of Akron. New directors are J.D. Robinson of Independence and Carl Pockrandt and Dr. E.L. Hackney, both of Akron.

Commenting on the objectives and goals of the canal society, President Findley said, "Our basic objective is to preserve and maintain the artifacts of the old canal systems of the state. The average historical society's field is so large that it can't concentrate on any particular thing. Our job is to bring the canal history to the front. We hope someday to have a museum where we can store and exhibit the tremendous amount of material we are accumulating. We just got started 20 years too late."

Governor Gets Plea

During the Canal Society of Ohio's meeting the members voted unanimously to ask the governor of Ohio to spare a beautiful section of the Ohio & Erie Canal that is scheduled for obliteration by highway department bulldozers.

The resolution, addressed to Honorable James A. Rhodes, reads as follows:

"Resolved that the Governor of the State of Ohio be asked to suggest to the Department of Highways that it review and, if necessary, reconsider the location of the centerline of the proposed highway on the north side of the Tuscarawas River, between West Lafayette in Coshocton County to Newcomerstown in Tuscarawas County to preserve as much as possible of the existing Ohio Canal structures for our posterity."

The letter from the society explains that: "According to our information, Lock 24, Lock 23 and Lock 22 south of Portage Summit will probably be demolished, as may the mill at Orange, Ohio. We would like to suggest that the sites of these locks could well become roadside parks and points of historical interest. We are afraid that the bulldozer may quickly destroy these interesting monuments of the early builders of beautiful Ohio."

Canoeists Increase

Members of the Canal Society of Ohio,

riding down the canal aboard Peter Neidert's pontoon boat, saw at least three canoes gliding smoothly along the surface of the old waterway.

Aboard their new fiberglass canoe were members of the Byron D. Keller family of Canton. Back in January, I wrote in this column that the Kellers and their four children found canoeing in rented canoes so much fun that they hoped to buy their own canoe and use it on the Ohio & Erie. Sunday the Kellers were enjoying themselves thoroughly. They had taken fishing poles along and, when they were not riding in their new canoe, they were trying their luck fishing.

Mrs. Keller's brother, Richard Kintz of North Canton, also got a canoe recently, a wooden one. He and Mrs. Kintz, their eight children and his father took turns Sunday canoeing on the canal. Even 14-month-old David enjoyed a ride.

The third canoe on the canal was an aluminum craft paddled by an unidentified couple from Canton. It was their first time out and they were thoroughly enjoying it, according to Mrs. Keller, who noted, "Everyone in our family was real tickled about it. In fact, on the way home, my husband said we would have to invite some of the other relatives and take them and have a picnic at Lock 4."

And that shouldn't be too difficult. For Mrs. Keller observed that her brother-in-law and sister, Mr. and Mrs. Eugene Whitmyer of Mantua in Portage County, recently got a canoe and they intend to come to Stark County to paddle on the Ohio & Erie.

Tells Canal Story

Down in the Sandy and Beaver country, Glenn Fishel of Magnolia spoke recently to the Rotary Club of Waynesburg about the canal that ties the two communities together.

He showed aerial photos he took of the canal, from the Elson Mill in Magnolia to the Sandy Creek dam at Waynesburg. He also showed pictures he snapped of the same area while he was walking the towpath. In explaining the pictures, Glenn discussed the possibilities of linking parks in each village by a ribbon parkway along the towpath and canal.

The Rotary Club is planning a box social in August at which time members and guests hope to look over the Sandy and Beaver with an eye to its potential development.

August 1, 1965
Legislators OK Canal Bill

Ohio was less than 25 years old when proponents of a canal system in the state first put their thoughts into words and action. Actually, Buckeye Land was only 14 years old when a resolution for constructing the Ohio & Erie Canal was introduced in the General Assembly. During the elections of 1818, canals became a major state issue. And, in their campaign speeches, a majority of the state legislators promised to support them.

A little over a week ago, 147 years later, an amendment to existing law, involving canals, was prepared by another state legislator, Rep. Ralph S. Regula of Navarre. It was introduced for him in the State Senate by Sen. Edward Garrigan of Summit County after having been approved by Sen. David Matia of Cuyahoga County. The amendment was passed in both houses and awaited only the lieutenant governor's and governor's signatures to become law.

The new legislation permits private companies or individuals who lease canal lands from the state to open them to the public for recreational use without fear of being subject to lawsuits. By removing the fear of liability in the event of mishaps on canal lanes, Rep. Regula and his co-legislators have brought closer the possibility of a three-county hikeway and canoeway as part of a ribbon-like system.

Some time ago, members of Rep. Regula's and this writer's families spent a Sunday afternoon exploring the Ohio & Erie Canal in Cuyahoga and Summit counties. We were delighted to find that the canal had been preserved intact in northern Summit

County and throughout almost the entire length of Cuyahoga County.

Metal aqueducts had been constructed to carry the strong-flowing water across streams in Cuyahoga County to provide a water supply for the American Steel and Wire Co., which holds a 99-year lease on the canal from the state.

Greatly impressed by the mile after mile of fully watered canal excellently maintained by the steel and wire firm, Rep. Regula and I enthused about its recreational potential and that of similar sections of the Ohio & Erie.

Following our exchange of thoughts, Rep. Regula conceived the liability amendment through which such leased sections of the canal could be made available for recreational use. Commenting on the legislation last week, he said, "I think it will mean that a number of areas throughout Ohio that are presently leased from the state by private interests will be made available to the public for recreational purposes. It is my hope that this legislation will facilitate the opening of Cuyahoga and Summit county canal areas so they can be tied in with the Stark County canal lands as part of the proposed Buckeye Trail."

With this enabling legislation on the books, the day comes ever closer when individuals or families in populous Cleveland conceivably could sling on their packs or launch their canoes and travel the towpath, or the waterway itself, the more than 50 miles to Massillon. And their Stark County counterparts could hike or canoe north through some beautiful historic countryside to the suburbs of Ohio's largest city.

Although it was almost overshadowed by the multitude of highly publicized bills processed through the legislative mill during recent months, the canal lands amendment holds forth promise of considerable historical, educational and recreational benefit for Ohioans.

Lynda Goes Canoeing

I continue to receive calls from Stark County residents interested in canoeing on the canal and wanting to know the best launching places, weed conditions, water depth, etc. It is another indication of the growing interest in canal canoeing.

Telephoto pictures from Minnesota this past week focused national attention on canoeing as a recreation. When the President's daughter, Lynda Bird Johnson, went on a four-day canoe trip through Minnesota's Superior National Forest, she was photographed smiling from the bow of a canoe, the stern of which was occupied by Secretary of Agriculture Orrville Freeman. Wonder if she could have learned how to paddle on that stretch of the Chesapeake and Ohio Canal in our nation's capital?

August 8, 1965
Studies … They're Wonderful!

Studies are always with us. They are everywhere — and of all kinds. Our bureaucratic government thrives on them.

We, as citizens, frequently are part of them — being studied, that is (our habits, our mores, our likes, dislikes, etc.). But then everything else is being studied, too.

Studies keep some of us busy, some of us involved and some interested while they simply get in the hair of others (like maybe a gimlet-eyed efficiency expert giving the office force the treatment.)

Headline writers use the word "study," meaning "a rendering of anything made as a result of careful investigation," so often a study may be made to see if another word can be substituted.

Studies… we thrive on them.

Comes now a study of special interest to those who read this column — not a study of canal towpaths, but very close to it — a "nationwide system of trails study." It was announced at Cabinet level last month by Secretary of the Interior Stewart L. Udall through the Bureau of Outdoor Recreation.

Make no mistake about it, this study has merit. It has tremendous recreational potential for millions of Americans and Americans yet to come. Perhaps it even

48

may touch Stark County and its developing towpath trail as a proposed section of the Buckeye Trail.

Plans call for a detailed study that could lead to the establishment of a nationwide system of trails as recommended by President Johnson in his "natural beauty message" to Congress. A four-man steering committee will conduct the study and make suggestions to Secretary Udall for his consideration in making recommendations to the President by the end of this year.

Objectives of the study will be to evaluate present trail programs and recommend a comprehensive plan to develop and use the trails so their full potential for outdoor recreation can be realized now and in the future.

In the course of the study, the committee will consult representatives of the Bureau of Sport Fisheries and Wildlife, Bureau of Public Roads, Bureau of Indian Affairs, Corps of Engineers, Bureau of Reclamation and other interested federal, state and local public agencies and private organizations.

President Johnson, in his message to Congress, requested a cooperative program to encourage the augmentation of trails now established in our national parks and forests. In his message, the President said:

"The forgotten outdoorsmen of today are those who like to walk, hike, ride horseback or bicycle. For them we must have trails as well as highways. Nor should motor vehicles be permitted to tyrannize the more leisurely human traffic.

"Old and young alike can participate. Our doctors recommend and encourage such activity for fitness and fun...

"There are many new and exciting trail projects under way across the land. In Arizona, a county has arranged for miles of irrigation canal banks to be used by riders and hikers. In Illinois, an abandoned railroad right-of-way is being developed as a 'Prairie Path.' In Mexico, utility rights-of-way are used as public trails.

"As with so much of our quest for beauty and quality, each community has opportunities for action. We can and should have an abundance of trails for walking, cycling and horseback riding, in and close to our cities. In the back country, we need to copy the great Appalachian Trail in all parts of America, and to make full use of rights-of-way and other public paths."

Three general classes of trails will be considered for inclusion in the system:

Trunk Trails — Scenic and historic trails of national significance intended to permit extended hiking or riding trips. Such existing and proposed trails typically might be 500 miles or more in length, pass through two or more states, have overnight shelters at appropriate intervals, and be interconnected with other trunk trails.

Specific Area Trails — Trails primarily on public lands that enable people to make full use of the outdoor recreation opportunities. An assessment will be made of the adequacy of existing trail systems in national parks, national forests, public domain lands, national wildlife refuges, and other federal and state lands.

Regional and Local Trails — Trails intended primarily for day use that are directly accessible to people living in urban centers or which can be reached readily from urban centers. Such trails are built because of their proximity to populations and their capacity to satisfy needs for limited hiking and riding experiences. They include existing and potential trails operated by public agencies and private organizations.

The study will consider the acquisition, construction, operation and maintenance of trails by one or more appropriate federal, state or local public agencies, or by private organizations.

How can a study of such magnitude possibly overlook the Ohio & Erie Canal towpath and its potential as it is being demonstrated here in Stark County?

Discovery in Summit

Talk about digging up canal history and unearthing remnants of old locks and docks. Up in Summit County, they pulled a switch on the usual procedure. They discovered a fairly well preserved guard lock of the old Pennsylvania and Ohio Canal — not by unearthing it, but by "unwatering" it.

For canal buffs, the discovery was a real treat. It happened this way:

Last May, workmen emptied a dam in the Cuyahoga River under the downtown Route 8 bridge in Kent so they could build supports for a new bridge. When the water receded, lo and behold, there was the old guard lock.

Ted Dettling of Akron, a director of the Canal Society of Ohio, says the lock has been inundated for 123 years. He explains that the lock is in the area where the canal entered the Cuyahoga River. The Pennsylvania and Ohio Canal joined the Ohio & Erie Canal in the heart of Akron.

Canal enthusiasts interested in seeing and taking pictures of the old guard lock before it is again covered by the waters of the dam, perhaps for another 123 years, have about six weeks to do so. Then, Kent Service Director Larry Wooddell says, the dam will be closed and the waters of the river again will rise above the old lock.

————

Editors note: *Along the Towpath* did not appear for the next three weeks while Simpson took a vacation.

September 5, 1965
Western Ohio Has Canal Boom

Back "along the towpath" again after a three-week vacation, I find there has been a boom in canal restoration interest in western Ohio. News stories originating in cities along the Miami and Erie Canal tell of big plans for restoration and utilization of the old waterway in that historically rich area. The activity seems to have resulted, in part, from Gov. James A. Rhodes' recent "tour of the Wonderful World of Anthony Wayne." Consequently, state aid is in the offing for the reconstruction project.

As a part of the development, seven miles of the canal along the Maumee River,

between Independence Dam in Defiance County and Florida in Henry County, will be made into a canoe run by the State Division of Parks and Recreation. The canal runs the length of Independence State Park.

Debris and silt, which found its way into the canal during the last half century and before, will be dredged during the winter, Melvin J. Rebholz, state parks and recreation division head, said, adding that the state will set up a canoe rental concession and construct docks from funds provided through the capital improvements program. The canoe run is reported to be one of 20 sites scheduled for development as part of a multimillion-dollar program for recreation along the Maumee and Auglaize rivers.

Here in Stark County, we have the potential for as nice or nicer and as long or longer a canoe run than the state plans in the western part of the state. This column has been plugging for its development for nearly 18 months and, in recent weeks, interest in the Ohio & Erie Canal as a canoeway has been picking up. More and more canoes have been gliding over its waters. Without the benefit of vast state funds to work with, however, the development of Stark County's canal lands as a hiking path and canoe run proceeds at what seems a snail's pace. But there is progress and there are growing numbers of interested persons willing to help the project.

Again in the western part of the state, farther south on the Miami and Erie, the city of Delphos has a new project under way. The city council and civic organizations plan to restore a part of the canal within the city as a historic landmark. After Delphos received the deed to the canal within the city limits from the state, civic groups raised $37,500 for the project and merchants and the city council added $10,750. Again, state funds are expected to help pay for the project.

State funds could serve as a magic wand in helping to bring the Stark County canal lands to the point of restoration and beautification envisioned by those who would have it become a beautiful, recreational and historical parkway. But, as of

50

now, there have been no state funds made available.

River-Canal Run

Another organization urging the restoration of the Miami and Erie Canal in western Ohio is the Maumee Valley Society of Professional Engineers. The engineers submitted a plan to dredge the canal to the state. The plan calls for installation of a lift to transfer boats from the Maumee River into the canal. When completed, the river-canal waterway would be navigable for 25 miles.

Here in Stark County, at least 25 miles of a combined Tuscarawas River-Ohio & Erie Canal waterway is potentially navigable by canoes. In fact, it was so navigated last Sunday.

Arden Gill, 31, of North Canton, Jim Harper, 29, of Massillon, and Earl Roberts of Wadsworth stepped into a canoe at the north edge of Canal Fulton at 9 a.m. Nine hours and 15 minutes later they stepped from their canoe on a bank of the Tuscarawas River near the old canal aqueduct piers north of Bolivar.

They were "really beat" but enthusiastic, Arden said, reporting, for those who may wish to follow their course (perhaps not so far the first time), that they paddled down the canal until it started to get weedy. Then the going was slower, although they could still get through. When the canal ran out of water, they portaged a short distance to the Tuscarawas River. The river, at this point, polluted with industrial wastes and sewage, is unsightly and often offensive to the nostrils. And it gets worse before it gets better.

"The river is a mass of corruption south of Massillon to Navarre," Arden declared. "Then, south of Navarre, it really begins to look nice. It begins to clear up and you start seeing more wildlife. Except for a few people on the bridges in Massillon, I don't think there were more than three or four persons who actually saw us during the entire trip. It was that much away from it all. The scenery was really beautiful and there were lots of woods. It was just like you said it would be — a real park area with beautiful scenery.

But I'm glad we made it to the last stretch or we would have had a different opinion of it."

And I'm glad that Arden's wife, Donna, who is a reader of this column, suggested the canoe trip to her husband and his friends. For, after talking with him, I believe Arden Gill sees the potential in our Stark County canal lands and supports the efforts being made to restore them for all who would use them and benefit from them. We need more like him.

September 12, 1965

It's Fine Time for "Towpathing"

Fall is for hiking. When the air is bracing and the scenery a blaze of color, that's the prime time for hiking, and especially "towpathing" (that's hiking along a canal towpath).

Nobody knows this better than our senior citizens.

Next Friday, 25 to 30 members of the Canton YMCA Senior Center plan to do some towpathing approximately a mile along the Ohio & Erie Canal towpath in the vicinity of the county's Lock 4 Park south of Canal Fulton. The seniors will ride the YMCA bus to the canal, which they have been studying. As part of their research, they have heard talks by State Rep. Ralph Regula of Navarre and Ted Findley of New Philadelpia, president of the Canal Society of Ohio.

So here is to the best of weather for your hike, seniors. And good towpathing!

Canal Boat Sold

Peter Neidert's "canal boat" has been sold. Those who rode up and down the canal this past summer aboard the pontoon excursion craft and those who planned a trip in the future will be interested to know the canal craft has become a lake launch. Otis Clay, owner and operator of Clay's Park, southwest of Canal Fulton, has purchased the boat and plans to add it to

51

the recreational attractions at the park.

The pontoon boat made numerous runs from Canal Fulton to Lock 4 Park and back during the village's sesquicentennial. In July, it was charted by the Canal Society of Ohio as a special feature of the group's annual meeting.

Mr. Clay, in adding the pontoon boat to his flotilla of rowboats and canoes, plans to use the launch to ferry sightseers around the park's two lakes.

Now, more than ever, there is a need for a canal boat.

How about building a real one?

Canal Section Doomed

When the Canal Society of Ohio met last July at Canal Fulton, it passed a resolution urging Gov. James A. Rhodes to save a beautiful stretch of the Ohio & Erie in Coshocton County that is to be destroyed by the construction of a highway along the canal bed.

The society received a reply from P.E. Masheter, director of the Department of Highways, that the use of the canal lands was the only economically feasible way "to safely serve the area and anticipated traffic needs."

"We regret the use of canal lands for highway purposes, but the prevailing conditions in this area made it impracticable to do otherwise," he concluded.

Military Had Role

Canals and information pertinent to them crop up in the least expected places. This week, while attending an Air Force Reserve meeting, I was looking over a command study on counterinsurgency when I came on a section titled "Roads and Canals." The section stressed how the growth of the nation required early emphasis on the construction of roads and canals. It went on to explain that the government called on the military for its trained engineers to execute a development program. In 1824, Congress acted to specifically authorize the use of the Corps of Engineers in constructing roads and canals with government aid.

In 'Wonderful World'

In case you missed it, the September issue of *The Wonderful World of Ohio* contains an article and color pictures of the Ohio & Erie Canal in Stark County. The article, which will be read statewide, may well bring tourists from throughout the Buck-eye State to the Canal Fulton area.

September 19, 1965
Who Will Build New Hills?

Will America someday be bulldozed as flat as the deck of one of its mighty aircraft carriers — its treeless hills and mountains eroded and leveled as smooth as the rapidly increasing number of parking lots? Or will a "wilderness bill of rights" come in time to save our beloved "America, the Beautiful" from ourselves?

This week, this column is devoted to editorializing in an effort to enlist support for a tremendous idea advanced by one of America's greatest conservationists — Supreme Court Justice William O. Douglas.

The concept of a "wilderness bill of rights," advanced by Justice Douglas, would "protect those whose spiritual values extend to the rivers and lakes, the valleys and the ridges, and who find life in a mechanized society worth living only because those splendid resources are not despoiled."

It would protect and aid those who would preserve and restore the Ohio & Erie Canal and the Stark Wilderness Center with its stand of virgin timber.

The justice, who was responsible for a last-minute save of the Chesapeake and Ohio Canal, which terminates in the nation's capital, classifies himself and other ardent lovers of the outdoors as a minority. But he says it is the government's duty to protect their beloved wilderness from "mechanized society."

The 66-year-old jurist, who currently is mountain climbing and hiking with a backpack in some of the undisturbed primitive areas of the Pacific Northwest he wants preserved, makes two proposals. He would create a special federal office of conservation with direct access to the President and sufficient stature to advise the President on matters affecting natural resources. And he would bring into being a wilderness bill of rights designed to "save the outdoors from progress and people who don't fully appreciate it."

The conservation office would speak out in defense of conservation interests when other federal agencies advanced "proposals destructive of conservation values."

In putting forth his arguments on behalf of nature lovers, the justice said:

"Even though a wilderness is thought of only in terms of those who canoe or hike or backpack or ride horses or climb mountains, the values are important in our pluralistic society. Though these actual participants constitute a minority, they have rights that the majority should respect.

"The Bill of Rights, which makes up the first 10 amendments to our Constitution, contains, in the main, guarantees to minorities. These are guarantees of things that government cannot do to the individual because of his conviction or belief or other idiosyncrasies.

"When it comes to wilderness, we need a similar bill of rights. The ingredients of a wilderness bill of rights must be reflected in laws, regulations and administrative orders that reflect governmental purpose through all levels — from the village, municipality, county, state and on up to the federal government. Such measures, to be effective, must stem from wide public approval and undertake to accommodate the conflicts between preservation of wilderness, on the one hand, and the traditional American concept of industrial or other business use of forests, waterways and beaches for commercial purposes, on the other.

"The wilderness cannot be preserved against the pressures of population and 'progress' unless the guarantees are explicit and severely enforced, and unless wilderness values become a crusade."

Mr. Douglas, in his nineteenth and newest book, *A Wilderness Bill of Rights*, warns that more ground is lost annually in the field of conservation than is gained. He writes that the "pressure of commercial interests, of motorized recreationists, of our mounting population, threaten to overrun the meager wilderness areas left, fill them with the debris of civilization, and leave only Alpine areas in primitive condition."

Here in Stark County, the truth of this statement can be seen in that mining and lumber interests threatened the destruction of the Stark Wilderness Center's virgin timber prior to the center's creation and individual and other interests have caused and still are causing the eradication of many areas of the Ohio & Erie Canal.

The justice speaks out strongly against the disfigurement of our natural beauties, the pollution of rivers and the decimation of our wildlife. Close at hand, the pollution of the Tuscarawas River, which flows through Stark and Tuscarawas counties, is a graphic case in point.

Observing that local parks take much of the automobile pressure off wilderness areas, the justice writes: "As the population increases, state parks and other local preserves must multiply, if our wilderness areas are to be preserved."

A wilderness bill of rights, as he envisions it, would include the following ingredients:

"The multiple use concept, but not from the view that this allows every section of the public domain to be put to all possible uses; proper provision for public hearings and fair decisions on matters affecting use of public lands and resources; proper control of fencing of public lands; control of motorized vehicles, power boats and aircraft; restriction of mining claims in wilderness areas; protection against sewage and industrial wastes; protection against dams; preservation of wild rivers and of wetlands; safeguards against highways; and a new conservation land ethic.

"We must learn to live with the land, not off the land," Justice Douglas says. "We need a new land ethic that restates man's relation to the earth from which he comes. One indication of the arrival of the new land ethic will be the tolerance of the majority, who want the automobile to take them everywhere, for the minority who want sanctuaries free of the noise and debris of civilization."

When the justice speaks of "safeguards against highways," we are reminded of another local case in point — the beautiful stretch of the Ohio & Erie Canal extending westward into Coshocton County from Newcomerstown in Tuscarawas County. Despite protests of a minority who would save this natural and historic beauty spot, a highway very soon will eradicate it.

In California, where a minority has gained more support, conservation-minded individuals and groups have so far prevented road builders from slashing through a magnificent stand of giant redwoods. But the highway supporters yet may win. With their modern equipment, they can level in one day what it took thousands of years to grow.

Here, in our part of America the Beautiful, the magnificent oaks, maples and beeches of the Stark Wilderness Center are comparable, for a hardwood stand, to the redwood groves of the West. And the Ohio & Erie Canal is as much worth saving as the Chesapeake and Ohio was. It took the redwoods and oaks a long time to reach their lofty stature. We can't wait a long time for the new land ethic. We need it now — along with a "wilderness bill of rights."

September 26, 1965
The Lady Had Problems

Well, it had to happen. I knew it would, sooner or later. Someone hiked the towpath and didn't enjoy it. And I heard of it. It seems there were two couples making the trek. The one couple enjoyed the hike. The other couple didn't — especially the wife. And she had reasons not to. Lots of them. All with wings.

I have hiked the towpath many times in many places and I can't recall being both-

ered by mosquitoes. But this wasn't the case with the two couples. The mosquitoes were waiting for them. They seemed to show a distinct preference for Mrs. T (that's T for target), and especially for her head. They came from everywhere and practically formed a cloud around her head. Relentlessly they pursued her down the towpath, dive-bombing her head in squadron strength. They couldn't seem to resist her hair.

It's safe to say that if Mrs. T ever hikes the towpath again during the mosquito season, she won't be "wearing" hair spray. The mosquitoes in that area still are buzzing about how irresistible she was.

Seniors Enjoyed Hike

I had the opportunity to talk with two members of the Canton YMCA senior citizens group that hiked the towpath near Canal Fulton two weeks ago.

H.J. Berger, who is 80 and chairman of the group's historical division, said, "There were 32 present and we had a lovely time."

Emmett E. Urwin, who is 85, nodded his head in assent, and said, "Everybody I heard speaking about it spoke favorably and I didn't hear anyone speak against it. One thing though, that sun was sure hot." (It was 89 degrees.)

Both men took pride in telling me of the senior member of their group, Frederick Croad, who hiked the towpath. Last week the club had a birthday party for Mr. Croad. He was 102!

The two seniors were appreciative of the efforts of Paul Marks, general foreman of canal reconstruction, who "opened the lock for us, showed us how it worked and then gave us a nice little talk," Mr. Berger said.

"What do you think of the idea to build an authentic canal boat and put it in operation on the canal?" I asked.

"I think it is a very good idea," Mr. Berger responded. "It will attract a lot of attention to Stark County."

"Would you like to ride on it?" I inquired.

"Yes sir, I would," he assured me.

With the mention of the canal boat, Mr. Urwin came into his own. As a boy, he had lived on the canal aboard a houseboat.

Housing was hard to find at the time, he recalls, and so his father, a miner, bought the houseboat and the family set up housekeeping on the canal about three miles from Canal Dover (Dover) in Tuscarawas County.

Mr. Urwin recalls seeing the canal traffic every day the boats were moving. And because he lived near where the canal boats were loaded, he had the experience of working as a mule skinner for three days. It took that long to take a load of coal up the canal from Canal Dover to Akron and return empty.

Young Emmett was only 14 or 15 at the time. But one of the canal boat crews was in dire need of a mule skinner and so they asked if Emmett could drive the mule, horse and burro that towed the boat. With great reluctance, Emmett's mother permitted him to go but only after extracting the promise from the skipper that the boy could sleep in the stern cabin with the captain's family and not up in the bow.

Questioned as to the difficulty of the trip, Mr. Urwin recalled that it wasn't bad at all.

"When you got tired walking, you could mount the mule and ride a piece," he explained.

Once, when approaching a lock to operate the gates so the canal boat could pass through, young Emmett ran into an unpleasant but common canal era situation. A crewman from another boat that was approaching from the opposite direction attempted to set the locks so his boat could get through first, despite the fact that the boy had gotten there first.

Mr. Urwin recalls his captain jumped off their boat and told the crewman "what was what," dressing him down for attempting to take advantage of young Emmett's youthfulness. Although the incident ended without blows being struck, canal history is filled with stories of similar incidents that didn't end as peaceably.

The two senior citizens had a good time at the canal and they seemed to enjoy talking about it. I certainly enjoyed listening to them and observing the twinkle in their eyes as they recalled stories and experiences out of the past.

Having taken the towpath trip in stride, the two octogenarians were looking forward to the club's next excursion, a picnic outing at Happy Valley near Stanwood — and perhaps some square dancing.

October 3, 1965

Is Metro Park the Answer?

Medina County, which adjoins Stark's neighboring counties of Summit and Wayne, is not a canal county. As far as having the potential to restore and develop a historical canal and create a recreational canal parkway — Medina is a "have not" county. But sometimes it takes the "have nots" to point the way for the "haves" and make them realize their favored status, their material blessings and their opportunities.

Canalwise, Stark, with roughly 25 miles of the Ohio & Erie Canal reclaimable, is a "have" county. It has the potential for a beautiful cross-county canal parkway, historically significant, educationally useful and recreationally fun-filled.

But after nearly a year of effort, the county's canal lands development advisory board, charged by the county commissioners with the development of the canal lands, finds itself able to dream and plan but not fulfill. There is and has been no money for the canal project.

The commissioners, willing and desirous of developing the canal into a useful, pleasurable recreational facility for public use, have had no funds to allocate to this project.

Medina County, likewise, had no money for such a project. But residents there decided to do something about it.

No, they didn't decide to build a canal. They decided to have a canal-less park system — a metropolitan park system.

As a result, 75 advisory committeemen from all walks of life, including farmers, housewives, doctors, public officials, businessmen and civic and church representatives, are working together to develop such a system.

To get the money for their project, they are spark-plugging a drive for a three-tenths mill countywide levy. The levy would provide $60,000 a year for 10 years to buy land and develop parks. Estimates are that it would cost the average Medina County family about a dollar a year.

Stark County could do wonders with its canal restoration and park development — with $60,000.

But Medina County is expecting more. Park project leaders there anticipate federal matching funds would double the income from the levy, thus providing $120,000 a year and $1,200,000 in 10 years.

The extensive River Styx conservation complex proposed for that area would become a part of the Medina County park system, according to plans. This would include a lake for boating and fishing and campsite facilities.

Plans for the Ohio & Erie development also call for a lake and campsites as part of the recreational facilities.

Just as a Stark County landscaper donated flowering crab apple trees to beautify the canal towpath, so a Medina County landscaper donated 10 of the trees to the park group.

And the Medina Junior Chamber of Commerce offered to install playgrounds in the park system.

Eighty-five persons were invited to attend the organizational meeting for the Medina park project. Seventy-five, willing to work, turned out.

In Stark County there have been many offers of assistance and some donations of material. But the project creeps forward instead of leaping ahead — not because of the lack of leadership but due to the lack of funds.

Consequently, Cochairmen Ralph Regula of Navarre and Mayor William Keen of Massillon have been thinking in terms of a metropolitan park system for Stark County and a countywide levy to provide needed funds.

Mr. Regula, who as a member of the State Legislature is also a member of the metropolitan area committee of the House of Representatives, sees the metropolitan park system and levy as "a means of pro-

viding a stable base for continuing development of Stark County's potential. We are the architects of the recreational future of our county and we must assume this responsibility."

Mayor Keen says, "The only way we are going to get a park system in Stark County, that is something more than we have now, is to create such an agency at the county level and ask people to support it through an increase in taxation. The present level of taxation simply will not support such an additional county government function."

All they need in Medina County to obtain their objective and establish a metropolitan park system for the county is a favorable vote of the people.

Perhaps, in this regard, Stark County must follow instead of lead. Certainly the course being chartered in Medina County seems the logical way.

Canal Gets More Fish

There are 2,999 more largemouth bass swimming in the Ohio & Erie Canal near Canal Fulton today than there were last week. There would have been 3,000 but Raymond Katler of Massillon caught a dandy 15-incher shortly after the division of wildlife of the Department of Natural Resources put the 3,000 in the canal at Lock 4 Park.

Down at the other end of the county, at Navarre, fishing should be improving also. Mayor David Mayer said he put 1,300 bluegills in the canal fishing pond there Thursday. The mayor obtained the fish from the Senecaville hatchery through the U.S. Soil Conservation Service. He says there are also bass and catfish in the canal pond.

October 10, 1965
Another County Canal Boat-Minded

We've been talking for nearly a year now about building an authentic canal boat for use on the Ohio & Erie Canal in Stark County. During this past year, similar suggestions were made in Summit County. Now we hear the same kind of proposal from Columbiana County.

The Columbiana County Forests and Parks Council, an organization of interested citizens promoting the development of Beaver Creek State Park, is restoring Gaston's Mill in the park in cooperation with the Columbiana County Historical Association.

With the development of the state park, extending from Elkton to the Ohio River, under way, officers of the council are excited about the possibility of establishing a museum at Elkton in conjunction with a typical country store of 100 years ago. They also are publicizing the fact that "the Elkton project could well include an exhibit of a typical blacksmith shop and possible horse-drawn boat rides on a portion of the old Sandy and Beaver Canal."

Will Summit or Columbiana have a canal boat before Stark?

Item in the News

Fred J. Milligan, former president of the Ohio Historical Society, announced in Columbus last week that $105,000 in state funds will be used on the Miami and Erie Canal at Lockington in Shelby County for rehabilitation of locks and a locktender's house and museum-information center at the highest point of the Miami and Erie system.

Girls on the Towpath

"Let's be the first cadet troop to do it."

Do what? Why, hike the Ohio & Erie Canal towpath, of course. After all, several Boy Scout troops had done it. So why not a Girl Scout troop?

According to their leader, Mrs. Willard Hambleton, this was the spirit of Cadet Troop 346, Girl Scouts of America, when they decided to hike the towpath from Canal Fulton to Massillon. All 15 members of the troop, which is sponsored by Zion EUB Church, are seventh-grade pupils at Edison Junior High School in Perry Township.

Barring rain, the girls will make the seven-mile hike October 17. And Mrs. Hambleton has promised to report on the outing. Take your color film and cameras girls, the canal and towpath are especially photogenic when the trees are dressed in their fall colors.

Towpath Trimmers

If the Girl Scouts find the towpath from Forty Corners Road south to Massillon well maintained, they can thank another troop of Scouts, Troop 906, Boy Scouts of America.

The Boy Scouts, under the leadership of H. Fred Beyer, asked for and were given permission to maintain the towpath from Forty Corners Road to Massillon. The 25 members of the troop, which is sponsored by First Christian Church of Massillon, have worked two Saturdays clearing brush, cutting weeds and mowing the towpath. Later they will burn the collected brush. They spend three or four hours each weekend on the project and expect to work at least once a month through the winter. The work is considered part of their community service and conservation project.

October 17, 1965
Why Not a Canal Stamp?

I wonder when they will put out a postage stamp with a canal scene printed on it. They ought to. Just think of the beautiful scenes they could reproduce. And from the historical standpoint, such a stamp would be a natural commemorative.

This thought came out of a conversation with Mrs. James Halter, general chairman of the Stark County Stamp Club's fifth annual exhibition and bourse. Mrs. Halter suggested I might be interested in one of the feature exhibits at the stamp show, as it pertained to canals. I found the exhibit interesting and informative. It was composed of several frames, one of which was entitled "Ohio Canal Scenes." Another was labeled "Ohio Canal Business."

The display, a special attraction, was by Rendell Rhoades, a professor at Ashland College. The professor, who, unfortunately, was unable to be present at the show, is reported to have collected some 200 historical items or documents pertaining to the canal.

His frame on canal scenes was made up of 16 brightly colored, nearly perfectly preserved postal cards of canal views. The exquisite postal card detail gave the viewer a historically accurate look at 16 canalera scenes in Stark County. These included views of Lock No. 1 and Lock No. 2 at Massillon, a lock at Navarre, the falls at the reservoir in Massillon, the canal in the center of downtown Massillon and the canal at the Cherry Street bridge there.

The old canal days came alive as I looked at each bit of postal history. One card showed a man wearing a derby, which looked just exactly like my grandfather's dress-up derby. The man was sitting on the canal bank gazing at the waterfall from the lock bypass as it spilled water back into the canal. Just behind him I could make out the hoofprints of horses and/or mules in the sandy towpath. Another card afforded an excellent view of a flotilla of canal boats near Navarre, with the Tuscarawas River flowing along beside the canal.

The frame titled "Ohio Canal Business" included a canal shipping bill and a listing of the "Regulations in Relation to the Navigation of the Ohio Canal and the Payment of Tolls Thereon."

There also were two letters written by persons who were traveling on the Ohio & Erie Canal by canal boat. One was by a woman passenger on a packet traveling south from Cleveland. This letter was written while the boat was between Akron and Massillon and it revealed that the writer hoped to meet her brother in Cincinnati if she could brave the cholera.

Another historical frame on display was captioned "Canal Towns." It was part of the exhibit of Ross K. Lindsay Jr. of the Tuscora Stamp Club of New Philadelphia and Dennison in Tuscarawas County.

The full exhibit was titled "Dead Post Offices in Tuscarawas County." It contained cancellations from post offices in Canal Dover, Tracy, Bernice, Rock, Gilmore and Port Washington, most of which have been discontinued.

One envelope, with a 4-cent stamp of the pony express rider, bore this historical information: "Historic Port Washington, Ohio... Terminus of the Old Port Washington Road where covered wagons met canal boats." The commemorative envelope was postmarked July 20, 1860.

Although not a philatelist myself, I was impressed by the outstanding collections displayed and the work and thought that went into them. I was especially fascinated by the historical frames of the canal era.

If we ever are to have a postage stamp bearing a canal scene, it most likely will be due to the efforts of clubs such as the Stark County Stamp Club and its associate club, the Tuscora Stamp Club. It surely would be nice to have a stamp featuring one of the most picturesque canal scenes including a sunset, a canal boat, a waterfall and a team and mule skinner moving "along the towpath."

October 24, 1965

Canal Committee Is Year Old

It is hard to believe — but a year has passed since the first meeting of the Stark County Canal Lands Development Advisory Committee at Lock 4 Park south of Canal Fulton.

The weather was raw the afternoon of October 9, 1964, and so the meeting was adjourned and quickly reconvened at the B&M Grill in the village. There, over cups of coffee and tea, the committee members became acquainted and, with considerable enthusiasm, began making plans to restore and develop the Ohio & Erie Canal and its adjoining lands within Stark County.

A lot of water has flowed down the canal since then. Likewise, a lot has been accomplished by the committee in its advisory role to the Stark County commissioners. On the other hand, some of the committee's goals seem as far away today as they were on that first meeting day. But the momentum of the restoration program is forward and always there is the hope that there will be a major breakthrough in the form of unexpected funds, state assistance or help from established organizations, which will enable the restoration program to leap ahead.

Because I was nudged nearly into the "position" of committee secretary, I have recorded the minutes of all the meetings and have them at hand. A review of the minutes reveals the committee's activities during the past year:

Leaks in the canal were plugged, low places in the banks were raised, bridges were built over spillways to provide a continuous towpath, the towpath was cleared of brush and mowed, many dead trees were cut and burned, a mechanical weed cutter was used to cut the water weeds in the canal.

Benches were made for the towpath at Lock 4 Park, bird houses and bird feeders were placed near the canal by the Canton Audubon Society, a historical marker was erected at Lock 4, responsibility for maintaining sections of the towpath was given various organizations, maps of the canal were made with an eye to zoning.

State officials were invited to inspect the canal, efforts were made to tie in the canal towpath with the Buckeye Trail, fish were placed in the canal by the state, the county's regional planning commission was asked to develop an optimum development plan for the canal lands park, Paul Marks was deputized to police the canal lands.

An ice skating area was prepared, plans for a canalside museum and an authentic canal boat were begun, donated trees were planted along the towpath and efforts were made to obtain donations for the advancement of the canal park system.

There were numerous other activities during the year. And, as a result, the residents of Stark County, in ever increasing numbers, are coming to use and enjoy the maintained sections of the canal parkway.

The Girls Did It!

Well, they did it. Twelve Girl Scouts, members of Cadet Troop 346 at Zion EUB Church, hiked the towpath from the north edge of Massillon to Canal Fulton. The girls' leader, Mrs. Willard Hambleton, said it wasn't easy, especially on the lower end of the towpath where the weeds had grown high again.

"But it was wonderful," she said, "and we all are ready to go back."

The girls, along with three mothers, one father and Rev. Richard Appel, pastor of the church, made the hike last Sunday. Indicative of the spreading interest in the canal, the girls met hikers who had traveled 80 miles to see and walk along the canal. The girls plan to make a map of the canal and towpath for the benefit of other Girl Scouts who may wish to follow in their footsteps. The influence of Stark County's garden clubs was also in evidence. When the girls left the canal, they all had handfuls of weeds and colored leaves to make dry arrangements.

Canal Tour Was Fun

Two weeks ago, Mrs. Stanley Odar, volunteer chairman of the travel and tour Wonderful World of Ohio series of the Canton YWCA, called to say that a group of 70 women planned to go to Canal Fulton in two buses October 21. They expected to eat in the village and then go to Lock 4 Park to see the canal and perhaps hike up the towpath. Mrs. Odar promised to report on the outing. And she did.

Seventy-three women made the trip, and although the weather was not very good, they still enjoyed the tour.

"They had a real wonderful time and are really enthused to support the canal restoration," Mrs. Odar said.

Before leaving for Canal Fulton, the group heard a talk about the canal by Ted Findley of New Philadelphia, president of the Canal Society of Ohio. And when they got to the canal, Paul Marks, general foreman of canal reconstruction, explained the workings of the canal lock and answered questions. Despite occasional raindrops, some of the women walked for a short distance "along the towpath."

59

Late Thoughts by the Fireplace

It's late at night as I begin this column — not far from the midnight hour. The telephone has fallen silent and the house has grown quiet. Only the miniature explosions of the burning willow logs in the fireplace punctuate the stillness.

Outside the windows, all is darkness.

But the picture I see in my mind's eye is just the opposite. It is bright and colorful — a summer day. The kind of a day that sets the birds to singing. And there are all kinds of birds in this picture.

But it is the flashing, darting bits of blue that attract me most. They are everywhere, these small birds with the soft voices.

This last sentence tells you that picture I see is of the future. It can't be of today. For the scene is, of course, the Ohio & Erie Canal in Stark County and the eastern bluebird is rarely seen in this part of Ohio today.

In fact, the bluebird population in the nation has been declining for the last 75 years. Then, in the winter of 1957-58, an unusually cold winter, thousands of bluebirds either starved or froze to death.

Most birds can endure extremely cold weather if they can get enough food. But when ice and snow cover the ground and trees during much of the winter, the wild berries and insects which bluebirds love become unavailable.

The frozen bodies of bluebirds were found scattered on the ground that year from Ohio to Virginia and from Tennessee to Florida. It has been estimated that one-third to one-half of the eastern population of bluebirds was destroyed.

It is believed that most of those that survived had learned to come to bird feeders for sustenance.

Successive harsh winters continued to kill off the species until the population reached its lowest ebb in 1963. Seeing them return in fewer numbers each year, those who love them wondered how long the bluebird, so vulnerable in winter, could survive.

To compound the problem, the aggressive European starlings and English sparrows were preempting the nesting cavities in trees the bluebirds, already suffering from a "housing shortage," needed.

Then, seemingly at the last minute, a way was found to help the bluebird and to slowly but surely rebuild its population. The technique was to build "bluebird trails." This involved the building and placing of a number of bluebird nesting boxes about four feet above the ground and about 400 feet apart. Specially constructed to discourage occupation by starlings and sparrows, the boxes serve their purpose well.

The bluebird trails have been remarkably successful in various parts of the country; hundreds, perhaps thousands of baby bluebirds have been hatched in bluebird trail houses built by doctors, lawyers, educators, insurance men, engineers, construction workers and housewives. In one section of North Carolina, the bluebird once again is almost as common as it was prior to the cold winters of the last decade.

In Stark County, where it is a rare treat to see a bluebird, we need bluebird trails. We need someone to build them.

Homer Fulton of Lake Cable thinks the canal towpath would make an ideal bluebird trail. I heartily endorse his idea and suggest that the section of towpath between Crystal Springs and Butterbridge Road would be the ideal location.

This section of the towpath, which already is being improved by the Canton Audubon Society, could become known as "Bluebird Trail" because of the great number of bluebirds to be found there.

But somebody will have to take up the project, make the houses and establish the trail.

Every good idea needs implementation.

It is past the midnight hour now and the logs in the fireplace are but a pile of glowing ashes. But that picture in my mind's eye is brighter than ever. It's the towpath on a summery day in June a few years hence. There are people, young and old, strolling along the path beside the old canal. And the sky — it's blue — blue like with bluebirds.

Canal Gets Feeders

Last April, the Canton Audubon Society placed a number of birdhouses at strategic spots along the canal. Just recently members of the society did the same thing with bird feeders. Throughout the snowy winter months, the birds along the canal will find feed available close at hand, for an Audubon committee plans to supply the feeders at regular intervals, probably twice a week.

Each feeder holds four pounds of feed and there now are four feeders, although more may be added later if there is no vandalism. Paul Marks, general foreman of canal reconstruction, made and donated the feeders and the Buckeye Feed Mills of Dalton provided 400 pounds of feed at cost.

The society's purpose in supplying the feeders is to keep the winter resident birds in this area so everyone can enjoy them as they walk along the towpath.

Jack R. Minger, president of Canton Audubon Society, said, "This area of the canal, from Crystal Springs north to Butterbridge Road, has been set aside as a wildlife sanctuary and no hunting or shooting is permitted." He said the society also plans to put picnic tables in the section for public use.

In addition to the many varieties of birds he has seen in that area, Mr. Minger said he has observed muskrats, mink, woodchucks, possum, weasels, shrews, chipmunks, rabbits, squirrels and raccoons.

One of the remote sections of the canal accessible to hikers, the Crystal Springs to Butterbridge Road stretch, lends itself to development as a wilderness sanctuary. As a comparatively primitive area, it would be a welcome contrast to the more civilized park-like sections of the canalway.

November 7, 1965
Building Boom for Bluebirds?

Things may be looking up for the few remaining bluebirds in Stark County if others are motivated by last week's column about the plight of the bluebirds in the same way that James Pitz of Massillon was. Mr. and Mrs. Pitz, who live near the canal and walk there frequently, read the column and decided to do something about it. Mr. Pitz, a carpenter skilled at making things with his hands, plans to go down into his basement during the long winter months and make bluebird houses. All he needs is the pattern.

Homer Fulton of Lake Cable has drawings of two bluebird houses and detailed instructions for building them. Mr. Fulton, who first brought the need for bluebird trails to my attention, has offered to have copies of the house plans made for free distribution to anyone desiring to build one or more bluebird houses. Copies of the plans, one of which appears with this column, and instructions may be obtained by writing to "Along the Towpath."

Canals in Cartoons

Although I haven't seen it, I understand that the story of the construction of Ohio's canal is being told in cartoon form and is appearing in the *Columbus Sunday Dispatch*. Also, this story of the canals, Book Two of Jim Baker's cartoon series *Ben Hardy and the Ohio Adventure,* has been published by Pioneer Press at Worthington and is available in booklet form from the Ohio Historical Society at Columbus.

Barging Must Be Fun

The canal scenery and atmosphere near New Hope in Bucks County, Pa., must really be something. I have never been there but people keep telling me about it and I hope some day to barge the Lehigh Navigation Canal there.

Last week I received a telephone call and a letter, both of which emphasized the beauty of that area.

The phone call was from Mrs. Charles Lynch. She and her husband had just returned from a trip during which they traveled beside the Delaware River and the Lehigh Canal or the Delaware Canal Locks as it is also known. She describes the highway from New Hope to Easton as a "beautiful drive well worth seeing." New Hope, she said, is a resort town for artists in the summer, and a happy hunting ground for antique collectors due to the many antique shops in the vicinity.

While driving near New Hope, they saw two barges being pulled by mules. The barges were filled with people.

"They waved as we went by and they all looked very happy. There must have been 25 or 30 in each boat," she recalled. "They were smiling and having a great time and one fellow was playing the accordion. The weather was just a little brisk and it was a delightful day. We saw quite a few people walking along the towpath, which is beautifully kept up."

The experience was so interesting to Mrs. Lynch that she confided: "I was thrilled all the rest of the day."

Then came the letter and a booklet from Mrs. Enid Kerry. Published monthly by the Unity School of Christianity in Lee's Summit, Mo., the religious pamphlet featured a color photograph of a canal scene on its cover.

The peaceful panorama was a summer scene of the canal and towpath at New Hope. A youth was riding one of a team of white mules on the graveled towpath and the team was towing a red canal barge. The calm waters of the canal reflected the summer foliage above it. The picture was titled "In Restful Quietness."

I have seen boats or pictures of operating canal boats in three states. But I have yet to see one built to the original specifications. Stark County, to the best of my information, has the opportunity to become the first canal area to have such an authentic craft. We have the canal and we have the drawings and specifications of an original canal boat.

November 14, 1965

Bluebirds Get Helping Hand

Stark County's tiny bluebird population ought to be full-throated with happy song today. Massive help is on the way and it's not the federal-aid kind. It's volunteer help from the home front. Twenty-one persons have indicated they wish to build bluebird houses. Building plans and instructions will be mailed to them in the near future.

It means housing, and lots of it, for the few remaining blue-backed, rusty-breasted thrushes. And this may mean that the mellow warbling of this gentle-dispositioned harbinger of spring will be heard again throughout Stark County — and especially along the Ohio & Erie Canal. For once established in an area, bluebirds will return yearly. Nesting usually produces four to six eggs and two nestings a season are common.

Among those who have written to "Along the Towpath," in care of *The Canton Repository*, for plans are the advisers of the Reedurbanaires 4-H Club, Mr. And Mrs. Walter Swigart. The club plans to build bluebird houses as its woodworking project this year.

And from Massillon comes word that Steven Horner, a retiree, has already built some bluebird houses in his workshop and has them ready to be put up. And he hopes to build more.

Letters have come in from Paris, Waynesburg, Millersburg, Minerva, Sandyville and North Canton, as well as Canton, requesting the plans.

Several letters, from the more rural areas, told of the writers' good fortune in having one or more pairs of bluebirds near their homes.

Anyone who has built or plans to build bluebird houses and wishes to donate them toward the establishment of bluebird trails, under the supervision of the Canton Audubon Society, should contact Jack R. Minger, president. The society plans to establish one or more bluebird trails along the towpath of the Ohio & Erie Canal and at other places in the county if enough houses are constructed and donated.

The houses need to be properly located and placed relative to their immediate environs and the experts in the society have the know-how to accomplish this.

The bluebirds will amply "pay" for any help they are given as their diet consists of about 70 percent insects — good news for towpath hikers and bad news for mosquitoes.

The brightly colored orange-and-black orioles, yellow warblers and wild canaries, and the perky redbirds already are numerous in the canal lands now.

Add the bright blue of the bluebirds, a bluer sky, flowering crab apple blossoms and reflect all this in the waters of the canal and a towpath walk next spring becomes nature's own color spectacular.

Still Time for Canal Tours

Activity along the Ohio & Erie Canal in Stark County is fast fading away as winter approaches.

Oh, the hardy hiker will still have a go at it. And the Boy Scouts may do some winter camping along the towpath. But the major volume of recreational activity along the canal has disappeared and won't return until spring sets the frogs to croaking and buds the pussy willows.

There still is time, however, to make some interesting canal tours. And the officers and members of the Canal Society of Ohio are doing just that. Last Sunday and again today some of the society's members made a tour of the route of the Sandy and Beaver Canal from its junction with the Ohio & Erie at Bolivar to the Lusks Lock of Elkton. They plan a later tour to cover the section from Lusks Lock to the Ohio River. The Sandy and Beaver, by the way, was formed as a private company to establish a connection from the Ohio & Erie to the Ohio River and provide a shorter route to Pittsburgh.

Ted Findley of New Philadelphia, president of the society, reported 18 persons, some from Akron and Cleveland, left Bolivar in "pouring down rain" last Sunday for the 70-mile trip. However, by the time the group reached Dungannon in Columbiana County, the sun was shining. The group began the tour at 9:30 a.m., had lunch in Minerva, made stops at points of historical significance and reached its destination at 5 p.m.

Ted observed that since the leaves now are off the trees, many of the 14 locks originally built in Furnace Hollow, on the way to the McKinley Homestead, can be seen.

A chance meeting resulted in an interesting experience for the officers of the group. While they were admiring the pic-turesque A.R. Elson Co.'s Magnolia flouring mills, built in 1834, Mack A. Elson drove up to check on the water level in the millpond, swollen by rain. Mr. Elson and his sister, Miss Lorene Elson, are the present owners of the mill.

Upon learning the identity of the canal society members, Mr. Elson graciously opened the mill, invited them in and showed them about, explaining the mill's operation. Then he opened the gate to let in some of the excess water from the millpond to operate the old mill wheel within the building before flowing back into the canal. The sight of the canal water operating the overshot waterwheel was a real treat for the members of the society.

As for the Sandy and Beaver tour, Ted said, "It's really something worth seeing. It makes a real trip."

Mr. Findley has said the canal society will make available, without charge, copies of the informative stop-by-stop itinerary of the Sandy and Beaver tour.

November 21, 1965

Snowflakes Stir Spring Thoughts

The first snow has fallen on the towpath and spring is a long way off. But people are making plans already involving the use and enjoyment of the canal and towpath next spring.

Just for example, there are Katherine and Steffanie Buehman of Minerva. The Buehman sisters are new residents of Ohio. They like to travel, ride bicycles and hike. And they are artists and take many photographs. As newcomers, they are interested in the canals and towpaths in this part of the state. In requesting information about the towpaths, Katherine wrote: "We would like to start planning our trips for next spring to hike, paint and explore."

At the same time, others throughout the district are engaged in a project that could add a touch of color to some of the pictures the Buehman sisters might paint.

They are building bluebird houses.

I came home the other night to find a neatly constructed bluebird residence had been left at the side of my garage door. A fine looking house, it obviously had been made from the plan published with this column two weeks ago. It had been made by Steven J. Horner of Massillon. I'm looking at it as I write this column and, frankly, I don't see how a bluebird could resist it — especially since it is rent free.

Since it was one of the first three made by Mr. Horner and was donated for a bluebird trail, it will be placed along the towpath of the Ohio & Erie Canal when the first bluebird trail is established by the Canton Audubon Society. Someone, incidentally, has supplied Mr. Horner, a retiree, with lumber and he is busy making more houses.

From the number of letters I have received asking for the plans for the bluebird houses, I believe we may expect enough of the box-like dwelling places to create a bluebird trail the entire length of the canal towpath from Summit County to Tuscarawas County. All who desire to donate the houses they build for this bluebird trail should call or write to Jack R. Minger, president of Canton Audubon Society.

Another friendly note from the mailbag last week was accompanied by still another plan for a simple bluebird house along with pertinent and interesting information. There also was an article from the *Ford Times*, which told the story of Thomas Edgar Musselman of Quincy, Ill., who was described as "Godfather to a Million Bluebirds."

The note was from Mrs. Harry Reed of East Canton. Commenting on the house plans she enclosed, Mrs. Reed wrote: "We made these boxes a few years ago. Our bluebirds have had 15 young during the summer, 5 in each nesting. Hope you can use this plan and anyone can get a copy by sending a stamped, self-addressed envelope to Dr. T.E. Musselman, Quincy, Ill.

A plan sheet also may be obtained from another dedicated friend of the bluebirds. William G. Duncan of Louisville, Kentucky. Mr. Duncan has erected more than 5,000 bluebird boxes in his area.

The magazine article claims that if it

were not for Dr. Musselman, the bluebird would be rarely seen along the upper stretches of the Mississippi Valley. Bluebirds, especially around his area in Illinois, are no longer as rare as they were because, late in life, he made a career of providing nesting boxes for the bluebirds and encouraging others to do so.

But they are rare and are seldom seen in Stark County. They need help if they are to multiply and return to this area.

Dr. Musselman advocates the erection of bluebird boxes as an enjoyable project for high school classes, Boy and Girl Scouts, 4-H Clubs, vacation Bible school groups and garden clubs. Dr. Musselman has labored hard and long to preserve and perpetuate what once was probably America's best-known bird. All the compensation he asks is that he be known as the godfather of millions of bluebirds.

The way I see it, Stark County's bluebirds, happily, are going to have a lot of godfathers — and godmothers, too.

November 28, 1965

A Look Backward in 1901

I had hoped to title this week's column "Thanksgiving on the Canal" or "Turkey on the Towpath." But the paucity of canal literature defeated my plans. I was unable to find a Thanksgiving story associated with the canal.

I did have something to be thankful for, however. Several weeks ago, Gervis S. Brady, director of the Stark County Historical Center, brought to my attention a copy of *The Roller Monthly*, dated September 1901. The 64-page pamphlet described itself as "A High Class Illustrated Magazine From the Home of President McKinley." In its 17th year of publication, it sold for five cents a copy.

This issue contained an article by C.C. Newkirk, titled "Old Canal Days." It was complete with historical facts about Communists, a president's family and even canal pirates. It reads as follows:

"The proposed abandonment by the Legislature of the old Ohio State canal, one of the most historic and interesting old waterways in the United States, seems to be a certainty and with its passing will go the memories of the time when it was the throbbing vein of trans-State traffic between the lakes and the Ohio River.

"Two years ago, the State Legislature came near abandoning the Ohio State canal, but the strong rally of its friends to the rescue saved it for the time and secured the necessary appropriation for its maintenance.

"The Ohio State and the Miami and Erie canals have been operated in recent years at a loss of $100,000, in round numbers, per annum. If it were not that in their prosperous days these two canals were veritable bonanzas and placed in the State exchequer the sum of $5,000,000, all profit, the canals would have been abandoned long ago.

"The losses in recent years make it probable that some action will be taken with reference to this State property at the next session of the Legislature.

"That canal traffic in the past sorely crippled railroad traffic there can be no doubt, and even today, the proportion of freight traffic it secures is sufficient to induce the railroads to take up arms against it. The tonnage hauled today on the navigable portions of the canal is considerable and this will be thrown to the railroads when the canal is abandoned.

"There is somewhat of a pathetic side to the abandonment of the old Ohio canal. When it is abandoned about 500 people will be thrown out of a livelihood. They are principally lock-keepers and freight boat owners, many of whom are well advanced in years and, since the construction of the canal, have made and lost on its surface.

"The Ohio canal from Cleveland, Ohio, where it leaves Lake Erie, to Portsmouth, Ohio, where its sluggish stream empties into the Ohio River is 308 miles long, and in that distance has 146 locks. Its original depth was four feet and its width 40 feet. To construct it, the Buckeye State paid out $4,695,203.69.

"Its construction was begun on July 4, 1825, and it was formally opened to navigation from the lake to the river in 1830. The construction work was let out by contract to the lowest bidders. These contracts consisted of sections from one to five miles in length. In some instances they were let out to individuals and in others companies undertook the work.

"The building of the Ohio canal proved to be a most opportune boon for the Society of Communists, which was established at Zoar, Ohio, early in the last century. The Zoarites obligated themselves heavily for their lands to found a colony and almost despaired paying off their debt when the Ohio canal was projected.

"Over 150 able-bodied communists went to work helping build the canal and received a fair wage. The Zoarites alone built many miles of the canal north and south of their colony and in this way filled their depleted exchequer.

"Abraham Garfield, father of the martyred president, was one of the men who took a contract to build a portion of the Ohio canal. His contract was for a half mile between Port Washington and Newcomerstown, in Tuscarawas County, and there are yet men living in that community who remember working under Mr. Garfield, and who today speak in the highest terms of his sterling qualities.

"Mr. and Mrs. Garfield lived in temporary quarters near the route of the canal. It is related that they were most amiable people and that their humble quarters was often the scene of festivity in which young and old from miles in many directions took part.

"The present navigable portion of the canal is between Coshocton and Cleveland, the southern end being out of repair and useless. The bulk of freight nowadays goes north and consists mainly of wheat, coal and lumber.

"Navigation began in the spring and will continue busily until ice interferes with it. What is called the 'canal year' begins November 15 each year, after which date new records are kept of traffic.

"While the canal is most picturesque and inviting in summer it is correspondingly dreary in mid-winter, the one season dreaded by the canal folks.

"The boatmen and their families are obliged to tie up wherever the ice freeze catches them and must establish quarters aboard until they can get loose in the spring. They live and stable their mules on the profits of the boating season.

"The palmy days of the Ohio canal are past. The contrast of the bustle, which prevailed on this old waterway half a century ago, with the lazy, humdrum traffic of today can scarcely be imagined. At one time there were over 1,500 freight and passenger boats plying on the Ohio canal between the lake and the river.

"These ran day and night and there was scarcely a minute in the 24 hours that lockers were not busy getting the boats through. Blockades, collisions, runaways and upsets were everyday affairs. Many a score was settled by the brawny-fisted drivers for right of way on the towpath. It takes the veteran canal boatman to recount the stirring events of those days."

To read more of canal events during the last century, including comment on the canal pirates of that day, see next Sunday's *Along the Towpath.*

December 5, 1965
Complete With Apple Cobbler

Took a trip the other day — an imaginary one. But it was nonetheless delight-
ful. Went with a journalist crony. Maybe you've heard of him. Name's Jack Leggett and he's an old pro at this business of gathering and writing the news. Jack does it with a flair.

Jack had stopped by my desk to tell me that he found last week's column interesting due to the historical information about the canal at the turn of the century.

"You know," he mused, "if they ever develop that time machine, you and I will take a trip back into the past. It'd be great. Yes sir, if we had one of those machines, we could go back and ride the old canal boats."

It was getting near lunchtime, so Jack's next observation came naturally.

"I'd like to go get some of that old-fashioned food in one of those old-time inns. I'd REALLY like that," he said wistfully. "Yes sir, I'd like to go in there and pay a quarter and get all that food — get some of that old apple cobbler like we don't get anymore."

He fairly drooled.

"You know, at those prices, you could have a real swell vacation," he continued. "You could travel in another century, spend 10 bucks instead of a couple of hundred and have a real great time. We could see how it would be to have a leisurely pace and no ulcers. If they ever do get that machine, we could get back to where it was peaceful. We'd just take a little bit of money with us and live like kings. Of course, we'd need old coins. Where could we get them? They cost too much from today's collectors. Maybe we could take some modern flashlights along and barter with the folks back there."

Mindful of Clyde Gainey's huge antique canal-boat lantern, I said, "Not a bad idea. How about laying in a supply of flashlights?"

As Jack moved off across the newsroom to his own desk, I assured him I would let him know if and when we could return, via a time machine, to the last century and ship out on one of the old canal packets for a downstate excursion.

"Just book me passage," was his parting quip.

But since we don't have a time machine yet, I will have to take you back to the canal era via the second and final installment of a two-part serial from *The Roller Monthly* magazine published in Canton and dated September 1901.

It picks up talking about canal boats:

"A good boat could be built for about $1,600, although some of the boat owners expended as high as $2,000 or $3,000 when they wanted something in the way of a boat to take the 'shine' off the other boats along the line. The freight boats were from 60 to 75 feet long and carried from 75 to 85 tons. At the stern end of the boat was the living and eating apartments of the canal boat captain and his family. The hired crew slept in the bow of the boat and midway of its length were the stables in which one force of mules were housed on board. In the old days when the boats ran day and night, each boat had two crews made up as follows:

"Captain, two steersmen, two drivers, two bowsmen (or lockers) and the cook, not to speak of the captain's family, if he had any. The old-time canal boat captain was a very much spoiled and indulged individual. He dressed in the best the tailors could make; wore a ruffled shirt and not unfrequently a silk hat. He was a gentleman of leisure; his hands were white and he would have been insulted if asked to soil them with work. He did nothing but pose on the deck from time to time, and direct the movements of the boat, or, if it were not too hot, fling a few choice epithets at the obstinate and slow-moving mules just to let them know that he was in charge of the boat. He slept well, dined well and made money. He was lavish in spending his earnings and was known as an all-around good fellow.

"There used to be some gorgeous turnouts in the way of dress teams along the Ohio canal. Mules, of course, had the call. Some horses were used, but not as many in proportion to the whole number as will be found on the towpath today (1901). The drivers took great pride in vying with each other in decorating the harness and in keeping the mules slick and well fed. Frequently a string of mules almost covered with ivory rings would be met or again the harness would be silver or nickel-plated, and these trappings would be polished to a hue that made the harness of the common mules along the towpath dull by comparison.

"Before the advent of railroads in Ohio, the Ohio canal passenger packet did a flourishing business and there are many people yet living who doubtless remember some pleasant journey over the Ohio canal behind the slow plodding mules. These passenger boats were run entirely across the state and tried to observe a regular schedule, but the great volume of freight traffic made it an uncertain thing to depend on the time of arrival or departure of the passenger packets. The latter were constructed much in the form of a long, narrow houseboat, but much lighter than the freighters and under favorable circumstances could make 30 or more miles a day.

"Relays of mules were kept along the canal and fresh mules were hitched to the boat at given intervals. The passenger boats were also run at night. Josh Billings has described a trip on the Ohio canal, and in his droll way referred to it as the 'raging canawl,' which term is yet in popular favor.

"The poor canal boat mule has been made the butt of many a jibe and jest but, nevertheless, he is a paragon of strength, patience, docility and stubbornness. He soon learns all the tricks of the business whereby he may avoid work and it takes the driver's constant eye to keep him from shirking. When there are three mules tandem then the veteran mules let the two green mules pull the boat, while to all appearances he seems to be doing his full share. Occasionally a mule can be found which will pull the boat along steadily without a driver, but he is the exception, and there is surely something lacking in his intellect. What becomes of the canal boat mules is a mystery. They are rarely sold; they don't seem to die; they are not given away, but in some manner or other they disappear occasionally, and their places are filled by others.

"During the early spring and winter the vocation of the canal boatman is not an enviable one. The steersman and driver can never leave their posts, no matter what the weather may be. Nowadays the captain's wife is not above the dignity of steering a boat, and in the busy season, women may be seen on the upper deck directing the craft's movements. Many of the quaint characters along the Ohio canal have reached their allotted three-score-and-ten, and it has been observed that there is something about canal life that tends toward longevity.

"The Ohio canal has its pirates as truly as large streams. For many years a species of small craft have plied along its banks. These are usually in the form of houseboats, which are either pulled by the inmates or allowed to float with the current. The owners of these boats usually depend on the crops of the farmers along the route for sustenance. Some of them are veritable dens of vice, and the reputation borne by the houseboat contingent is none of the best. An effort was made last summer to drive these boats from the navigable portions of the canal. Lockmasters were ordered to forbid them passing through the locks but there are many of them afloat this year (1901). Derelicts of many of the old-time boats built when the canal was opened are strewn along the waterway from the lake to the river.

"The curious names borne by some of the boats which ply today on the Ohio canal are interesting: Charlotta, Favorite, Hattie, Hazel, Belle, Iowa, Lillie, Spray, Soppo, Two Brothers, Bolivar, W.J. Bryan, Banner, Alliance, Ben Harrison, Akron, Colonel Dick and Governor McKinley, named after the President when he was candidate for governor."

Wonder which one Jack would like to book passage on.

December 12, 1965
Let's Paint the Canal

An idea thought of in Canton and then fired off to New Philadelphia has ricocheted back here. As a result, it ultimately may end up as a reality, here and there along the Ohio & Erie Canal in western Stark County.

The idea was conceived by Dr. John M. Van Dyke. He directed it to Ted Findley,

president of the Canal Society of Ohio, in New Philadelphia, and Ted, in turn, referred it to me, thinking this column might help to bring the idea to life.

Dr. Van Dyke's idea, which is to be considered by the canal society's board, already has the approval of the Stark County Canal Lands Development Advisory Committee.

The doctor, who calls himself a "Sunday painter," suggests there are many amateur and professional artists in this area. He says there also are many classes of students receiving instruction in schools and colleges and from numerous private teachers. Some of these are members of organized groups of artists, he notes.

In view of this interest in art, Dr. Van Dyke asks if it wouldn't be worthwhile to plan an extended contest for those artists with prizes and exhibits. He suggests a three-year period with a better schedule of prizes each year.

Watercolor and the other media would "compete separately." But here is the kicker — all pictures would be of scenes along the canal. Dr. Van Dyke would give some advantage for scenes depicting the canal "in early use."

Although he does not suggest a specific sponsoring agency, the Canton physician says there are "agencies like the Junior Chamber of Commerce which foster exhibitions and sales of pictures."

"I should like to see easels set up (along the canal) weekends throughout the summer season," the doctor wrote.

Dr. Van Dyke's idea has a great deal of merit and considerable potential. Conceivably, it could result in a lot of canal art appearing in area homes and perhaps large murals of canal scenes, painted by local artists, in some of our leading business places.

Anyone who has seen the magnificent canal mural on the lobby wall of the Coshocton National Bank can hardly forget it.

Why not turn the artists loose? Who knows, perhaps they can make Stark County known far and wide for its abundance of canal paintings. Some day art collectors and hobbyists may come into Stark County from all parts of the country in search of authentic "Stark County" oils and watercolors of life on the old Ohio & Erie.

Remember Grandma Moses and her "New England primitives?"

Bluebird Trail Report

It has been several weeks since the last report on the bluebird trail project. During that time, plans for constructing bluebird houses were mailed to 31 persons who wrote to "Along the Towpath" requesting the plans.

Already 18 completed houses have been donated toward the creation of a bluebird trail along the Ohio & Erie Canal and more have been promised. The more houses built and contributed, the longer the bluebird trail can be. Anyone interested in obtaining plans for the houses should write to "Along the Towpath" in care of *The Canton Repository*.

And anyone wishing to donate bluebird houses for the trail should contact Jack R. Minger, president of Canton Audubon Society. The society will supervise construction of the bluebird trail.

Scouts Track, Stalk

Most of the summer canalside strollers have given up towpath tramping until next spring. But the Boy Scouts, always a hardy group, are still at it. Sixteen members of Troop 251, sponsored by Shiloh Baptist Church at Massillon, recently hiked from the church to Canal Fulton via the towpath trail. They stopped to have lunch at Lock 4 Park. Scoutmaster Jesse Evans reported that Scouts of second-class rank were tested on their trailing, tracking and stalking skills between the park and Canal Fulton.

December 19, 1965
Canal News: Good and Bad

Canal news is both good and bad this week. Down in Tuscarawas County, the news, to say the least, is discouraging. But up in Summit County it is just the opposite.

So let's take the disappointing news first.

The Ohio Department of Highways, which recently severed the canal bed and towpath at Fort Laurens near Bolivar in northern Tuscarawas County while constructing an approach to Interstate Route 77, and which currently is eradicating miles of extremely scenic canal lands stretching westward from Newcomerstown in southern Tuscarawas County, now plans to fill and obliterate more than half a mile of the canal near Dover in the central section of the county.

The highway department expects to spend in the vicinity of $60,000 to permanently erase this section of the canal, claiming it is a traffic hazard to Route 8 due to narrow berms. Poor drainage and stagnant water also were cited as causes for the projected fill. Bids are to be opened Feb. 8 and the canal-filling job is to be done sometime next year.

Meanwhile, Stark County continues to plan and work for the preservation and reconstruction of its share of the Ohio & Erie by digging out filled-in sections of the canal and restoring flowing water wherever possible, looking toward the day when a county-long canal parkway may become an integral part of a metropolitan park system within the county.

And up in Summit County a bit of the old canal lands is being put to good use in a markedly educational way.

Stumpy Basin, once a storage area and turnabout spot for canal barges in northern Summit County near the village of Peninsula, has been acquired from the state by Kent State University. The transfer of title of 22.4 acres of land, including the roughly 8-acre basin, resulted largely from the efforts of J. Arthur Herrick, professor of biology at the university and leader of the natural areas project of the Ohio Biological Survey.

Mr. Herrick, who had been interested in the basin, as "a rare gem of nature," for 15 years, describes the basin as "rather unique in a lot of ways." It is isolated and rather inaccessible as it is bounded on the north by the Ohio Turnpike, on the west by the Cuyahoga River, on the east by a very steep hillside and on the south by relatively wild terrain. The professor, who says acquisition of the basin had been one of his many dreams, explains that the area will be used primarily by biology department students but that other students also can use it for field work and research.

"We are especially happy to have it because open-space wild areas are rapidly disappearing in this part of Ohio," he said, adding that regularly scheduled classes will now go there for outdoor study.

Calling the basin and adjoining lands "more or less virgin territory," Mr. Herrick said the university will maintain it as "a nature sanctuary for educational, scientific and aesthetic purposes."

The basin long has been drained and today is a cattail swamp or marsh containing lots of interesting ecology for students. And the surrounding land supports a wide variety of plant life. The professor describes part of the area botanically as a prairie and says prairie grasses found there "belong" further west.

"Many wild flowers grow there which are found in the West," he declared, observing that the wooded area just south of the old canal basin has countless wild flowers and "trilliums by the thousands."

The Akron Garden Club and Cleveland Garden Club, working through the Nature Conservancy organization, recently explored the possibility of purchasing this adjacent land but ran into an "insurmountable purchase price," Mr. Herrick disclosed.

So while part of the canal will be filled up to provide a bed for more blacktop highway, another part of the old waterway is being restored to life and still a third section, old Stumpy Basin, will become a natural and highly interesting outdoor classroom for students of Kent State University.

Bluebird Report

A lot of bluebirds are going to receive some nice Christmas presents from a number of Stark County Santa Clauses — but they are going to have to wait until spring to use them. Last week I reported 18 bluebird houses had been built and donated for the establishment of a bluebird trail along the Ohio and Erie Canal towpath. This week that figure has climbed to 42,

with more promised. Letters requesting bluebird house plans continue to come in.

Lester J. Wells of Louisville writes that he will retire in a few months and would like to keep busy. He's going to start out building a few homes for bluebirds.

Carl H. Bechtel of East Canton says, "My son and I will be glad to build some and donate them for the bluebird trail."

And A.J. Jarrett of Canton sees three benefits to be derived from building the houses. He says it will provide recreational activity during the long winter evenings, result in at least two houses for the bluebird trail and additional houses for the family's summer retreat in Holmes County, where bluebirds have been seen in the past and where the Jarretts hope to attract many more.

— Merry Christmas

December 26, 1965
Crystal Ball Gazing

It's that time again. Time to haul out the old crystal ball and peer into its depths, trying to see what lies ahead in 1966. As far as the Ohio & Erie Canal and its restoration are concerned, the Stark County Canal Lands Development Advisory Committee is not making any New Year's resolutions.

But the committee has some hopes and a number of plans for the new year. Hope is a thing called money as far as the committee is concerned. A number of plans for advancing the restoration are being held up by one thing — lack of money. A few thousand dollars here and there would unlock the door or, more appropriately, open the lock gates, enabling a great deal of progress to be made with volunteer effort and equipment on hand or available.

The committee hopes, in 1966, to rewater the canal all the way to the north edge of Massillon, provided it can latch onto a dragline for a period long enough to dredge out filled-in sections of the canal bed.

An extensive parking area and picnic site just north of Massillon, at the termi-

The closed lock gates are visible in this view of Wilson Mill at 14 Mile Lock in June 1965.

nus of the rewatered section of the canal, is a pretty realistic hope of the committee for 1966. In fact, work is already under way on this project, which will provide easy access to the canal and its towpath for thousands of Stark residents and visitors to the county.

Looking deep into the crystal ball, the committee sees the shadowy form of a canal lands museum at canalside. Its configuration cannot be determined and the date of the cornerstone defies recognition. But the committee has seen enough to have hope.

Equally nebulous in the crystal sphere is the long low shape of an authentic canal boat docked near the museum and waiting for passengers. But the form is there and again the committee is encouraged.

As the panorama within the crystal globe changes, the committee sees the lovely section of the canal from Navarre south and it seems like work is going on there to restore and beautify the towpath. There even seem to be efforts directed toward rewatering that section, which passes through some very scenic countryside.

And then, suddenly, the crystal ball is illuminated, glowing on and off incandescently. It seems to be messaging three words over and over. Clear enough to be recognized, they are: "Metropolitan – Park – System."

The crystal ball has revealed much and, obviously, the climactic way it presented the metropolitan park system leaves little doubt in the minds of the committee members but that this must be their goal. For such a system can most readily produce the necessary funds and organization to bring the canal restoration and development plans to fruition – for the benefit of all.

HAPPY NEW YEAR!

71

Lock 169 was overgrown with weeds and strewn with boulders when this photograph was taken in 1963. The lock was between Trenton and Port Washington in Tuscarawas County.

Canal Society of Ohio

Book Three·1966

January 2, 1966
Good News To Start 1966

There's good news this week — news that should make for a Happy New Year for all who are interested in the preservation and restoration of the Ohio & Erie Canal.

In one of their last official acts of 1965, the Tuscarawas County commissioners approved a resolution to apply for title to all of the former Ohio & Erie Canal lands in the county, outside the municipalities, which have not otherwise been conveyed. Copies of the resolution are being forwarded to the Ohio Department of Public Works and to the director of its real estate division. The resolution states that the land is needed for public recreation, parks, historical sites, drainage courses, roads, highways and other programs of a public na-ture.

Tuscarawas County, in applying for title to the canal lands, is following the example of Stark County, which now has title to its canal lands. The action comes as a welcome climax to efforts by individuals and organizations in both counties to bring about county ownership of the canal lands in Tuscarawas.

Among those primarily responsible for the drive for county ownership were Ray Crumbley, city editor of the *New Philadelphia Daily Times*, who worked diligently to publicize the project; the newspaper, which supported the plan editorially; Ted H. Findley of New Philadelphia, president of the Canal Society of Ohio, who has given innumerable illustrated lectures about the canal to stimulate interest in its preservation; the New Philadelphia Kiwanis Club, and the Tuscarawas Chamber of Commerce.

State Rep. Ralph Regula of Navarre made a number of talks in Tuscarawas County outlining the procedure of obtaining title to the canal lands and acquainting organizations with their recreational, educational and historical potential. He also acquaint-

ed them with the progress being made in Stark County through its canal lands development advisory committee, which was host to the Tuscarawas commissioners and canal project proponents at one of its meetings and encouraged them to acquire title to the canal lands.

Jacob Dummermuth, chairman of the Tuscarawas commissioners, observed that, although application has been made, it will take time to get title of the land. Like Stark County, our neighbor county to the south has no money to restore the canal and consequently the commissioners have no immediate plans to develop it.

But at least their action puts the canal and its adjoining lands into the "safety deposit box" and preserves it for future development. The action of the Tuscarawas commissioners may speed similar action by the communities of Port Washington, Tuscarawas and Bolivar. Officials of these towns have expressed interest in getting title to the canal lands within their village limits.

The city of New Philadelphia is already in the process of obtaining title to its canal lands including Lock 13 and an old canal basin. Plans call for the basin to become a city park.

In view of this widespread and increasing interest in Tuscarawas County, perhaps the commissioners will appoint an advisory committee similar to Stark County's to advise them and to shoulder much of the work involved in the development of the canal lands.

Mr. Crumbley and Mr. Findley are planning to make slide presentations to various organization, apprising them of what the county is acquiring in its canal lands and what can be done with them. City Editor Crumbley, in thanking the commissioners and commending them for their action in acquiring the canal lands, said, "I

73

consider it one of the most important steps ever taken in the county for future generations."

Mr. Findley, speaking as president of the state canal society, said, "We are immensely pleased and our board of directors will probably prepare the history and make applications for historic markers from the Ohio Historical Society. We want to get the different service clubs, the historical societies, the Boy Scouts and Girl Scouts, the garden clubs and other civic organizations interested in the canal development to help us make certain restorations."

Observing that 12 of the original 14 locks in the county are still in existence, he said the scenic Bolivar-Fort Laurens area is probably the place to start the restoration.

"It lends itself so beautifully for a start," he said, expressing hope that the Boy Scouts could be prevailed upon to clear the towpath for hiking in that area.

An officer of the New Philadelphia Kiwanis Club said his organization plans to continue its efforts in support of the canal project.

The action of the Tuscarawas commissioners reaches beyond the county borders and holds forth the promise that the canal and towpath in Tuscarawas one day may be joined with the same waterway and hiking path in Stark, Summit and Cuyahoga counties, making possible canoe travel and hiking from Cleveland to Coshocton County. And if Rep. Regula is successful in his plan to have the canal towpath used as the northern section of the state-long Buckeye Trail, the Tuscarawas section of the towpath will become the major link that up to now has been missing.

January 9, 1966
Keep an Eye on Erie Canal

Sometimes we must look far afield and into the lives and activities of others before we appreciate our own possessions, heritage and the opportunities available to us.

Maybe it is like that with our Stark County canal preservation and restoration project.

For more than a year, the county's canal lands development advisory committee has been at work, under the authority of the county commissioners, to develop the Ohio & Erie Canal into a county-long parkway and recreational area. But the committee has had to work without funds and consequently progress has been limited.

The committee is now hopeful that a metropolitan park system can be established in Stark County through which money could be obtained for the canal park development.

Up in scenic Syracuse, New York, where the Erie Canal flows through hills and fields not unlike our own Ohio country, they have a similar problem — and similar plans. But, perhaps they are ahead of us in solving their problems.

State Rep. Ralph Regula, who must be given the credit for igniting the spark that touched off the "save the canal" project here and has been advocating the metropolitan park system, recently called attention to the canal park project in the Syracuse area.

Last November, an eight-column headline in the *Syracuse Herald-Journal* read: "U.S. Funds Available for Erie Canal Park." The news story began: "Federal monies are available to finance a major portion of the proposed 35-mile Erie Canal Park project, Undersecretary of the Interior John A. Carver Jr. revealed here today." The article revealed that three counties had approved the park, which would stretch from DeWitt to Rome along the site of the old Erie Canal. Facilities would include boating, fishing, marinas, horse trails, camping and picnic areas.

The Erie Canal Park Planning Committee, composed of residents of the three counties, had been pressing for state support of the project for a year. Undersecretary Carver, in expressing strong support for the project, said federal funds are available and that all that is needed to obtain federal money for the park is state urging.

"Our experts consider this to be the most valuable single potential outdoor recreational resource of several park projects in the county," the Washington official said. "Restoring the quality of our environment presents the single biggest challenge of our generation. America must not only restore the natural beauty of its countryside, but also clean up the air, water, and natural environment or live in the 'dungheap' of its own creation."

Much that has been said about the Syracuse canal park project and its planning commission fits the Ohio & Erie Canal park project and its advisory committee like a glove.

Here in Stark County we have an excellent outdoor recreational resource, we have a planning committee and we have a canal. But we need money — or a vehicle to obtain it. All indications are that a metropolitan park system is the most logical and best-suited vehicle to enable Stark and its neighboring counties to accomplish what is being achieved with the Erie Canal in New York State.

Unexpected Help

Speaking of the need for money to advance the cause, the canal advisory committee was pleasantly surprised recently to receive an unsolicited check for the canal project. It was the second such check to be received.

The donor said, "I would like to help the restoration project. It won't be a great deal but it will be a little bit. I was real thrilled about it when I heard they were going to restore the canal."

The donor, originally from Wayne County and now a Canton resident, recalled that her great-grandfather had hauled wheat from west of Wooster to the canal at Massillon more than 100 years ago.

January 16, 1966
Research Results in Canal Paper

Back in November of 1964, in one of the first "Along the Towpath" columns, I reported that Robert L. Witmer of Louisville, then a junior at Malone College, had been in to see me about the Ohio & Erie Canal research paper he was planning. The months rolled by and then one day I received a letter from Joseph L. Grabill, associate professor of history at Malone. It was accompanied by a 13-page paper written by Mr. Witmer and titled "The Ohio & Erie Canal in Stark County."

Mr. Witmer, now a teacher of world and American history at Central Christian High School in Kidron, has given me permission to reprint parts of the paper. And so, from time to time, I plan to share its contents with you.

It seems hard to believe that so little should have been recorded for posterity about so vital and significant an economic factor in the development of our nation, and Stark County in particular, as the "big ditch." But this seems to be the case, judging from the experience of those who try to put together the recorded pieces about the boom days of the canals. Only fragmentary information is available.

Mr. Witmer has rendered a service to all of us in writing his paper. One of his painstaking, time-consuming tasks was to visit the Canton Public Library and carefully scan every page of every issue of *The Repository* from 1819 to 1840.

Some of the most interesting data compiled by Mr. Witmer pertained to the regulation of canal-boat traffic.

Quoting now from Mr. Witmer's paper:

"There were three different types of boats which operated on the canal waters. Passenger boats, freight boats, which carried supplies and products, and excursion boats, which were gaily decorated pleasure crafts. The state had patrol boats, which were seen once in a while.

"The canal boats were sometimes pulled by horses but more often by mules. The mules moved along on a dirt bank at the edge of the canal. They were hitched to the boat with long leads (ropes), usually double ropes. Sometimes there were five or six ropes. The mules pulled the boats at a rate of about four miles per hour. The speed was regulated by state law so as to prevent excessive wave action on the banks, which would, in time, cause the canal to become shallow. Tow mules, which were kept at the weigh stations along the canal, were exchanged periodically. Sometimes the mules were kept on the boat in the middle compartment, much to the discomfort of the passengers.

"There were various laws concerning the operation of the canal. Some of the most important ones were: $5 fine for driving an animal on the towpath other than an official tow animal; $10-$15 fine for improper operation of the locks; $1,000 fine for damage to canal drainage; $1 fine plus damages for running into anything; $10 fine for use of steel guard plates on the front of the boat because it might cut tow ropes; $10 fine for traveling in excess of the speed limit."

Mr. Witmer writes that there were changes in social life during the canal days. This certainly was associated with increased volume of traffic on the canal.

Quoting again from his paper:

"Hotel upon hotel opened, boarding houses opened, restaurants opened, taverns opened; little cities were born overnight. The great traffic on the canal brought many visitors into canal towns.

"The canal, naturally, was used by passengers going for pleasure cruises or to see friends. Even party boats traveled up and down the canal. They say that on a quiet night near the canal one could sit on the steps of his home in the summer and hear the singing of the groups of pleasure-seekers cruising up and down the canal. People did not gather to see movies, but to talk in taverns or attend the opera. In the 1840s and 1850s, nearly 300 canal boats ran back and forth between Massillon and Cleveland on a regular schedule. At least one-third of these boats were pleasure crafts."

Today's pleasure boats are a far cry from the cumbersome canal boats. But I predict, if Stark County ever gets a canal boat of its own, it will prove to be a popular pleasure craft — today.

January 23, 1966
Finest Walk in Ohio?

A spectacular hiking trail in one of the emptiest lands in the world will be built in the near future in British Columbia, a Canadian province larger than Texas and with less than two million inhabitants.

I can testify to the tremendous atmosphere of this province, having traveled across its northern section from Dawson Creek to Watson Lake in the Yukon Territory. It should make a wonderful setting for the 150-mile "British Columbia Trail." The Canadians think so, too, and have asserted that the trail will compare with the 32-mile Milford Trail in New Zealand, which has been described as the "finest walk in the world."

Roland Wild, writing in the *New York Times*, observed that "the British Columbia Trail may never compare with the Appalachian Trail, which took 20 years in the making, or with the 480-mile Bruce Trail in Ontario, also to open in 1967. But it will claim to be the 'finest walk in the West' and will serve to introduce the rugged interior to thousands of Canadians who only see their vast empty land through a car windshield."

Visualizing what breath-taking scenery will unfold before the eyes of the British Columbia Trail hiker, it is difficult not to make an unfavorable comparison with the rather prosaic views offered hikers along Stark County's Ohio & Erie Canal towpath trail. The comparison must be that of an absolutely ravishing and exciting beauty with a pretty, but rather commonplace, local belle. But there is more in the comparison than beauty alone. Take, for example, usage.

The Canadian trail will cross a vast land, very sparsely populated. Add to the native population those who will travel great distances to hike the trail and, chances are, you still will not have much vacation usage of the trail. For it will take those in rugged health to traverse the 15-day trail which will "experience sudden and unexpected changes in terrain" as it passes from high farmlands of the Fraser River delta into rugged mountain areas and then into cowboy country of sagebrush and high plains. And then, of course, there is the hazard of fire.

The Ohio & Erie towpath, on the other hand, will be within short driving distance of more than a million people in Canton, Akron and Cleveland and hundreds of thousands more in the sprawling suburbia surrounding these cities. Particularly this will be true if current efforts to make the canal towpath the northern terminus of the state-long "Buckeye Trail" are realized. The trail then would be twice as long as the Canadian trail. It would be readily accessible to more millions. And it would pass through some of the most scenic spots in Ohio in its long sweep through the southern Ohio hills to Cincinnati.

Surely its potential use greatly exceeds that of the British Columbia trail. The Canadian trail will be usable eight months of the year. The Buckeye trail ought to be hikeable even longer. And with a multitude of getting on and off places, in contrast to the remote Canadian trail, it should provide healthful exercise and enjoyment for untold numbers of hikers who simply are not "in condition" to make the British Columbia trail hike.

Another comparison that must be made between the two trails is the difficulty encountered in bringing the trails into existence.

Acquiring the land (stimulating governmental officials to act for acquisition), winning public interest and financial support and trying to prevent continuing destruction of sections of the canal and towpath trail by the highway builders is difficult, and at times discouraging, here in Ohio.

But in British Columbia, where they are not in danger of running out of natural beauty as we are in Stark County, the government has given special rights so their trail can pass through private and crown land. Hostels will be built every 10 miles along the trail and in the larger ones there will be "resident parents."

The Royal Engineers are to be called into service to construct bridges and access roads to the trail, which is to be open by the end of 1967. It is estimated the first 10 years of work will cost $20,000 plus the cost of hostels. And it is considered a bargain.

Here in Stark County and its neighboring counties, there also is a tremendous bargain — recreational, historical, educational and probably even commercial. In the Ohio & Erie Canal towpath trail, hopefully a part of the Buckeye Trail, we could have the finest walk in Ohio and perhaps the finest walk in the Midwest. Unfortunately, its true worth, as a bargain, may not be appreciated until too late.

January 30, 1966
Resurgence of Canals

For the second time in recent months, I have been surprised while studying an Air Force Reserve staff development course, to come upon material pertaining to canals. This time it was during the study of problems in the developing nations — specifically "Transportation." The textbook, in stressing the significance of inland waterway transportation as it applies to developing nations, provides insight into the major role canals and rivers played in the development of our country in the pioneer days.

Stressing the low-cost transport on both long and short hauls provided by waterways, the text contends that: "Ocean highways and inland waterways are as vital to a country as its airlines and rail and highway systems. Because waterways transportation is relatively inexpensive per ton-mile, it often makes possible the savings necessary to render mineral, agricultural and forest resources competitive in world markets."

That's the way it was in the early days of the Ohio & Erie Canal. Ohio was a "developing country." And for its pioneer citizens to purchase finished products, they had to depend on earning necessary funds through the export of raw materials, such as wheat.

Purely in the realm of conjecture, it is interesting to speculate as to the volume of use the Ohio & Erie would be experiencing today if it had been restored after the 1913 flood and then maintained and modernized through the years.

The Air Force manual, in treating the subject of water transportation on inland waterways today, says the increasing interest in this method of transport is due to its "inherent capacity to move hundreds of

millions of tons of cargo with great economy in fuel and manpower." The manual observes that since World War II, thousands of industrial and distribution plants have located along inland waterways to take advantage of low cost movement of bulk cargo.

The economy inherent in the floated ton becomes obvious when one realizes that the average barge loads five times its weight; the average railroad freight car only twice its weight. Another way of looking at it is to consider that a 6,000 horsepower diesel locomotive can efficiently handle 6,000 to 8,500 tons while a 6,000 horse-power towboat can handle 14,000 to 20,000 tons.

Quoting from the manual:

"The extent to which the inland waterways contribute to the growth of the gross national product is best appreciated when one considers that they handle annually over 400 million tons of freight. This freight is moved over 29,000 miles of navigable rivers and canals by some 4,200 barges with a total capacity of over 16 million tons. What is even more significant, at a time when the railways have had to abandon over 32,000 miles of right of way, navigation is being extended on such rivers as the Missouri, the Snake and the Columbia; also, new canals — the Tennessee-Tombigbee, Trans-Florida and Lake Erie-Ohio River — are either projected or under development."

The circle seems to have come full around and we once again find ourselves in canal-building days while the railroads, which put the canals out of business, are consolidating, merging and abandoning right of way.

Currier and Ives

It was a long time getting here but there's no question about winter finally having arrived. If one needs further proof, all he needs to do is to drive along the Ohio & Erie Canal or hike its towpath on a weekend when the ice skaters create living Currier and Ives winter scenes. The colorfully garbed skaters darting up and down the canal ice today are the forerunners of many more who will someday enjoy the winter recreational value of the canal after more of it is rewatered.

The most ambitious canal skaters I have heard of are Perry High School students Bob Campton and Larry Gesen, who skated the canal from Crystal Springs to Canal Fulton, roughly six miles, in an hour and 30 minutes. And then they turned around and skated back just ahead of the big snow. Larry reported the ice was good and that they left the canal surface only twice, once due to a fallen tree and once because of thin ice. They saw other skaters along the way and once were invited to warm themselves at a canalside fire. Larry said he, Bob and four other boys expect to make the trip again because the first trip was so enjoyable.

Bluebird Houses

I learned that one of the bluebird-house builders to whom I had sent plans and instructions had failed to receive them. I sent him another set. If there are others who failed to receive the free plans, please let me know.

A Hand Across the Sea

Since I began writing this column, one of the pleasures has been the receipt of letters from totally unexpected sources. Some were letters of encouragement for the canal restoration project, some sought information, others supplied interesting and helpful information for the column and one even contained a cash donation for the canal-boat project.

Last week I received a particularly interesting letter, which was especially appreciated because of its international flavor. It was postmarked "London" and it came from "Illa Upper Mulgrave Road, Cheam Surrey, England." The writer, Clifford H. Heard, describes himself and his family as canal "fanatics." Consequently, I hope he won't mind my sharing some of his letter as it is in the interest of saving, restoring and enjoying our canals.

Mr. Heard became aware of Canton, *The Repository* and "Along the Towpath" through his acquaintanceship with Phillip Dannemiller, son of Mr. And Mrs. Franklin T. Dannemiller of Canton. The Heards, who entertained Phillip during the recent holidays, said that Phillip "by his charm and courtesy, has been a great ambassador for his country."

Mr. Heard was equally complimentary about this column. He wrote:

"We have been delighted to make the acquaintance of the splendid work you are doing in America to save your canals. This has quite amazed us, as we felt this was something peculiar to England, and that no other country had canal problems, and certainly that no one else was taking energetic steps to prevent this loss of our heritage. From what we have read so far, it seems you have regional groups or societies devoted to particular parts of a canal system; but this is something about which we have no information.

"I am sure you will be interested to know that in Great Britain we have a national body, the Inland Waterways Association, whose object is to maintain the canals in being and to prevent their abandonment. This is entirely voluntary and without their vigorous action much of our waterway system would have just disappeared.

"With this group is associated a number of local associations concerned with a particular waterway, the outstanding example of which is the Stratford on Avon Canal Society. This canal was quite derelict five years ago and this band of enthusiasts took the job in hand and overrode the many difficulties. Help was enrolled from all over the country. Army and Air Force units, and even prisoners from a Midland Gaol all helped. This last summer, with great rejoicing, the canal was reopened by the Queen Mother. This really was an occasion and a wonderful job they made of it — now completely navigable.

"I hope you will find this letter an encouragement in your undertaking. And we do wish you well in an effort, which, if not performed now, will be too late tomorrow."

In my travels about the world I have encountered many expressions of international goodwill but Mr. Heard and his letter rate among the finest.

Did You Know?

The question of the week: What was the name of the first newspaper in Akron?

The answer: *Ohio Canal Advocate.* In 1825, Laurin Dewey set up a handpress to publish the paper to promote the building of the canal. But by the time the first edition of the paper came out, on September 28 of that year, the name was changed to the *Portage Journal* because the building of the canal had been assured.

More About Bluebirds

Letters requesting free plans for building bluebird houses continue to come in as an increasing number of persons volunteer to help bring the blue harbingers of spring back to the local scene, where they seldom have been seen in recent years. Roy P. Wise of North Canton, may have put his finger on the cause for the increased interest in birdhouse building in his request for the plans: "This weather is a good time to stay indoors and build houses."

Mrs. Yolanda Dacar, a second-grade teacher at Summit School, wrote: "I have a jigsaw, wood materials and a class full of children eager to begin this project... a new experience for the class." Mrs. Dacar plans to cut out the bluebird-house sections on the jigsaw and then have the 15 girls and 11 boys in her class assemble the homes.

The Bluebird Trail, to be established along the Ohio & Erie Canal towpath, should have special meaning for Mrs. Dacar's pupils when they hike the towpaths— especially if some of "their" houses are in evidence.

February 13, 1966

Dawn-Redwood Mile Proposed

Exotic Pre-Ice-Age Trees Could Line Ohio & Erie Canal Towpath

This is the tale of a tree — from 20 million to 100 million years out of the past — with a direct tie to today and a meaningful usefulness for tomorrow.

This is the story of Metasequoia (glyptostroboides), the exciting Dawn-Redwood, which lives and thrives today after it was believed to be extinct for thousands of centuries.

And this is a proposal to establish a "Dawn-Redwood Mile" along both sides of a rewatered section of the Ohio & Erie Canal, somewhere between Massillon and Canal Fulton, along with a planting of these "living fossils" at the Stark Wilderness Center.

The fact that this ancestor of the giant California redwoods was able to survive undiscovered in the hidden Valley of the Tiger for 200,000 centuries after it had become extinct in the rest of the world is one of the greatest marvels in the history of botanic discovery.

But to explain why countless thousands of Ohioans, today and in the years to come, should view this botanical "missing link" with admiration and awe, as they walk along the canal towpath beside more than 200 of these ornamental trees in the Dawn-Redwood Mile, it is necessary to go back 1944.

It was in that year that a Chinese student botanist employed by the Chinese government came upon a tree such as he had never seen before in a remote section of Central China near the village of Mo-tao-chi in Szechuan Province.

The student, who once had studied botany under a Harvard professor in the Philippines, thought there was a remarkable similarity between this unusual tree and the ancient Metasequoia fossils. Curious, he returned to Nanking and reported his findings with the result that several eminent scientists were convinced the specimens were not only similar to the fossil Metasequoia but were identical. This represented a botanical occurrence without precedent.

The student, whose name was Wang, then sent pressed samples of the twigs and needles (they are similar to hemlock in appearance) to Harvard University, where officials immediately saw that it was, indeed, the fossil tree Metasequoia. Excitedly, they cabled Wang to return to Shui-sha Valley to obtain a supply of seeds to send to America.

There was great disappointment, however, when they learned that the valley was being closed off because of advancing Communists. But, Wang said, he might be able to fly in by charter plane for $1,500,000. This news demoralized Harvard officials until it was realized that Wang was speaking in terms of Chinese money and that this translated into a sum of $150 in American money. The money was sent. Wang carried out his mission successfully and sent a large number of seed-bearing cones to Harvard.

When World War II was over, a botanist-paleontologist from the University of California walked across the rugged mountains of Central China to the Valley of the Tiger to see for himself the grove of native Metasequoia. Deep in the valley, which is surrounded by tall peaks, he found many of the trees towering more than 100 feet high. They were at least 300 years old.

The natives called the area "Shui-hsapa," meaning "place of the water pine." This tiny dot on the map of the world, halfway between the Pacific Coast of China and the Tibetan Plateau, the Gobi Desert and the China Sea, was the only place on the face of the earth that the tree had survived, despite the fact that it apparently was very abundant throughout the present North Temperate regions before the Ice Age, ranging from Iceland to Siberia and as far south as New Jersey.

Harvard distributed the seeds to interested agencies throughout the United States. In time, plantings established in most of these places proved highly successful. Here in Ohio, Oliver D. Diller, then chairman of Ohio's Department of Forestry at the Agricultural Experiment Station at Wooster, received a packet of Dawn-Redwood seeds in 1948. He planted them in the Secrest Arboretum at the experiment station where they have grown vigorously.

Constantly being subjected to tests relative to its physical and chemical properties, ability to withstand heat and cold, drought and moisture, insects and disease, the Dawn-Redwood has, so far, scored very well on all counts. It seems little affected by weather changes or extremes of temperature and is resistant to insects and disease. It seems to prefer, however, a mild, moist climate. The tree grows rapidly with an annual growth of 5 feet having been recorded in some locations.

In China, the tree is planted for aesthetic purposes along the banks of streams and the margins of rice paddies.

The Dawn-Redwood has flattened, greenish-yellow, needle-like leaves, which drop off in the fall. Its bark is thin and its wood pale red in color, light and not particularly strong. Its most promising use seems to be for ornamental growth and as pulpwood.

What more interesting tree could be planted along the Ohio & Erie Canal to create a forested avenue and scenic change of pace for towpath hikers?

Prof. Diller and Prof. Arthur Herrick of Kent State University have expressed the belief that the Metasequoia will adapt readily to the canalside terrain as long as there is adequate open space and the sun-light can reach them. This should be no problem.

There should be no more difficulty in finding a suitable spot for a planting of the "living fossils" at the Stark Wilderness Center, where they would become another highlight of botanical interest for young and old. Informative signs at each end of the avenue of Metasequoias could inform all towpath hikers through the years of the continuing legend of the enchanting tree from China's Valley of the Tiger.

And Stark County's canal parkway could claim a botanical attraction without duplication in Ohio in its "Dawn-Redwood Mile."

February 20, 1966
Bluebird Trail Is 'Go'

Just thinking about winter won't make it go away. And, anyway, there are a lot of ice skaters, skiers and sled riders who aren't ready for winter to disappear just yet.

But for those who have had enough of the snow and slush season, I can tell you that something is being done to make spring "springier" along the Ohio & Erie Canal towpath. That "something" is the construction of bluebird houses by many persons in Stark and surrounding counties. Because more than 100 of the houses have been built and donated to the Canton Audubon Society, I can tell you that a "Bluebird Trail" definitely will be established along the towpath.

One of two Audubon Society committees charged with the responsibility for constructing and maintaining the bluebird trail expected to start putting up the houses this weekend. Come the mating and nesting season, it is hoped the word will get around among the rarely seen bluebirds that there is high quality housing, abundantly available, near the old canal towpath. Once the shy harbingers of spring begin to repopulate the canal vicinity, a towpath hike will become a more interesting and colorful experience.

"We were overwhelmed by the enthusiasm people have shown for the bluebird project along the canal and their desire to see the bluebirds return to this part of the county," Jack R. Minger, president of the Audubon Society, said.

Reporting on the bird feeders placed along the canal last year, he added, "There is no doubt in my mind but that the bird population along the canal has been greatly increased by the feeding and a much greater variety of birds can be seen there. From Oct. 1 to the present time, the society has put out 700 pounds of birdseed along the canal."

In placing the 100 houses between Lock 4 Park and Massillon, the society will put up as many as possible where they can find suitable trees and posts. In the spring, when the ground thaws, posts will be erected to accommodate the remaining houses.

Mr. Minger said that if the society gets the approval of the canal lands development advisory committee, it "may call on volunteer bluebird-house builders again this fall to extend the trail south of Massillon toward Navarre." Within two years, he said, the bluebird trail could extend from Navarre to Canal Fulton and, ultimately, reach the length of the county, from where the towpath enters from Summit County to where it crosses the Tuscarawas River into Tuscarawas County.

With a county-long bluebird trail, there should no longer be any difficulty in taking children to where they actually can see bluebirds — alive and out of a museum.

They're Real 'Jewels'

I received a letter addressed in red ink. It arrived just before Valentine's Day, so I am going to consider it a valentine as it contained a truly sweet (and thoughtful) gift from the Emerald Valley Dinner Belles 4-H Club, over East Canton way. The girls' secretary, Anita Bosler, wrote: "We have read about the bluebird houses being built for use along the Ohio & Erie Canal. We would like to inquire whether you would like sunflower seeds for the birds along the canal to eat. If so, we will grow some for them this summer. If you would like the seeds, do you want them in the flower heads or picked out?"

Well, girls, I asked the Audubon Society about your generous offer and this is what I was told:

"Most of the seed-eating birds like sunflower seeds. They'll eat them right away. It would be easier for the Audubon Society to handle the seeds, however, if they are picked out of the heads. Please tell the girls we appreciate it and thank them for their cooperation in the bluebird venture."

How's that for a valentine?

Fund Gets 'Valentine'

I received a second letter that also contained a "gift." This one was a check sent by the Damascus Garden Club in Mahoning County — the money to go to the canal-boat fund.

It seems that Mrs. Mary Regula, wife of State Rep. Ralph S. Regula of Navarre, accepted a speaking engagement for her husband, whose schedule as a legislator in Columbus prevented him from making his presentation of the Ohio & Erie Canal restoration story. Because her husband is cochairman of the Stark County Canal Lands Development Advisory Committee, Mrs. Regula had developed an interest in and acquired considerable knowledge of the canal. She carried off the "substitute" assignment effectively and went on to develop her own historically-oriented canal talk, which has caused her to be in demand in her own right.

Regarding Mrs. Regula's talk in Damascus, the club's program chairman wrote: "Mrs. Regula spoke to our garden club and asked us to send whatever we would have given her to the canal-boat fund. She aroused much interest and gave a most informative talk about the canal and its history."

And so the canal-boat fund got a valentine, too!

February 27, 1966
Longest Canal in the World

Somewhere along the way toward obtaining an education, most of us read or were told about the Great Wall of China. A defensive fortification, the wall extended 1,500 miles from the Yellow Sea to the gates of Central Asia.

But I'll bet very few of us ever heard of the Grand Canal of China. I first learned of it last week while snooping among the bookshelves at Canton Public Library. Looking for something new or different about canals, I came across a book I hadn't seen before. Published in 1964, it is about the canals of the central United States and it contains much of interest I hope to discuss in future columns.

In tracing the history of canals back to earliest time, the book reveals that the oldest canal in Asia was the Grand Canal of China, a 1,000-mile ditch, which linked Tungchow and Peking in the north with Hangchow in South China.

This 13th-century waterway generally was recognized as the longest in the world. Apparently it had no locks, as it was necessary to portage goods in moving shipments from one level of the canal to another. Mindful of the tremendous engineering feat accomplished by the builders of our own Ohio & Erie Canal, consider the engineering involved (and the labor utilized) in constructing the Grand Canal of China.

Builder Memorialized

Monuments there are, someone once said, to almost everything. Well, at least great numbers of monuments have been erected to a multitude of notable persons and events.

But until this past week I had not heard of a monument memorializing a canal builder. Then, while looking through the February issue of the Ohio Historical Society's publication, *Echoes,* I came upon an article about such a monument. The accompanying photo showed a squat stone obelisk in the small community of Texas in Henry County, southwest of Toledo.

The shaft memorializes James Durbin, surveyor and builder of canals, who completed a section of the Wabash and Erie Canal between Texas and the Providence lock in 1842. The Wabash and Erie ran from Toledo to Lafayette, Ind., and once was a prosperous waterway. Durbin, who also received contracts for other sections of this canal, had been a prime contractor in excavating the Miami and Erie Canal.

Rhodes Plugs Parks

I see where the governor has been out hobnobbing with the campers in Hueston Woods State Park near Oxford. The chief executive's overnight trailer campout included a chipped-steak supper, an open-pit barbecue breakfast, a songfest around a campfire and a tour of the 3,500-acre park.

The campout was part of the governor's program to boost tourism in Ohio and prove it's a "year-round Wonderful World of Ohio." Observing that tourists brought the state 1 billion last year and declaring that he wanted to up that to 2 billion, the governor said: "Parks like these have psychological impact on our workers. This may be a form of escapism but when you work a 40, 50 or 60-hour week, you need a place where you can escape to."

But, as it has been pointed out by proponents of the Ohio & Erie Canal parkway here in Stark County, few of us can get away to Hueston Woods for a weekend. We need our own park system close at hand.

If and when a metropolitan park system is established in Stark County, it could bring state and federal funds on a matching basis. This would enable the county to develop a strip park along the canal, which would provide recreation in abundance and, at the same time, help to attract those tourists the governor sees just over the horizon.

Latchstrings Out

The latchstrings on some 70 prefabricated houses are out today to bluebirds that may wish to become Stark County residents. That was the number reported in readiness for bluebird families this spring, following the work of the Canton Audubon Society last weekend in establishing a bluebird trail along the Ohio & Erie Canal southward from Canal Fulton.

Since first writing about the bluebird trail October 31, 1965, I have mailed out 58 sets of bluebird house plans.

The first person to respond to that initial "bluebird" column was Mrs. James Pitz of Massillon. She said her husband, a car-

83

penter skilled at making things, "plans to go down into the basement during the long winter months and make bluebird houses. All he needs is the pattern."

Well, we saw to it that he got the pattern. After Thanksgiving, Mr. Pitz started to make birdhouses. He called me several days ago to report that he had (coincidentally) 58 houses stained and ready for delivery — and that he would enjoy helping to put them up.

So the Audubon committee will be out again this weekend, extending the bluebird trail farther south along the canal towpath. And the number of "welcome" signs on bluebird houses will go well beyond the 100 mark, thanks to the interest and industry of the Pitzes.

March 6, 1966

Have You Heard of the Hennepin?

It is nice to be first and nice to be unique. But, as we are reminded so often in the newspaper business, uniqueness and "firstness" are often hard to come by.

That's the way it is with the Ohio & Erie Canal and the project to preserve and restore it as a recreational parkway. The Ohio & Erie certainly was not the first canal in the United States. That distinction is believed to belong to a 7-mile ditch dug around the falls of the James River in Virginia in 1784. Nor is the Ohio & Erie unique. There are many other early-American canals in varying degrees of abandonment in a number of states.

Even our canal restoration project is not new. The federal government's restoration of the Chesapeake and Ohio Canal, running into Maryland from our nation's capital, is well advanced and is recreationally oriented.

And in Illinois, which, it is claimed, tops the nation in total mileage of old, new and partly abandoned canals, canalized rivers and plans for canalization of additional rivers, the Illinois and Mississippi Canal, more commonly known as the

Hennepin Canal, is undergoing extensive rehabilitation work intended to make the 104-mile waterway one of the most popular recreation spots and tourist attractions in the nation.

The Hennepin has an interesting history. Leslie C. Swanson, in his book *Canals of Mid-America,* writes that the Hennepin was practically obsolete before it was completed in 1907, just six years before the big flood of 1913 washed out the Ohio & Erie. According to Mr. Swanson, the Hennepin was the last small canal of any length built in the United States in the last half of the nineteenth century. He believes it will be the longest such canal to be preserved in the United States and probably will become the longest state park in the nation.

After the canal rehabilitation program is completed, officials estimate that $20,000,000 more will be spent in a broad development program over the next 15 or 20 years. That is nearly three times the cost of building the canal.

More than 50 miles of continuous usable waterway for small boats will be provided by the Hennepin; claimed to be the longest man-made course of its type in the nation.

The Hennepin, like the Chesapeake and Ohio, was the subject of a massive "save the canal" campaign after federal engineers announced plans for its abandonment in 1951. The announcement dropped like a bombshell among the sportsmen of Illinois. Protests were heard from all sides. Newspapers, chambers of commerce, the Illinois Federation of Sportsmen's Clubs and many other groups joined individuals in protesting.

The combined efforts prevailed and ultimately, after a great deal of buck-passing between Washington and Springfield, it was agreed that Illinois would take over the canal as soon as the federal engineers had completed its rehabilitation.

The Hennepin no longer carried any commercial traffic in 1948 but it had become "one of the most popular recreation spots in the state." It quickly came into its ultimate role, that of a great outdoor area for millions of Illinois residents and visitors from other states. As a recreation spot, it has repaid many times the money spent on it. The public soon identified the canal as a fisherman's paradise. Flathead catfish weighing 50 pounds and lunker bass have been caught in its waters. The state of Illinois has kept the canal well stocked with fish. The waterway passes through some of the most beautiful scenery in Illinois, including stretches of woodland, rolling countryside and interesting towns. Aqueducts, dams and locks tie the waterway to some of the most picturesque rivers in the state.

Author Swanson writes about the Ohio & Erie Canal and old canals in other states but he comes across rather strongly as a booster for the canals of Illinois, his own state.

Proponents of the Ohio & Erie restoration project who chafe at its slow advance can take heart from the story of the Hennepin Canal.

Author Swanson sums up the future of the Hennepin with these words: "When work is completed, the Hennepin will take its place among the top recreation spots in the nation. The popular waterway has long supplied material for many feature stories in newspapers and national outdoor magazines. Millions of words have been written about it but none are more deftly phrased than a sentence by one Moline (Illinois) outdoor writer who describes the waterway as a 'big overgrown boy who doesn't like to work for the U.S. Engineers but who would rather relax with the folks who love him for what he is — a 104-mile-long playground.' "

March 13, 1966
Post Cards Are Canal Days Link

Some of the most graphic and colorful reproductions of old canal days scenes are to be found on well-preserved postal cards. I was reminded of this again this past week when I received several cards from readers.

Mrs. Anna Embly of Canton sent two cards. One was postmarked "Zanesville" and dated "1913." The other was stamped "Cumberland, Md." and dated "1908." The card from Zanesville pictures the Ohio & Erie Canal and the Muskingum River flowing side by side through the city. Two canal boats are visible on the calm waters of the canal. The other card pictures the Chesapeake and Ohio Canal as it sweeps through the Maryland city. Purple and green mountains in the background add to the "color" of the canal community as it appeared at the turn of the century.

Some time earlier, I received 26 postal cards of canal scenes from Mr. and Mrs. Harold S. Weber of Canton. These well-preserved cards showed canal-life scenes at Newcomerstown, Tuscarawas, Navarre, New Philadelphia, Coshocton, Zoar, Seventeen, Canal Dover, Port Washington and Bolivar. It was interesting to note that many of the cards, postmarked in 1911 and 1912, were made in Germany.

Equally interesting was Mrs. Weber's identification of the canal boat picture that appeared with this column in the Sunday edition of May 2, 1965. The boat, which was shown on the canal at Lock 17 in Tuscarawas County, and the people aboard it were unidentified until Mrs. Weber recognized them from the identical scene on a postal card. The people on the roof of the rear or stern cabin of the boat were her cousin, great-uncle and great-grandfather, and the boat was the "Col. Charles Dick," her great-grandfather's state canal boat. He was L.P. Wilson, superintendent of that section of the canal.

Mrs. Weber recalls that, as a very young girl, she accompanied her grandmother for a trip on the boat from Newcomerstown to Zoar. The regular cook was ill or absent for some cause and her grandmother filled in as cook during the trip. She remembers the bunk beds in the cabin and the old wood-burning stove. She also recalls playing on the towpath as the canal boat made its slow way along or waited in line to pass through one of the many locks.

Asked if she would like to see a canal boat like her great-grandfather's afloat today on the rewatered section of the Ohio & Erie Canal, Mrs. Weber replied emphatically: "I certainly would."

Justice Hikes Again

I see by the *New York Times* that Justice William O. Douglas of the U.S. Supreme Court was out hiking again and, as usual, in the interest of conservation. This time the 67-year-old justice led hiking groups along both shores of the Hudson River. Walking along the Croton Aqueduct near Ossining, New York, and later along the turbid river itself, the justice set his usual stiff pace for some 225 hikers who accompanied him.

Looking back at the conservationists, schoolchildren and politicians that followed him, the bareheaded justice observed: "It looks a little like Coxey's army." He was referring to the hundreds of jobless men that Jacob S. Coxey led in an historic march from Massillon, Ohio, to the nation's capital after the panic of 1893. The 500 or so men who survived the long hike to petition Congress for help were arrested for walking on the lawn of the Capitol.

The Croton Aqueduct runs from the Croton Reservoir into The Bronx. The ground above the aqueduct used to be an unbroken walkway through beautiful wooded valleys and along sparkling streams. While a student and teacher at Columbia Law School in the '20s, Mr. Douglas would hike along the path.

But today the hiking path is blocked in dozens of places by roads, fences and parking lots.

Many groups are urging its preservation now, however, and recently Governor. Nelson Rockefeller's Scenic Hudson Preservation Commission proposed that the walkway be made into one of the world's longest and narrowest parks — 32 miles long and 66 feet wide — something like the parkway proposed for the Ohio & Erie Canal here in Stark County.

In the afternoon of the same day, Justice Douglas led another large group, which he met at Nyack Beach Park, along a path between the Hudson River and the face of Hook Mountain. The "Beach" in the park's name should be changed, as no swimming is permitted because the Hudson is polluted.

"This is beautiful walking country, country that should be preserved," the jus-tice said as he was departing to board a plane back to Washington.

I suspect the justice could say much the same about our "Ohio & Erie Canal country" for it, too, is beautiful walking country that should be preserved. It also borders a mightily polluted river — the Tuscarawas.

March 15, 1966

Buckeye Trail Group Meets at Massillon

Back in the days when Ohio was a wilderness, the state was crossed and criss-crossed by Indian trails. And the part of the state that is now Stark County had its share of them.

Historians tell of The Great Indian Trail, which passed along the valley of the Little Sandy just south of Minerva in Carroll County. It was a natural roadway from east to west. In Stark County, the trail from the present Canton to Ravenna passed through the Hartville-Congress Lake area. The Indian trail through Newman's Creek bottom northwest of Massillon was another.

But the only trails officially recognized in the county today are concrete or black-topped and they are designated as route this and route that. Not even the Boy Scouts have an official trail in the county. All this could change as the result of a meeting Sunday. Out of it could come an honest-to-goodness, officially-recognized trail linking Lake Erie to the Ohio River and passing through some of the most beautiful sections of what passes today for Ohio's wilderness.

The Buckeye Trail Association will hold its annual meeting in Massillon Sunday, marking the first time the statewide hiking organization has convened in Stark County since it was conceived in 1958.

Hiking Along Towpath

The Stark County Canal Lands Development Advisory Committee invited the trail association to meet in Massillon so its members could hike the Ohio & Erie Canal towpath to Canal Fulton. State Rep. Ralph S. Regula of Navarre and Mayor William Keen of Massillon, cochairmen of the canal lands committee, said the officers and members of the trail association will hike the towpath with an eye toward incorporating it into the developing Buckeye Trail.

Association president William Miller of Logan invited the public to attend the annual meeting and to hike the towpath with members of his organization. Robert R. Paton of Columbus, Ohio Forestry Association executive director and an officer of the trail association, said he believes the Stark County meeting will mark a new era for the Buckeye Trail project, "setting the stage for a continuous trail from Cleveland to Cincinnati through the beautiful hills of Ohio."

Southern Ohio Active

Most of the trail association's activity in the past has been centered in southern Ohio, where more than 150 miles of established trail exist today. The southern terminus of the trail is Tar Hollow State Park in Ross County and the northern terminus is near Senecaville Reservoir in Guernsey County.

Mr. Miller, noting that the Tuscarawas County commissioners recently acquired title to canal lands in that county, said this

would aid substantially in providing access to the towpath in Stark, Portage and Cuyahoga counties and thus to Lake Erie.

Discussion of these developments will take place during the annual meeting, following lunch at 1 p.m. in the Towpath Inn at Massillon. Other events in the program include church services at 8 a.m. at Central Presbyterian Church in Massillon, a bus ride to the canal north of Massillon, a 6-mile hike along the towpath from Crystal Springs to Canal Fulton, with a rest stop at Lock 4 Park, and bus transportation back to Massillon.

March 20, 1966
Welcome, Buckeye Trail Hikers!

Along about the time many readers of this column turn to this page today, I hope to be hiking along the towpath of the Ohio & Erie Canal or getting ready to hike it. Perhaps some of you will be along with me.

Did you notice the big canal and towpath news of the week in Tuesday's editions of *The Repository* — the announcement that the Buckeye Trail Association would be holding its annual meeting today in Massillon?

The news was big because of its portent. If things go right on the towpath between Crystal Springs and Canal Fulton today — and in the association's annual meeting afterward — Stark County's developing towpath trail may become an integral part of the projected state-long Buckeye Trail.

The Ohio version of the Appalachian Trail now reaches root-like toward Cincinnati and Cleveland from its 165-mile central core in the cave country of southeastern Ohio.

The officer corps and active membership of the trail association were to meet in Massillon's Towpath Inn today, after hiking the towpath for nearly 5 miles of the rewatered section to evaluate it for possible designation as a northern section of the Buckeye Trail.

The Stark County Canal Lands Development Advisory Committee, host to the Buckeye Trail group, was greatly encouraged by the earlier action of the association's board of directors in tentatively approving the Stark section of the towpath trail as part of the Buckeye Trail. The committee members also were heartened by the fact that the trail association postponed its annual meeting from November until March to deal with the "new interest in the Buckeye Trail in Northern Ohio, especially in Stark County."

If the towpath becomes a part of the Buckeye Trail, it will be due primarily to the efforts of Cochairman Ralph Regula of the canal advisory committee.

I well recall the meeting of the canal committee, more than a year ago, when Mr. Regula waved a copy of the "Ohio Conservation Bulletin," predecessor of the magazine, *The Wonderful World of Ohio*, before the committee and reported on an article about the Buckeye Trail.

Since then he has promoted the idea of rerouting the northern section of the trail, which originally was to have passed between Youngstown and Warren and terminated near the Pennsylvania border at Conneaut. Regula would have it come north through Tuscarawas, Stark, Summit and Cuyahoga counties on the already existing towpath of the Ohio & Erie Canal wherever possible, terminating in Cleveland, where more than a million persons would have ready access to it.

The Buckeye Trail Association, in a recent letter to members, expressed appreciation to Mr. Regula, saying, "Rep. Ralph Regula of Stark County, an enthusiastic booster of the Buckeye Trail, has given us his valuable help in the legislature and in discussions and arrangements with the Ohio Department of Natural Resources, Gov. James A. Rhodes, Stark County agencies, organizations..."

Cochairman William Keen, wearing his other hat as Massillon's chief executive, assumed a major part of the planning for the association's visit in his city.

The hiking organization's newsletter also reports that interest in the Buckeye Trail has been indicated by the new U.S. Bureau of Recreation.

The association, incidentally, is a non-profit organization. All labor for scouting out the trail and clearing it has been voluntary. And, except for a small amount of secretarial assistance, all effort on behalf of the trail has been donated.

These facts give the Buckeye Trail a close kinship to the Ohio & Erie Canal towpath trail here in Stark County. It, too, has been developed to its present stage through volunteer efforts and with donations.

A wedding of the two walkways should be a real happy affair, full of benefits for everybody concerned. For example, the next time a national holiday comes along and the traffic fatality predictions occupy the headlines; if you fear to venture out onto the interstate raceways, why not just hop over to the canal, adjust your hiker's pack comfortably on your back and join "Hiking Unit 777" which is about to pad off downstate at a leisurely, healthful, safe and sane pace.

Bluebirds Return!

The bluebirds are back and house hunting!

Mrs. George Klein, who lives near Paris, wrote a thank-you card for the bluebird house plans I mailed to her and reported that she had several male bluebirds in her backyard since March 12. Mr. Klein had made a number of houses and placed them in strategic spots on their 53 acres. Describing the action of one of the bluebirds she had seen, Mrs. Klein said: "He was looking over all the houses. You know, they house hunt more than some people."

Now if only some of the house-hunting bluebirds discover the Ohio & Erie Canal towpath, they'll find more than 100 homes from which to make a selection — and, in so doing, will make the canal Bluebird Trail a complete success.

March 27, 1966

Towpath Trail Has 'Status' Now

They came... they saw... they hiked. Then they departed. But not before they had put the stamp of approval on Stark County's Ohio & Erie Canal towpath and claimed it as a part of their own.

"They" are the officers and members of the Buckeye Trail Association from many sections of the state who held their annual meeting in Massillon last Sunday and hiked 5 miles of the towpath from Crystal Springs to Canal Fulton.

For those who did not read the stories covering the visit of the association (last Monday's edition), suffice it to say that a significant step was taken in the development of the proposed state-long Buckeye Trail and our own canal parkway Our canal towpath has new status now. It is part of the Buckeye Trail, albeit sort of an island unto itself. The bulk of the completed trail is in southeastern Ohio in the scenic cave country. Segments of the trail are being constructed in various counties along the planned route but there still are gaps to be filled in. Such gaps exist between Seneca-ville Dam in Guernsey County and the Stark County section of the trail, and between Stark County and Lake Erie.

There was new hope this past week that Tuscarawas County may be one of the next counties to offer its roughly 40 miles of towpath as a section of the Buckeye Trail. Then only a few remaining miles in Guernsey County would separate Stark County from the new Salt Fork State Park and junction with the established trail near Senecaville.

Under the leadership of Chairman William Winters, Tuscarawas County commissioners have approved formation of a canal advisory committee similar to the one in Stark County. Composed of persons interested in the preservation and restoration of the canal, the committee would plan a program of improvements for consideration by the commissioners.

In addition to the commissioners, others in the forefront of the move to obtain title to the Tuscarawas canal lands are Ted Findley of New Philadelphia, president of the Canal Society of Ohio; Ray Crumbley, city editor of the *New Philadelphia Daily Times*, and E. Richards of Bolivar.

Mr. Findley has pledged his organization to do all it can to assist the Buckeye Trail Association establish itself in Tusc-arawas County. And so, if the county gets title to its canal lands, it is a good bet that the Tuscarawas towpath also will become a much-needed section of the Buckeye Trail.

Summit County has its hiking enthusiasts, too. Some of them were with the Buckeye Trail Association members who hiked the Stark County towpath last Sunday. An organized effort there conceivably could put still another county in the Buckeye Trail fold.

I guess there were a lot of hikers out last Sunday despite the rather cold and overcast day. Up in Hinckley Reservation of Cleveland's metropolitan park, nearly 300 Greater Clevelanders turned out to take a hike sponsored by the Cleveland Geological Society.

Harold E. Wallin, the park naturalist, said it was the best turnout for a society walk in four years. And there probably would have been more hikers if it hadn't been Buzzard Sunday in Hinckley. Some 18,000 visitors arrived in town, including Gov. James A. Rhodes, to eat sausage and pancakes and see the turkey buzzards, which come back to roost in Hinckley every year, about March 15.

There's no question about it — more and more Americans are taking up hiking, in sort of a holiday from the wheels on which we all live and move. A report from the Federal Bureau of Outdoor Recreation indicates that walking for pleasure (hiking) is second in a list of 12 favorite recreational activities of Americans. Of these 12, at least eight could be enjoyed in conjunction with a trip to the Ohio & Erie Canal towpath.

The report listed the activities in order of popularity and I have capitalized those that can be enjoyed in connection with the canal: DRIVING FOR PLEASURE (to and from the canal), WALKING FOR PLEASURE, PLAYING OUTDOOR GAMES OR SPORTS (at Canal Fulton Village Park or Lock 4 Park), swimming, sightseeing, BICYCLING (on the towpath), FISHING, attending sports events, PICNICKING, TAKING NATURE WALKS, BOATING (canoeing) and hunting.

Lawrence N. Stevens, associate director of the bureau, which is a Department of the Interior agency, said; "Today we are pushing toward a population that is 70 percent urban and this will continue to go up. As more people live in cities, the more they desire open space and outdoor recreation. We are trying desperately to keep ahead of urban sprawl, to encourage states, cities and counties to make adequate provision for recreation resources as they grow themselves."

Mr. Stevens said the big news today is the availability of money by which the federal government and the states can evenly split the cost of developing recreation resources.

Translated in terms of our urban Stark County, this means the creation of a metropolitan park system, which would bring funds to develop the canal towpath parkway and other parks throughout the county. For 150 years, Stark County, like most of the rest of the nation, was primarily agricultural. And the last thing farmers wanted was outdoor recreation. 'Tain't so today. 'Tain't.

Then there was the card from Harold E. Nutter of Canton. Nutter, who said he has been interested in the canal since he was a small boy, sent me a postcard bearing a picture of an abandoned canal lock being taken over by weeds and trees. An elderly man and a young girl stand at the entrance to the lock. The caption on the card reads: "Last Canal Boatman at First Locks on Ohio & Erie Canal." The man is identified as William Kneeland, last known boatman in Newark, who drove mules on his first trip on the canal in 1879 when he was 9 years old. The girl is his great-grandniece, Roberta Johnson.

The lock, south of Newark on Route 79, is a part of Four-Mile Locks, the site of the start of the Ohio & Erie Canal. It was on this spot that Gov. DeWitt Clinton of New York took out the first spadeful of earth to launch the canal construction, July 4, 1825.

Coincidentally, I was in Newark shortly before receiving the card. En route from there to Buckeye Lake, I passed this lock, noting that it was constructed of a different kind of stone than the locks in Stark, Tuscarawas and Summit counties. The colors of the huge blocks were a warm tan and rust color in contrast to the gray stone used in the northern counties. But at Newark, as in other areas of the state, the highway builders have eradicated much of the canal, just as they are doing in Coshocton and Tuscarawas counties.

While visiting Newark, I picked up the magazine section of the *Sunday Columbus Dispatch*. On the cover was a colorful picture of two young men and two young women riding an assortment of bicycles on a pathway through a woods. The caption

April 3, 1966
Canal Towpath a Bike-Hike Trail

Last week was a dandy — mailwise. A number of letters and cards reached my desk, each interesting in its own way.

There was the note from Grandma Emma Gatewood down in Cheshire, thanking me for sending her clippings of "the write-up" about the Buckeye Trail Association's meeting in Massillon and hike along the Ohio & Erie Canal towpath.

"It was very encouraging, the way folk turned out for the meeting and hike on the tote road," Grandma wrote. "I am very anxious to see the Buckeye Trail completed."

Grandma, who is 78, was one of the pacesetters for the hike. She was present when William Miller of Logan, president of the trail association, nailed the organization's official marker on a tree along the canal in Canal Fulton, designating the towpath in Stark County as a part of the Buckeye Trail.

on the picture read: "Freeway for Bicycles, Trail Network Planned" (See Page 8). Turning to Page 8, I found an article telling of the plans of the recreation department of the City of Columbus and the Columbus Council of American Youth Hostels to provide special trails for bicyclers. The article reported that more than five million bicycles were sold last year and that this figure may be doubled by 1975.

If the recreation department's plans materialize, someday it may be possible to ride a bicycle or take a hike all the way through Columbus, in a north-south direction, along the Scioto and Olentangy rivers without once crossing a street or having to compete with automobiles.

Future plans call for extending the bike-hike trail well beyond the city. Melvin Dodge of the Columbus recreation department stresses the physical fitness benefits to be derived from use of the trail. He sees hiking working in very well with the bicycling on the trail where no motorized vehicles will be permitted. Families will be able to rent bicycles for a few hours or a day of togetherness on the trails.

The youth hostel group is excited about plans. As far as its members are concerned, anyone who can ride a bicycle is classified as "young." The organization today is placing emphasis on family participation in its activities.

There are other bikeways in the state today and more in the planning stages. One near Kettering is eight miles long.

Bicycling enthusiasts, thinking big, are talking of one or more bikeways extending from coast to coast. Cycling always has been popular but in recent years it has been increasingly difficult to find safe places to ride. It is to restore safety bicycling that the bicycle trails are being established. People of all ages ride bicycles and Dr. Paul Dudley White, nationally known cardiologist, finds this good. He has recommended cycling to many of his patients as a method of keeping fit and he advises it for healthy people who want to stay that way.

In Stark County, eight miles of towpath, from north of Canal Fulton to south of Crystal Springs, is in good condition for cycling, a ready-built bikeway with scenic environs.

There were other interesting letters but I shall mention only one more. It contained a check from the Arboretum Garden Club of Canton and it was made out to the "Canal-boat fund." The unsolicited fund has grown to $65 contributed by persons who would like to see and ride on an authentic canal boat afloat on Stark County's section of the Ohio & Erie Canal.

April 10, 1966
Homer and the Bluebird

Sometimes things turn out just right — appropriately nice — a happy happenstance. That's the way it was with Homer Fulton and the bluebird. Homer, who first suggested I use this column to help bring back the bluebirds to Stark County, has done a great deal to provide good housing for the spring songbirds. He made copies of house plans available to the public, provided lumber for the construction of many houses and helped to collect the houses, which were donated for the bluebird trail along the Ohio & Erie Canal towpath.

And yet Homer had never seen a bluebird!

Not until last Sunday, that is.

Then, while gazing through the windows of his Lake Cable home, he saw his first flashing blue wings through the falling snowflakes. The bluebird was inspecting some of the houses Homer had placed on a fence near his home.

Here's hoping the bluebird takes up residence near the Fulton home. It couldn't happen to a more deserving guy. After all he did to help bring the bluebirds back to Stark County, it seems almost like poetic justice that he should be among the first to see the fruits of his labor in the form of a house-hunting bluebird. Homer's first sight of his first bluebird was a thrill — a well-deserved one.

Word Gets Around
News of Stark County's canal-lands

restoration project is getting around the state. A letter from Springfield brings word that the *Springfield News-Sun* is planning a nine-picture Sunday layout and story about the recent hike along the canal towpath by members of the Buckeye Trail Association and the designation of the towpath as part of the Buckeye Trail.

Two members of the Springfield newspaper's staff drove to Massillon to make the hike and work up the story. While on the towpath trek, the Springfield newspapermen learned of the Stark Wilderness Center and, as a result, they plan another trip to Stark County. They hope that, by showing what Stark County has done to save and develop its wilderness area near Wilmot, they may be able to save a "natural area" near Springfield.

Canoe-Canal-Circus

E.J. Bissler of Alliance, who says he has been a canal buff since the '30s when he traveled by canoe from Cleveland to Akron via canal and river, sent in several interesting items. One article, which appeared in a trade magazine, indicates that Stark County is not the only place in Ohio where an effort is being made to float a canal boat once again.

Mr. Bissler quotes the following paragraph from the magazine *Western Electrician*: "Thomas N. Fordyce has ordered the equipment for his canal-boat scheme on the Miami and Erie Canal (in western Ohio). The Westinghouse Co. furnished the motors, which are slow-speed machines. A standard track will be laid along the canal and the boats will be towed by the motors."

Sounds interesting but hardly historically authentic.

In a separate note, Mr. Bissler adds a bit of mystery and adventure by telling of a canal boat carrying "some sort of valuables," which supposedly was sunk in the backwater in the Jaite-Boston-Peninsula area in Summit County. He is searching for more information about the "sunken treasure."

I never thought about it until I received Mr. Bissler's letter but how do you suppose circuses got around the country before there were railroads?

Well, at least some of them traveled by canal boat.

Mr. Bissler writes that the Van Amburgh Circus traveled the Sandy and Beaver Canal as far west as Minerva. The circus needed four canal boats to carry the entire show.

In lieu of a parade, the owners of the circus would have elephants bathe in the canal basin at Minerva. This event was probably well advertised as it drew a good attendance.

April 17 and 24, 1966
Hat's Off to a Sharp-Eyed Reader

The serial about the voyage of John Quincy Adams through Stark County aboard the canal packet ROB ROY, contained a minor error. I wonder how many readers caught it. One who did was C.P. Miesmer of Canton, whose hobby is presidents of the United States. He has visited and photographed the birthplace, home (where standing) and the burial site of every president since and including George Washington. He showed me his photo album and pointed out the historical error.

John Quincy Adams was not president when he floated through Stark County on the Ohio & Erie Canal in 1843. He was a former president. John Tyler was president then. JQA was 76 years old and a member of the House of Representatives at the time of his trip. Elected a representative after his term as president, he served his country until his death at age 81, while speaking in the halls of Congress.

John Quincy Adams and the Canal Boat

Believe it or not, a (former) president of the United States once passed through Stark County as a canal boat passenger — and he wrote about it in his memoirs. I came upon the published excerpts of these memoirs in the April issue of "Towpaths," official publication of the Canal Society of Ohio, which is shared here with permission:

"In 1843, the Astronomical Society of Cincinnati invited the president of the United States, John Quincy Adams, to lay the cornerstone of a new observatory to be built in that city. The President accepted with reluctance, his interest in science overcoming his distaste for travel. The journey involved going from Boston to Buffalo by train, to Cleveland by lake steamer and then to Cincinnati by canal boat and stagecoach. The small presidential party shared a packet boat with numerous other passengers and the Chief Executive enjoyed no more privacy or comfort than the others. The following excerpts are from Vol. XI, *The Memoirs of John Quincy Adams, 1876.*

"Nov. 1. — From this place (Cleveland) there are two modes of proceeding to Columbus, distant 232 miles — one by land stages traveling night and day, with excessively bad and very dangerous roads; the other by canal boat on the Ohio Canal, which will take us four days to reach Columbus.

"We were advised by all means to take the latter mode, which we concluded to do, and took passage in the canal boat ROB ROY, Captain Phillips. She was to depart at two o'clock p.m., and in the meantime I was to undergo a reception.

"Mr. Andrew made the address to me, which I answered as usual, and shook hands with the men, women, and children; after which we dined at the American Hotel, and embarked in the canal boat ROB ROY.

"Akron, (Nov.) 2nd. — I came on board the canal packet boat ROB ROY yesterday very unwell with my catarrh, hoarseness and sore throat, and some fever. This boat is eighty-three feet long, fifteen wide and had, beside the persons I have named, about twenty other passengers.

"It is divided into six compartments, the first in the bow, with two settee beds, for the ladies, separated by a curtain from a parlor bed-chamber, with an iron stove in the center, and side settees, on which four of us slept, feet to feet; then a bulging stable for four horses, two and two by turns, and a narrow passage, with a settee for one passenger to sleep on, leading to the third compartment, a dining hall and dormitory

for thirty persons; and lastly, a kitchen and cooking apparatus, with sleeping room for cook, steward and crew, and necessary conveniences.

"So much humanity crowded into such a compass was a trial such as I had never before had experienced, and my heart sank within me, squeezing into this pillory, I reflected that I am to pass three nights and four days in it.

"We came on board the boat at two o'clock, the time she was to depart, but it was four before she left the wharf. We were obliged to keep the windows of the cabins closed against the driving snow, and the stoves, heated with billets of wood, made the rooms uncomfortably warm.

"(Nov.) 3rd. — In the course of yesterday and this day we passed through the places named in the margins of Wednesday's page (the names of 45 towns between Cleveland and Columbus).

"We reached Massillon last evening after dark, and, it being a considerable place, there were symptoms of a desire on the part of its inhabitants to give me a reception. We finally persuaded them to let us pass on quietly.

"As acquaintance became familiar with my fellow passengers, time slipped away more cheerily. They are all kind and obliging, the young ladies very lively and good-humored.

"The weather has been so harsh and churlish that we have not been tempted to open our windows, or to stand on the deck of the boat to see the country around us. The banks of the canal are so muddy that there is no comfort in walking.

"We see that we are in a beautiful country, with a deep rich soil, but much of it along the borders of the canal is woodland, and with the wood cut down, and the stumps standing, like the pins of a bowling green, and presenting an aspect rather of desolation than plenty.

"In the common dining room and dormitory I made out no small trouble and inconvenience to write for about two hours in the forenoon of yesterday and this day, and one hour of each afternoon, in this diary...

"I write amidst perpetual interruptions,

in the presence of half a dozen strangers, who seem to think me a strange, sulky person, to spend so much time writing. The most uncomfortable part of our navigation is caused by the careless and unskillful steering of the boat into and through the locks, which seem to be numberless, upwards of two hundred of them on the canal. The boat scarcely escapes a heavy thump on entering every one of them. She strikes and grazes against their sides, and staggers along like a stumbling nag.

"We passed, in the course of last night, through a settlement of Germans, called Zoar, a community under an absolute ruler, and this day through Gnadenhutten, originally a Moravian settlement, but now fallen into the ordinary track of breeding towns.

"This afternoon the sky cleared off, and on approaching a place called Roscoe, several of us landed, and walked about a mile, when we were obliged to return to the boat...

"(Nov.) 4th. — About one o'clock this morning Mr. Grinnel came to my settee and awoke me to communicate to me a letter just received... inviting me to visit... that place (Newark) where we were to arrive about sunrise.

"On reaching Newark we landed. After breakfast we went to the Town Hall, I believe, crowded with good-looking persons of both sexes, and there a gentleman welcomed me with a complimentary address.

"We returned to the boat, and proceeded, to terminate our navigation at Hebron. Here we took leave of the Macy family, Mr. Russell, and Miss Langdon, whom we had found charming traveling companions. They proceed in the boat to Portsmouth, where the canal reaches the Ohio River. We are henceforth to go by land stages to Cincinnati."

And so ends the narrative of John Quincy Adams' passage aboard the canal packet ROB ROY.

But, having read it, I, for one, will look at Lock 4, south of Canal Fulton, with even greater interest than before as I visualize the ROB ROY, with the ex-president aboard, thumping and bumping its way through the lock and staggering, as he said, "like a stumbling nag."

Canal Boat Dollars

Encouragement and financial support for the canal boat project continue to come in unexpected ways. The most recent boost was a cash contribution from the Canton YWCA Garden Club. The money was given in appreciation of a talk to the members by Mrs. Arthur Christenson of Canton. Mrs. Christenson spoke about "A Bird Walk Along the Towpath" and then pointed the honorarium toward the canal-boat fund.

It's a Grand Time for Hiking

It's a grand time for hiking along the towpath — right now. Last Sunday nearly 200 persons participated in the Stark Wilderness Center-sponsored hike up the towpath. It was the largest group to hike along the canal since it was deeded to Stark County.

May 1, 1966
New Canal Developments

Developments to the north of us, action to the south of us and all of it seemingly good news for the preservation and utilization of the Ohio & Erie canal lands.

Up Cleveland way, the concept of establishing a canal parkway is finding support. There is talk of making the section from Cleveland's outskirts to Akron into a national park.

U.S. Rep. Charles A. Vanik, D-Cleveland, has written to the advisory board on national parks of the Interior Department in Washington proposing just that. His proposal is being considered in Washington. If approved, the restoration project would become eligible for federal funds.

Readers may recall that two years ago this month Ralph Regula of Navarre and I went to Washington after traveling the length of the Chesapeake and Ohio Canal, and spoke with officials of the Interior Department. We proposed substantially what is being sought now except that we suggested the possibility of a state-long parkway, similar to the Chesapeake and

Ohio Park, which would serve people in communities all along the old canal route from Cleveland to Portsmouth. We reminded the officials, as did Rep. Vanik, that Ohio has less than 90 acres of the more than 26 million acres of land controlled by the National Park Service.

No action from Washington was forthcoming and so Stark County has gone ahead on its own to restore and develop its canal lands, to such an extent that its accomplishments are being pointed to and cited as an example of what can be done for the recreational benefit of thousands.

Rep. Vanik has strategic political position in his effort to make a federal park of the northern section of the canal. We certainly welcome his efforts and wish him success.

Meanwhile, down in Coshocton County, an "historic preservation recreation study" has been conducted the last four weeks under auspices of the department of architecture of Kent State University. The study centered about the old canal town of Roscoe, near Coshocton. This historic community grew as a direct result of the canal.

Today, a number of persons in Coshocton are interested in Roscoe and concerned about its preservation. The city owns parcels of parkland, which include part of the canal, its towpath and the unusual triple locks, which are in excellent condition for restoration.

It was about a year ago that Rep. Regula and I drove to Coshocton to talk with the commissioners and citizens there in an effort to stir interest in preserving a particularly beautiful section of the canal east of Newcomerstown. But no organized effort to save the canal developed at that time and the highway department has marked the scenic section for obliteration. Consequently, the news of the project at Roscoe is welcome indeed.

Students in the third-year design class of Clyde A. Patterson Jr., associate professor in Kent State's department of architecture, have just completed their program for the restoration and preservation of the Roscoe community.

Three prizes, $25, $50 and $100 from the Montgomery Foundation, await the students whose plans are judged to be the best by a professional jury of architects. The prizes were arranged by the Coshocton Chamber of Commerce, which will sponsor an awards dinner in Coshocton.

The competing students were reminded that architects must recognize the need as a professional person to be aware of the architectural heritage of our country and to preserve its best examples before they are lost to the community forever. Architects must consider themselves as guardians of important spaces in the town complex as well as important buildings and other architectural forms.

I was particularly interested to note, in the suggestions offered to the students for their planning, that "activities should not only include adults but also children as e.g., a trip on a canal packet boat."

The program instructions recommended to the students that "Roscoe should not be thought of as a museum, but every effort must be made to bring interest and activity to it as it is a part of a total recreational complex."

The students have studied the problem from many angles, they have visited Roscoe and Coshocton, they have collected data and they have planned their proposal phases and methods of presentation. Lastly, they have collaborated to construct a three-dimensional model of Roscoe and its adjacent areas. What these budding architects have come up with in the way of a restored historic canal community should prove quite interesting.

During our visit to Coshocton, Rev. Russell Hoy of Canal Lewisville took Rep. Regula and me on a tour of Roscoe and showed us some of the old canal-days buildings still standing. These structures, along with the unusual triple lock, could become the central units of a remarkable canal park.

Many months ago, "Along the Towpath" suggested that a healthy competition among canal counties to preserve and develop their respective historical sites and canal lands could prove beneficial to all. With the current developments in Cuyahoga County and the project in Coshocton County, this may be coming to pass.

A Phone Call Brings Hope

My nebulous plans for this week's column have just gone out the window — put to flight by a telephone call. As a result, I write tonight of what is on my mind and in my heart, namely — a canal boat for Stark County's Ohio & Erie Canal. The telephone brought heartening news — real hope for the missing link in the chain of needs required to build the boat — manpower.

There have been other calls recently, all encouraging. One caller said he had the promise of three big oak trees, to be donated by three different residents of Jackson Township. The "green" oak, he said, should meet the requirements for this particular type of wood in the framing of the boat. He also told of a businessman whose firm will help.

Other calls have brought offers of help. And then the letters bringing in donations for the canal-boat fund — they are wonderful. The fund now contains $115. There have been other offers of lumber for the boat — one extremely generous one. And we have a place to build the boat — this, too, has been offered.

But the big bottleneck has been manpower. Now, maybe — just maybe — a happy solution.

A Towpath 'First'?

In the old days, hikers along the towpath of the Ohio & Erie didn't have what members of Boy Scout Troop 159 of Canton will have when they hike the towpath May 22. In fact, it may be a first among scouts who have hiked the towpath.

So what is it? Dehydrated food — enough for the meal the scouts will "cook" at Lock 4 Park. Al Salasek, troop committeeman, said the dehydrated foods were ordered from Chicago. The scouts will carry the food with them on their 5-mile hike from Crystal Springs to Canal Fulton and should find it considerably lighter than their standard provisions. Zion Lutheran Church at Seventh Street and Raff Road SW sponsors the troop and William D.G. Stewart is scoutmaster. Most of the 45-member troop is expected to make the hike.

"The boys are really hepped up about it," Salasek said.

Attention Hikers

This item should be of interest to hikers who have been getting into condition for summer by hiking the canal towpath.

Arthur Jones of Massillon reports that 300 miles of the 500-mile Bruce trail in Ontario, Canada, are completed and awaiting hikers. The trail starts at Queenston, Ontario, near Niagara Falls, and stretches northwest along the Georgian Bay to Tobermory in the same province. At one point it crosses the busy Welland Canal from Lake Ontario to Lake Erie.

B(blue)FOs Sighted!

The first two reports of bluebird sightings along the new bluebird trail beside the Ohio & Erie Canal came from a husband and wife. The sightings were made by William and Ruth Bender of Canton on widely separated occasions.

Mr. Bender spotted four or five of the blue songsters several weeks ago while he was filling the bird feeders along the trail. A member of the canal committee of Canton Audubon Society, Bill, helped to keep the feeders supplied with seed through the winter. Then last Monday, while Ruth was leading members of the Chechahco Garden Club of North Canton along the towpath, she spotted a bluebird.

The Audubon Society has not reported any bluebirds nesting in the more than 100 bluebird houses in the bluebird trail. But at least the bluebirds have found the trail — and its rent-free houses.

Let's 'Metropolitanize'

The May issue of the Cleveland Metropolitan Park District's nifty newsletter, "The Emerald Necklace," arrived containing hints of things to come in Stark County — provided a metropolitan park district is established here. The four-page monthly encourages residents of metropolitan Cleveland to leave the hard-surfaced city for a while to enjoy the displays of wild flowers in the park system reservations. In three of the reservations, North Chagrin, Rocky River and Brecksville, the flowers along the trails are labeled.

Similarly, along some of the wilder undeveloped stretches of the Ohio & Erie Canal towpath in Stark County, there are clusters and uncultivated beds of some of the more unusual wild flowers. They are not labeled, of course. But someday they may be.

In the Cleveland metropolitan parks, bird walks are conducted at 7:30 Sunday mornings. Leaders "help you identify" the birds by sight and sound.

The canal towpath in Stark and its immediate environs constitute a fine "bird land." Mrs. Judson Case, a member of Canton Audubon Society, has counted 93 different birds while supplying bird feeders along the canal. There should be no problem in establishing regularly scheduled bird walks comparable to those in Cleveland once a metropolitan park system is created here.

The "Emerald Necklace" also tells of a 5-mile hike scheduled for May 22 by the Cleveland Hiking Club. The major part of the hike, which is open to the adult public, will be on back trails that "are seldom traveled by the casual visitor."

Now that Stark County's section of the canal towpath is officially part of the Buckeye Trail, all that is needed to match Cleveland is the organization of a county hikers group.

This summer, in the Cleveland Metropolitan Park District, there will be 29 day camps operating in 17 areas. More than 2,000 children are expected to participate in outdoor experiences at the camps. Agencies sponsoring the camps will include the Girl Scouts, Camp Fire Girls, CYO, YMCAs, YWCAs and neighborhood and community centers.

Stark County's canal lands could provide the setting for such day camps. The same organizations and others like them need only a "go ahead" to duplicate the Cleveland program. The "go ahead" seems to be spelled "m-e-t-r-o-p-o-l-i-t-a-n-i-z-e."

Canal Artist Goofed

Harold E. Nutter of Canton, who has been interested in the Ohio & Erie Canal since he was a boy, dropped in to see me the other day. He brought along an interesting book, *Pioneers on Early Waterways.* A supplementary reader in American history from the Frontiers of America series of Edith McCall, the book is at the third-grade reading level although it's interest level extends to the eighth grade.

The book includes a chapter titled "Jim Garfield, Canal Boatman." The Jim Garfield referred to later become James Abram Garfield, president of the United States. A paragraph in the introduction to the book reads: "Jim Garfield falls off his canal boat about once a week before a fight leads him to think he should go on to better things."

The introduction also states that the book contains "true stories of real people."

Unfortunately, the artist who drew the sketches for the book did not always present a true or accurate picture — at least where the canal-boat era was portrayed.

Mr. Nutter called my attention to the fact that the canal-boat teams were not hitched in tandem, there was no motive power at all in evidence on one boat passing through a lock, the lock was much too wide and unrealistically constructed, there was no rudder or means of operating one on another boat, and the canal boats were being towed from the bow of the boat, which any canal buff knows just wasn't so.

At least in these sketches the artist has done a disservice to the author. Maybe the third graders won't notice these errors but, on the other hand, if this book gives them their first understanding of the canal era, the pictures as well as the text should be authentic.

But perhaps the book will inspire the third graders to search out other books and pictures about the canal days. If it does, it is fulfilling a useful purpose in helping to tell the story of our American heritage.

May 22, 1966
Miami & Erie
Had Electric 'Mules'

Newspaper writers and editors, probably more than most people, are careful about what they say and write. They are trained that way. They have to have the facts to back up their statements or they can be in trouble. And it seems, at times, that the public is just waiting for them to make a statement that can be successfully challenged.

I take particular pride in keeping "Along the Towpath" free from challenge. But, in 18 months of writing this column, I have been challenged twice. And both times I was in error.

The last time, I was commenting on an article telling of a scheme to use motors to tow canal boats on the Miami and Erie Canal in western Ohio.

This short afterthought sentence of six words brought forth the well-deserved correction:

"Sounds interesting but hardly historically authentic."

John P. Wunderle of Kent read the column and wrote to tell me the "electric mules" were authentic.

"The Miami and Erie did have this system through Cincinnati," he wrote. Mr. Wunderle went on to explain that the electric-powered "mules" were used on standard gauge tracks to pull the canal boats but that their existence was short-lived because the 5 mph speed caused the banks of the canal to wash away.

Except for having to "eat" all six words in that sentence, I am glad Mr. Wunderle wrote to me. His letter led me to the information for today's column — a very unusual and interesting chapter in the Ohio canal story.

I put in a call for help to Ted Findley of New Philadelphia, president of the Canal Society of Ohio, and Ted wrote back: "I don't think you were out of line with your 'electric mules.' They were not used on the Ohio & Erie — just the Miami." Ted sent along a copy of the society's "Towpaths" magazine, containing an article titled

"Power on the Towpath" by L.W. Richardson of Cleveland, editor of the magazine.

Almost at the same time, I received a letter from Mr. Richardson, who said he had just read the column. He, too, called my attention to the error and enclosed a copy of his article and pictorial proof of the existence of the "electric mules." In doing his research, Mr. Richardson found that "very little information on the electrification of the towpath is to be found in the Ohio histories" and that the best account is in the *Street Railway Journal*, Nov. 7, 1903, "although this is written for the electrical and interurban professionals rather than for the 'canawler'." Mr. Richardson explained that the picture of the "electric mule" he sent to me was a copy of the builder's photo and was obtained from the Smithsonian Institution after nearly a year of fruitless searching in newspaper morgues, libraries, etc., in southwestern Ohio.

To tell the story of the "electric mules," I quote from Mr. Richardson's article "Power on The Towpath":

"The most expensive experiment in the use of mechanical power on the Ohio canals began in 1901 on the Miami and Erie and, although ostensibly designed to revitalize the ailing canal, it was actually an attempt to seize control of canal rights-of-way into Cincinnati for the electric interurban interests. The Board of Public Works in that year granted a lease to Thomas Fordyce to operate an electric towing company, the Miami and Erie Canal Transit Co., between Cincinnati and Dayton.

"It was revealed later that the company stock was controlled by the Weidner interurban combine of Philadelphia and, in 1904, bills were introduced in Columbus to grant the transit company perpetual rights to canal property for railway purposes. Canal supporters rallied to the cause, the bills failed to pass and the transit company soon went into receivership.

"Regardless of the real reason for its existence, construction on the line began in 1903 and... reached Dayton in 1904... The system was the first three-phase AC railroad in this country and is believed to have been the longest continuous track towing system in the world. Seven road engines and one low, cableless switcher were used. The track and the two trolley wires required by the three-phase operation followed the canal bank and no existing bridges were raised. Minimum clearances were very low, in Cincinnati as little as six feet. For this reason the switcher was used exclusively in the Cincinnati city limits. Power was held to 390 volts in the city, 1,170 volts elsewhere. With the bare wires within reach of any active boy, the fact that numerous electrocutions were not reported is a cause for wonder.

"The engines had on each side a double hook for a 200-foot towing cable and a 50-foot line was used between each tow. The original plan was to tow 10 boats but in practice it was found that no more than five could be handled and the usual tow was two or three. After the failure to the company, the engines, powerhouses and the copper wires were salvaged but for many years afterward the patient teams had to walk the track."

And so ended an unusual but interesting chapter in the canal story of Ohio — with the "electric mules" being put out "to pasture" in the salvage yards of southwestern Ohio.

May 29, 1966
Letter with Bluebird on it

There must have been a dozen letters dropped on my desk when the office mail delivery was made the other day. One of them caught my eye immediately. It was sealed with a brightly colored bluebird sticker. I figured the letter contained information pertaining to the bluebird trail along the Ohio & Erie Canal — and it did.

Mrs. Dorothy Corner, historian of the Ohio Gourd Society, had written to tell me of a project involving the canal, gourds, people and especially bluebirds. Mrs. Corner wrote that the gourd society, meeting recently in Dover, "went on record as wishing to contribute gourd birdhouses to help the Canal Society of Ohio establish a bluebird trail across the state of Ohio."

Wholeheartedly endorsing Stark County's canal bluebird trail, the gourd society would like to extend it through the use of bluebird houses made from gourds. At the society's big fall gourd show Oct. 9 at Mt. Gilead, members from throughout the state will bring gourd bluebird houses for distribution next spring prior to nesting time.

In response to my request for assurance that bluebirds would make their homes in a gourd house, Mrs. Corner brought two of them in for me to see, one of which contained a nest.

She also submitted printed publications supporting her statements, including a U.S. Department of Agriculture bulletin, which states: "Gourds of the spoon, dipper and bottle types make excellent nesting quarters for certain birds, because they are weatherproof and can easily be made ready for use and fastened in place; furthermore they are so easily and cheaply grown that they make very inexpensive nesting quarters. In the southeastern states especially, groups of gourds put up for purple martin nests are a common sight."

The bulletin states that "use of gourds as homes for birds need not be restricted to martins," and lists a number of birds and gives the number of inches of all inside dimensions of the gourd houses for the various birds. For the bluebird it is 5 inches.

Another publication tells the story of Connie N. Watts of the Dixie Martin-Bluebird Co-Operative Club:

"In northwest Georgia, where birds were once plentiful, the destruction of nesting places in old dead trees and post stumps sadly depleted their number. After years of decreasing bird-life, he realized something must be done to coax back these valuable friends in an area where insects, unchecked, would do great damage.

"He began to put up boxes and gourds for birdhouses. Gourds of the hardshell variety (Laganaria) were easily grown and prepared for bird occupancy by first drying, then cutting out an entrance hole.

"Knowing that he could do but a small share alone, he conceived the idea of a club for bird lovers in search of a hobby. So on Oct. 8, 1939, with one other member, this club was launched — with no dues and no publicity. To encourage the preparation of birdhouses, he offered to send 25 gourd seeds free to anyone who would send a three-cent stamp for postage. Then came the phenomenal response and an increase from 26,000 seeds sent the first year to 300,000 (by 1942) to every state in the United States."

The article concludes by noting that the bluebird, "a blue flash of sheer beauty, has never been accused of preying on crops or garden, feeding mostly on the ground on our common insect pests."

And now for those interested in making gourd birdhouses, Mrs. Corner tells how to do it:

"After cleaning off the outer surface, the entrance should be made about the middle of the gourd, to prevent the fledglings from falling out. If you cannot remove the pits and seeds easily, put in small sharp stones, shaking the gourd vigorously. If it is not convenient to remove the material through the entrance hole, the bottom of the gourd may be removed, and then wired on again. A few holes should be drilled in the bottom for drainage.

"Most birds like a perch. Insert a grapevine tendril near the entrance or make small holes with the wood-burning needle, and use strong twigs for the entrance as well as the top of the gourd, so it may be easily suspended. To hang the houses in the trees use copper wire as it will not rust. Small pebbles in the bottom of the gourd houses will act as ballast, so they will not sway too freely in the wind."

Bluebirds Move In

For the many persons who built and donated houses for the bluebird trail, there is good news this week. At least one of more than 100 houses near the towpath contains a bluebird family. Mr. and Mrs. William Bender, members of Canton Audubon Society, followed up their earlier report of bluebird sightings by confirming that one house is occupied. The Benders stood in the rain 25 minutes, watching with binoculars, to be sure. Perhaps, after

a reasonable length of time for bluebird "gossip" to get around, we can expect to see the development of a bluebird allotment along the canal.

June 5, 1966
The Old Canal

There's a little silver ribbon runs across
the Buckeye State,
'Tis the dearest place of all this earth to
me,
For upon its placid surface I was born
some years ago,
and its beauty, grandeur, always do I see.
Cleveland is the northern end and
Portsmouth is the south,
while its side cuts they are many, many,
Pal.
And where e'er we went we took along our
Home, Sweet, Home,
you know, in those balmy days upon the
old canal.
There's naught in all creation that to this
can compare.
Good times, rounds of pleasure were our
lot dear Pal.
No other people e'er were known to have
such times as we,
in those balmy days upon the old canal.

Songs Along the Canal

It's too bad this column can't come to you with sound track attached because it concerns the "sound of music" on the canal. As a matter of fact, I came directly to the typewriter keys from the piano keyboard — before I wrote the first word. I had been playing the melody lines of a little canal mood music from an interesting pamphlet titled *Scenes and Songs of the Ohio-Erie Canal.*

Published by the Ohio State Archaeological and Historical Society, the booklet contains photographs and songs collected and recorded by Capt. Pearl R. Nye, who lived all his life on or near the Ohio & Erie Canal. The songs were transcribed and edited by Cloea Thomas of the school of music of Ohio State University.

100

We're just lit-tle sweet-hearts, our home is the can-al, We
fro-lic a - long in a life full of smiles, No po-ten-tate

Before we leaf through the booklet, let me tell you how it came into my possession.

Mrs. B.W. Sebring came upon it while she was searching for some old schoolbooks in the basement of her Canton home and thought I would like to have it. She had purchased the booklet at a national music convention in Columbus principally because she read in the preface that along the banks of the canal "once were heard the lyric songs of the Irish laborers still mindful of the old homeland but mindful for the new one as they helped dig the canal."

Mrs. Sebring's great-grandfather, William Dunlap, and his wife, who was Lady Eleanor Rennison, came to Ohio from Ireland in 1825-26 when the canal was being dug. Actually, they eloped. William was a gardener and stonemason employed on the estate of his future wife's parents. He heard about the work on the canal in the "Ohio country" and so they came to America and settled at Frazeysburg between Newark and Coshocton. William Dunlap worked on that section of the Ohio & Erie Canal and became one of the thousands of Irishmen to carve the big ditch out of the rich soil of the Buckeye State.

Mrs. Sebring's husband, Ben, well-known retired Canton abstracter, also has personal memories of the canal days. Now 88, he was a lad of 11 when he and his buddy decided, on the spur of the moment, to ride a canal boat from their home in Columbus toward Canal Winchester. It cost five cents each. And as that was all the money they had, they had to walk the four

miles home along the towpath. Ben recalls they arrived home about 10 p.m. and that although he was given his supper, he also got the "silent treatment" from the members of his family who were concerned and angry about his escapade.

Back to the canal song booklet. In its preface, the editor wrote:

"The canallers served a real function in our musical growth by keeping alive favorite ballads as well as disseminating the newly developing American music of the camp meetings, minstrel shows, and showboats. They also helped to keep song-making alive by composing their own songs, related to the work and life on the canal. In the following pages an attempt has been made to give the reader a glimpse into the culture of this bygone day and into the personal philosophy of one canaller, Captain Pearl R. Nye, who loved his way of life so deeply that he painstakingly collected and preserved both the songs and scenes from the era in which he played so vital a part."

There are many stories of the brawls canal crews engaged in while trying to be first through the locks. One song, *Get That Boat,* tells about it in all too plain lyrics.

Capt. Nye said that often there would be a solid string of boats for two miles approaching a canal station. Crews, eager to get their loads weighed so they could continue on their run would attempt to pass other boats even if they had to tip them over to do so. With long poles, they would ram and fight to get ahead. *Get That Boat* depicted such a scene and was sung in a "rough, boisterous style."

Another ballad, *Last Trip in the Fall,* describes the approach of winter and some of the rigors of life on the canal. But it concludes with an ecstatic tribute to the canal:

"But who in God's creation
Can enumerate this life?
'Tis so unique and lovely
Where the heart is free from strife
I'm a died in wool a Canaller;
I don't care what be the sky,
I'll stay upon the Great Big Ditch
Until the day I die!"

And then there is *The Clever Skipper,* which has its setting in Akron but tells a tale of a philandering tailor and a faithless wife. Told in humorous verse, *The Clever Skipper,* according to Capt. Nye, was much in demand at gatherings of the canallers.

There are other songs: About the gospel boat, a canal dance and a song sung in dialogue between Mollie and Johnnie.

But certainly one of the most impressive is titled simply *The Old Canal.* Captain Nye considered this song his masterpiece. It contains 80 stanzas, which describe the canal from the northern end to the southern. There is some comment in the lines about virtually every town, lock, store, mill or mine along the way.

Captain Nye, reputed to be a fine folk singer, sang for several meetings of the American Folk Song Society in Washington and Philadelphia. And many of his songs were recorded for the Congressional Library collection of American folk songs.

Seems like there might be an opportunity for one of our modern young folk singers to "make it big" by becoming a specialist in songs and ballads of the old canal. All he needs is a good voice, a little musical talent and a "gimmick." The many legends of the Big Ditch surely could provide the gimmick.

June 12, 1966

Canal at the College Level

The project to preserve, restore and develop the remaining sections of the Ohio & Erie Canal has been described as beneficial historically, educationally and recreationally. Its recreational benefits are obvious and have been discussed in this column many times. Its historical value also has been well delineated. But the project's value in the field of education has not been spelled out as clearly — especially as it applies to formal education.

But as of this past week the educational values of the canal are being recognized on the college level. Malone College is conducting what is believed to be one of the first travel courses in Ohio history offered by an Ohio college. Professors Joseph L. Grabill and Fred G. Thomas explain the purpose of the course is to study Ohio history in relation to American history and to learn how to use sites, museums and libraries in the studies.

In addition to hearing an illustrated lecture by Ted Findley of New Philadelphia, president of the Canal Society of Ohio, and visiting Lock 4 Park, members are assigned reading, which includes a research paper, "The Ohio & Erie Canal in Stark County," by Robert Witmer, a former Malone student and now a teacher at Central Christian High School in Kidron. The course involves travel throughout the second week. The class will visit Stark and Tuscarawas counties, then range as far as Cleveland, Sandusky, Marion, Columbus, Chillicothe, Cincinnati and Marietta.

It would seem that field-trip history taught at the site must make the subject come alive. What visual aid could be better than Stark County's Lock 4 gates to "carry the student back" to the canal era? And how could he get the feel of the old days along the canal better than by laying hold of the huge timbers of the lock gate?

Towpath Hike-o-Ree

Most of us, from time to time, have read about the Boy Scout camporees. But how many have heard of hike-o-ree — especially a towpath hike-o-ree? The Buckeye Council's Nimishillen District is holding one this weekend and more than 100 Scouts and leaders are participating. The schedule called for the Scouts to assemble at Crystal Springs, then hike toward Canal Fulton, carrying their gear, a trail lunch and fresh water. Nature study and canal history were to be emphasized. They were to camp Saturday night at Lock 4 Park.

A recreational feature was to be a canal fishing derby, with prizes for the largest fish, the most fish, the smallest fish, and the most different varieties. A campfire program was to feature Indian dancing by members of the Order of the Arrow. Also, Paul Marks, foreman of reconstruction work, was to speak about the canal and the operation of Lock 4. Religious services were to wind up the hike-o-ree. But sometime in the future the Scouts plan to do a good turn for the towpath project, details of which are being worked out.

New Life for C&O

The Chesapeake and Ohio Canal was the subject of a June news bulletin issued by the National Geographic Society. The 185-mile waterway, which has been called "a magnificent ruin," may get a face-lifting. The National Park Service has been asked to restore some of the sections by hikers, canoeists, naturalists and fishermen.

Today, sediment fills large parts of the canal bed and sections of walls and embankments have crumbled. But in 1871 the Chesapeake and Ohio was a successful operation and more than 500 canal boats floated 850,000 tons of coal from the West Virginia mines to the tidewater area.

An old-timer, reminiscing about the vanished era in a *National Geographic* magazine article, said, "I'd lie abed at night and watch the barges inch their way up and down. The lights from their bow lamps shone on the water and flashed on the trees. I could hear the music of fiddles, and people singing and laughing in the cabins."

It must have been like that here in Stark County back in the 1870s as the canal boats worked their way from one end to the other on the Ohio & Erie. But reconstruction of "our" canal will be much more difficult to achieve than the restoration of the Chesapeake and Ohio. The latter waterway is a national monument and, as such, is eligible for federal funds. "Our" canal, on the other hand, has no funds available

at the present time. The only hope seems to be through the creation of a metropolitan park system, which would include the canal lands and make it possible to obtain federal monies on a matching basis.

The Chesapeake and Ohio has great potential as a national monument. But it would be a mistake to underestimate the potential of our Ohio & Erie Canal for development under a metropolitan park system.

June 19, 1966
Hearing About Hocking

When a pebble is dropped into a pool, the ripples reach out in ever widening circles. So it is with a good idea. Perhaps this explains, in part, why more and more reports of canal restoration and development throughout the state's canal counties are reaching us here in Stark County.

We sort of like to think that Stark County is in the forefront of the current effort to save and develop the surviving sections of canals — particularly those within its borders, the Ohio & Erie and the Sandy and Beaver.

Word has reached across the state in many ways of the program and plans we have here for developing the canals and their towpaths. And now from north and south of us come reports of efforts to do the same thing in other counties.

The latest report, sent to me by Richard A. Williams of Canton, was a Sunday magazine section from the *Columbus Dispatch*, which featured a colorful natural bridge on the Hocking Canal. The sandstone bridge, which gave the Hocking County town of Rockbridge its name, is by-passed today by motorists speeding along new Route 33. But the huge stone span once attracted sightseers from afar and was "the mecca for excursion boats."

The Hocking Canal extended from Carroll, 20 miles southeast of Columbus, to Athens. It came into being because citizens of Lancaster feared their town would fail if it were not connected with the Ohio

& Erie Canal. The "Lancaster Sidecut" was completed in 1836 and then the state legislature decided to extend the canal to Athens. It has been said that the first canal boat on the Hocking, in 1841, was greeted by crowds all along the towpath and by "many incredulous people who had never seen coal before."

Nothing is left of the 80-foot aqueduct, which crossed Monday Creek, and many of the stone canal locks have vanished without a trace, as they have in other canals. But remnants of the Hocking Canal still are in existence, such as the large stone-arch aqueduct at the east entrance of Logan. Smaller stone culverts that transported the canal across streams below Lancaster at Pleasant Run and north of Rockridge are still intact.

Twelve of the original 31 locks on the Hocking can be seen today. Sheepskin Lock, probably the best known, is preserved in a roadside park along Route 33 north of Nelsonville. Many of the locks throughout Ohio had descriptive picturesque names and Sheepskin Lock is no exception. It got its name because a farmer sheltered his sheep in it before it was completed.

The Hocking Canal, like the other canals of the state, had its special moments in history — like the time in 1863 when Confederate Gen. John Hunt Morgan made his mad dash across Ohio and burned a covered bridge and a dozen canal boats at Nelsonville. Lancaster's General William Tecumseh Sherman helped to survey the canal and Thomas Worthington, Ohio's first governor to endorse state-supported canals, built a pioneer grist mill, which was standing when the Hocking was built and still standing during its heyday and decline.

The Hocking has been described as the canal that was carved through the hills. I have not had the pleasure of hiking what remains of its towpath but I certainly would like to.

James Murphy, in his canal story in the *Columbus Dispatch*, describes the Hocking as passing through "territory of interest to the naturalist as well as the local historian." He writes that Clear Creek and Crystal Springs, northwest of Sugargrove, "harbor numerous plant rarities including rhododendron, trailing arbutus and native orchids. He reports along nearly all the canal route from Lancaster to Nelsonville "tall hemlocks and sycamores rise against a backdrop of rugged sandstone cliffs."

Just recently, according to Mr. Murphy, there has been renewed interest in the old waterway and the remains of the locks and other stone works. Largely through the efforts of the Institute for Regional Development at Athens, which represents Ohio's efforts in the federal Appalachia program, the canal route is being investigated for its park and recreational potential.

The Columbus writer winds up a surprising disclosure touching on this column's current special project — building a canal boat for Stark County's Ohio & Erie. He observes that almost none of the remaining canal relics are under government protection and that some people have suggested that a portion of the canal be restored, complete with a canal boat and a set of working locks. This is the third or fourth county from which I have heard talk of building a canal boat.

Although Stark County has no federal funds to draw on to build a boat, it has many other resources, which, if volunteered in sufficient amount, could make such a boat possible. Will we be the first?

June 26, 1966
Canal Boat Patterns Made

I thought I was doing something the other day that no other man in Ohio had done in this century. And I was almost right — but not quite. I was one of a group of men laying out and cutting the templates for a 60-foot canal boat. For me, it was the beginning of what I hoped would be the realization of a cherished idea — construction of a canal boat.

Smelling the fresh sawdust and listening to the whine and rasp of the saws, I could picture the reconstructed freighter, accurate in every detail, plying the waters of the canal with cargoes of happy passengers.

To check whether any canal boats had been built during this century, I called one of the foremost authorities on the canal era in the state, Ted Findley of New Philadelphia, president of the Canal Society of Ohio.

Known as State Repair Boat No. 9, it was built at Akron and launched in 1907. Six years later, during the canal-destroying flood of 1913, the boat was pushed into the big triple lock on the Walhonding Canal at Coshocton, where it ultimately rotted away.

Today, not far from Lock 4 south of Canal Fulton and just a stone's throw from the canal, a new canal boat may rise, almost like a phoenix, to float again on the tranquil surface of the old waterway. If it does, it will be the direct result of the efforts of many people. If it does not, at least the wooden patterns and blueprints of such a boat out of the past will be preserved for some future generation whose members may have greater zeal for such a project.

It was to preserve these patterns in solid form that the men were at work in Peter Neidert's farm equipment service building in Canal Fulton. Neidert also provided power tools for work on the canal boat and donated the service of a large truck to haul oak timbers. Paul R. Baird, president of Notnac Mfg. Co. of Canton, did much of the preliminary work making possible the day's activity.

But it was a third man, obviously the "boss" of the group, who was the key figure in the pattern making and without whom the project probably would grind to a halt. Arthur P. Sweany of New Philadelphia, who will be 86 years old on his next birthday, is the man with the know-how to build the boat and the energy to supervise it. Assisted by Mr. Baird, he did practically all the work in making the templates, displaying a knowledge of the job and a confidence in himself that made the rest of us marvel.

Mr. Sweany, who worked as a flour millwright and in timber construction, was a carpenter 62 years before retiring 10 years ago. A native of New Philadelphia, he remembers the canal-boat days. He has constructed two scale model canal boats

and, to make blueprints for an authentic canal boat, he went to the locks and measured their width. Then he obtained as much information as he could from books and manuals and drew on his rich experience for the rest. He made the blueprints available to the Stark County Canal Lands Development Advisory Committee to build the boat with his supervision.

The lumber from which the patterns were cut was purchased from funds donated for the construction, primarily by individuals and various women's and garden clubs. Some live white oak trees also have been donated to make the hull timbers but more are needed. Only green wood can be used for the part of the boat that will be "in water."

Volunteer manpower will also be needed, primarily carpenters or those handy with tools.

And, of course, money will be required where donations of materials are not forthcoming. A canal-boat fund has been established at the Harter Bank & Trust Co. and contributions may be made there in person or sent to the bank.

Last week U.S. Secretary of the Interior Stewart L. Udall inspected the Cuyahoga River valley and the Ohio & Erie Canal in Cuyahoga and Summit counties with an eye toward creation of a national park. Before leaving the canal village of Peninsula at the end of his tour, the secretary left this bit of encouragement for the assembled park boosters:

"You have a beautiful valley, a watershed, which can provide a lot of water, and a river, which should be cleaned up. You also have history. When you combine all these things, you could indeed make an oasis. I wish you well."

Paraphrasing the secretary, it could be said that we, too, have a beautiful valley (the Tuscarawas), a watershed, which can provide a lot of water (for the canal) and a river, which should be cleaned up (the Tuscarawas). We also have history. And if we combine all these things, we, too, could make an oasis. If Secretary Udall knew that we were planning to float a real honest to goodness canal boat up and down the core of such an oasis, I'm sure he would say to us also: "I wish you well."

105

T-I-*M-B-E-R-r-r-r-r-r-r*

If Stark County once again is to have a canal boat sail up and down its Ohio & Erie Canal, a number of things must happen. Some of them have. The most recent development was the cutting Saturday of two white oak trees from which will come the first "green" wood for the boat's hull — provided several other problems can be surmounted.

The trees, which leaned out over Mudbrook St. NW from a wooded tract on Bruce A. Crissinger Jr.'s farm near Jackson High School, were donated by Mr. Crissinger and cut, without charge, by Kenneth D. Ferguson of Canton. Asked why he contributed the oaks for the canal boat Mr. Crissinger replied, "I'm interested in seeing it built. I'm interested in local history."

Towpath Garden Club

Among the organizations most in tune with the canal restoration and park development project are the women's garden clubs. Several have contributed money to the canal-boat fund. Now one club has identified itself closely with the canal by adopting a name unmistakably canal-oriented. The Towpath Garden Club of the Dover-New Philadelphia area in Tuscarawas County was organized by Mrs. Judson Case, regional vice president of the Garden Club of Ohio. The club elected Mrs. William Stevens of Dover as its first president and then selected as an initial project the extension of Stark County's towpath bluebird trail into Tuscarawas County.

Congratulations and best wishes to the Towpath Garden Club from "Along the Towpath."

Canal Between the Lakes

All across America interest in parks is growing. And, in a surprising number of cases, canals, old or modern, are key features of the recreational planning. A case in point is the "Land Between the Lakes" in western Kentucky, one of the nation's newest recreation areas.

The lakes, which did not exist a generation ago, were formed when the Kentucky Dam impounded the waters of the Tennessee River and the Barkley Dam backed up the Cumberland River to form Lake Barkley. The lakes now fill entire valleys but high ground keeps them separated. However, a modern canal permits boats to pass from one lake to the other. This enables boat skippers to explore more than 3,200 miles of shoreline.

Just as plans call for the development of a strip park along the banks of the Ohio & Erie Canal in Stark County and perhaps other counties, so the Tennessee Valley Authority is developing the 40-mile-long Land Between the Lakes to demonstrate how an area with a declining economy can be restored to meet the recreational needs of an urban society.

The area's development will require several more years but many recreational facilities are already available, including camping and day-use areas. And, of course, the core of the recreational development is the canal.

Father-Son Hike

Speaking of recreational use of the canal and towpath, the Boy Scouts are finding them very useful in their advancement program. Just recently, Troop 129 of Zion EUB Church at 1023 Whipple Avenue NW enjoyed a father-son hike along the towpath from Crystal Springs to Lock 4 Park. It was the first time members of the troop had hiked with their fathers and apparently it was a great success.

The fathers had planned merely to drop the boys off at the lower end and then drive to the upper end and wait for the Scouts to arrive. But instead, the fathers hoofed it too. Arriving at the park, they built a campfire and had a wiener roast in the shadow of the old lock. They sang songs around the fire and the Scouts presented skits for their fathers.

Mrs. Harry Staley, whose husband is assistant scoutmaster of the troop, reported the Scouts saw a number of nests in the bluebird-trail houses along the towpath.

Fish Testing Report

The recent testing of the fish population in the Ohio & Erie Canal by District 3 of the Division of Wildlife of the State

Department of Natural Resources resulted in a "fair" catch. Nets were placed north and south of Lock 4 for four days. Division personnel said they netted catfish, crappies, bluegills, largemouth bass, a few black suckers, northern pike up to 23 inches and many big carp up to 26 inches.

July 10, 1966
Ohio & Erie Has Birthday

It was 139 years ago this past week — the Fourth of July to be exact — that the Ohio & Erie Canal was born.

In the lusty days that followed, the young state of Ohio stepped out of its swaddling clothes and grew fast. That period of economic growth, stimulated by the new artery of water commerce has since been referred to by historians as the "canal days" or the "canal era."

Throughout the heyday of that period the village of Canal Fulton was a bustling canal town of the first water.

Today, once again there is bustling in the village as its citizens and organizations get ready for the community's first annual Old Canal Days Exposition. Residents will commemorate the "old days" when they stage the festive exposition. There will be a parade next Sunday, a two-day fishing derby with lots of prizes (at the canal of course), a casting exhibition (also at the canal), and games, amusement rides, refreshment stands and concessions on Main Street.

And, naturally, there will be photographs and other memorabilia of the old canal days on exhibit.

The village plans to open its picnic grounds and swimming pool to the public without charge during the event.

Mayor John Cullen, expressing the hope that the exposition will be well attended, stressed that the canal and its history do not belong alone to Canal Fulton but to all the residents of Stark County, wherever they live.

Meanwhile, a few miles to the north, in Summit County, the next town along the canal will wind up a three-day sesquicentennial celebration today. Clinton, named after De Witt Clinton, the governor of New York who was known as the father of the Erie Canal in that state, once was a thriving center for shipping grain on the canal.

A pageant showing the history of Clinton will be presented this afternoon in the Northwest High School stadium. Participating in the pageant will be the high school band, community band, children's chorus, adult choir, dancing groups, vocal soloists, the Stark County sheriff's posse and many individuals from the Clinton area. More than 1,000 pictures, including many of the Ohio & Erie Canal, will be displayed in the Clinton Elementary School building.

What with the Clinton Sesquicentennial and the Canal Fulton Old Days Exposition, the birth of the Ohio and Erie 139 years ago this month certainly is being observed in grand style.

Too bad there isn't a canal boat between the two towns to transport celebrators from one village to the other. That would do it up right.

Father of the Canals

A recent news story told of the efforts of the German Village Society of Columbus to have the city rebuild the Alfred Kelley mansion in Schiller Park and designate it the City of Columbus Museum.

Why should this item be of interest to readers of this column? For a very good reason. Alfred Kelley has been described as Ohio's "Father of the Canals."

Born in Connecticut in 1789, he moved to Cleveland in 1810, was admitted to the bar and appointed prosecuting attorney on his 21st birthday. In 1814, he was elected to the Ohio House of Representatives, which then was meeting in Chillicothe. In and out of the Legislature, he was the master spirit of Ohio's canal policy, urging it is as a necessary means of developing the resources of the state.

When the system was decided upon, Kelley, having been the prime mover and having framed the statutes that authorized the canals, was made a canal commissioner. He accepted the trust, abandoned his profession and sacrificed his health by exposure to the wet and malaria. Then, in the financial crash of 1837-41, he pledged his individual notes to an amount twice what he was worth in order to save Ohio from repudiating its debts as other states were doing.

In order to see that everything was done honestly, he personally inspected the work, living at one time in a cabin along the line of the canal with his family. He often carried a long iron rod with which he would probe the embankments to discover the tricks of contractors who were apt to fell huge trees, cover them with earth, and then draw pay for dirt fill.

The Ohio & Erie Canal was Alfred Kelley's life work. And although it was a public work, he gave so much to its origin and construction and was so economical in management that when the canal, which connected the Ohio River with Lake Erie, was completed, the cost did not exceed the estimate.

After retiring from public life, he gradually declined in strength. Broken in health by his arduous labors for Ohio, he died Dec. 2, 1859. It has been said of him that he "lived a life of as great if not greater usefulness to the people of Ohio than that of any other one man the state has known."

His Greek-style mansion was dismantled on the site of the Christopher Inn in Columbus in 1959 and the bricks and pillars stored in an East Side park. Today there are groups at work to have the marked bricks rebuilt as a museum.

And today also, in Stark County and in other counties other groups are at work to restore the Ohio & Erie Canal for recreational, educational and historical purposes. In so doing, they also would be creating a living monument to Alfred Kelley, the man who was known as the "Father of the Canals."

Hear Ye!

Prospects for the construction of a canal boat to become the property of Stark County grew brighter this week as the result of two announcements. First, the Stark County commissioners said they would accept such a boat if and when constructed. Then Mayor John Cullen of Canal

Fulton announced that the village council is wholeheartedly in favor of the canalboat project and has offered the use of the village park as a construction site, including special surveillance of the area by village police.

July 17, 1966
Easels Along the Canal

The snow was flying last December when a part of this column was devoted to an idea suggested by Dr. John M. Van Dyke. The doctor suggested that he would like to see the many amateur and professional artists in Stark County painting canal scenes. He thought it would be nice if some organizations would sponsor a contest for the best paintings of such scenes.

"I should like to see easels set up (along the Ohio & Erie Canal) throughout the summer season," the doctor wrote.

Well, Dr. Van Dyke ought to be pleased with the picture accompanying today's column. Although no contest has been set up, at least the artists are finding the canal — and like hummingbirds finding the fragrant honeysuckle and the scented bergamot, once the discovery has been made, others are attracted.

For example, Mrs. James Stiles of Massillon "discovered" the beauty of Lock 4 Park recently and decided to paint it in company with her sister, Mrs. Richard Durius of Massillon and her daughter, Mrs. Thomas Price of Canal Fulton. Mrs. Stiles gives private painting instructions, and when members of her class saw the canal paintings, they decided they, too, wanted to paint canal scenes. So the entire class may pick a sunny summer day and go canal painting.

And perhaps other artists may be inspired to "do" some canal painting if they see the two canal-lock scenes painted by Mrs. Stiles and her sister.

Clyde Gainey of Canal Fulton, a member of the Stark County Canal Lands Advisory Committee, is exhibiting the paintings, along with old photographs and other memorabilia of the canal era, at the Old Canal Days Exposition, which ends today in Canal Fulton.

Mrs. Stiles, commenting on her day at the canal, said, "It's so beautiful out there. People think they have to travel far and wide to get beauty and yet it's right here in our own county."

Seniors Want Boat

A good speaker frequently delights his audience. Not so frequently, but occasionally, an audience delights a speaker. That's the way it was Wednesday afternoon at the Amherst Park Civic Center when Mrs. Ralph (Mary) Regula spoke to 300 senior citizens about the romance of the Ohio & Erie Canal.

"They were wonderful," Mary enthused. "Many of them had lived along the canal. They watched the canal boats as children and some remembered riding them. So many of them want us to hurry up and build the canal boat. They are enthusiastic about it and they keep track of everything about it in the newspapers. And they are so glad that it is going to be authentic."

Mrs. Regula said many of the senior citizens spoke with her after her talk and that their message to her, in regard to the canal boat, seemed to be: "Hurry, because we don't have so many years left and we want to be able to ride a canal boat again."

For the next three or four Sundays, this column will not appear in the *Repository* as I will be "on vacation." "Along the Towpath" will return in August. In the meantime, good "towpathing."

August 21, 1966

Denver Has Canal Street, too

If I needed to be reminded about the cause of the canal era's decline and fall (the railroad), our vacation trip this year was made to order as a reminder. We spent seven days hiking and climbing in the Colorado wilderness and had a wonderful time.

We rode a train to and from Colorado, traveling some 1,500 miles in 24 hours. At four miles an hour, it would have taken us nearly 16 days to get to Colorado by canal boat — if we traveled 24 hours every day.

Getting off the speedy Denver Zephyr and walking into the big terminal in Colorado's capital, we seemed a long way from a canal of any sort. Imagine our surprise then to look for street exit signs in the terminal and see, in foot-high letters cut in stone, the words "Canal Street." I do not know the story behind the naming of the street but there it was — not "Wilderness Street," which really wouldn't have surprised us, but "Canal Street" — like in Navarre or Canal Fulton.

Although this column has been shut down for a month there has been action of one kind or another involving the canal and towpath.

The towpath continues to provide enjoyment for hikers. The last group I heard of to hike from Crystal Springs to Lock 4 Park was from the "G" Teen Center, which is sponsored by the First Methodist Church of Massillon. Led by Mrs. Arthur Christenson, the teenagers asked many questions about the canal and its history. They also observed that there were many nests in the bluebird houses, which had been placed along the towpath early in the spring. Now they are talking of a bicycle "hike" on the towpath.

More Trees for Boat

The canal-boat project, while moving very slowly, still is moving. Paul Baird, who has been working hard on the project, has 10 more oak trees lined up from which hull timbers can be cut. But still more oak trees are needed, especially white oak. Anyone wishing to help the project along by donating one or more white oaks for the hull should contact Paul.

More and more people are hearing the story of the canal — its history and its potential for the future — principally through talks by State Rep. Ralph Regula and his wife, Mary, and Ted Findley of New Philadelphia, president of the Canal Society of Ohio.

I received three more checks this week that were endorsed to the canal-boat fund by the Regulas. All were from garden clubs that had heard Ralph or Mary speak.

And Ted Findley, in his July letter to the canal society's membership, told of the canal-boat project and capped his comments with an appeal to the members to send any spare dollars to me or to him for the furtherance of the project.

Incidentally, the canal society and the University of Akron's student radio station are planning a series of 15 radio programs on the history and future of the Ohio & Erie Canal.

In examining the history of the canal system in Ohio, the series will feature a discussion conducted by members of the canal society. Discussion on each program will be supplemented by interviews with people who lived and worked on the canals.

David Lieberth, a sophomore at the university, is producing the series for WAUP and Mr. Findley is coordinating the production with members of the canal society. The station will broadcast the series of programs this fall and then offer them to other Ohio radio stations and boards of education.

The university feels the programs are particularly appropriate now that the U.S. Department of Interior has shown an interest in helping to make one or more sections of the canal into a strip park.

Park News Is Big

With future massive recreational use of the canal lands hinging directly on the success or failure of the metropolitan park concept in Stark County, probably the biggest news last week was the approval of the park proposal by Canton and Alliance. Massillon, Louisville and North Canton, the county's other three cities, already had approved the proposal to create the park district. Nine of the 17 townships and nine of the 14 villages in the county have also endorsed the metropolitan park proposal as of this date.

Metropolitan Parks Grow

While members of Stark County's Metropolitan Park and Recreation Committee are working to obtain widespread endorsement of the metropolitan park district proposal, nearby counties continue to increase their metropolitan parks through land purchase supported by federal matching funds.

For example, a $120,840 federal grant from the Department of Housing and Urban Development soon will be sent to Akron to cover half the cost of purchasing land for a new metropolitan park in that area. The 391-acre site is in both Summit and Medina counties with its southern border coinciding with the northern border of Wayne County. To be known as Silver Creek Metropolitan Park, it will be the ninth metropolitan park in Summit County. The local share of the cost of acquiring the land will be paid from the park district revenue accumulated under a 25-mill levy. Park commissioners said the two-county site was selected because it is in the center of a fast-growing area and convenient to several communities.

Meanwhile, Stark County's metropolitan park committee met last week and learned that its efforts have resulted in 70 percent of the county's political subdivisions approving formal resolutions favoring establishment of a metropolitan park district. The committee also is seeking similar resolutions of approval from groups such as garden clubs, service clubs, sportsmen's groups and other civic organizations.

If and when such a park is established in Stark County, it is expected that the Ohio & Erie and Sandy and Beaver canal lands would be an important part of the park district.

Surprise Visit

Clyde Gainey of Canal Fulton, a member of the Stark County Canal Lands Development Advisory Committee, was surprised to receive a visit recently from John

W. Walker of the National Parks Service in Washington. Clyde and Gale Hartel of the Canal Fulton Rotary Club talked with Mr. Walker for some time about the prospects of including Stark County in the proposed canal parkway through Cuyahoga and Summit counties.

The National Parks Service representative was surveying the canal lands as a result of Secretary of the Interior Stewart Udall's recent visit to the two counties.

In his effort to "sell" Mr. Walker on the idea that Stark County should be a part of the strip park, Clyde gave him his huge color map (9 feet by 3 feet), which shows the location of all the canal locks from Cleveland to Coshocton as well as an elevation profile of the entire route.

The government official, during his visit to the Clyde Gainey Museum, expressed surprise that so many pictures and other memorabilia of the canal days had been collected.

Steamers on the Canal

In case you missed it in this newspaper's "Up Through a Century" column, I am repeating a news item from 100 years ago. *The Repository* reported, just a century ago, that "two steam-propelled boats, the Superior and Ontario, of the Kingman line of Buffalo passed through Massillon on the Canal. They were en route to Red River, Tex. They were the first craft of that kind to pass through Massillon and attracted considerable attention."

Landmark Razed

Speaking of a century ago, an old landmark at Canal Fulton recently was razed so a residential garage could be constructed on the site. The old frame structure on S. Canal St. was used to store ice cut from the canal about 100 years ago. It was located on the property formerly owned by the late Charles A. McLaughlin, a Canal Fulton boat builder and repairman.

Canal Figures in Bet

Not quite so long ago — about 77 years — a rather unusual bet was made involving the canal. It was a political bet. According to "Echoes," a publication of the Ohio His-

torical Society, "Dr. J. C. Pence and S. F. Richardson have made a rather 'strong' bet on the election. If Harrison is elected, Richardson is to drink a glass of water out of the canal or forfeit $5, and if Cleveland is elected Doc is to undergo the same ordeal. Doc says if he wins, it will be cheaper for Richardson to pay the $5; for one glass of canal water means 10 weeks of typhoid fever and that means $100..." The punch line to the anecdote, as reported by "Echoes," came in the next paragraph:

"On Monday, March 4th on the Fourth Street bridge, S.F. Richardson will drink a glassful..."

Sandy-Beaver News

Moving into this century, to last week in fact, we find the news about canals is of a different sort.

Down in the Magnolia-Waynesburg area, action has been taken to incorporate the Sandy Beaver Canal Society. The incorporators are Paul Muckley and James France of Waynesburg and Glenn Fishel of Magnolia. The incorporating trustees are W. S. Janson, Augustus Elson and Joseph Tovissi, all of Magnolia. Officers will be elected in September. Oh yes, the society proposes to restore and develop the Sandy and Beaver Canal in the Waynesburg-Magnolia area for recreational, historical and educational purposes in much the same way that the Ohio & Erie Canal is being restored.

September 4, 1966
Mail Brings Inspiration

The mail continues to provide inspiration to those dedicated to the preservation and development of the Ohio & Erie Canal and its towpath as an integral part of a hoped-for metropolitan park system. This mail, almost without exception, endorses the project and creates hope of a vast reservoir of support for the canal restoration program.

Speaking of "hope," I received three postal cards of canal scenes last week that are probably the most colorful I have seen. The scenes of the Delaware Canal and its towpath near New Hope, Pa., show a beautifully manicured grass-covered towpath; weed-free water reflecting autumn foliage and picturesque bridges raised enough to allow the passage of a canal barge being towed by two white mules.

Miss Alice B. Embly, who sent me the cards, saw the canal during a trip she and her mother, Mrs. Anna Embly, made to the East. She wrote that the canal "is very beautiful, especially in Bucks County."

The pictures serve to point out the potential along our Ohio & Erie Canal for such development. If they can do it in Bucks County, why can't it be done in Stark County? Someday then, visitors to this section of Ohio might be able to write of the Ohio & Erie as Miss Embly wrote of the Delaware: "The canal is very beautiful, especially in Stark County."

Canal Era Recognized

Milan, the Erie County birthplace of Thomas A. Edison, recognized an era in its history last week by dedicating an Ohio historical marker. The village became a leading Great Lakes port after completion of the 3-mile Milan Canal in 1839.

Foot Travelers

The short labor supply, combined with lack of funds, has made it very difficult for the county to do much this summer in the way of maintaining, let alone improving, the towpath along the Ohio & Erie Canal.

But in spite of this, individuals and groups continue to derive enjoyment from hiking the towpath and canoeing the open-water sections of the canal. The area from Crystal Springs north to Canal Fulton seems to be the most popular and is in the best condition for hiking. Groups often stop at Lock 4 Park for sack lunches or other refreshments.

That's the way 12 members of Girl Scout Troop 636 of Trinity United Church of Christ in Avondale did it. The girls, accompanied by two mothers, enjoyed their adventure up the towpath. According to their leader, Mrs. Roger D. Yohe, the girls saw snakes, bugs, frogs and "all sorts

of things" in their natural environment. "It was so peaceful along the way." Mrs. Yohe observed.

September 11, 1966
Canal Boats in Millersburg?

According to a map of Ohio showing existing, abandoned and proposed canal routes, none of these was a part of the life or history of Holmes County. But, according to the October 14, 1925, edition of the *Holmes County Hub*, weekly newspaper published in Millersburg, canal boats figured in the life and history of the county.

Maurice Amos of Beach City, who heard about the plans to build a canal boat in Stark County, brought a copy of that 1925 Holmes County newspaper to the *Repository*. The article Mr. Amos found interesting was headlined "Canal Boats Once Ran to Millersburg" and "Big Dredge Turns One of the Craft Over on Killbuck River Bank" and read as follows:

"The digging up of an old canal boat from the bottom of Killbuck River near Killbuck recently has brought back to the minds of some of the older residents the fact that Killbuck River was once used as a canal and boats plied between Millersburg, Killbuck, Coshocton and Zanesville.

"Hughes Croskey, 84-year-old Killbuck citizen, says that he remembers a little of the days when Killbuck River was used as a canal and that he had often heard his father talk about it.

" 'It was about 115 years ago that canal boats first ran between Zanesville, through Coshocton, and through this part of Holmes County,' he (Hughes Croskey) said.

"On the Killbuck River at the Duncan mill at Killbuck, there still remains a part of one of the old locks. Near the steel bridge south of Millersburg, just south of what was known as the old Sharp mills, another lock was located."

The article concluded by stating the old canal boat dug up by the dredge was left on the bank of the Killbuck River about

100 rods north of the Duncan mill at Kill-buck in 1925.

Real Encouragement

Shortly after it was suggested in this column that a canal boat be built for use on the Ohio & Erie Canal near Canal Fulton, I received a check in the mail. The accompanying note indicated the money was to go toward a board or two for the canal boat. This unsolicited check from Mr. and Mrs. Jay C. Foltz established a fund that has reached $223. Now comes another check from the Foltzes, with another note of encouragement: "Here is another small piece of wood for the canal boat... and we hope to send more help in the near future."

Meanwhile, behind the scenes, work goes on to make the boat a reality.

To Tear Out Lock

Down in Tuscarawas County the State Highway Department is about to tear out another historical lock of the Ohio & Erie Canal. Known as Tucker's Lock, just east of the village, it is scheduled to be eliminated to make way for the new Route 36-250 bypass. Built in 1827, the lock has stood near the present road, serving as a reminder of the canal era to passing motorists. It seems a shame the new road couldn't have curved slightly to miss the lock, thus preserving it as a historical roadside attraction for travelers in the years to come. Surely such a monument to the canal era and its people would do more than a couple hundred feet of new highway for what has been described as the "Wonderful World of Ohio."

Canal Yields Fish

There's fish in that old canal. If you don't believe it, just ask Robert W. Motz of Massillon. One of Bob's friends recently went to Canada to get in some good fishing. Bob, meanwhile, went out to the canal, where he has been fishing for about five years. His friend "didn't get a thing" according to Bob who pulled a 25-inch northern pike from the canal after a 20-minute battle. "I had to wear him down because of the weeds," Bob explained.

The pike was the largest fish Bob has caught in the canal and, according to Mayor John Cullen of Canal Fulton, an avid fisherman, it is the largest pike he has heard of being caught there since the canal was restocked by the division of wildlife of the Ohio Department of Natural Resources.

Bob's son, 9-year-old Denny, also did well fishing the canal. He landed a 3-pound bass last Monday, just north of Canal Fulton.

"I got more of a thrill out of Denny than I did in catching the pike," Bob laughed. "The nice thing about the canal is it's close and it's in Stark County. There aren't many places you can go after work and fish where there are a lot of fish. When my friend who went to Canada heard that I caught a pike that big in the canal, he didn't want to believe me. He about flipped when I told him."

Discovering Rogues' Hollow

"Rogues' Hollow was the toughest (censored) spot in the whole United States."

That's the way it has been described by those who knew it when people all over northern Ohio were talking about it.

According to Russell W. Frey of Rittman, former publisher of the Rittman Press and author of the historical book, *Rogues' Hollow,* the hollow's reputation was downright disagreeable — so bad that people avoided going near it.

Mr. Frey writes, "It is commonly believed that Rogues' Hollow was given its name because of the rascals and unprincipled persons living in that area about 100 years ago."

But what does Rogues' Hollow have to do with the Ohio & Erie Canal? The connection was a direct one, although not by water. It was a narrow-gauge tram road that linked the hollow with Clinton on the canal. The tram road, which was five miles long, made it possible for mule-drawn cars to transport hundreds of tons of coal from the mines in the hollow to the waiting canal boats every day.

In his book, Mr. Frey lists 51 mines in the hollow but he told me the other day that further research has shown there were more than 100.

"The availability of the canal and cheap transportation led to the opening of the coal mines," Mr. Frey wrote, explaining that the mines, in turn, attracted all types of characters and rogues "who made the hollow into a tangled jungle of hard, crusty life."

There were seven saloons and they played their part in gang fights and brawls that were a way of life in the hollow, especially on Saturday nights and holidays.

Author Frey writes that "the 'law' back in those days, which was the county sheriff, avoided the hollow for long periods of time, being content to stop at the top of a hill leading to the hollow, look down and decide that life would be safer if the doings in the hollow were not interfered with."

Of the gang fights, Mr. Frey writes, "The lads from England, or from Wales, or Ireland, or from Germany would stick together. They would joke back and forth, maybe kidding one another until the kidding got a bit more embarrassing than the others could take. Then they would settle the argument with fists. Maybe the whole gang would join in and there would be a lot of bruised knuckles, bloody noses, black eyes, smashed furniture and even broken windows. There were farm boys from all around who visited the hollow to test their fists against the braggarts. There were some real bruisers who came in swaggering from the canal boats on the Ohio Canal, especially when they tied up at Clinton several miles away or at Canal Fulton, a short distance further."

Mr. Frey told me, during our telephone conversation, that the old Blue Goose Saloon between Clinton and Canal Fulton was the scene of many battles between the miners and the canal-boat crews, because many of the miners went there to "wet their whistles."

"Let me tell you, this was a fabulous era," Mr. Frey said with conviction.

Where is Rogues' Hollow?

Having read this far, you are entitled to know. The hollow is tucked away in the hills about a mile south of Doylestown in Wayne County. The northern edge is about a mile from the south edge of Doylestown. If you walk from the square in Doylestown to the center of the hollow, it's about 2½ miles. Take Clinton St. south cut of Doylestown Square and it will take you into the hollow. It's County Road 100.

The hollow today is a pretty place according to Mr. Frey, just as it must have been when the Indians called it Nibrara or Beautiful Valley.

The author, who has added new maps to the second printing of his book, expects to spend more time in the months ahead compiling new information, which will result in a larger volume about Rogues' Hollow. He also is thinking in terms of a museum in the hollow, which would display records and artifacts of the days when Rogues' Hollow was infamous — in the roaring 1860s and '70s.

The first printing of the book includes one chapter on the importance of the Ohio & Erie Canal in spurring the development of the coal industry in the hollow. And primarily because of this chapter, the book was brought to my attention by Dr. and Mrs. Bruce D. Harrold of Lake Cable. Dr. Harrold and his daughter, Sharon, were riding their motorbikes when they "just stumbled" onto the hollow. They found it such an interesting place the family has returned a number of times.

The hollow today is a peaceful place. But in its heyday it was a rip-roaring rendezvous for rampaging rogues with alcohol in their veins, fire in their eyes and fury in their fists.

September 25, 1966

More About Rogues' Hollow

Last week's column about Rogues' Hollow was difficult to write — not because of a dearth of material but because of too much. The problem was to tell the story of this fascinating hollow (about which a 100-page book has been written) in the length of this column. Because I couldn't do it justice in so few paragraphs, Rogues' Hollow is the subject again today.

But since writing last week's column, I have visited the hollow, talked with some of it residents and searched through the woods for the bed of the old tramway, which ran from the hollow to Clinton on the Ohio & Erie Canal.

Using a map printed in Russell W. Frey's book, my eldest son, Heath, and I tramped the area where the map indicated the tramway had been located. We are fairly certain that we were able to distinguish the flat bed of the tramway in some places, though farmers and others had dug up the wooden ties for firewood many decades ago.

A reader who was interested in the story of Rogues' Hollow — because he had lived near Doylestown and trapped muskrats in Silver Creek, which runs through the hollow — is Milo Gillespie, a *Repository* printer. As young boys, he and his playmates were scared of the hollow.

"We stayed out of there," Milo declared, explaining that all the boys were warned that it was "an undesirable area to be in."

Milo tells of the flourishing bootleg business, which was at its height from 1900 to 1910. In the hollow's wildest days, whiskey figuratively flowed from the hollow's seven saloons. But in the bootleg era, according to Milo, "whiskey was running out of those abandoned coal mines like water because the area was overrun with bootleggers that had stills in the mines."

A hazardous place to be when the coal miners and crews from the Ohio & Erie's canal boats got into fights before the turn of the century, the hollow, from 1900 to 1910, still "wasn't safe to be caught in after dark," Milo asserted. "You might be suspected of being a government agent." The whiskey was being shipped to Cleveland, he explained.

Milo's father, W. R. Gillespie, was editor and publisher of the *Doylestown Journal* for 11 years shortly after 1900. From issues of this paper, author Frey learned much about Rogues' Hollow.

Not only was Rogues' Hollow tied to the Ohio & Erie Canal economically by the tramway, which enabled the hollow's mine operators to ship their coal to other parts of the state via the canal, but the two also were linked in that some of the hollow's residents arrived there by way of the canal.

For example, Mr. Frey tells how the canal made it possible for David Lyon, grandfather of Miss Deborah Chidester, to move his family by boat from Salisbury, New York, to Clinton in 10 days back in 1849. The family took a canal boat on the Erie Canal to Buffalo, then changed to a lake boat to reach Cleveland and then transferred to another canal boat to come down the Ohio & Erie to Clinton. From there they went by carriage to the Doylestown area. Ultimately, Deborah married Samuel Chidester, founder of the Chidester Woolen Mill in Rogues' Hollow.

Mr. Frey devotes considerable space in his book to the Chidesters, a pioneer family in the hollow, and the legend of the ghost of Chidester's Mill — an apparition reportedly "seen by a number of persons."

But the hollow being the kind of place it was, there were many legends and ghost stories associated with it.

Perhaps some of the rogues who frequented the hollow also came there as a result of the canal. Mr. Frey writes that "the canal attracted many laborers from the east and many crooks who lived by their wits at the expense of the laborers."

But most of all it was the brawls that gave Rogues' Hollow its unsavory reputation. Many old-timers said the hollow was at its worst in the 1860s and '70s.

A record book from the justice of the peace court in Chippewa Township (Wayne County), found about 10 years ago, confirmed this belief. The record of cases heard before the court shows the period during and after the Civil War was the roughest, toughest era in the life of Rogues' Hollow.

And to think that one of the fastest ways out in those days was by canal boat — at three to four miles an hour.

October 2, 1966

Sudden 'Drought' Hits Canal

For a short while recently, it looked like someone had pulled the plug in the bottom of the Ohio & Erie Canal. The water level dropped 5 inches suddenly and unexplainably, then stabilized at the lower level.

Mayor John Cullen of Canal Fulton assigned Richard Simmons, village water and sewer department foreman, to accompany Paul Marks, canal foreman for the Stark County commissioners, in a search for the trouble. All three men feared the bank of the canal feeder stream had given way at some point, thus halting the inflow of fresh water.

The foremen found the trouble in a wild area of dense undergrowth between Canal Fulton and Manchester, where the canal feeder was close to a stream feeding Lake Lucern.

Instead of a break in the feeder dike, they found a dam and two partially completed ones were backing up the water of the canal feeder and spilling it over a low bank into the stream feeding the lake. Who built the dams and why?

The two men had an idea. They knocked a hole in the dam and stepped back to see what, if anything, would happen. It wasn't long before the dam builders — three sharp-toothed beavers — arrived. Satisfied as to the cause of their problem, the men removed the dams, letting the water again flow into the canal. They expect the beavers to start work on a new set of dams but the division of wildlife of the Ohio Department of Natural Resources may have something to say about that.

Canal Span Redecked

There has been little work done on the canal this past summer for various reasons, among these the lack of funds and manpower. One definite improvement was made, however, by the Stark County Engineer's bridge department. Under the supervision of Richard Teeter, bridge supervisor, the picturesque wrought iron footbridge across the canal in the vicinity of the Canal Fulton village park was redecked. Canal Fulton Mayor Jack Cullen, in announcing that the 8-foot-wide span again is ready for use, said a horse had stepped through one of the rotting planks, making the bridge unsafe.

Call for Canoeists

With fall advancing rapidly and its leaves becoming more colorful daily, the time for some of the most enjoyable canoeing is at hand. No mosquitoes for one thing. And few, if any, water weeds.

I know of at least two canoe trips planned.

Melvin J. Rebholz, chief of the parks and recreation division of the Ohio Department of Natural Resources, announced a 6-mile canoe trip down the Mohican River would be made Saturday. Open to beginning and seasoned canoeists, the trip was to start at the Mohican Canoe Livery at the junction of Routes 3 and 97 south of Loudonville.

Mr. Rebholz was to speak briefly on the state's plans to develop nearby Mohican State Park and then the canoeists were to head downstream. Free transportation was available to return participants to their cars and the Loudonville Jaycees were on hand at the finish line with refreshments. Canoes from Loudonville and Brinkhaven liveries were added to those of the Mohican livery to make the total of rental canoes available more than 100.

And then there is the all-day canoe trip planned Oct. 22 by the Cleveland Hiking Club as one of its many scheduled activities for October. The Clevelanders will travel to the Portage Lakes south of Akron, arriving in time to begin their day of canoeing at 9 a.m.

Having made the Mohican trip twice, and also canoed the waters of all the Portage Lakes, I can safely predict that both trips should be especially nice at this time of year.

But then so should a trip on the Ohio & Erie Canal in Stark County. There is lovely scenery to behold between Canal Fulton and the present termination of the rewatered canal south of Crystal Springs. And if you get tired, the towpath is always right at hand for you to pull up to and rest. The water is not deep (4 feet), as in a lake, or swift, as in a river.

River, lake or canal, the fall offerings canoeists are varied, interesting and inviting.

October 9, 1966

Britisher Tells of Yankee Canals

Earlier this year, to my great surprise, I received a letter from Clifford H. Heard of Cheam, Surrey, England, in which he wrote in support of the "work you are doing in the restoration of your canals." He had been introduced to this column by Philip Dannemiller of Canton, who was in England. At that time, I wrote a column in which I quoted liberally from Mr. Heard's interesting letter.

And now, I have received another welcome letter from Mr. Heard in which he provides a bit of canal history, which should prove of interest to readers.

In his pursuit of canal history, Mr. Heard came upon an English newspaper report, or rather a letter to the editor, published in the *Hereford Times* November 14, 1838.

The background of the letter was this:

The Hereford and Gloucester Canal Co. was proposing to complete its unfinished canal and carry it on to Hereford and the newspaper was publishing a number of letters on the subject. It also published letters on canal travel in England and America. The latter letter, copied from a reprinted collection of canal items in the Hereford City Library, is as follows:

"Having seen in your valuable paper... an article on canal traveling, I beg to offer a few remarks on the subject. I have often wondered that canal traveling is not more in use in this country, as it is carried to such an extent in the United States of America.

"The passage boats there are of two descriptions: packet boats and line boats. The packet boats are built long and narrow, to accelerate their speed, and are, of course, fitted up for the convenience of passengers with a cabin, cooking place, etc. They have three horses attached to them, the rider or driver riding the last horse and driving the other two before him.

"Stations are upon the line of the canal, at distances of about 14 miles, where they change horses. The rate of traveling averages about 9 miles an hour, including locks, stoppages, etc. The charge (per mile) is five cents... They carry only passengers with their luggage. The line boats are only second rate; both as regards speed and comfort — the average speed of these is 5 miles an hour. They have two horses attached to them and carry freight as well as passengers, and are, of course, cheaper than the packets.

"Last summer I traveled upwards of 700 miles in this way, upon different canals in the United States, and I consider it not only a cheap, but very pleasant mode of traveling. There is also an advantage besides cheapness; the passenger can take a greater quantity of luggage with him by this conveyance than by coach.

"Few persons have an idea of the number of boats upon the canals in America. The beginning of last summer I was traveling upon the Erie Canal, which runs from Albany to Buffalo in the state of New York, a distance of 363 miles. When within 40 miles of Buffalo, the canal burst. We therefore could not proceed until the break as they called it was mended. In a few hours, upwards of 70 boats were waiting to pass. The break was, however, soon repaired and on we went. It is proposed to widen this canal so as to admit of steamboats plying upon it.

"The Ohio Canal runs through the state of Ohio 310 miles from Cleveland upon Lake Erie to Portsmouth upon the Ohio River. At this place it empties in the Ohio River. Hundreds of boats are constantly plying upon these canals. There are also many pretty towns built upon the line of these canals where passengers may provide themselves with whatever accommodations they may require. The Pennsylvania Canal also, and various others, in fact all the canals in the United States, have boats of this description plying upon their waters. I do not think the canals are any wider than they are here. Neither did I perceive that the swell caused by the boats, making headway at all into the banks.

"Now why may not boats of this kind be introduced upon the canals of England? And I further ask where any new canals are projected for the Ledbury and Hereford Canal — why may they not be made sufficiently wide and deep to admit of steamboats plying upon their waters? It is true that the outlay would be considerably increased: but would it not pay the shareholders, inasmuch as passengers and goods would be conveyed so much quicker and cheaper than at present? And by this internal communication, every part of the country would be brought within a few hours of any of the ports of this kingdom.

"I do not doubt that this will ultimately take place. This is the age of improvement. Steam is making rapid strides and it is just as reasonable to suppose that we shall see it propelling vessels upon our canals as it was, a short time ago, to suppose we should see it triumph over the foaming billows of the Atlantic."

The 1838 letter was signed simply "A friend to improvement."

Mr. Heard, in concluding his contemporary letter, said he thought I might also be interested to know that steps are being taken for the retention of the canals in Ireland.

Thank you, Mr. Heard.

October 16, 1966

Washington, Franklin, Dickens and Canals

Many of the readers of this column know the approximate dates of the canal era in America — when it reached its peak and when its decline began.

But I wonder how many know that George Washington conceived of a great network of canals — linking every section of the new nation — many years before the first shovelful of dirt was dug for the first "big ditch."

And how many know that Benjamin

Franklin, far ahead of his time, saw the feasibility and value of canals. As far back as 1770 he wrote from England to the mayor of Philadelphia concerning a canal to tie together the Susquehanna and Schuylkill rivers: "Rivers are ungovernable things, especially in hilly countries. Canals are quiet and always manageable... I warmly wish success to every attempt for improvement of our dear country."

Charles Dickens once wrote about a trip he made aboard a canal packet. Displeased with the sleeping arrangements, he wrote the following description in his *American Notes*:

"I have mentioned my having been in some uncertainty and doubt, at first, relative to the sleeping arrangements on board this boat. I remained in the same vague state of mind until ten o'clock or thereabouts, when going below, I found suspended on either side of the cabin three long tiers of hanging bookshelves, designed apparently for volumes of the small octavo size.

"Looking with greater attention at these contrivances (wondering to find such literary preparations in such a place), I descried on each shelf a sort of microscopic sheet and blanket, then I began to dimly comprehend that the passengers were the library, and that they were to be arranged, edge-wise, on these shelves, till morning... I was at first in uncertainty as to the best means of getting into it. But the shelf being a bottom one, I finally determined on lying upon the floor, rolling gently in, stopping immediately, I touched the mattress, and remaining for the night with that side uppermost, whatever it might be. Luckily, I came upon my back at exactly the right moment.

"One of two remarkable circumstances is indisputably a fact, with reference to that class of society who travel in these boats. Either they carry their restlessness to such a pitch that they never sleep at all, or they expectorate in dreams... All night long, and every night, on this canal, there was a perfect storm and tempest of spitting..."

For Mr. Dickens' description of night-life aboard a canal packet and for the information about George Washington and

Benjamin Franklin, I am indebted to Calvin G. Shinn of the Barber Trailer Court at Alliance. Mr. Shinn, who has a keen interest in covered bridges, came into possession of a book titled *The Story of American Roads* by Val Hart.

The book, which he sent to me, has a chapter devoted to the Erie Canal, New York's "big ditch." After all, the Erie Canal was indeed a road; after it came into the American transportation scene, thousands of travelers used it to reach the frontier country in Ohio.

In 1825, the year the Erie Canal was opened, there were about 8,000 immigrants a year from foreign nations. Five years later more than 50,000 were coming into the United States annually. Many of these pioneers who were to become Americans preferred to go into the West, where they could buy land for $1.25 an acre. The Erie Canal became their turnpike of that day. And as a result, Ohio, which had been the 13th state in population in 1810, became the third by 1840.

The frontier beckoned. The canal provided comparatively easy access to it. And so thousands endured the difficulties of which Mr. Dickens wrote. Hardships and all, the Erie Canal was a tremendous success. Soon canals were being built throughout the country. And one of the greatest was our own Ohio & Erie.

Teens on the Towpath

Teenagers from the New "G" Teen Center, sponsored by First Methodist Church of Massillon, planned to spend Saturday trimming the undergrowth and making the towpath between Crystal Springs and Butterbridge Rd. more attractive for autumn hikers. Due to the lack of manpower and funds, maintenance on the canal lands has been practically nonexistent this past summer. So the efforts of the teenagers, under the supervision of Mrs. Dee Lanier, director of the teen center, and other adults, is welcome.

Mrs. Lanier said the work crew planned a hamburger fry at Lock 4 Park after their work was done. This was to be concluded in time for the group to get back to Massillon for the football game.

October 23, 1966

To Cleveland via Canal

Anyone setting out on his own to find facts and figures, anecdotes and legends, in fact anything recorded about the canal era, will find slim pickings.

But, because of this column, I have been given or permitted to borrow books, papers and articles about the canal days that I may never have come upon myself. Through the helpfulness and generosity of these people, I have been able to share canal history with the readers on a continuing, if irregular, basis.

My eldest son, while seeking canal-boat data for me at a Cleveland museum, came upon a book, which he purchased, thinking I should have it. Although you would never know from its title, *Cultural Story of an American City, Cleveland - Part 2,* it contains considerable information about canals. Authored by Elbert Jay Benton, the study was published with monies from the Philip L. Cobb Memorial Fund as one of the publications of the Western Reserve Historical Society.

In reading the various books and pamphlets about the canal days, I have felt that the personal, "I was there" accounts of travel give the greatest insight into the realities of life in the canal era. And so, from the pages of Mr. Benton's cultural story of Cleveland, here is another description of canal-boat travel between 1825 and 1850:

"Prince Maximillian of Wied, a German scholar traveling in the United States in 1834, came to Cleveland over the Ohio Canal. He arrived early on the third day from Portsmouth. The packet, he says, was built in the same style as the keel boats of the Missouri, but had many convenient small chambers.

"It was between 70 and 80 feet long, 14 feet in breadth and drawn by two horses, tandemwise, on one of which the driver was seated. The boat, he found, was not as well arranged and fitted up as those of the Erie Canal over which he traveled to Albany.

"The Erie Canal had distinct boats for passengers and freight, this was a combination. The Ohio Canal boat was slower because it used fewer horses. In the middle of the boat on which he traveled was the space for the goods; in front two cabins; at the rear was the saloon or dining room. At the side of the room, which, as well as on the floor, the beds were arranged at night. In the cabins were the berths for the ladies. His description of the towns and valleys through which they passed is interesting, of Zoar with its red tiled houses and German population, of the long descent by locks at Akron, and the sight of Lake Erie as they neared Cleveland. The sealike expanse and bluish waters of the large lake fascinated him. 'A most agreeable journey,' it had been 'during which we sat quite at ease on the dock,' like on an ocean voyage.

"In Cleveland he was surprised to meet many Germans, the advance guard of a great migration. 'Cleveland,' he wrote, 'is a large, rapidly improving town, with several thousand inhabitants, full of life, trade and business... It contains many large buildings, several churches, a school or academy, a prison, good inns, and numerous shops and stores; the trade is very considerable in consequence of the junction of the great lakes with the Ohio and the Mississippi.'

" 'Numbers of canal boats are assembled here, and also two-masted schooners which navigate the lake. Several large, commodious steamers, generally full of passengers, come and depart daily.' As a result of the new system of waterways it had come about that the business horizon of Clevelanders was bounded by Portsmouth, Pittsburgh and Buffalo, with Philadelphia, New York and Montreal not too distant for such contacts."

Today the business horizon of Cleveland reaches to all corners of the world and water commerce throughout the seven seas has been achieved through the St. Lawrence Seaway. But, even today, this would not be possible if it were not for a canal — the Welland Canal — and a series of locks, which raise and lower boats in the same manner as did the locks of the old Ohio & Erie Canal when Cleveland first became a canal town.

October 30, 1966
Canal Is Election Issue

The Apaches and the Cherokees will be locked in a battle for power during the next seven days — in a big wigwam just an arrow's flight from the old Tuscarawas Indian Trail. Preparations for the battle are under way, tribal leaders are rounding up support and, all in all, it promises to be a major engagement — fought entirely by little Indians. Regardless of the outcome, the Ohio & Erie Canal from Massillon to Clinton will have been involved in a major way.

If you need an interpreter, here is the translation:

The two tribes are opposing political parties in the first five grades at Clinton Elementary School. The battle is the political campaigning to elect public officials ranging from the local level to the governorship. The pupil candidates must give speeches telling why they should be elected. The wigwam, of course, is the school building in Clinton, a canal community.

The Apaches and the Cherokees are busy making stickers, badges and signs supporting their candidates. Monday, Nov. 7, the day before the adult general election, the pupils will cast their ballots in the same booths that their parents will use the following day in the school. Some of the regular Election Day precinct workers have volunteered to make an official count for the pupils.

Even the first graders will vote. Each classroom is a "city" and there are seven "cities" — Cleveland, Columbus, Akron, Canton, Massillon, Canal Fulton and Clinton.

The plan is the brainchild of Principal Thompson C. Roberts, who conceived it as an effective way of teaching the children the basic system and purpose of American elections. Each "city" will have its own school issue and special levy to vote on and there will be county and state issues.

The big issue to be voted on by the pupils is a $5 million bond issue envisioning the restoration of the Ohio & Erie Canal between Massillon and Clinton. The multiple purposes of this "state level" bond issue is to make the canal usable for regular canal boats and barges, to restore the locks

120

and feeder lakes, to provide for fishing and picnicking along the canal and beside the feeder lakes, to construct museums at several points along the waterway and to establish tours for children and adults.

Mr. Roberts explained that, as part of the election experience, the pupils who live along the canal will have to convince their fellow voters of the benefits to be gained by the canal improvement plan if they hope to muster enough votes for passage of the bond issue.

As a result of the mock election, Mr. Roberts expects the pupils to learn a great deal about the system of government under which they live. I believe he is right and will be anxious to learn what our very young "voters" decide.

(Editor's note: The outcome was reported Nov. 13. The issue was approved by a vote of 133 to 58.)

Stone-Lift Addenda

Perhaps you read in Thursday's editions about Stark County acquiring the 140 –year-old stones from Tuckers Lock near Newcomerstown in Tuscarawas County. Destined for burial, the stones have been given a new lease on life and hopefully will become part of a canal museum at Lock 4 Park.

A handful of people played key roles in making the stone-lift a success. Most were recognized in the Thursday article but, due to a space problem, the story had to be trimmed and some of the names were left out.

Bob Ries, Canal Fulton contractor, donated his services and used his front-end loader to unload all 62 of the heavy stone blocks at Lock 4 Park.

Mike Pierry, superintendent of the Route 36-16 bypass project for Great Lakes Construction Co. of Cleveland, flashed the green light for acquisition of the stones when he granted permission for their removal.

Floyd Breyer, owner of the Breyer Exchange Inc. at New Philadelphia, donated services of a driver and truck to haul the last 18 stones to Stark County.

One of the biggest contributors to the success of the two-county project was Richard Robinson of the Department of Highways, whose cooperation in arranging key details of the stone-lift was a fine example of public relations.

The space problem also made it necessary to cut out historical information about Tucker's Lock. Ted Findley of New Philadelphia, president of the Canal Society of Ohio, revealed that Abram Garfield, father of President James Abram Garfield, had a contract to build a mile of the canal between Port Washington and Newcomerstown. It could have been the section containing Tucker's Lock.

The possibility of the presidential association with the stones of Tucker's Lock should add interest in the years to come for all who visit Stark County's canal museum, which today is just a grand dream of a few men, based on a pile of stones — beautiful, historical, 140-year-old stones — etched with character and full of promise.

November 6, 1966
Pupils Learn Canal History

During the first half of the 19th century, when the canal era was at its peak, schoolchildren probably never got more than a few miles out of town on an educational trip. In those pre-Civil War days, there wouldn't have been much for them to see, only wagon roads or canals to travel on and only wagons or canal boats to ride in.

Today, with our modern highways and multitude of school buses, educational tours to many places of historical interest are within range of classes everywhere. Illustrated textbooks, slides, motion pictures, television and other visual aids are remarkable tools to be used in the educational process, but they can hardly equal the impact of the eyewitness, on-the-scene, "I was there" type of learning.

It was this type of learning that 35 fifth and sixth-grade pupils in Minerva's Mary Irene Day Elementary School experienced when they took a "canal" trip. They made

the 160-mile round-trip on a Saturday, riding a school bus and paying for the trip themselves. And, according to their teacher, Mrs. Janette McAvoy, they thoroughly enjoyed it.

The Minerva pupils were especially fortunate to have as their teacher-guide Ted Findley of New Philadelphia, president of the Canal Society of Ohio and one of the most knowledgeable men in the state on canal history.

Apparently, the pupils realized the specialness of their learning experience with Mr. Findley, for they sent him 32 letters in which they told of their appreciation of the trip and thanked him for making it so interesting. The relationship was one of mutual admiration, for Mr. Findley, in telling of the 32 letters, said his charges were "very well behaved."

Mrs. McAvoy's pupils started their study-tour in their own village, where traces of the old Sandy and Beaver Canal still are discernable. Next they observed the same canal and the millrace at Elson's picturesque old mill at Magnolia and then drove to Dover Dam.

From there, they followed the Ohio & Erie Canal towpath into New Philadelphia and then went to historic Schoenbrunn and Lock 17 near Tuscarawas. From there it wasn't far to Newcomerstown, near which they saw an old stone fort. Then it was on to Coshocton, where they viewed the canal mural on an inside wall of the Coshocton National Bank. After studying the mural they drove to nearby Roscoe where some buildings portrayed in the mural still are standing.

The pupils saw where the old canal aqueduct stood and visited the unusual and ex-cellently preserved triple lock at Roscoe. They concluded their tour with a visit to the museum in Coshocton.

While visiting the burial site of a number of Christian Indians at Gnadenhutten and noting that David Zeisberger, a Christian missionary, was buried there too, one young miss observed rather timorously, "I don't think that I'd like to be buried with all those Indians."

As a follow-up to their trip the pupils have filled their room with material pertaining to the tour in preparation for open house at the school Nov. 15. This includes photographs they took, scrapbooks, maps showing the different canals and clippings of this column. Mrs. McAvoy will show four rolls of motion picture film she shot during the tour.

Pilgrimage to Clinton

The Ohio & Erie Canal and some of its history will receive considerable attention during the pilgrimage to Clinton Monday by the Akron chapter of the Daughters of the American Revolution. The chapter, which has invited DAR members everywhere to attend, expects to "really turn back the pages of history."

The village, which is bisected by the canal, celebrated its sesquicentennial in July. Those who make the pilgrimage will tour the waterway, visit Lock 4 Park in Stark County and see the preserved log cabin, which is part of Clinton's early history. At the conclusion of their tour, members will have a buffet supper at the 126-year-old home of Mrs. W.J. McIntosh on Main St. in Clinton. The house is believed to have been built by a wheat grower during the heyday of the Ohio & Erie Canal. Mrs. Catherine Dobbs, a former mayor of Barberton, will speak on the history of the canal.

State Rep. Ralph Regula of Navarre, co-chairman of the Stark County Canal Lands Development Advisory Committee and Rev. Ray Seeley, pastor of Columbia United Church of Christ at Barberton, will assist in the dedication of a new but historically old gavel.

The gavel was made from a piece of the 1812 White House salvaged after the historic fire. The gavel base was made from a piece of the first canal boat on the Ohio & Erie Canal, the "State of Ohio," which was built in Akron, officially opened the canal July of 1827 and continued in service until it sank near Navarre in 1848. Years later, during a dry season, the timbers were exposed and Stephan Gladwin obtained a section of the boat and made the gavel base for his wife, who was fifth regent of the Akron chapter of the DAR.

November 13, 1966
Robert Fulton Helped Canal Boom

The column this week shapes up as a potpourri. I have a little information on "this" phase of canal history and a bit more on "that." I have a smidgen of facts on one aspect and a smidgen of data on another. Just bits and pieces — but all related in some way to life along the towpath.

For example, did you know that the invention of the steamboat by Robert Fulton is credited with doing a great deal to stir up interest in and create a demand for canals in Ohio?

That's what it says in my daughter April's eighth-grade Ohio history textbook. The book states, "while steamboats could not run on the canals, they greatly increased the shipping on Lake Erie and the Ohio River."

One of the numerous color photographs and paintings in the textbook shows a steamboat with a side paddle wheel churning along while a number of people in smaller craft shout and wave their hats and handkerchiefs. The caption beneath the painting says "Robert Fulton's steamboat, the *Clermont*, ushered in the steamship and canal era." The book devotes five pages to the canal era and includes a color photograph of an abandoned lock that is unidentified but looks much like one I have seen in Summit County.

It is heartening to know our schoolchildren are learning much of the history of their state, including the important part played by the canals and the boats that used them.

Major Undertaking

Speaking of the importance of canals in early America, a recent "filler" in *The Repository* revealed that: "The building of the Erie Canal in the early 19th Century, from north of Albany westward to Buffalo, was the biggest construction project ever undertaken in the young United States."

Canals Advertised

I was leafing through a national travel magazine the other day when I came across an advertisement about canals. Although the sales pitch was for jet travel, the lure was — come and see the canals.

I thought it interesting that the advertisement for "Surprising Amsterdam" should use canals to attract visitors to one of Europe's most popular cities. The ad featured a color photograph showing a canal scene and beneath it this message:

"Glorious, tree-lined canals... divide the city into 70 islands with 36 bridges. The water... is remarkably clean. Reason: the tidy Dutch change it every week (by opening and closing floodgates). The best way to explore Amsterdam is to cruise through it. You can take a 75-minute trip in a glass-topped boat for 70 U.S. cents. You'll see miles of leaning, canal houses, barges ablaze with flowers, the house where Rembrandt lived and dozens of other surprises."

Perhaps Stark County's canals can't offer all that but the Ohio & Erie and the Sandy and Beaver can offer much that would be worthwhile for travelers to see.

Of course much of this "offering" is in the future, but steps have been taken on a number of projects that someday could make our canals rival, in interest, those of Amsterdam.

For example, the project to build an authentic canal boat for use on the Ohio & Erie is going ahead. White oak trees for the hull timbers are being collected and donations of money continue to come in slowly but steadily for the "Canal Boat Fund."

The canalside museum project was advanced recently when three truckloads of stones from a Tuscarawas County lock marked for destruction were brought to Lock 4 Park for possible use in constructing a museum for canal memorabilia.

Down at Magnolia the picturesque Elson Mill stands close to the Sandy and Beaver, a delight to tourists with a sense of the artistic.

As for barges filled with flowers, we may not have them. But we could have canal banks filled with wild flowers or cultivated flower beds if some of Stark County's garden clubs were authorized to work their floral wonders.

Project in Illinois

Just read about another canal project similar to ours here in Stark County. This one is in Illinois. The following excerpt is from a letter written by the conservation chairman of the Great Lakes Chapter of the Sierra Club:

"Conservation interests are hoping to bring about establishment of a recreational area on the right-of-way of the Illinois and Michigan Canal. If this goes through, it will consist of hiking and bicycling trails as well as provisions for camping and canoeing along the entire length of 100 miles from Chicago to Peru, Ill. In a letter to Jean Leever (an officer of the chapter), Governor Kerner indicated he is cognizant of the recreational values of this strip of land. Many problems must be overcome, however: Some portions of the land (and waterway) are being used as a dumping ground for industrial wastes. This must be stopped and the canal cleaned of all pollution. We hope it's soon."

November 20, 1966
Lights for Lock 4 Park?

Last Sunday was a dandy day to be out-of-doors. The air was sharp but the sun was bright — an invigorating sort of day, ideal for hiking or riding horseback. Both were being enjoyed along the Ohio & Erie Canal towpath near Lock 4 Park south of Canal Fulton. During a visit to the park, I saw at least eight horsemen pass the lock on their way up or down the towpath and a number of persons who preferred using their own feet to stroll along the canal.

Paul Marks, foreman in charge of the canal reconstruction for the county, says horse traffic on the towpath is increasing and that usage by hikers remains high despite the approach of winter.

Paul, who is constantly thinking of ways to improve the canal lands when county funds become available, has come up with a nifty improvement idea, which he thinks he can accomplish without funds. He says he may need a little assistance through donations of material but basically he hopes to make it a "do it yourself" project.

Paul's plan is to build a waterwheel 20 feet wide and fit it into the spillway of the canal bypass at Lock 4 Park. By using the water that pours over the spillway the year around to operate the waterwheel, Paul figures enough electricity could be generated to light the small park 24 hours a day. If he is able to accomplish this hydroelectric project, it won't be the first time waterpower has been used for man's benefit at this location. According to the foreman, the spillway is located at the terminus of the raceway that once brought water to the waterwheel of an old gristmill at the site of Lock 4 Park.

Rowing Up the Canal

Horseback riders and hikers were not the only ones enjoying the canal and its towpath last Sunday. Ralph Romig of the village of Tuscarawas, author of the book *Cy Young, Baseball's Legendary Giant*, and friends Robert Zorn and Albert Ulrich drove to Lock 4 Park to go boating on the canal.

Ralph, a teacher at Claymont High School in Uhrichsville and farm editor of the *Uhrichsville Chronicle*, has been writing about the Stark County canal project to arouse interest in Tuscarawas County in a similar restoration project.

The three men report they enjoyed rowing Ralph's boat up the canal toward Canal Fulton.

Viva Chechahcos!

The canal-boat "crew" (all who are working to build a canal boat for Stark County) received a big boost last week. The mailman brought the canal boat fund a check for $100 from the Chechahco Garden Club. It was the largest single contribution received to date from any organization and was a much appreciated "shot" of encouragement. The Chechahcos assisted the Stark Wilderness Center last year with a comparable contribution. Maybe the club is among the first to extend a financial helping hand to new projects its members consider worthwhile because the name "Chechahco" means "newcomer."

November 27, 1966
Thanksgiving on the Canal?

This is the second year that I have searched in vain for a true Thanksgiving story related to life on the canal or along the towpath. Canal literature is scarce and anecdotes linking Thanksgiving with canal travel, seemingly nonexistent.

Somewhere, in an old yellowed letter or faded newspaper, there must be an account of Thanksgiving Day aboard a canal boat. We know so little about the canal era —maybe the boats were not operated on the November holiday. But, if they were, the crew and passengers probably were served a special dinner. We know that the packet boats, which carried passengers, were equipped to serve meals. This is attested to in the periodical *Ohio Cues*, which is written especially for young Ohioans.

In an article titled "Notes on Canawling," the following description of the interior of a packet is given:

"On a packet, the crew's cabin with five or six bunks was in the bow — passengers could freshen up in the washroom with water dipped from the canal, and with a massive comb and brush chained to the wall of the room — women and children slept in the ladies cabin and had their breakfasts served there at 6 a.m. After breakfast, families assembled in the largest compartment where the baggage was stored, also where the other two meals of the day were served on trestle tables set up each time, and where the men slept in tiers of bunks at night — at night passengers hung their clothes on lines strung across the cabins."

And so we see that the cumbersome, slow-moving and rather rough-appearing canal boats had the facilities aboard to prepare and serve a turkey dinner. If the traditional fowl were the main course of the holiday meal aboard canal boats, it probably was a wild turkey, which had not yet been driven from the Ohio country.

More Stones Saved

Apparently, Stark is not the only county to save old hand-cut stones from the Ohio & Erie Canal installations near Newcomerstown. Francis McMasters, manager of the northeast district of the Ohio Historical Society, was successful in salvaging some stones from a drainpipe associated with the canal. The stones are now at Fort Laurens near Bolivar in Tuscarawas County, adjacent to another section of the canal, awaiting a decision as to their ultimate use.

December 4, 1966
Canal Boat Lumber Stockpile Grows

What with the holiday and all, another special day slipped by and was almost forgotten — "Along the Towpath's" birthday. Last week this column began its third year.

During the past year, several promising

projects associated with the restoration and development of the canal lands were either started or advanced. One was the plan to build a canal boat. Much of the work to advance this project went unreported but not unappreciated.

One of the key requisites for building the canal boat is lumber for the hull — special white oak and a lot of it.

Early last spring, Paul R. Baird, president of Notnac Mfg. Co. of Canton, began a search for suitable white oak trees and people who would donate them to the project. During the spring, summer and fall, Paul was in the woods of Stark County whenever he could get away from his business duties. He drove hundreds of miles and walked many more in his search.

As of last week, Paul had 30 logs in a pile at the sawmill in Canal Fulton ready to be cut into hull timbers. He had five more ready to be hauled to the mill and several more trees promised. Meanwhile, Paul continues to search for trees big enough to provide the timber required for a 60-foot boat.

After the logs had been found, donated and cut, there remained the problem of getting them to the sawmill. Several persons solved this problem by donating the services of themselves and their trucks. Foremost among these is Peter Neidert of Canal Fulton, who has hauled more of the logs than anyone else. Pete, who is the "Neidert" of Neidert & Sons of Canal Fulton, has a sturdy truck, which he uses in the operation of his farm machinery and lawn and garden equipment business. Donating his time and his truck, Pete has brought the lion's share of the trees to the sawmill.

The formula for getting the logs to the mill has evolved into a two-man effort: Paul finds them and Pete hauls them.

After this "Gemini" phase of the program has been completed and sufficient lumber has been provided, we will be ready for the "Apollo" or final phase — construction. The need then will be for manpower — men with know-how and desire to build the boat.

Zigzagging the Canal

For two years now, I have been reporting how individuals and groups enjoy hiking the towpath and boating on the canal. And so I find it interesting to read what someone else has written about these activities. Ralph Romig, farm editor of *The Evening Chronicle*, daily newspaper for Uhrichsville-Dennison, recently explored part of the Ohio & Erie near Lock 4 Park in a rowboat. Then he wrote about it in the *Chronicle*.

Quoting one of his companions, Ralph wrote: "I'm impressed with the number of people hiking along the towpath. See that mother and dad and two little kids over there? That's my idea of what a family's Sunday afternoon should be."

Speaking for himself, Ralph wrote: "The number of hikers was large for a crisp November day. There were also quite a few horseback riders taking advantage of the car-free towpath trail."

Ralph and his two companions estimated they paddled three miles on the canal. Later, they were told they had actually covered about 1½ miles. The three visiting boatmen made no boasts as to their prowess with the paddles but they did staunchly maintain they had traveled three miles.

"If you count our number of zigzags, I'm sure we made three miles." Ralph declared.

December 11, 1966
Volunteers Make the Difference

If Stark becomes the first Ohio county to operate an authentic canal boat, it likely will be due to volunteer efforts and donations of funds. For it is the volunteer that makes the "impossible" possible in situations such as this.

I recently learned that if it hadn't been for what was considered prohibitive cost, one or more canal boats probably would have been built elsewhere in the state.

Requests for blueprints and specifications of early canal boats addressed to the State Department of Public Works were honored but the cost of building the boats apparently discouraged any follow-through.

And it seems there were not enough dedicated volunteers to do the "impossible." And so Stark County, with a dedicated core of volunteers (but needing more), apparently has a good chance to become the first to accomplish the boat-building feat.

It would be nice if the boat could be built for what they cost in 1880. According to Hall's *The Shipbuilding Industry in the U.S.,* a canal boat cost between $1,100 and $1,200. Some cost more. A paragraph from the *Last Ohio Canal Boat,* published by the Ohio Archaeological & Historical Society in 1926, reads: "The itemized cost for one of the first boats used on the Ohio canal totaled $2,123.34, including six horses for towing... and two gallons of whiskey at 24 cents a gallon for the 'hands'."

Both statements on the cost of canal boats were published in "Towpaths," quarterly journal of the Canal Society of Ohio.

The article from Hall's book contained further interesting information:

"The old time boats of Ohio were able to carry only about 45 tons of cargo each. They were then, as now, 80 feet long, 14 feet wide, and 4 or 4½ feet deep, drawing 3 feet of water, and were rather sharp and fast boats. But in late years they have been built fuller and given 4 feet draught, so that their capacity has been increased 80 or 90 tons.

"They are neat boats, but not large enough; and, considering that the large 240-ton boats in the State of New York find it hard to hold their own against railroad competition, it is not surprising that the smaller craft of Ohio have been hard pressed since the war (Civil War), the discouragement among the boatmen being so great that very few new boats have been built for 10 or 12 years.

"About 1870 the old Philadelphia and Erie Canal was abandoned and about 40 canal boats were taken over to the Ohio canal. There has been almost no building on the latter since, not to exceed five or six boats being built in any one year. The Ohio boats were all framed, the object being to secure as light a hull as possible. The model is the same as that of the bull-head

of the Erie Canal.

"The house is not continuous from stem to stern, but consists of three small houses, one in the bow, one amidship for a stable, and one away aft for the captain, with a little roof or gangway 3 feet wide running from one to another. A few are completely housed and are called two-deckers.

"The frames are sawed out of 1¾ inch oak, molded 11 or 12 inches over the keel, 9 near the bilge, and 3 at the gunwale, spaced about 14 inches. There is a light ceiling of 1 or 1½ inch oak or 2 inch white pine. The outside is planked with 1¾ inch oak.

"There are three fenders on the bow, one at the planksheer height, the other two a foot apart below, extending around the curve of the bow and ironed with 2 by 3/4 inch straps. The stem is oak, 12 by 4 inches, ironed on the face with 3 by 1-inch strap. Houses are white pine.

"The stern overhangs just enough to house the rudder stock. About 13,000 feet of wood, a ton of iron and 80 pounds of manila lines are required for one of these boats."

As to the legal speed of the canal boats, the General Assembly of the State of Ohio passed "An Act to Regulate Navigation" Feb. 23, 1830, Section I of which specified that: "in no case shall any float (boat) move on either of the canals faster than at the rate of four miles an hour."

There is a great deal yet to be accomplished but Stark County's canal boat project is advancing, albeit at a canal boat's speed.

December 18, 1966
Surprise Telephone Call

Back in the early days of this writer's career, I wrote a feature story about "The Greatest Miniature Show on Earth." And it had nothing at all to do with canals or canal boats.

It was, I thought, a good story. Apparently, the editor thought so too, for he rewarded me with a byline, which, in those days, was hard to come by.

But if the story was good, it was largely due to the fact that its subject and main personality were fascinating.

Robert W. Harned, who lived in Akron at the time, had spent 27 years accomplishing an amazing feat. He toiled for more than 25,000 hours carving, painting and costuming some 300 tiny circus folk and 370 animals, fashioning them from the ends of orange crates and joining them so they could be animated.

Faithfully reproduced and accurate to the smallest detail, each tiny figure added a little more authenticity and "atmosphere" to the miniature circus, which its creator said was valued at $1 million and insured for $700,000.

I remember that I started my story, back in 1948, with this quotation from Bob Harned: "The last circus that America will ever see will be the miniature circus."

Realizing that the circus, with all its gaudy color and flamboyant showmanship, was a vanishing part of America, he wielded his carving knife many hours every day to keep it alive in miniature form. He even mechanized his circus street parade, using a bicycle chain 80 feet long.

But to shorten a long story — imagine my surprise and pleasure when I received a call two weeks ago from Mr. Harned, whom I hadn't seen in 18 years. He and his wife, formerly Ruth Gonder of this city, had moved back to her hometown for retirement and were living in a Heritage House apartment. They saw this column and wondered if I was the same reporter who had written the story about their circus.

The telephone call renewed our acquaintance and — to make the story even shorter — when Mr. Harned hung up he went to a hobby shop and purchased a 28-cent knife and some balsa wood. Bob Harned, circus carver extraordinary, was going to carve a model canal boat.

Two weeks passed and another call from Bob brought the anticipated announcement: "The canal boat is done." I wasted little time in getting over to the Harneds' apartment to see the boat and take some notes on its construction.

Mr. Harned had designed and fashioned

the boat entirely from memory, as he had been unable to find a picture at the library of a canal boat similar to the one he planned to make. His boat is of the packet or passenger-carrying type. And despite the fact that it was fashioned from Bob Harned's memory, it looks remarkably like the canal boat pictured on several State of Ohio Canal Stock certificates recently turned over to the Stark County Historical Center. The certificates date to the 1850s.

Bob's boat, which he finished off in a bright coat of white paint and green trim, bears the name "Ohio Belle." It is constructed of balsa wood and required two weeks to make.

Craftsman that he is, Bob still experienced considerable difficulty in bending the balsa planking of the hull to the proper contour. Each time he managed to get one of the miniature timbers bent to the correct degree, it would snap. Finally he struck on the same technique that was employed to bend the hull timbers of some of the original canal boats. He steamed the balsa trips until they could be bent into place to give the trim little packet the lines it has.

In addition to the tiller and rudder and ladders on the cabin, the "Ohio Belle" has a miniature bilge pump and several cargo boxes or trunks fastened securely to the deck.

Bob has presented the "Ohio Belle" to the historical center, where it has been placed in the center's model canal lock to help portray more vividly the little-known story of the canal era in Ohio.

A Talk and a Donation

A Tuscarawas County resident, who knows the history of the Ohio & Erie Canal like few others, came to Stark County last week to share his knowledge with nearly 300 eighth grade pupils who study Ohio history at Sauder Junior High School in Jackson Township. And then he donated his honorarium to Stark County's canal-boat project.

Ted Findley, president of the Canal Society of Ohio, spoke and showed slides of canal scenes to the pupils who, according to Principal Dale Haverstock, found the presentation interesting and very informative.

Incidentally, Ted and Mrs. Findley have an unusual Christmas card this year. It features a photograph of the Ohio & Erie Canal in New Philadelphia taken 100 years ago. Two canal boats are seen on the canal. One of them, from a head-on view, looks remarkably like the model presented to the historical center by Bob Harned. The scene, moreover, includes the area where the Findleys' canalside home is located today.

December 25, 1966
A Babe in a Canal-Boat Manger

Through the generations there has been speculation as to how the world would receive the Christ child if He were born "in our time."

Down through the centuries, the Christmas story — the story of Christ's birth — has been so universally portrayed in its true Palestinian setting that it is difficult to conceive of it taking place elsewhere and at a different time. It simply seems impossible to think of Jesus coming into the world in New York City in 1966 or in Chicago, San Francisco, London, Paris, Moscow.

And yet there are places on the face of the earth which remain today almost exactly as they were nearly 2,000 years ago. In many of these nations, shepherds guide their flocks across the hills and fields as did their fathers and forefathers before them. But the story being as it is, it seems essential that the birth take place in a stable — not in a precinct police station or a suburban motel room.

During the past week, hundreds of thousands of Christmas cards arrived at homes throughout Christendom — countless numbers of them bearing artists' conceptions of the nativity scene in the stable.

Sitting down to write this column, with some of these cards in view, I couldn't help but wonder what the history of the world would be if Christ had been born about

135 years ago in the rolling hills of western Stark County.

For one thing, it was good sheep country and large numbers of the docile animals grazed over the hills and fields.

There were stables to be found in the area, of course. But probably few were more humble than those to be found aboard the canal boats, which moved slowly up and down the Ohio & Erie Canal between Canal Fulton and Navarre (which is in Bethlehem Township).

Since Joseph, the husband of Mary, mother of Jesus, was a woodworker, he may well have been employed in one of the yards where canal boats were built (had he lived in the 1830s).

It would not have been unlikely then for him to have taken Mary, about to be delivered, aboard a canal boat and made her as comfortable as possible on the straw in the boat's center cabin where the horses and mules were stabled. Turned away from the inns in the nearby village and with the ribald songs and curses of drunken boat crews ringing in their ears, they would have found the boat's stable welcome indeed.

And so it came to pass that Mary "gave birth to her first-born son and wrapped him in swaddling cloths, and laid him in a manger, because there was no place for them in the inn."

And when the wise men came, they were from the tribes of the Wyandot and the Delaware and the Shawnee. When they saw the star, which had gone before them, leading them to the Christ child, they "rejoiced exceedingly with great joy" and went aboard the boat and saw the child

The Ohio & Erie Canal, Lock No.4 at Canal Fulton, featured a waterwheel designed to provide electric power to Lock 4 Park.

with Mary his mother "and they fell down and worshipped him."

Then the Bible tells us that an angel of the Lord appeared and told Joseph in a dream to take the child and his mother and flee the country.

If it were, in truth, in 1830 in western Stark County, Joseph may well have hitched the horses and mules to the towline of the canal boat and moved slowly and quietly away on the waters of the placid canal.

"This was to fulfill what the Lord had spoken by the prophet."

What might the world be like today if, indeed, the Christ child had come among us not 1,966 years ago, but a short 135? The answer to this hypothetical question, although interesting, is unimportant. What is important is that the babe was born in Bethlehem and the world has never been the same since. Merry Christmas and a Happy New Year to all!

130

Book Four·1967

Canal Plans for the New Year

Here it is again — New Year's Day! And most of us are wondering what 1967 has in store for us. A logical time, it would seem, also to wonder what is in store for the various canal-lands development projects.

The old canal and its towpath have been around a long time — at least 140 years. And they have "seen" a lot more New Year's Days than any of us. But it has been a century or more since prospects for developments associated with the canal have been as bright as they are today — at least as they apply to the section of the canal within Stark County.

To find out just what is in prospect, I put a series of questions to State Sen. Ralph Regula of Navarre and Mayor William Keen of Massillon, cochairmen of the county commissioners' canal lands development advisory committee. And I called Gervis Brady, director of the Stark County Historical Center, for a report on the proposed canalside museum. This is what they had to say:

Sen. Regula: "I foresee increased use of the canal in 1967 for recreation purposes. I believe there is ever-increasing activity on the canal and that this will continue to be true. Lock 4 Park, for example, has been and continues to be a very popular park area. One of the things I hope we can accomplish there is to repair and restore the lock gates so as to keep them functional."

Mayor Keen: "I hope that we will be able to move more dramatically in developing the canal lands during 1967. We are looking toward further development of the 1,200-foot park north of Massillon on the filled-in section of the canal just north of Route 21. And we are hopeful that the city of Massillon and Perry Township can cooperate to improve the entrance to this park."

As a part of its program to name unnamed alleys, Massillon city council passed an ordinance December 19 officially identifying a 20-foot alley, just south of the city's north boundary and leading into the filled-in portion of the canal, as Towpath Ct. NE. The name was suggested by Mayor Keen.

Mr. Brady: "We see, eventually, a canal museum, operated by the Stark County Historical Society. And we hope that 1967 will see it at least started. The society already has a committee organized to cover the future development of the historical center and it is that committee's wish to include long-range planning for a canal museum. The board of trustees, in authorizing the committee in 1966, directed its planning to include all aspects of the future building program."

Sen. Regula: "One of our goals, which I hope we can complete early this year, is to establish a metropolitan park district. I am hopeful that we can make real strides in completing a plan for the development of a metropolitan park system for the county. I also hope that we will be able to bring the water further down the canal this year — to the area of the proposed park at the north edge of Massillon. Another related project I would like to see successfully completed this year is the establishment of an official Boy Scout trail to be used for the purpose of earning hiking awards."

Mayor Keen: "The acquisition of additional property between the canal and Tuscarawas River is one of our goals for 1967. We also hope to see the completion, by the Stark County Regional Planning Commission, of the general development plan as it applies to the canal. And then, of course, we would like to see the state purchase Lake Lucern, north of Canal Fulton, so that it could be made into a state park and used as a source of additional water for the canal."

Mr. Brady: "With the acquisition of the stones from the old canal lock at Newcomerstown, we hope that the canal museum building, itself, will be a historical monument to the Ohio canal lore. We think that a canal museum built of this stone and containing one of the finest collections of canal history in the state should be a major addition to the educational enrichment of our county. It also will be, along with the projected canal boat, a major tourist attraction. What we hope to have, if our plans work out, is the most authentic and finest canal museum in the nation."

As for the canal-boat project — it continues to move along at somewhat less than canal-boat speed. But there is progress. More lumber is being obtained for the hull. Additional drawings have been provided by Arthur P. Sweaney, 85, of New Philadelphia, who drew up the plans for the boat. Small checks continue to augment the canal-boat fund and more persons express an interest in the project.

Manpower to build the boat and more money to be used for its construction are the prime needs of the canal-boat project for 1967. If the canal boat could be built and launched in 1967, it certainly would be one of the most dramatic developments of what, hopefully, will be a progressive year — along the towpath.

January 8, 1967
Historical Center Gets Canal Stock

The Stark County Historical Center received a gift of stock recently from a donor who prefers to remain anonymous.

Although the stock cost the original purchasers a goodly sum, it would have no value on today's market. For the certificates are "State of Ohio Canal Stock," and the state retired its last canal bond in 1903.

The three certificates presented to the historical center are interesting and attractive. Printed on American Bank Note Co. paper, with black and red ink, and bearing the required revenue stamps, the certificates are signed by the attorney general of Ohio, the secretary of state and the auditor of the state.

Each bears an engraved scene highlighting a canal boat in operation. A muleskinner is astride a horse, which is pulling the boat through a lock, and two other men are operating the lock gate. Visible on the far side of the canal is a group of farmers forking hay onto a hay wagon. In the background, a coal-burning railroad train is crossing a bridge over the canal, its smokestack belching black smoke.

Beneath the picture is inscribed the words: "Office of the Commissioners of the Sinking Fund."

The oldest of the three certificates was dated September 6, 1858. It was issued, with a face value of $1,400 to Samuel L. Hart, in trust for Maria Hart. Mr. Hart indicated his residence as being Old Saybrook in Connecticut. This certificate paid 6 percent interest and was payable after the 31st day of December in 1886.

The most interesting certificate was purchased April 26, 1859 and it also paid 6 percent per annum, payable after December 31, 1886. It was in the amount of $7,038.54, an impressive sum for those days. But even more interesting than the sum is the fact that it was purchased by an Englishman, George Nicholson of Whitehayes near Ringwood in the County of Hampshire in England. What prompted Mr. Nicholson to buy the stock and spend such a large sum for it is not known. But it is known that he sold it December 5, 1867 in the city of London.

The third certificate was for $3,000. Purchased March 12, 1863, by W.H. Neilson, it was payable a short time later — December 31, 1865. It paid only 5 percent.

The act that authorized the stock was passed by the Ohio General Assembly in 1856. The state, it seems, had to keep borrowing money in order to retire the debt it incurred in building the canal and in maintaining it.

Ohio never realized enough from the canal tolls to pay for the construction and the necessary maintenance. But while the

Ohio canals never paid for themselves from a purely financial point of view, they did pay for their cost many times over in that they made possible the tremendous development of the state in its early history. In fact, records show that the value of some properties in the interior counties increased 400 percent during a period of 20 years as a direct result of the canal being constructed.

It was through the purchase of canal stock certificates, like those presented to the historical center, that the people of Ohio and other states, and even England, made possible the operation of the Buckeye State's "big ditches."

January 15, 1967

The Canal Town That Almost Was

Canton was almost a canal town. It actually tried to be. But it wasn't cut out for it. Too much of an inland community, which is just another way of saying there wasn't enough water available to make the town a canal port.

There was incentive — and plenty of it — to build a canal to the city. Nearby Massillon was booming due to its location on the Ohio & Erie Canal.

This was in the 1830s when the canals were in their heyday — "intravenously" feeding the heartland of the young nation, making it stronger and healthier by the day.

But while Massillon grew in importance, Canton was in a bad way. It just had to have a canal. And so a group of its citizens formed a company to build one. The company's name — a real "Swinger" — was The Nimishillen and Sandy Slackwater Navigation Co. And a moneymaker it was not.

The irony is that Canton had the opportunity earlier to have the Ohio & Erie Canal pass through it but said "no thanks."

Historian John Struthers Stewart described the missed opportunity this way:

"An interesting point in connection with the routing of the canal, which directly interests this history, is the fact that from the Akron summit through Stark County two routes were about equal in feasibility; one through Canton, and the other through Massillon. For some reason the leading citizens of Canton raised opposition to the canal and it was thereby routed through Massillon, a fact which was the making of the latter city, and on the other hand reacted against Canton to such extent that the Canton people later on made a frantic effort to connect with the ill-fated Sandy and Beaver Canal."

Of this frantic effort, historian Stewart wrote: "A branch (canal), called the Nimishillen, projected to connect with Canton and thus correct that town's original error, also proved a failure."

Stark County historian E.T. Heald described Canton's catch-up attempt in these words:

"The Ohio Canal quadrupled the living standards overnight, doubling the prices farmers could get for their crops, and bringing to them outside articles of commerce at one-half their previous cost. The construction of the canal gave employment and cash to hundreds of nearby farmers, thus helping them to pay for their lands. Cantonians tried to get into the canal game but lost heavily in the ill-fated Sandy and Beaver Canal, and in the fantastic Nimishillen and Sandy Slackwater Navigation Co."

Still another historian, commenting on the Canton-Massillon canal involvement, adds some tidbits of information about Canton's abortive canal-building attempt. W.F. Gilmore, in the History of Sandy & Beaver, writes:

"Massillon, with its port on the Ohio Canal, was prospering at the expense of Canton and something had to be done. A stock company was organized with the alluring title: Nimishillen and Sandy Slackwater Navigation Co.

"A gala day was set in Canton for the grand opening of this pretentious project. An immense plow with 10 yoke of oxen started excavation on N. Walnut St.; the channel was to be kept full for boats by means of Shriver's Run. This stream headed near N. Market St., and from large springs above 12th St. NE. At Tuscarawas

St., a bridge crossed the canal excavation. The channel was to proceed to the main creek whose channel was to be dammed and locked at intervals as the fall of the creek required. The old canal bed in N. Walnut has been filled in and paved and Shriver's Run has disappeared into underground sewers."

Although Canton's canal outlet to the seven seas failed dismally, apparently it was used for shipping for a short while.

William Henry Perrin, writing in the *History of Stark County*, which was published in 1881, observed that "every navigable stream was regarded as an inestimable feature of the country through which it passed."

Of Canton and Nimishillen Creek, he wrote: "Canton in the forks of Nimishillen Creek, was at the head of navigation. Boats called pirogues, capable of carrying a ton, were in common use for ordinary transportation, and flatboats for flour, bacon and whiskey. These started just below town and their usual destination was New Orleans. In the earlier days, before the country was cleared up, the usual stage of water in the Nimishillen and Tuscarawas was much higher than after, and this made navigation, at least part of the year, possible for light craft, but at best it was difficult and attended with much risk of property. The pirogue and flatboat furnished a partial relief, but by no means all that the wants of a rapidly developing country called for."

While doing extensive research for information about Canton's canal, I called on Ted Findley of New Philadelphia, president of the Canal Society of Ohio, for an assist.

Ted, as usual, was extremely helpful and traced the course of the canal for me: It started about 6th St. NE and Walnut Ave. and ran due south to the site of the present Pennsylvania Railroad depot and then swung westward across the property now occupied by the Hercules Engines, Inc. From there it went south along the east side of Market Ave. to Navarre Rd. where it cut across to the west side of Market Ave. It then continued south until joining Nimishillen Creek.

From that point on, the canal was in and out of the creek, depending on the depth of water in the creek and whether or not the stream made a big arc. Wherever the water was too shallow in the creek at any given section, the canal had been dug. Wherever a shortcut was possible across a big bend in the creek, another section of canal was dug.

The canal followed the creek south through North Industry and Howenstine and then on to East Sparta, finally crossing into Tuscarawas County. It terminated at the east side of Sandyville where it joined the Sandy and Beaver Canal between Magnolia and Bolivar.

After describing the canal's course for me, Ted offered to guide me on a ride-and-hike tour of the route of the watercourse. I accepted. And so in next week's column, Ted and I go canal hunting — in search of the vestiges of Canton's last-gasp canal with the grandiose name — Nimishillen and Sandy Slackwater Canal.

January 22, 1967
Our Quarry Was Vanishing Canal

Ted Findley and I went canal hunting the other day — and enjoyed it. The weather wasn't just the best, but it wasn't the worst either. It was the traces of our quarry that gave us problems. They were scanty, well camouflaged and drastically altered by time. In fact, one couldn't be positive that everything that looked like it had been a canal was, indeed, the old waterway. After all, the "spoor" was really cold — about 130 years cold.

I had read in a number of history books about our quarry, the ill-fated Nimishillen and Sandy Slackwater Canal. Usually, though, there was only brief mention of it. Ted — just about the best possible guide one could have on a canal hunting trip — had read much more about it through the years. But just as there are large areas missing in the route of the canal today, there is much missing information about it.

Obviously, the canal was dug in Canton and at the lower end where it tied into the Sandy and Beaver Canal at Sandyville. But there is disagreement as to whether it was built through North Industry to East Sparta. Ted believes it was and points to locations where he is convinced the canal existed. Some residents of North Industry say there were millraces there but no canal. And, of course, there is nobody alive today who can say, "I know — because I was there." The history books don't agree.

The canal passed within a block of the present *Repository* building as it came straight south on Walnut Ave., once called Canal St. Ted observed that 30 years ago, when he worked and lived in Canton, the canal was much more discernible. Now railroad tracks, large trucking concerns, blacktop parking areas, houses and buildings have drastically changed the landscape.

Our first sighting of the "canal" was to the rear of a row of houses on the west side of Market Ave. S, north of 15th St. SW. Ted pointed to a depression, which ran through the yards behind the houses, and said, "There she is."

We stopped next at the north edge of North Industry and walked to the rear of the Evangelical Lutheran Church, where a watercourse exists today. Although only a rather unsightly trickle of water is flowing now, Ted says it is the old canal bed. Others claim it was a millrace and not the canal.

Those holding the latter opinion can point to Chapter 10 of *The Sandy and Beaver Canal* by R. Max Gard and William H. Vodrey Jr., which states: "The Nimishillen and Sandy suffered a collapse at the same time that the Sandy and Beaver shutdown occurred. When the Sandy and Beaver was finally rejuvenated and completed, it was too late to interest Canton in a canal. The P. & O. Railroad had stolen the spotlight position. The Nimishillen and Sandy was never completed."

On the other hand, in support of Ted's position, John Danner, in his first volume of *Old Landmarks of Canton and Stark County, Ohio*, wrote: "At that time, there were still visible all along past the Willett farm to the creek, evidence of the old canal that was finished a number of years before, but never used or even filled with water."

And last week my daughter, April, showed me a map of the canals in Ohio in her school textbook on Ohio geography, history and government. Clearly shown on the map was a canal connecting Canton with the Sandy and Beaver Canal. It had to be the Nimishillen and Sandy Slackwater Canal. Whether it was completed in the North Industry area or not, there seems little question about it having been completed between East Sparta and Sandyville.

It is interesting to note that in the microfilm copy of an 1834 issue of the *Ohio Repository* there is a report of an election held Christmas Day by the Nimishillen and Sandy Slackwater Navigation Co. Directors were elected and two days later the directors elected as officers "John Harris, president; Lewis Vail, secretary; Lewis Fogle, treasurer. Joshua Malin was employed as engineer and had the first division of four and one half miles located by January 30, 1835."

The Repository of January 30, 1835, reported that the canal would be finished to the Ohio & Erie Canal even though the Sandy and Beaver should fail. On February 5, 1835, the *Ohio Repository* displayed an advertisement for bids for clearing, grubbing, excavating, etc., the first five miles of the canal. The contract was taken by Rodman Lovett and J. Gilbert advertised for 100 good canal hands to report September 18, 1835.

We concluded our hunting trip at Sandyville, where we clearly could see the distinct outline of the Sandy and Beaver and the less distinct profile of the Nimishillen and Sandy.

Canton's canal was sort of a nebulous thing from the beginning. And just little bits of its shadow remain today. But it did exist although it has become only an intriguing paragraph or two in one of the early chapters of the Ohio story.

January 29, 1967
Hiking the Buckeye Trail

Parks have been big in the news the last week or two. The biggest news was the latest step forward in the plan to establish a metropolitan park district in Stark County.

State Senator Ralph S. Regula and C.J. Kurlinski, president of Stark Tri-County Building Trades Council, presented Probate Judge Reuben Z. Wise Jr. with information indicating more than 90 percent of the county's population favor establishment of a metropolitan park system. The two men are cochairmen of the Stark County Regional Planning Commission's metropolitan park and recreation committee.

Once such a district is established, state and federal money will be easier to obtain for development of a park system. And there is where the county's two canals come into the picture. Although no specific park areas have been designated yet, it is safe to assume that the Ohio & Erie Canal in the western part of the county and the Sandy and Beaver Canal in the southeastern section will be strongly considered as potential parks within the system.

With money available, the canal parks could flourish and blossom in a way that has been impossible to date.

Continuing to look ahead to the day when Stark County has its own metropolitan park, Sen. Regula drove to southern Ohio a week ago for a firsthand look at one of Ohio's finest park areas — the Hocking Hills. Accompanying him were his two sons, David and Richard, and this columnist.

We participated in a 5-mile hike sponsored by the Ohio division of parks and recreation and the Buckeye Trail Association. Starting at Ash Cave in Hocking Hills State Park (near Logan), we hiked through the beautiful hemlock forest and past the frozen ice cascade, which is Cedar Falls in the winter, to Old Man's Cave, considered by some to be the most scenic attraction in the state.

Last year, with the temperature near zero and the ground covered with snow, 140 hardy hikers made the trek. This year, an estimated 600 enthusiasts, dressed in all manner of brightly colored clothing, walked the distance. Several factors may have been responsible for the unexpectedly large attendance. But surely one must be the increasing popularity of this type of recreation.

One of the encouraging aspects of the hike was the large number of children and family groups making the walk. However, two of the stoutest hikers on the trip were the two oldest — Leo Armstrong, 81, and Grandma Emma Gatewood, 79.

Grandma, wearing her crepe-soled tennis shoes, raincoat and bright red tam-o'shanter, was with the first group on the trail, as is her custom. Mr. Armstrong was with the group led by Norv Hall, recreation supervisor of the division of parks and recreation. This group included the "delegation" from Stark County. Looking hale and hearty at the end of the hike, the octogenarian made the trip much easier than some of the hikers many years younger.

There were seven groups on the trail, led by William Miller of Logan, president of the Buckeye Trail Association; Mr. Hall; five members of the division of parks and recreation staff, and two volunteers, one of whom was from the Columbus Metropolitan Park District staff. Portable radios were used to keep the various groups in contact as they strode through forests, over the hills and into the canyons.

On all sides large works of ice sculpture, looking like giant pieces of milk glass, hung from canyon walls or glistened from behind the dark green branches of screening hemlock. Ice stalactites and stalagmites added to the wintry decor of the hollows and scenic gorges.

During short rest periods, some of the leaders told of the organization of the Buckeye Trail, outlined its plans and commented on the organization's goal of establishing the trail from Cincinnati to Cleveland. Primarily through the efforts of Sen. Regula, more than a year ago, the Ohio & Erie Canal towpath in Stark County was designated officially as a segment of the Buckeye Trail.

At several scheduled halts during the hike, Melvin J. Rebholz, director of the division of parks and recreation, and his wife and daughter looked in on the hikers. I had the privilege of speaking with him and learning of the state's interest in developing the state parks for year-round use.

Sen. Regula, noting that a number of Boy Scouts were on the hike and that there were many family groups with a wide range in areas, observed that the facilities for hiking and trail riding that are a part of the Hocking Hills State Park could be made available, much closer, to the people of Stark County through the preservation of open spaces in a metropolitan park district.

"The great number of people that participated in the hike and the great distances they traveled to get there is graphic evidence of the interest people have in hiking," he said. "I had looked forward to the hike but the reality was even better than the anticipation. It was a delightful day."

Of the same opinion were two casual hiking acquaintances who passed one another at the end of the hike.

"Nice hike," said one, on his way to his car.

"Sure was!" replied the other.

Boy Scouts Plan Canal Trail

Since the earliest days of the contemporary "save and restore the canal" project, the Boy Scouts have been involved in one way or another. I won't list the ways in which troops have contributed to the program. Suffice it to say that they have. And naturally so, for the canal and its projects are ready-made for them.

From the outset of the restoration project, it was felt that the Ohio & Erie Canal towpath through Stark County would make a fine hiking trail for the Boy Scouts — safer than some of their officially recognized trails because of its distance from the highways.

It remained, however, for a Scout to get the ball rolling. Charles (Chip) Balough, chairman of the trail committee of Sippo Lodge 377, Order of the Arrow of the Boy Scouts of America, took up the trail idea as a personal project.

Chip wrote a letter to State Sen. Ralph Regula of Navarre and Mayor William Keen of Massillon, cochairmen of the Stark County Canal Lands Development Advisory Committee, asking permission for the Order of the Arrow to develop a historic trail along the canal from Lake Lucern, north of Canal Fulton, to the city limits of Massillon.

Chip said the trail would be for hiking and learning some of the history of the canal. The trail would be open to all members of the Boy Scouts of America regardless of race, creed or color. Scouts from other areas would be encouraged to participate in the program and an official patch would be designed for those who successfully met the requirements of the trail hike.

The Order of the Arrow would refer to the trail as the Lock 4 Segment of the Buckeye Trail. Stark County's canal towpath is an official section of the cross-state Buckeye Trail.

The Scouts hope, in the future, to extend their trail down the towpath to the county's southern border. In the meantime, they asked for permission to set up a camping area in the field between the canal and the Tuscarawas River at Lock 4 Park.

Chip stressed that the camping area would be under the administration of the Order of the Arrow with supervision from the Buckeye Council of the Boy Scouts. Safety precautions would be observed and each group of campers would have at least one adult present for every 15 boys.

Less than two weeks later, a letter from Cochairmen Regula and Keen to Chip informed: "On January 17, the mayor and council of the village of Canal Fulton unanimously authorized the use of village property adjacent to Lock 4 for your campsite. Therefore, we are pleased to grant permission to the Sippo Lodge of the Order of the Arrow to develop a historic trail along the Stark County canal lands as described... in your letter of January 10, 1967. We are pleased with the initiative you have shown and hope that the use of these facilities will be adequate for your purpose."

I talked with Chip last week and he was enthusiastic about the "go-ahead." He explained that there are three more administrative steps requiring approval from Scout headquarters and then the trail officially will be on its way. He is hopeful that by late spring the Order of the Arrow will be in action along the towpath.

Canal Delineations

One of my coworkers brought a book into the office the other day that had been in his family many years. It contained a number of pictures of canal boats in various settings. Because of Russell McCauley's thoughtfulness, I was able to get a better perspective of early canal traffic and related activity. Probably the most informative of these pictures accompanies this column.

The book, published in 1874, is titled *Picturesque America* or *The Land We Live In*. The title page describes it as "a delineation by pen and pencil of the mountains, rivers, lakes, forests, waterfalls, shores, canyons, valleys, cities and other picturesque features of our country... with illustrations on steel and wood by eminent American artists." The book, incidentally,

was edited by William Cullen Bryant.

The canal-boat drawings show the boats in various locations. Some are "aerial" views showing a boat or boats being towed through forested countryside. Others show the cumbersome craft within cities and one portrays two boats crossing a picturesque stone aqueduct. Of the book's 576 pictures of early America, just six feature canal scenes, further evidence of the scarcity of information, pictorial and written, dealing with the canal era.

Help the Bluebirds!

Spring certainly isn't here yet but we are over the hump of the winter. We can see March and its thaws just over the horizon. And before we know it, the birds will be back from the South — and house hunting.

Mindful of this, Homer Fulton of Lake Cable, whose idea led to the establishment of the bluebird trail along the towpath of the Ohio & Erie Canal in northwestern Stark County, already is at work making replacement homes for those in the bluebird trail that were damaged or destroyed by vandals. And he suggests that while we still are "holed up" by these long winter nights, we might give some thought to making some bluebird houses and either extending the bluebird trail along the canal or building our own trails.

Homer has agreed to supply bluebird house plans for anyone wishing to build a house. And Robert E. Ball, president of Canton Audubon Society, has agreed to mail them out in response to written requests. The society will also accept the houses for distribution if the builder desires.

February 12, 1967

They'll Read Way 'Down Canal'

Louisville, the Constitution Town, may not be a canal town but it is a major community in a canal county. And, I have learned, there are citizens of Louisville who are

138

as interested in the history and restoration of the Ohio & Erie Canal as many Stark residents who live much closer to the old waterway.

One of these is Mrs. Joyce L. Moser, who is employed by the Louisville Public Library as a librarian-decorator.

Each year, during the summer, the library conducts a reading program for children in which a map, chart, or picture is used as a chart upon which each child plots his or her individual progress in reading. The children's room is further decorated with pictures and models of the theme selected.

In recent years, the themes have tended to run to fairy tales and fantasy. But this year the library staff decided the children might learn more "of the world in which they live" if the Ohio & Erie Canal was selected as the theme.

Mrs. Moser, who describes the canal as a "wonderful part of our historical lore," believes the interests of the children will be served better by combining the summer reading program with a practical history lesson on a level the children can enjoy. She envisions construction of a large map of the canal route on which each child can plot his progress by stopping at various ports of call such as Massillon, Canal Fulton or Navarre or at numbered locks.

The climax of the summer reading program is usually a party. This year, Mrs. Moser is thinking about a picnic along the canal, probably at Lock 4 Park, where the children can see a working lock and a canal bypass.

In the meantime, she is seeking maps, charts, models, books, cards or any other pertinent information she can obtain to make the canal era display at the library more attractive and informative. Ted Findley of New Philadelphia, president of the Canal Society of Ohio, has agreed to assist her in obtaining material for the display.

It sounds like a lot of educational fun for the young patrons of the Louisville library as they read their way "down the canal."

Cubs Hike Canal

Another community in the eastern part of the county also has provided a little canal news for this week's column. And again it is the very young making the news.

Den 7 of Cub Scout Pack 36, which is East Canton based, recently hiked for a mile along the Ohio & Erie Canal south of Canal Fulton. They made the trip in conjunction with their theme of the month, which was transportation, specifically "Highways Through History."

After the hike, they made an exhibit showing the canal, towpath and lock. Using modeling clay, the boys fashioned little boats and a lock, a towpath and trees. Their den mother, Mrs. Darrell Henderson of East Canton, assisted them by coloring the clay with wall paint and watercolors and in helping them establish two levels of "water" at the lock. In observance of Boy Scout Week, the display was exhibited in the window of the Sypolt Chevrolet garage on the village square.

February 19, 1967

Waiting for the Canal To Thaw

Tired of winter and ready for spring!

Sounds like the beginning of an advertisement or commercial, doesn't it? Well, maybe it is at that. Like maybe a teaser to go fishing… along the Ohio & Erie Canal? I imagine, along about this time, there are quite a few fishermen anxious to get their lines wet in the old canal. I know at least one.

A friend of many years, Ian (Scotty) MacCartney of Perry Heights, retired recently and has more time for fishing. He went to Florida earlier in the winter, planning to stay for two or three months. But he was back home in Ohio a month later. Never one to sit around doing nothing, Scotty found Florida too "full of old fellows just shuffling around." And his unsuccessful attempts to catch some of those Florida lunkers proved to be only hard work. And so it was back to the Wonderful World of Ohio for Scotty and his wife, Audrey, where the grass is always greener except when it's covered with snow and ice.

In a recent letter, Scotty wrote: "I fish the canal quite a bit and am only waiting for spring to get started."

When I asked him if the canal was one of his favorite fishing spots, he put it this way: "Let's say it is one of my handy places."

This statement, although I'm sure it wasn't made for that purpose, supports the backers of the proposed metropolitan park district for Stark County. For they have said repeatedly that the recreational facilities, such as the canal lands and other park areas, should be "where the people are"... or as Scotty puts it, "handy."

Perhaps many Stark County residents know Scotty best as the director of the MacGregor Bagpipe Band and Dancers. Although retired, Scotty still is teaching youngsters in the band how to play the bagpipe. One of his fondest hopes, unrealized as yet, is to see a nucleus of the many bagpipers he trained through the years form an adult bagpipe band to represent the Canton area.

In the meantime, if you see a tall, slender, very erect man, with an uncovered head of white hair, striding along the canal towpath with fishing rod in hand, chances are it will be Scotty MacCartney, enjoying one of his favorite pastimes along the handy old canal.

Atlas Has Canal Maps

Maps intrigue me and I am always ready to stop and look at one. Consequently, when Rev. Richard E. Appel, pastor of Zion EUB Church, stopped up to show me a book of maps, he found me very much interested.

The book, *Harper's Atlas of American History*, with map studies by Dixon Ryan Fox, contains 128 maps, which show the progress of American life. The maps clearly picture a variety of developments in our young nation. One shows the frontier line of the United States in 1800. The frontier then stretched westward from what now is Maine to a point on the Ohio River between Kentucky and Indiana (west of Louisville) and then back to the Atlantic Ocean south of Savannah, Ga.

Especially interesting is the fact that the frontier ran due north and south along the Tuscarawas River, which served as part of the boundary line between the United States and the Indian territory, in accordance with a treaty concluded in 1785 with the Indian tribes. Ohio had not yet been admitted to the Union as a state.

One of the maps clearly shows the network of early waterways and highways east of the Mississippi River, including completed canals and those under construction.

The Ohio & Erie Canal shows up plainly as one of the major canals completed between 1826 and 1830, the period covered by the map. Several other maps also feature canals and one, of the "principal routes of trade and migration from 1840 to 1850," shows the Ohio & Erie as a major artery.

Maps like these, showing the canals of early America, are few and far between. But they graphically trace the history of our young nation as it began "to feel its oats" economically and grow swiftly to become a world power. The maps also make it clear that the canal era, although of comparatively short duration, was a period of great development and expansion in our state and nation.

February 26, 1967

It's 'Go' for Metro Park

The light is green, the signal "go" for Stark County's Metropolitan Park District. Probate Judge Reuben Z. Wise Jr. officially breathed life into the district when he found the application for its establishment "properly filed and properly before the court" and then filed a journal entry making his decision official. In so doing, he declared "the creation of the Stark County Metropolitan Park District will be conducive to the general welfare."

No legal step has been so important and so filled with potential for the development of the Ohio & Erie and Sandy and Beaver canal lands within Stark County since the deeding of the Ohio & Erie lands to the county by the State of Ohio in September of 1964 and the appointment of the Stark County Canal Lands Development Advisory Committee.

The proper sequence of events now calls for the appointment of three commissioners to organize the district. Judge Wise has indicated he will appoint them in the near future. The commissioners then will develop a park program for the county. Once the plan is established, the best way to finance it will have to be determined.

Melvin Rebholz, chief of the division of parks and recreation of the Ohio Department of Natural Resources, who came to Canton for the public hearing on the park district proposal, spoke in support of the county park system and said there will be state and federal funds available for land acquisition and development in communities that have metropolitan parks systems.

The state's park chief complimented Stark County for having built a good solid foundation of information before embarking on a metropolitan park program. This foundation consisted primarily of a parks land study completed in 1962 by a Stark County Regional Planning Commission committee and work accomplished more recently by the commission's parks committee, which is headed by State Sen. Ralph Regula and C.J. Kurlinsky, president of Stark Building Trades Council.

It is interesting to note that as Stark County gives birth to its metropolitan park district, the city of Cleveland's giant metropolitan park system is 50-plus years old.

One can only dream about what Stark County's metropolitan park system will be like 50 years from now. But one thing is certain — when Judge Wise signed it into existence, it was a great day for all who visualize (and benefit from) the many improvements to come "along the towpath."

March 5, 1967

Things Were Fine in... Metamora!

Do you remember Brigadoon — the lovely little Scottish village that was the setting for Lerner and Loewe's fanciful musical of the same name? And how once each century the village would reappear in the Scottish highlands and pick up life just where it had left off 100 years a before? Can you recall how the two young American men came upon the village and entered into its life for a "wee bit" — before Brigadoon disappeared again into the mist of the heather hills for another 100 years?

Last week two other American men traveled across the state of Ohio into the snow-daubed hills of southeastern Indiana. And, for a brief span of time, they too left the 20th century to live a few fleeting moments in a captivating little American community from out of the past.

I was one of the men and the other was State Sen. Ralph Regula of Navarre. The American Brigadoon was the delightful little Hoosier village of Metamora.

But unlike Brigadoon, Metamora's quaint charm will not disappear at the blink of an eye. One need not wait another century to see it again. For although to walk along the strong-flowing waters of the Whitewater Canal, which runs the length of the village, is to walk back through time, one need have no fear of Cinderella's clock striking.

Metamora will not vanish. It is neither Brigadoon nor Glocca Morra. It is very much a living page out of history — a tintype community from the 1840s, alive and breathing in 1967. Preserved and restored, the canal runs through one of the most scenic sections of Indiana, an area that long has been a mecca for artists, photographers and, more recently, tourists.

Metamora and the Whitewater Canal State Memorial could be a wonderful prototype for development of the Ohio & Erie and Sandy and Beaver canals in Stark County.

It was to see what the state of Indiana had done with its canal heritage that Sen. Regula, as cochairman, and I, as a member of the Stark County Canal Lands Development Advisory Committee, made the pilgrimage to Metamora.

It was a cold but bright and sunny February day when we rolled into the roadside rest park east of the village and got our first close-up view of the Whitewater

Canal. The ice-choked waterway was a ribbon of white stretching east and west from the tidy little park.

Neat, clean and nicely landscaped, the park features a good road and attractive signs. It has that spruced-up look that indicates someone cares about it. But its basic potential cannot equal that of Lock 4 Park south of Canal Fulton.

On down the highway a lock was visible — and beside it a boat. It was the "Valley Belle," a launch-type boat built by local people, which, in 13 weeks of operation in 1965, carried 4,243 passengers up and down the canal and through the lock.

The "Belle," which was in A-1 condition, was drydocked in the lock bypass, from which all water was removed for the winter. Canvas panels, securely attached, protected the boat's interior from the weather. The light-gray-stone lock and its wooden gates also were in excellent condition.

It was necessary to leave the highway and drop down into the village to see the Duck Creek Aqueduct, which was built in 1843 and reconstructed in 1949 by the Indiana Department of Conservation's division of state parks. The wooden aqueduct, in a fine state of preservation, carries the crystal clear water of the canal across Duck Creek. Its heavy timbers and arched trusses have the look of authenticity.

Stark County's canals have no aqueduct but the piers of the old aqueduct, which spanned the Tuscarawas River at the Stark-Tuscarawas county line, still exist and conceivably one could be reconstructed there, possibly as a feature of the new Metropolitan Park System.

Metamora's buildings, which are set back from both banks of the canal as it passes through the village, are quaint and picturesque. Most of them have that last-century look. One large residence overlooking the canal is a beautiful example of early American architecture, complete with all the "gingerbread." In front of one tiny store, an antique shop, an old school desk attracts the visitor's eye. In the windows of another store, paintings by local artists are displayed.

On a Sunday afternoon in February, life is relatively dormant in Metamora. Occasionally a young boy or girl will come out of a house and skip or run across the footbridges over the canal in the center of town — much as they must have done in years gone by. None of the stores was open and neither was the roller mill, which is the canalside museum. Standing at the west edge of the village, the old mill was built in 1845 and rebuilt in 1900.

As the water entered the lock opposite the mill, it activated wheels, which, through a system of gear reduction and drive shafts, operated the roller mill. The wheels and gears are on display at the mill.

In some way, Stark County may find it difficult to equal Indiana's Franklin County in bringing its canal to life. But, in other ways, it can. In some ways it can even surpass it.

Seeing is believing, however. So if you want to see what can be done to an old weedy, dried-up canal to make it young and free-flowing — really a thing of beauty — take a trip to Franklin County in Indiana. Having been there and having fallen under the village's spell of enchantment, already I find myself wondering (to paraphrase the title of a song from Finian's Rainbow) "How Are Things in Metamora?"

March 12, 1967
Riders' New Trail Adds to Canals

My teenage daughter, April, can do a split with the effortless ease of a trained gymnast. But not me. Years of dance instruction, being a cheerleader and just being a teenager make doing a split easy for her. But none of that helps me. Maybe that's why I never took up horseback riding. With my short legs, when I get aboard (whoa!) astride a broad-beamed horse, I'm already halfway into a split. And that's my limit. But split or no split, I'm actually eager to saddle up one of these days (horse willing) and trot off into a new (for me) and intriguing kind of trail adventure.

Hardly anybody knows it, but through these cold wintry months — since November — 30 horsemen have been working, mostly on weekends, to clear and mark a trail, sections of which are between the Tuscarawas River and the Ohio & Erie Canal, and between Sandy Creek and the Sandy and Beaver Canal. Their efforts have resulted in the creation of a 45-mile trail in Tuscarawas and Stark counties that can be enjoyed by both horsemen and hikers. The trail, which is 98 percent marked, can be ridden in seven hours.

Organized as the Tri-County Trail Association, the group's membership is from Stark, Tuscarawas and Carroll counties. It is fitting that they named their trail the Tri-Co Trail. "Top gun" of the trail riders is Al Zaleski of East Sparta, president and founder of the association, which now has 94 members. Al, who has been riding horses all his life, has been secretary of the Ohio Quarter Horse Association seven years.

"I love horses and I love the outdoors," Al enthuses. His healthy complexion attests to the latter.

Putting his two "loves" together, it was only natural that he should come up with the idea for the scenic horse trail. Then, last September, Al and the special brand of horsemen he calls "trail people" organized their association and began their trail.

The trail, which is in the shape of a top-heavy figure 8, has its junction at Bolivar Dam. Generally, it extends from Fohl Street in Stark County (southwest of North Industry) to just south of Zoar in Tuscarawas County and from Bolivar on the west to Sandyville and East Sparta on the east. The trail follows the Ohio & Erie Canal towpath southeastward from Bolivar a distance of four miles. For a shorter distance it also coincides with the towpath of the Sandy and Beaver Canal.

Al says the trail is now passable and much of it has been marked with red and orange markers placed on trees. In some places, metal arrows indicate turns. The oblong, 2-by-6-inch, two-color markers will prove helpful to riders and hikers.

The trail was designed so as to keep it "as natural as possible," Al says. He describes the trail as being picturesque and says most of it is on "back in" type of land. You don't have to walk or ride on any roads and, in fact, you stay as far from "civilization" as possible, Al points out with satisfaction.

Tri-Co Trail passes through strip mines, follows an old railroad bed for a ways, and then comes out of the back country for a short distance, passing right through the middle of Zoar and past the historical Zoar Gardens. It also comes within visual distance of what Al claims is one of the tallest stands of pine trees in the state.

The trail is continuous so that riders do not have to retrace their route unless they want to. But neither do they have to ride the entire 45 miles as they can select sections of varying lengths, depending on how long they wish to ride. And there are many cross trails between points on the main trail. This permits shorter rides and hikes while adding to the total number of miles available to riders. One special 3-mile trail, which loops off the main trail west of Zoar, winds through high hills and deep woods and is particularly "interesting."

Wherever hazards exist, the trail goes around them, according to Al. If a rider wishes to avoid a river fording (a standard scene in every good Western film), he can do so by taking another route. The trail people hope to make signs highlighting historical points along the trail and already have found 15 places worth marking.

Most of the land over which the trail passes is under the jurisdiction of the Muskingum Watershed Conservancy District or the State of Ohio. But some of it is private

143

property whose owners have granted the trail riders permission to use. Presently there are two staging areas on the trail. One is at Cricket Valley south of North Industry and the other is at Bolivar Dam.

The next extension of the trail will be north along the towpath of the Ohio & Erie Canal toward Navarre, according to trail-boss Zaleski. When cleared and marked, this section of the trail will permit hikers and riders to enjoy probably the most scenic section of the old waterway within Stark County.

The trail association plans to prepare maps of the trail area and make them available to the public. Members also encourage use of the trail by Boy and Girl Scouts, other youth groups and the general public.

Because of the interest and industry of a small group of volunteers, the Stark-Tuscarawas area has another recreational facility, linked usefully and effectively to our canals and their towpaths.

March 19, 1967

New Planner 'Delighted, Surprised'

"I was delighted, really. And I was surprised!"

And in these two statements there is a great deal of hope and bright promise for Stark County's canal restoration program. It works up this way:

The speaker was Mrs. Jane Staehli, new senior planner of the Stark County Regional Planning Commission. She was talking about Stark's section of the Ohio & Erie Canal, which she toured a few days before. Her reaction is important and significant, for she will head the open space program in Stark County for the commission.

Consequently, what Mrs. Staehli thinks of what has been accomplished and what remains to be done to restore and develop Stark's canal lands is important.

She and her boss, commission director Larry Summers, made the inspection tour of the canal by car, from Canal Fulton to Navarre. Although she said she would prefer to hike or bike the towpath, the auto-

mobile tour showed her enough that she is eager to see more.

During a pleasurable interview, I found myself caught up in her enthusiasm, being sold something I have been trying to sell for over two years — the canal and its historical-educational-recreational potential.

"You have here this mecca, which is much more than recreational, as I see it," Mrs. Staehli said with conviction. "It should appeal to all age groups because of its historical, educational and recreational interest in the broadest sense. The list is practically endless in recreational activities — hiking, canoeing, bicycling, etc."

The young planner, who arrived in Canton Feb. 20, is working under a federal grant to prepare a comprehensive open space plan for the county within a year. When completed, the plan will serve as a flexible guideline for the county's metropolitan park board directors in their development of the canal lands, she said.

"The canal has one of the top priority ratings for recreational development because the county already owns most of the canal lands," she said. "Step one has already been taken... I hope within a year we will see things begin to snowball."

I have a hunch we will.

Gift From Sportsmen

Several months ago, Paul Marks, foreman in charge of the canal reconstruction, and I spoke to members of the Game Reserve Association about the canal, plans for its development and its needs.

Last week, the association got in touch with Paul again — to tell him the membership was contributing $75 to meet current needs on the canal or to make improvements associated with fishing activity. Paul accepted the check from Richard Stambaugh, association president, at its annual landowners appreciation dinner.

Scouts Help Bluebirds

Twenty-five new bluebird houses were placed along the Ohio & Erie Canal towpath recently by members of Boy Scout Troop 20 at Dueber Methodist Church. Scoutmaster Eugene Nolte said the Scouts were assisted and directed by Scout committeemen Owen Nolte and Lowell Riley. They began the project last fall as part of their conservation project.

Others are making birdhouses, too. Some 30 persons had requested plans for houses as of March 4. Robert Ball, Canton Audubon Society president, has said the group will collect the houses and place them properly on a bluebird trail if the builders will contact him.

March 26, 1967

Action Along the Sandy & Beaver

One day in May or June of 1965, I received a telephone call from a resident of Magnolia who wondered if anyone associated with the Ohio & Erie Canal restoration project in Stark County could help him get a similar project started on the Sandy and Beaver Canal.

His name, he said, was Glenn Fishel. I assured him of our interest and told him some of us would assist him in various ways. Since then a lot of water has flowed through the Sandy and Beaver from Waynesburg to Magnolia. And today Glenn Fishel is the newly elected first president of Sandy Valley Canal Society, Inc.

Other officers of the society, which held its charter meeting earlier this month, are Donald C. Shine of Magnolia, first vice president; A.R. Elson of Magnolia, second vice president; Mrs. James France of Waynesburg, secretary; W.F. Janson of Canton, treasurer, and James A. France of Waynesburg, historian. Irvin F. Fritchley of Magnolia, Paul E. Muckley of Waynesburg, George W. Colton of Waynesburg and Joseph L. Tovissi of Magnolia are trustees.

Purposes of the society are: to collect and preserve for posterity information relating to the history and memory of the Sandy and Beaver Canal in the Sandy Valley area and other canals; accumulate and catalog such books, papers, documents, relics and articles of interest as will tend to illustrate the history of the canals; receive by deed, devise, bequest or other means, property having historical significance in relation to the canals; devote all such property and other historical material to the education of schoolchildren; awaken the interest of adults in the history of the Sandy and Beaver and other canals.

Additional purposes of the society are to: preserve and restore as much of the canal in the Sandy Valley area as possible; establish a recreational park and facilities in the vicinity of the canal; conduct the affairs of the society without profit, using all money and property received by the society for the benefit of the people in the Sandy Valley area.

Any person who shows an interest in the history of the Sandy and Beaver and other canals is eligible for membership. Glenn said the drive for charter members, which started last week, will close July 1.

"As the membership expands, committee work will be assigned in the various areas of development," he explained.

In regard to collecting canal memorabilia, Glenn said the society will make duplicates of pictures or papers loaned to it and preserve the duplicates for display in a hoped-for museum in the area. Some historical canal material already has been promised to the society by area residents.

Waxing enthusiastic about the cooperation of the people in Sandy Valley, Glenn declared, "All of the organizations in our valley have been very active in organizing the canal society. We have had wonderful cooperation from all of them. I have encountered widespread interest in the canal wherever I have spoken about it. Many people I have met on the street have asked how the project is progressing and what the plans are."

The cooperating organizations listed by the society are the Sandy Valley Chamber of Commerce, Sandy Valley Woman's Club, Sandy Valley Junior Woman's Club, Magnolia Grange, Magnolia Lions Club, Waynesburg Lions Club, Waynesburg Rotary Club, Waynesburg Village Council, Magnolia Village Council, Waynesburg Parent-Teacher Association and Sandy Valley Ruritan Club.

The new president said determination of water rights is the society's first concern. This will be followed by land acquisition, locating and acquiring access routes and determining how best to use the land.

"Our main interest right now, is preserving and beautifying what we have," he said. "We plan to clean up the towpath for hiking and the water for boating."

There is a fully watered mile and a half of canal between the dam in Sandy Creek at Waynesburg and Elson's flouring mill at Magnolia, which is ideal for development of an intervillage ribbon park. The recreational potential of the canal for southeastern Stark County is excellent.

April 2, 1967

Boating Is BIG on Britain's Canals

Several times since this column first appeared in *The Repository*, I have written about the canals of Europe —particularly those of England. The English canals are a little older than their American counterparts. Traffic was in full swing in the late 1700s, while activity on the American waterways didn't peak until half a century later.

But the canals of the two nations actually have much in common. Today there even is a similarity in the efforts to preserve and restore the canals in the two countries. But, in this respect also, the British apparently are ahead of us.

According to an article in the *Christian Science Monitor*, Britain's canals are making a comeback. Lionel Munk, chairman of the Inland Waterways Association in Great Britain, claims Britain is floating into its second canal age.

The following paragraphs are quoted from the *Christian Science Monitor*:

"A stroll along a towpath any fine weekend supports his (Mr. Munk's) thesis. The quiet-loving pleasure seeker is bringing the waterways back to life.

"More than 1,000 miles of these placid streams lace the countryside. Their away-from-it-all appeal today contrasts with the brisk commercial traffic of the late 1700s that opened up the canals and kept their

waters ruffled. Sixty years after that the railways took over as freight carriers and bought up most of these watery routes. Many miles of them have been abandoned or closed to navigation.

"Mr. Munk warns that if the Ministry of Transport lets any of the remaining waterways go down the drain, 'future generations will mourn a lost heritage.' Right now appreciation is keen. The canals boast at least 100 boatyards along their banks for pleasure craft. And new canals are in the picture for Thamesmead, a New Town planned on the Thames at Greenwich to accommodate 60,000 Londoners."

It is interesting to note the extensive use of the British canals for pleasure craft. In Stark County our two canals have a fine, but almost untapped, potential for pleasure boating. Properly regulated and controlled, this form of canal recreation could boom quickly. In time, small-boat canal travel between Massillon and Akron and Akron and Cleveland may be possible. In the meantime, there are a few obstacles to remove.

Conference on Canals

The morning after I wrote the preceding item about the canals in England, I received a letter containing a clipping on the identical subject. But the clipping was from a different newspaper. It was sent by Donald C. Steiner of Canton. Mr. Steiner, an attorney, had just returned from a business trip to England. While there, he read an article in the *London Times* of March 20, which he thought might be of interest to readers of this column.

Thanks to Mr. Steiner, here it is:

"The canals that lie neglected at the centres of Britain's cities may soon be turning into Arcadian scenes of leisure and amusement, if certain enterprising people get their way. Progress in this direction has already been made in London. Councillor Illtyd Harrington of the GIC has been looking into the possibilities, as chairman of the London Canals Committee, and he tells us they have at last found a way to overcome the legal difficulties involved in giving the public access to the canalside.

" 'Work has recently begun on a canalside walk near the Warwick Estate in Paddington,' he tells us. 'Mrs. Peggy Jay will be putting up a railing there to launch it officially next month. Eventually we hope to have boating and fishing on the canal between the zoo and Little Venice, where you will be able to walk 15 miles without seeing or hearing a motor car.'

"Birmingham City Council also has plans to develop part of their canal system, landscaping the canals into the new housing of the city's big development areas.

"Mr. R.B. Cowels, Birmingham's deputy surveyor, and Mr. Harrington will be describing their plans... at a three-day national conference on the waterways of Britain. The conference, organized by the Inland Waterways Association, is the first of its kind. It will be attended by about 170 people, mostly planning officers of local authorities, who are interested in developing waterways for recreation. Mr. John Morris, Joint Parliamentary Secretary at the Ministry of Transport, will be there to put the Government view."

To readers of "Along the Towpath," much of this should sound familiar. For the British program to restore the canals is similar in many ways to ours here in Stark County. And, although they are ahead of us, the goal is the same. It's nice to know that others share our concern for the preservation of the historical waterways and our desire to develop them for the educational and recreational benefit of our people.

April 9, 1967

Louisville Sportsmen Pledge Manpower

Volunteers Push Canal Boat Nearer Stark's Shore

Stark County is going to get its canal boat!

One of two major bottlenecks — money and manpower — that prevented construction from getting under way has been eliminated.

Manpower suddenly has become avail-able. The men, hammers and saws in hand, are ready to go — awaiting only completion of a scale model being built and delivery of the donated tough white oak timbers to the construction site.

This is how it happened:

I was looking over my personal file of "Along the Towpath" the other night, feeling rather disconsolate and a bit frustrated because it was just two years ago that I proposed in the column that a canal boat be built for use on Stark County's rewatered section of the Ohio & Erie Canal.

Admittedly, it was a dream — to build a canal boat, authentic as possible, which would be towed by horse-and-mule team up and down the canal between Canal Fulton and Massillon. Visitors would come from everywhere to see what must surely be the only historical craft of its kind in the nation actually in operation. It would be a real Disneyland ride right here on our own Ohio & Erie, which would take us back to the Indian days.

But two years! And the first two boards were yet to be nailed together.

Then the phone rang. It was Jim Cozy, whom I hadn't seen for a good many years. Jim, who now resides near Louisville, and I were neighbors when we were kids and members of the old Columbus Avenue "gang" back in the '20s and early '30s.

It was good to hear from Jim again. But it was what I heard that really excited me. Jim is president of the Louisville Sportsman's Club, and the club, he said, would like to help in someway on the canal restoration project. Did I have any ideas that they might adopt as a club project?

I thought a moment and then, jokingly, said, "Sure. How about building our canal boat for us?"

"You know, we just might do that," Jim replied. "Let me talk it over with some of the boys."

I couldn't believe what I was hearing because all our efforts to get an organization to build the boat had failed.

"You really think you could do it?" I asked, half expecting him to admit that be was just pulling my leg.

"If we take it on as a club project, we'll build your boat," Jim said emphatically. "We are fortunate enough to have a group

147

of skilled men... who are capable of carrying out this project."

Since that first phone call, there have been trips to Canal Fulton, Navarre, New Philadelphia and Cleveland, and many more phone calls to ready plans to get construction under way.

Jim, who has been shown two model canal boats and pictures of many others, now is building his own — tiny plank by tiny plank. It will serve as the exact detailed scaled model for the finished boat.

"We have 200 members... and we expect that 20 to 30 of them, working at various times, will spend about 400 man hours in constructing the boat," Jim estimated. "Some of our projects are to promote the club and some are strictly a service to the public. We expect no monetary return for this project. This is a conservation project as far as our club is concerned. We will be helping to bring back some of the history of Stark County."

Member Roy Preece, who lives near Canal Fulton, will work with Jim on the engineering and construction of the model. Both men are employees of the engineering shop at The Hoover Company in North Canton.

I asked Jim how long he figures it would take to build the boat. It really wasn't a fair question, for the last canal freighter like the one the club will build was constructed nearly 100 years ago.

Jim answered it this way:

"The men will be working in their spare time and this will govern the length of time required to build the boat. But I can tell you this. There has been a considerable amount of interest developed among our group as we discussed and planned the construction of the boat."

The club's offer involved a great deal of volunteer time and effort and some money.

It demonstrates something else, too, when members of a club from the eastern side of the county will drive 20 miles to build a boat that should be a source of pride and enjoyment for all residents of the county.

Maybe it's a little premature, but hadn't somebody ought to start looking for a bottle of champagne to christen out canal boat?

April 16, 1967
The Search for Recollections

In searching into the past, into another century, to learn the realities of an earlier era, one must seek out old records, old books and senior citizens.

The senior citizens are by far the most interesting source of information. Sometimes they may not be as accurate as reports written at the time of a historical event. For the process of aging often tends to erode the memory. But they ARE interesting! And it is fascinating to probe into their recollections of an earlier America in which they were eyewitnesses to events we want to know about today.

Last week I had the privilege, along with Ted Findley of New Philadelphia, president of the Canal Society of Ohio, of interviewing two very senior, senior citizens in our search for information about the canal era of Ohio.

In New Philadelphia, we talked with Edward R. (Uncle Ed) Reichman, who will be 95 years old in June. I asked the questions and Ted recorded the interview on tape. We used the same technique in North Canton the next day when we talked with Frederick George Croad, who was born September 13, 1863, during the Civil War. He will be 104 years young on his next birthday and is in remarkably good health.

Both men are residents of homes for the aged.

With Uncle Ed, we hit pay dirt. He knew quite a bit about the canal from firsthand observation and even built a model canal boat right after the 1913 flood, which ended the canal era. Our tip that Mr. Croad knew a lot about the canal proved to be erroneous. But interviewing a man who is approaching his 104th birthday is an experience in itself.

Uncle Ed Reichman began to work in the old Minnich mine near the canal town of Tuscarawas when he was about 12 years old. He recalled that this was during the administration of President Grover Cleveland. He was born "right close to the canal" near Lock 16, and when he said that he drove mules as a boy we thought he meant he drove mules that towed the canal boats. But he set us straight on this — he meant that he drove the mules that worked in the coal mine.

Despite his infirmities, Uncle Ed's mind is clear and his memory is surprisingly good. He recalled that the canal boats "went right past my house." Asked about the canal packets — the passenger boats — he said, "Every so often they'd go up and down. Yes, the women would be on them too. I used to know all those 'canal boaters.' But I sort of forget some of their names now."

In answer to Ted's question about loading coal on the canal freighters, Uncle Ed described the loading process and said, "I think they carried about 70 tons."

He recalled the trains of canal boats, how they were snubbed together and how, loaded with wheat, they would be towed up the branch canal to Uhrichsville.

When we told Uncle Ed that we are going to build a full-size canal boat in Stark County, his eyes lighted up and he exclaimed, "You are?"

Apparently not sure that he heard us right, he asked, "You're going to build a new one?"

We assured him that we were and then asked if he would like to ride on it.

"If I'd be able, I'd like to ride on it," he replied, favoring us with his brightest smile of the afternoon.

Mr. Croad was unable to tell us much about the canals. Apparently he could have replied truthfully that all he knew about them was what he read in the newspaper, for he has been reading *The Repository* since 1883, some 84 years.

He was born in England near the River Kent but, despite the fact that England has many canals still in use today, he recalls little about them.

Asked what he remembered about the McKinley era in Canton, the diminutive centenarian disclosed that President McKinley's mother was "one of the best friends I ever had."

"I could tell you a whole pile of stuff about that but it would fill a book," he declared. With his fantastic recall of names and events and the rapid-fire way he speaks,

it probably wouldn't take him long to fill that book.

Mr. Croad did hike the towpath a year or two ago as a member of a senior citizen group that visited Lock 4 and hiked a short distance along the canal. And he out walked many of his companions who were two or three decades younger.

In all of his 103 years, Mr. Croad never rode on a canal boat. But chances are very good that he will be able to ride on Stark County's promised canal boat either shortly before or shortly after his 104th birthday in September. And if he does, he certainly should be an honorary passenger.

Site Selected

Stark County's canal boat will be constructed by the Louisville Sportsman's Club at canalside just off Canal Street in Canal Fulton, opposite the Parker Motors, Inc., garage. The construction site is a short distance south of the village square. Jim Cozy, president of the club, said he expects work on laying the boat's keel will get under way this week.

April 23, 1967

Conference in Captain's Quarters

"The water pressure is from the outside in."

"Don't forget your expansion and swelling. You need some compensating clearance there."

"What about the stem?" (Answer) — "You'll have to laminate it."

"How about red lead?" (Answer) — "Fine."

Have you guessed what these questions and comments, heard at a recent meeting in Cleveland Heights, are all about?

If not, here are a few more:

"The block coefficient must be pretty close to nine-tenths."

"It has absolutely no elasticity."

"You should always paint the seams with a thin prime coat."

"Caulking? Drive it up snug."

"What are you going to fasten the planks

149

with? The outer half of your planks are splayed. Remember, we're working with green white oak."

Assuming you are a regular reader of this column, the last sentence surely told you what was being discussed at the meeting. The men, seated about the retired shipmaster with the close-cropped white hair, were talking shipbuilding or, more accurately, canal-boat building.

Present were State Sen. Ralph Regula, cochairman of the Stark County Canal Lands Development Advisory Committee; Paul Baird, president of Notnac Mfg. Company of Canton, who almost single-handedly "collected" the white oak trees needed for Stark County's canal boat: Paul Marks, foreman of canal reconstruction in the county; Jim Cozy, president of Louisville Sportsman's Club, whose organization is going to build the boat, and this writer.

The man they came to see was Herbert W. Dosey, who, retired from the sea, is chairman of the board of the Marine Museum of the Great Lakes Historical Society at Vermilion and corresponding secretary of the Canal Society of Ohio.

Capt. Dosey, a sailor 54 years, started his career as a cabin boy in 1913 and, at 26, was the youngest skipper on the Great Lakes. He sailed on a seagoing line in the coffee trade and "skippered" a number of big private yachts out of the port of New York. He also had been trial captain of naval vessels, including mine sweepers, built on the Great Lakes.

And he is interested in canal boats. In fact, he constructed a model of one on display in the marine museum.

In just a short time, with a few meaningful to-the-point words directed at problems bugging the Stark delegation of would-be boat builders, Capt. Dosey gave the canal-boat project a substantial push forward.

While gathering up plans and drawings for the canal boat as the conference drew to a close, Jim Cozy asked the captain if he would be free this summer "to come down a time or two" to check up on the construction of the boat.

The veteran shipmaster replied, "I will be glad to."

April 30, 1967
Canal Boat Gets Generous Gift

"As a kid, I had a lot of fun on the canal... the kind of fun kids today miss out on." Because he did have fun and is "a canal buff to a degree," Frank C. Wier of Newcomerstown made possible a generous gift to the canal-boat fund.

I learned of the gift last week when I received a call from John C. Lantz, president of Midstate Industrial Trucks, Inc., of Massillon. Mr. Lantz informed me that Mr. Wier, who is associated with the firm, suggested the gift from the company. He told me just enough about Mr. Wier that I wanted to meet and talk with him about the canal. When we did meet and talk, I learned the canal boat's benefactor had been a Canton resident 44 years and was superintendent of labor and materials at Timken Roller Bearing Company prior to his retirement.

As Mr. Wier reminisced about his boyhood along the canal at Newcomerstown, he recalled a Sunday School picnic when he rode on a canal excursion boat, pulled by horses, from Newcomerstown to Gnadenhutten and back. He also remembered seeing the state maintenance boats on the canal and their crews at work.

As a young boy, he was impressed by the sight of farmers using their pitchforks to pitch fish out of the canal when the lock gates were being repaired. It was necessary to drain a section of the canal to repair the locks and this would leave the fish exposed to the farmers and their pitchforks.

Mr. Wier asked me if I had ever seen a picture of a sailboat on the canal. "No," I said. "I've seen pictures of rowboats, canoes, many kinds of canal boats, a motorboat, a pontoon boat and even a steamboat — but not a sailboat."

The canal could hardly be considered good sailing water but he assured me he had a picture of his father sailing a small skiff on the canal near Newcomerstown in 1902. He produced the picture and it accompanies this column today.

Mr. Wier surprised me with another bit

of interesting information. When I asked him if he knew where we might locate a picture of a canal-boat bilge pump, he said he knew of a pump that had been preserved but he wasn't just sure of its location. If he can locate it, it may serve as a model for the bilge pumps to be built on Stark County's canal boat.

Motor Is Donated

Several weeks ago, this column told of the need for a motor to be used in generating electricity to illuminate Lock 4 Park south of Canal Fulton and used in conjunction with a waterwheel built by Paul S. Marks, foreman in charge of canal reconstruction. The response was gratifying and Paul's problem was solved by the American Mine Door Company of 2037 Dueber Ave. SW. The firm donated the first of several mo-tors offered by individuals and organizations. The motor soon will be converting waterpower to electricity, which, in turn, will bring light to the park.

May 7, 1967
Canals Do Things for Parks

Canals and parks — they seem to go together like ice cream and cake, especially in the spring of 1967. Rivers are wonderful and wild rivers are superb — the wilder the better. For the active nature lover, they can hardly be surpassed in appeal. But for parks, where people leisurely stroll along a footpath, stopping to look at the flowers or the birds or some form of aquatic life, still waters are tops in appeal.

That's why canals, in all their winding beauty and almost imperceptible slow-moving currents, are so ideally suited for central cores of park systems. Their relatively narrow width and shallow depth (four feet) make them comparatively safe. Most any able-bodied adult could wade in and rescue any child who accidentally fell into the water.

Canals are photogenic, too. And that's why, with the advent of spring, newspaper writers and photographers get out of the office and do photo-features about canal parks.

One of the most interesting features I have seen recently appeared in the April 23 issue of *The New York Times* under the byline of Hilda MacDonald. The headline read "Springtime Beside the Delaware at New Hope." "The Delaware" is the Delaware Canal and New Hope is in Bucks County in eastern Pennsylvania. I have written about this canal before because one can point to it and say: "Look, that's what we could have here in Stark County."

Accompanying the *Times* article is one of the loveliest water-and-woods still life photographs I have seen. Beautiful trees of considerable age form a vaulted arbor above the tranquil canal waters, which serve to mirror the leafy tunnel. The all-grass towpath is alternately shaded and sun-flecked.

In the article, the writer describes the coming of spring to the canal environs: "The dogwood covers the hills, woods and fields with a blaze of white. Later, peach and apple orchards blanket the sloping land with pink and white, and rhododendrons bloom in heavy masses on rocky hillsides."

By developing well-sodded canal banks and towpath, erosion on Stark County's Ohio & Erie Canal could be reduced greatly or eliminated, thus helping to prevent muddying of the canal's water. Trees planted on the far side of the towpath could, in years to come, duplicate the Delaware Canal scenery. And beautification through the use of rhododendrons and other flowers and trees can be accomplished as easily on the Ohio & Erie as on any other canal.

The following from the *New York Times* article could apply almost perfectly to the Canal Fulton vicinity:

"There is beauty here in every season… always open country, winding lanes, panoramic spreads of hills and valleys, creeks and ponds, little towns and the ever-present Delaware River (Tuscarawas River). In the middle of this enticing area is New Hope (Canal Fulton). It lies on both the Delaware River (Tuscarawas River) and the Delaware Canal (Ohio & Erie Canal), and they add extra joy to strolling its streets.

Many of the town's early homes are now occupied by picturesque shops (Canal Fulton residents take note). Also an 18th-century grist mill has been converted into the Bucks County Playhouse, while the Parry Mansion, built in the late 18th century by Benjamin Parry, a mill owner, is now owned by the New Hope Historical Society and houses arts and crafts exhibits."

The Delaware Canal is now part of the Theodore Roosevelt State Park and barges carry tourists rather than coal as they did in the last century. In the summer, excursions leave New Hope for a 5-mile tow to a picnic spot near Center Bridge. This, too, can be largely duplicated in Stark County.

Another spring canal park event, an annual one, is the walk led by U.S. Supreme Court Justice William O. Douglas —along the Chesapeake and Ohio Canal. This year the justice and his wife, leading 200 persons, set out from Oldtown, Maryland, April 29, on a hike to Paw Paw, West Virginia, 10 miles down the Potomac River. It was the 13th year the justice headed the hikers. The hikes are designed to arouse interest in creating a park in the Potomac River Valley and specifically in making the canal a national historic park.

Before starting off on the hike this year, Justice Douglas said, "The time has arrived for an organized program in the Potomac Valley. We can make the valley a showplace."

Canals and parks — in Pennsylvania it's the Delaware Canal and a state park; in Maryland and West Virginia it's the Chesapeake and Ohio Canal and a proposed national park; in Indiana, it's the Whitewater Canal and a state park, and here in Ohio it's the Ohio & Erie Canal and probably the Stark County Metropolitan Park. Our park, no less than the others, can be made a thing of beauty, of interest, of history — and just as much a showplace as the others.

Seedlings for Scenery

The Louisville Sportsman's Club has donated 700 evergreens to the Stark County Canal Lands Development Advisory Committee for use in beautifying the canal environs.

The seedlings have been planted temporarily by the Boy Scouts of Troop 120, sponsored by the North Nimishillen School Parent-Teacher Association. Their work, performed as part of their requirements to obtain soil and water conservation merit badges, is the latest fine example of volunteer service to the canal restoration project by Boy Scouts of the area.

Builders Begin

The cradle for the keel needed for building the canal boat was erected on the construction site off Canal Street in Canal Fulton last week. Members of the Louisville Sportsman's Club were to begin construction of the boat's hull Saturday.

May 14, 1967
Have Your Badge?

Want to be a canal-boat boss and help to restore the Ohio & Erie Canal? You can be — and wear a badge to prove it.

The Louisville Sportsman's Club is soliciting help of all kinds to advance its canal-boat-building project. Since the club accepted the responsibility for building the boat for the county, things really have begun to hum.

Club president Jim Cozy said contributions of labor, time, historic objects and money are needed to build and furnish the boat. In recognition of donations, badges will be given to contributors. Contributions with a value up to $5 will bring the donor a yellow badge with black lettering, while anything over $5 will rate a white badge with red letters. Large lettering in the center reads "Canal Boat Boss." Around the periphery are the words " Restore the Ohio Erie Canal."

The buttons can be obtained from members of the Louisville Sportsman's Club, Louisville Lions Club and the Canal Fulton Rotary Club. The sportsman's club would like to see the wearing of the badges become the "in" thing this spring and summer.

The first badge was sent to E.H. (Jerry)

Ebel of St. Petersburg, Florida. Jerry, who is 80-plus and a member of the sportsman's club, divides his time between Florida and Ohio. He left for Florida shortly after making a contribution to the fund, saying "I want the first badge."

So, if you want to be a boss and want to be "in" this summer, just get one of the badges and be sure to wear it when you visit the boat-building site at Canal Fulton. It will make you BIG.

At Last — a Stamp!

Back in October of 1965, this column featured a picture and report on the fifth annual exhibition sponsored by the Stark County Stamp Club. The column described displays of postal cards bearing canal scenes, canal-port postal marks, etc. I visited the exhibit and, after seeing the great variety of stamps on almost every subject, said: "They ought to make a stamp with a canal boat on it. After all, the canal and its boats were significant in the development of our country."

Well, they finally did make one, "they" being the Post Office Department. The new five-center honors the Erie Canal sesquicentennial. The Erie Canal was begun July 4, 1817, and the new stamp will be issued on the Fourth of July in Rome, New York, where the first dirt was dug on that day 150 years ago.

The stamp is not at all like I would have designed it. It is more impressionistic than realistic. But it does get the message across and it is a canal boat stamp. I would have preferred to see a profile of one of the distinctive freighters like the one we are building here in Stark County — with a mule team on the towpath pulling it into a lock.

But the horizontal stamp, which we should be seeing in a couple of months, shows just the stern of a canal boat. On it are the words "Erie Canal" in red. Beneath this, in black, are the dates "1817-1967." The cabin is light blue and a black ladder leans against it. The tiller is black and the hull is red. The water and sky are dark blue. Collectors desiring first-day cancellations may send addressed envelopes to the Postmaster at Rome, New York, 13440.

Ohio Bluebird Trail

Mrs. Dorothy Corner, historian of the Ohio Gourd Society, who was featured in "Along the Towpath" May 29, 1966, reports that considerable interest in promoting the Ohio Bluebird Trail was shown at the spring meeting of the society's Beta Chapter in Dover. Among the exhibitors of bluebird houses made of gourds were members of Girl Scout Cadette Troop No. 346 of Canton. This was the first Girl Scout troop to hike the Ohio & Erie Canal area near Lock 4. Their leader is Mrs. Walter J. Gowins.

See It Now

Probably the largest collection of model canal boats ever to be put together in this section of the state will be on display at the exhibits building of the Central Plaza. The boats, along with other exhibits associated with the Stark County canal-boat building project, have been collected by the Louisville Sportsman's Club, sponsors of the display.

May 21, 1967
A Man and His Museum

There's a little white frame building in Canal Fulton that reminds one of a two-story, slightly overgrown dollhouse. "Cute" would be a good way to describe it. It has a large clock over the street entrance and on the clock's face are the words "Old Canal Days Museum." Whenever the tiny museum's curator is at home, its latchstring is out.

Clyde Gainey is owner and curator of the museum. As a member of the Stark County Canal Lands Development Advisory Committee, Clyde has been active in planning the reconstruction of the Ohio & Erie Canal within the county. His interest in collecting memorabilia of the canal dates back only to August of 1964, when Canal Fulton celebrated its sesquicentennial.

"That put the burr under my tail," Clyde said.

It was about that time that he built his model canal boat, one of the finest in the area, which now is a feature exhibit in his museum.

As soon as the townspeople and area residents learned of Clyde's new interest, they began to bring him photographs of canal scenes, which he copied and enlarged. They also brought other items pertaining to canal history and soon Clyde and his wife had to find someplace else for the exhibits or get out of the house themselves.

A lot of people were attracted by Clyde's historical booth at the sesquicentennial and they continued to be interested in his hobby afterwards.

"It sort of struck the hearts of a lot of them," Clyde explains.

Looking around for a place to put his "canal collection," Clyde decided to use the small frame storage building at the back of his property. The building, at one time, belonged to the late Dr. Hiram Dissinger, who Clyde describes as a typical old-fashioned country doctor who "brought me into the world 72 years ago."

To conduct his medical practice by visiting families, Dr. Dissinger had a horse and buggy. To take care of his horse and keep his buggy in good condition, the doctor employed a man who lived in what is now the museum.

So much for the history of the structure.

When Clyde went to work on it, he lowered the upper floor to allow more headroom. Then he added a porch on the front and a stoop on the back. He cleaned it, polished it and shined it, arranged his exhibits neatly and effectively and now keeps it neat as a pin. As long as he is at home, the museum is open free to the public. Clyde has a register, which he likes visitors to sign, and he enjoys seeing them enthuse over his record of the "old canal days."

And more and more people are enjoying the museum. When groups go to the Canal Fulton area to hike the canal, they almost always stop to visit Clyde and see the museum.

Paul Marks, foreman in charge of canal reconstruction, conducts many of the tour groups along the canal, particularly school classes, and generally makes sure they see Lock 4, the canal boat, now under construction at canalside in Canal Fulton, and Clyde's museum.

Seventy-six pupils, members of the seventh-grade history classes at Loren E. Souers Junior High School in Canton, made the tour under the supervision of Principal Richard R. Dowding and two teachers, Miss Janyth Cooley and Mrs. Olivia Dearth, all of Canton. On another day a busload of pupils from Roosevelt Elementary School made the tour.

Last Tuesday, a group from the Canton Garden Center combined their annual bird hike along the canal with visits to the boat building site and the museum. Hiking the section of the canal between Crystal Springs and Butterbridge Road, where the canal is well removed from the highway, members of the group saw 34 varieties of birds. Observing that the orioles "sang beautifully" while the hikers ate their lunches at Lock 4 Park, a member said they all enjoyed the hike "thoroughly."

Mrs. W. Lewis Schaffer of East Canton, hike leader, was particularly interested in the tour, the canal boat and the museum. Her grandmother, the late Mrs. Christine Krabill, who had resided east of Louisville, was born in France in 1840 and, with her parents, rode a canal boat down the Ohio & Erie Canal from Cleveland to Canal Fulton when she was eight years old.

It is an interesting twist that Louisville, many of whose early families arrived there via canal boat to Canal Fulton, is the home of the sportsman's club, which is providing the bulk of the manpower to build Stark County's Canal Boat '67.

May 28, 1967
Follow-up on a Canal Hike

Much of the time, writing a "follow-up" story about a news event is pretty cut and dried — not the most exciting assignment in journalism. But sometimes something occurs after an event that really is exciting news. That's the way it is with the follow-up story I am writing today.

In last week's "Along the Towpath," I told of 76 seventh-grade pupils at Loren E. Souers Junior High School who hiked the Ohio & Erie Canal towpath between Lock 4 Park and Canal Fulton, had a look at Canal Boat '67, which is under construction, and visited Clyde Gainey's Old Canal Days Museum in the village.

Now comes the follow-up.

Do you know what those kids did? They returned to their school and members of the two classes went around to the other 12 seventh-grade classes to tell them what they had seen and they appealed to them to chip in to a fund to help build the canal boat.

The idea to raise the money originated with Tom Baker, 13, son of Mr. and Mrs. Donald Baker, while he and Principal Richard R. Dowding were walking along the towpath during the class hike. Back at the school, the Student Council representatives took up Tom's idea and through democratic procedure, decided to go ahead with the fund-raising. Tom was appointed chairman of the drive.

Seventh-grade teachers Miss Janyth Cooley and Mrs. Olivia Dearth gave the campaign an assist by suggesting canal-boat badges be made for contributors. Tom's father came up with the slogan, "Keep the Boat Afloat," which was printed on each badge.

Then, as sort of a climax to their fund-raising project, Ted Findley of New Philadelphia, president of the Canal Society of Ohio, spoke to the seventh graders and showed them film slides of canal history. In a special presentation during the assembly, Principal Dowding turned over to Ted the nickels, dimes, dollars, quarters and pennies the pupils had collected for the canal-boat fund, plus a check from the class treasury. Believe it or not, the magnificent total was $93.

With the Boat Builders

Cooperation and generosity are the lubricants to keep the boat-building "machine" operating and the project moving ahead. Several examples of both were noted last week.

Although they haven't quite reached that stage yet, the builders have been looking ahead to the time when they will need to steam and bend the tough oak planks to construct the bow and stern of the canal boat. So what happened? When the East Ohio Gas Company was apprised of the need, it generously made available a large section of steel pipe, 15 feet long and 20 inches in diameter.

Next, a special piece of steel large enough to seal one end of the pipe was needed. This was necessary so the pipe could be filled with water, planks inserted into it and sufficient heat applied to create steam. The Buck Hill Iron Works had a piece of steel that would do the job — presto, it was donated!

Before the green oak lumber being used for the boat's hull is bolted or nailed into place, it is painted with a powerful preservative. But painting it by hand is time-consuming and sloppy work. So Paul Baird, procurement expediter for the project, decided a tank was needed so the boat timbers could be immersed in the preservative. A visit by Paul to the C.R. Kurtz, Inc., heating and ventilating shop at Canal Fulton resulted in a galvanized metal tank 6½ feet long by 14 inches wide and 8 inches deep — compliments of Mr. Kurtz.

Then, because the preservative is "pretty wicked stuff" to handle, Paul decided a pair of heavy rubber gloves would be in order to protect the hands of the workmen. So Paul visited Canton's Wilson Rubber Company. Now there are three pair of sturdy neoprene gloves ready for use in dousing the lumber whenever needed — a donation of the rubber firm.

And so it goes. Cooperation and generosity — they're wonderful.

June 4, 1967

It Wasn't Exactly a Pony Express

"You walk a while and then you ride a while. Then you walk a while and ride a

while again."

The speaker was describing an experience of when he was a lad of 10. It wasn't riding a bicycle in hilly terrain. It was, in fact, an experience shared by few persons alive today.

Russell Darst of Canton was telling how he worked as a boy, during his summer vacations, as a mule driver or mule skinner on the Ohio & Erie Canal. That was about eight years before the big flood of 1913 ended the canal's usefulness as an artery of commerce.

Russell was born 71 years ago, alongside the canal at Lockport, which today is the south side of New Philadelphia. His grandfather, Jacob Darst, a prominent Civil War veteran in the New Philadelphia area, owned and operated two canal boats, the S.C. Cline, built in 1858, and the Levy Sargent, built in 1868. So, perhaps it was only natural that Russell would want to be a mule skinner when he was old enough.

Astride a mule, or walking beside one, he traveled from New Philadelphia south to Portsmouth and north to Cleveland, the entire length of the Ohio & Erie.

The freighters carried everything in the way of cargo but principally coal and lumber. Nearly every canal boat carried four mules. Two towed the boat while the other two were quartered in the midship stable. Mules were preferred to horses, Russell remembered, because they had a steady gait.

Russell ate and slept on the canal boat. The aftercabin contained the kitchen and sleeping quarters for the captain and his wife, while the crew slept in the cabin in the bow.

When it came to repairing leaks, Russell said, the canal boats provided their own repair material — mule manure. Tamped into the proper place to stop the leak, the manure did the job effectively until permanent repairs could be made.

During his trips, the young mule skinner crossed the aqueduct over the Tuscarawas River north of Bolivar and the floating towpath across Summit Lake near Akron. Neither exists today.

Sometimes the canal freighters would travel all night if there were adequate moonlight.

Russell laughs in telling of what he says was a daily occurrence — getting "doused." Usually, the dunking would occur when he misjudged the distance in leaping from the boat to the towpath. Probably his most dangerous fall into the canal occurred before he was a mule skinner, when he was just 5. While playing near his home, he fell through thin ice.

"If it hadn't been for our huge St. Bernard," Russell says, "I wouldn't be here today."

The big dog, Nero, went in after the boy, grabbed him by his brass-buttoned jacket and pulled him to safety.

Among Russell's keepsakes of the canal days were two of his grandfather's record books containing the cargo lists and prices of materials transported in his boats. These, along with some early canal-period photographs and a bootjack from one of the boats, were donated by Russell to the Canal Society of Ohio for possible placement in a museum.

More people will get to appreciate them there, Russell figures. And, besides, he still has all the memories of his boyhood days spent along the towpath.

Educational Canoeing

Marion (that's the wife) and I got our canoe out of winter storage the other day and went canoeing. On the canal, of course. But only after we affixed our state registration numbers and '67 license sticker. Then we had to wait out two heavy downpours. But it was worth it.

We sort of like to go on "first" things and so we joined the first Stark Wilderness Center-sponsored canoe trip.

We shoved off from the canal bank at Lock 4 Park about 7 p.m. last Sunday and paddled down the canal to Crystal Springs. The air, after the rain, was clean and fragrant, filled with all kinds of smells, including the aroma of an occasional honeysuckle in bloom. The delights to the nature lover were many and well worth the trip, although the weeds in some sections of the canal were so thick that only a canoe or swamp buggy could get through.

There were six canoes in our flotilla, which was under the supervision of Jeremy Felland, wilderness center director, and Robert Hawes, center naturalist. It turned out to be a family affair and the canoeists included wives and children.

To make the cruise educational as well as recreational, Bob Hawes tagged 67 "things to look at" along the canal banks. With identification sheets in each canoe, it was easy to use the canal and its environs as a living dictionary or encyclopedia. It was a novel and most enjoyable way of learning.

Many of the 67 "varieties" can be seen from the towpath, so for the benefit of hikers who may want to look for them, here is the list:

Great water dock, black currant, barberry, elderberry, sensitive fern, horsetail, wild mustard, American elm, silver maple, wild raspberry, wild grape, wild ginger, small-floured buttercup, choke cherry.

Wild black cherry, silky dogwood, hawthorn, Juneberry, sedge, jewelweed, cultivated cherry, slender bullrush, water flag, honey locust, red pine, poison ivy, golden ragwort, rush, climbing bittersweet.

Multiflora rose, corn salad, crabapple, mouse-eared chickweed, tent caterpillars, bittersweet nightshade, flower dogwood, common alder, osage-orange, musclewood, sassafras, wool-grass, cinquefoil, cattail, beaver gnawings, agrimoney.

Skunk cabbage, black walnut, arrowhead (watch for rose-breasted grosbeaks), weeping willow, elodea (under the canoe), oriole nest, smooth sumac, day lily, alumroot, purple angelica, bur-reed.

Gray dogwood, dewberry, crayfish, mud chimney, white ash, muskrat house, duckweed, water shield, water milfoil, hawthorn.

Have fun!

June 11, 1967
Facts From a Canal Boat

In my search for facts and figures about canal boats, I little thought that I would be acquiring information provided by Neptune — or more specifically, Neptune's Imps. But I am.

Neptune's Imps, incidentally, are not assistants to the mythological god of the sea. They are members of a Lisbon skindiving club of the same name. Their president is G.E. (Jerry) Linerode, who lives near Maximo. Jerry, a carpenter, has been diving for 10 years. He has gone down in every one of the Great Lakes, the Virgin Islands and many other places.

He and his diving buddies particularly like to hunt for wrecks on ocean and lake bottoms. So when they heard about the old derelict on the bottom of Coshocton's Lake Park, it was only natural that they should go down and have a look at it.

Because Jerry is a reader of this column, he thought I would be interested in the ribs, bolts and nails he brought up from the sunken vessel, which was a canal boat. And I was.

It was with considerable satisfaction that I learned the salvaged materials correspond in measurements to comparable wood and hardware being used in the current construction of Stark County's canal boat at Canal Fulton. It is reassuring to learn, directly from the entombed hull of the canal boat, that we are on the right trail to authenticity.

Jerry was accompanied in his search by Jim Berger of Leetonia and Alliance High School seniors Mike Draa and Paul Comer. They found the boat in water 15 feet deep. It was buried to deck level and there were several inches of silt on the deck, which was pretty well rotted away. Only the outer ribs protruded above the silt. The cabins had disappeared.

On their first trip to the park, the divers were underwater about an hour. Visibility, Jerry said, was two to three feet until they tore a rib loose or otherwise stirred up the bottom. Then visibility was zero.

Explaining why they didn't get more measurements the first time, Jerry said, "Initially, you don't do it too scientifically. You like to see everything you can."

Jerry originally estimated that the boat was 50 to 75 feet long. On his second trip, he measured it with a rope and it turned out to be roughly 70 feet in length. The ribs, he said, were about 13 inches apart.

I told Ted Findley of New Philadelphia, president of the Canal Society of Ohio, about Jerry's activity and asked what he knew about the boat. Ted apparently knew as much about it as is to be known. The boat was discovered in July of 1959 when the lake was drained so it could be cleaned preparatory to installation of a new bathing beach, bathhouse and other recreational facilities. According to an article in the *Coshocton Tribune*, no one seemed to know how the boat got there or how it sank. Nearby residents didn't even know it was there.

It was known that the lake was drained intentionally in 1907 and unintentionally in 1880 when a bank gave way. But a photo taken at the time of the 1880 drainage shows no evidence of a boat on the bottom.

Ted recalls that the editor of the newspaper called him when the boat first began to appear above the receding water and he, along with a group of historians, went to see what they could learn about the boat and whether it could be salvaged and preserved. They found it began to disintegrate when the air reached it and nothing could be done with it. The heavy bow piece and a

tool found on the boat were preserved and now are in the Coshocton Museum.

No name could be found on the boat, which was either a freighter or barge. But there it was.

And today it comes to light again, most appropriately, when it can be of some help in providing our current canal-boat builders with its vital measurements — thanks to Jerry Linerode and his fellow skin divers.

June 18, 1967
Ever Seen an 'Arkeologist'?

There is no term in the glossary of sciences that perfectly describes the activity I was engaged in last Sunday.

Perhaps "archaeology" would come closest. Archaeology is the scientific study of material remains (as fossil relics, artifacts, monuments) of past human life and activities.

But whoever saw archaeologists wallowing around in a shallow basin of mud and muddy water, snorting and blowing up bubbles from beneath the surface of the water, tugging and tearing at slimy blackened timbers and looking for all the world like playful hippopotamuses?

I did.

And because of the unusual and specific nature of the exploration of my friends in the black rubber skin-diving suits, I think a distinctive name for their "field of study" should be coined — how about "ark-eology?"

You see, they were searching for and, believe it or not, finding a long-sunken and buried canal boat (or boats).

The scene was Roscoe Basin at Coshocton. The "arkeologists" were G.E. (Jerry) Linerode, Rex Blair of Aliquippa, Pa., and Paul Comer, an Alliance High School student. The "towpath superintendents" were Paul Baird of 5905 Lakeside Dr. NW and this writer.

Hearsay and rumor were just about all we had to go on, although Ted Findley of New Philadelphia, president of the Canal

158

Society of Ohio, said he had seen dim shapes in the murky water that might have been parts of a long-buried canal boat. Ted told us about this after Jerry and fellow members of Neptune's Imps, a skin-diving club of Lisbon, had brought up pieces of another canal boat known to be on the bottom of Coshocton's Lake Park.

Ted wasn't able to be with us Sunday so we didn't know where to start the underwater search for the rumored remains. Fortunately we knocked on the right door. Edward Cupps, who lives at the edge of Roscoe Basin, had heard the rumors and knew where it was supposed to be.

He got in his rowboat and led the way out to the general area. He knew approximately where because a friend once caught a big catfish, which, during its flight to escape, had disappeared within the boat. The fisherman, reluctant to lose the fish, had stepped out of his rowboat into the basin, which was 3 to 4 feet deep at the spot, and attempted to work the fish back out of the sunken boat. In doing so, one of his legs broke through a decaying timber and he was in immediate peril. Fortunately only one leg went through the timbers of the canal boat or, as he said, he wouldn't have gotten out at all.

He was convinced of one thing — it was a boat and it had been there a long time. He was right, as we soon determined.

After repeated dives and underwater exploration, Jerry and his frogmen were able, by the use of floats, to outline pretty well where the boat is located. Then came a surprise. Some of the 12-foot ribs were found at right angles to others. Jerry surmised there must be two boats in the basin instead of one. Since the basins at either end of the canal aqueduct across the Walhonding River were early day marinas for canal boats and barges, it is reasonable to assume that more than one boat was sunk there, possibly during the devastating 1913 flood.

In addition to smaller pieces recovered, the "arkeologists" brought up three large ribs. These were delivered to Clyde Gainey's Old Canal Days Museum at Canal Fulton, where they may be seen when the museum is open.

While pondering how to conclude this column, I received a telephone call. Without realizing it, the caller provided me with a fitting conclusion.

Edgar C. Neptune of Canton had called to tell me that he had lived at Roscoe as a boy and had some pictures of the canal area that I might be interested in. He had read this column last Sunday in which I told about the skin divers' findings at Coshocton's Lake Park.

When I told him they had found at least one more boat in Roscoe Basin, he said he vaguely remembered seeing it. Several hours later, he called back to say he had found another old picture and it clearly showed the "mystery" boat. He is going to bring the picture to me and, if it is reproducible, you may see it next week in "Along the Towpath."

June 25, 1967
Mystery Boat Takes Form

Being an "arkeologist" (someone who searches for sunken mud-covered canal boats) is a lot of fun and a most uncommon avocation. "Arkeologists" make up a rather exclusive fraternity. It is unlikely that there are more than a dozen in the entire United States.

In the first place, there are very few places in the nation where one can look with any hope of finding one of the cumbersome vessels of a past era.

Rumor, hearsay, legend, chance and luck are some of the key elements in the "science" of "arkeology." It's sort of like being a detective or working a jigsaw puzzle. Bit by bit, clue by clue, the puzzle comes together, and the mystery surrounding the old vessels evaporates — if you are lucky.

That seems to have been the format of discovery associated with locating the mystery boat featured in this column last week. The surprising follow-up came in a telephone call from Edgar C. Neptune, who brought some old photographs of the Roscoe Basin area to show me.

159

They included several views of the aqueduct, which formerly carried the Walhonding Canal over the river of the same name to its juncture with the Ohio & Erie Canal; an old tintype of his grandfather, who was a corporal in the Union Army's 80th Ohio Volunteer Infantry; a general scene showing the basin and the lock tender's house, which was destroyed in the great flood of 1913, and — almost unbelievably — a clear shot of the mystery boat, apparently grounded a short way out in the basin from the lock entrance.

What a fantastic coincidence — that he should have a picture showing the boat the divers found but which no one seemed to know anything about.

The picture had been taken by Mr. Neptune's father, Charles, sometime before the turn of the century, while he was working at the Lee Milling Company flouring mill at Roscoe Basin. The photograph showed clearly that the mystery boat was a three-cabin canal freighter and not a barge. It was aground in a listing position in a spot very close to where its skeleton is today.

Mr. Neptune recalled that his father was in the mill the night of the disastrous 1913 flood and saw the raging torrent take out the Tuscarawas-Walhonding Valley and Ohio Railroad's substantial trestle across the basin. The railroad span went down under the relentless force of the flood despite the fact that carloads of coal were run out onto the trestle to hold it down.

In all probability, the flood moved the abandoned canal boat and sank it, perhaps overturning it in the process.

Mr. Neptune's picture is a revealing piece of the mystery boat puzzle. Perhaps someone reading this and looking at the picture can add another piece or two to the puzzle.

Shoulder Canal Boats

Stark County's section of the Ohio & Erie Canal soon may be publicized in a new way — through the shoulder patches of the Canal Fulton Ramrod Club, which claims to be the oldest muzzle-loading rifle club in the nation. The club has approved a shoulder patch design that features a canal boat as the central figure. Oval in shape, the 6 x 7-inch multicolored patch was designed by member Meta Stefanov of Akron. The canal-boat insignia ties in with the name of the club and with the history, which relates to the canal.

The patches will be worn on either the shoulders or backs of the shooting jackets. The jackets, in turn, will be worn by members of the club when they go to matches throughout the state and to out-of-state shoots as well.

The unusual patch (for a gun club) should arouse considerable interest in the gun world about Canal Fulton, particularly when those who ask questions about the patch are told that the village soon will have a canal boat operating on the canal, a reminder of the early days of America — days in which the muzzle-loaders also were an integral part of a young, developing nation.

July 2, 1967
Building the Buckeye Trail

They didn't say it in quite these words but each speaker at the 1967 annual meeting of the Buckeye Trail Association, held last Sunday at Burr Oak Lake in Athens and Morgan counties, said essentially "the trail must go through."

By "going through" they meant from Cincinnati to Cleveland — through state parks, over private farms, beside rivers, on top of strip mine ridges, around lakes, in and out of forests, and along the Ohio & Erie Canal towpath.

The towpath through Stark County was accepted as a part of the Buckeye Trail at the 1966 annual meeting of the association in Massillon. But the Stark section, part of which now is in use for hiking and riding, is a far-flung outpost separated from the main body of the trail by several counties.

It is hoped that the towpath, where it still exists in Cuyahoga, Summit and Tuscarawas counties, also will become part of the Buckeye Trail. The northern section of the trail then would be tied to the new Salt Fork State Park, under construction in Guernsey County. From there the "hikeway" would sweep through a series of state parks to Cincinnati.

Up to now, the trail has grown slowly, its development due to the dedicated efforts of a handful of volunteers — men and women. But things are looking up for the trail as the result of several major developments.

The Buckeye Trail, although far from completed, has been designated as the official trail of the State of Ohio by action of the General Assembly. Sen. Ralph Regula, R-Stark; Sen. Harry Armstrong, R-Logan; and Rep. J. Harvey Weis, R-Fairfield, sponsored the bill, a copy of which was presented to William Miller of Logan, retiring trail association president, by Gov. James A. Rhodes. The governor expressed pleasure in the legislative action, which supports a volunteer effort to restore public access to many of Ohio's scenic and recreational resources.

Now, expectations are that the state will support efforts to blaze the trail to completion.

Norv Hall, supervisor of the division of parks and recreation of the State Department of Natural Resources, said at the annual meeting the state will welcome suggestions as to how it best can help in establishing the trail. He declared the state will cooperate in the work of building it.

"We are obviously very happy to have the trail pass through the state park areas and we will do what we can to facilitate this," he assured the hikers.

He said the state wants local residents to help select the best approach routes to the parks.

The trail association is becoming a joint organization of hikers and horsemen, with the horsemen doing an increasing amount of the work.

Retiring president Miller, in speaking of the horsemen, said: "We are in business together." In telling of a joint effort of hikers and the Buckeye Trail Riders of Logan, he described it as a feasible relationship, adding, "It is a fact of life that if you don't clear a trail so horses can use it, you frequently lose it. If we hadn't found the hors-

es' hoofprints this morning (during a hike by association members), we might well have lost our way."

Al Zaleski of East Sparta, president of the Tri-County Trail Association (Stark, Carroll and Tuscarawas), told the members of the 45 miles of trail his organization has cleared and marked, part of which coincides with the towpaths of the Ohio & Erie and Sandy and Beaver canals. Having ridden on other sections of the Buckeye Trail, he extolled the recreational benefits of cross-state riding via the trail.

Statewide workdays are planned, in which members from throughout the state will come together for clearing or marking in a specific area. Stark County is one of the counties, high on the list for work-crew visitation.

The hikers were heartened by the report of a member of the American Walking Association that "at long last" the trail is under way in the Cincinnati area. The volunteer builders were forced to use the Ohio River bank, Boy Scout camps and state parks in the area. The southern terminus, he said, may well be "Fountain Square" in the Queen City.

Major emphasis in the push to expedite construction will be directed toward establishing Buckeye Trail chapters in each county through which the walkway passes. Chapter members then would assume the responsibility for developing the trail in their respective counties.

The new president of the state association is Dr. Victor Whitacre, a physician from Beverly. New vice presidents are State Sen. Ralph Regula of Navarre and this columnist. The secretary is Robert Merkle of Columbus, the treasurer is Robert Paton of Worthington, executive director emeritus of the Ohio Forestry Association, and the corresponding secretary is Joanne Baughman of Beverly. Five directors from various areas of the state will assist in guiding the development of the organization.

There now are more than 150 miles of established trail. But, as with Interstate 77 and other major thoroughfares, there are many gaps to be filled in. The potential, however, is tremendous. And when the trail is completed, Ohioans and others from all parts of the nation will be able to walk or ride through the Buckeye State's rolling hills, past its beautiful and productive farmland, along its rivers and beside its canals — from Cleveland to Cincinnati.

July 9, 1967
Special Week for Canawlers

Last week was sort of special for those of us who are interested in America's canals, their history, their impact on our country and their restoration today. It was 150 years ago the Fourth of July that New York State's Erie Canal was born, the forerunner and inspiration for our own Ohio & Erie Canal. They had a lot of hoopla over the anniversary at Rome, New York, commemorating the first ceremonial digging of the canal in 1817 and other events associated with the canal's first 150 years. It still is a working waterway.

I had an invitation to attend the sesquicentennial and would have liked to have gone but couldn't make it.

But due to the thoughtfulness of Jim Cozy, president of Louisville Sportsman's Club, whose members are building Stark County's canal boat, I received a first-day cover commemorating the sesquicentennial, complete with July 4 postmark from Rome and new red, white and blue Erie Canal stamp. The envelope also features a fine engraving of a canal boat in transit through the scenic New York State countryside, a portrait of Gov. De Witt Clinton, developer of the canal, and a map showing the route from Troy to Buffalo.

Readers of this column are well aware that canal towns frequently boomed and grew beyond the wildest expectations but I wonder how many know that one of these towns is "Big Town" itself, New York City. According to an article in *The New York Times*, the Erie Canal made New York City "the nation's preeminent city, with an access to the interior infinitely superior to the reach of Boston and Philadelphia."

Today, it appears the bright future of the canal may be in tourism. The Erie has become a "playway" for pleasure boats — about 20,000 last year. And this means tourists and vacationers who bring money for those who live along the canal's banks. The man who represents the Rome area in Congress sees the possibility of visitors spending $6 million annually by 1980.

Guess what they are planning to do in Rome? The Historic Rome Development Authority, organized to "revive the grandeur that was Rome," has announced it will issue $750,000 in bonds to put a 2-mile section of the Erie Canal back in service for tourists. It will be made to look as it did in the 1840s, complete with a canal packet and canal village.

Doesn't it all sound sort of familiar? It's almost exactly what we have been talking about and working toward at Lock 4 Park and Canal Fulton for nearly three years.

When we first planned to build a canal boat for Stark County residents, we were convinced it would be the only authentic one in the nation. Since then, at least two other boats are in the talking stage, with plenty of money designated for their construction. But both of these will be packets, not distinctive three-cabin freighters like Stark County's boat.

We have the lead now in Stark County. We don't have the big sums of money to see the job through but our canal boat is well under way at Canal Fulton. And we have something often better than money. We have volunteers.

Two of those volunteers, who are playing important roles in the boat-building drama but who have not been adequately recognized for their work, are Roy K. Preece, construction boss for the boat and supervisor in the pattern shop of the Engineering Division of The Hoover Company in North Canton, and Carroll M. Gantz, head of the industrial design section of the same engineering division.

The two men have spent many hours at the Stark County Historical Center taking measurements and contours from the large model canal freighter there. They use these as checks against their plans for the full-size boat.

Carroll, who says he has confidence in

the accuracy of the model, has found it contains a "lot of detail" and dimensions he has been unable to obtain from photographs.

At the "boat yard," Roy takes Carroll's drawings and supervises the construction. He also directs the volunteers who have been making the ribs, keel sections, etc., at Pete Neidert's farm machinery and lawn and garden equipment repair shop just south of the village.

Due to their combined efforts and the volunteer labor of a number of others, our canal boat is taking shape. Although there still are many problems, delays and frustrations ahead, launching day draws ever closer.

July 16, 1967

Pontoon Boat Plays Stand-In Role

The second annual Old Canal Days Exposition is over. But a part of it will linger through the summer as a teaser for those who are looking forward to the time when they can ride as passengers on Stark County's canal boat. I'm referring to the pontoon boat operated during the exposition by Canal Fulton Rotary Club.

Until the authentic 60-foot canal freighter is completed, the pontoon boat, powered by an outboard motor, will cruise the old waterway between Lock 4 Park and the footbridge across the canal in Canal Fulton from 1 p.m. to dark on Saturdays, Sundays and holidays.

Gale Hartel, chairman of the Rotary's canal-boat committee, says the round-trip, just under a mile each way, will take about 40 minutes. An interesting feature of the pontoon boat rides is the historical narrative to be presented by a member of the boat's crew as it glides along the canal. The information is a condensation from a talk on the history of the canal systems of Ohio prepared by Ted Findley of New Philadelphia, president of the Canal Society of Ohio.

The pontoon craft, which will be operated by Rotarians, will accommodate 25 passengers. If there are more than that awaiting the restful ride down the old waterway, they will be directed to Clyde Gainey's Old Canal Days Museum up the street. There they will find Clyde's excellent little museum will whet their appetites for the trip on the canal.

Plans call for Boy Scouts to be present at the footbridge to keep new passengers advised as to when the boat will return for them. Chairs will be provided and the village park shelter is close at hand in the event of rain.

Hoping to attract as many riders as possible, the Rotary Club will operate the pontoon boat on weekdays on a charter basis. Special arrangements can be made for groups of 25 or more by calling Edward Harriman of The Exchange Bank Company in Canal Fulton.

Gale, incidentally, believes Canal Fulton should have the largest chapter of the Canal Society of Ohio in the Buckeye State. And he's working to make it just that. He just requested more membership application forms.

Gale's right. Where in Ohio is there more canal restoration activity at the present time, more interest in developing the canal lands, a canal town in a better state of preservation and more interested citizenry than in Stark County? Success to Gale Hartel in his endeavor to make Canal Fulton the No. 1 chapter of the Canal Society of Ohio!

Reading 'Up the Canal'

Last February, I wrote about the summer reading program sponsored by the Louisville Public Library. It had a canal angle.

Last week I received a "ticket" to "summer reading travel down the historic Ohio Canal." The "ticket" was an advertising flyer from the Louisville library, giving the dates of the reading program and featuring a sketch of a canal boat being towed by a mule. Talking with Mrs. Joyce L. Moser, librarian-decorator at the library, I learned the six-week program is under way and the children's individual "canal boats" are moving right along on their canal progress chart.

Mrs. Moser has used the canal theme

for the reading program this year believing the children will benefit from the combining of the reading program and a practical history lesson based on the canal. She has decorated the library with material about the Ohio & Erie Canal and done much to stimulate interest in Stark County's historic waterway among residents of Constitution Town.

A highlight of the reading program was the lecture at the high school last Thursday night by Ted Findley of New Philadelphia, president of the Canal Society of Ohio. Ted showed his slides of the canal era.

The reading program will conclude with a party July 28. Featured speaker at the party will be Mrs. Ralph (Mary) Regula who will tell the "graduates" about the "Romance of the Canal."

July 23, 1967
Boom in Canalboating

I don't know if you can call it a boom yet, but canal boating seems to be growing more and more popular. Certainly, the number of canal boats is increasing.

The latest to become operative is the "John Quincy Adams," a barge modeled after the 19th-century canal barges. The "John Quincy" becomes the second boat in the Chesapeake and Ohio Canal "fleet." The other, the "Canal Clipper," has been carrying passengers up and down the C&O, out of Georgetown in our nation's capital, for some years. But its service has been suspended temporarily due to a rupture in the towpath.

Canal boats also are operating on the Delaware Canal near New Hope, Pa., and on the Whitewater Canal at Metamora, Ind. There are plans to build a canal packet to ply the waters of the well-preserved Erie Canal in New York State and equally definite plans to build a similar boat for use on the Miami and Erie Canal in western Ohio. And there are rumors of still others being built in the Buckeye State. But, as of now, Stark County's canal boat is further along than the others.

The boats operating today are the launch or barge type, while those that are planned are packets (passenger boats). But Stark County's canal boat will be a freighter and probably the only truly authentic canal boat in the nation.

It is taking time to build it that way — progress is slow but steady. Instead of being built of Mahogany or some other easily available lumber, Stark's freighter is being constructed of green white oak (the hull that is) as the boats were in the canals' heyday.

Some of the key men of the building crews are spending full days at the "shipyard" now, days of their vacation.

When their work is finished, the big freighter (it will be 60 feet long and 14 feet wide) will present a distinctive silhouette, unlike any other canal boat, as it moves slowly along the surface of the Ohio & Erie Canal.

The "John Quincy Adams" is 40 feet long and 11 1/2 feet wide. It is pulled by a mule and carries 60 passengers on a 4-mile trip, which takes about an hour. Visitors board the barge near the main parking lot at Great Falls, Maryland (a truly beautiful setting), Saturdays, Sundays and holidays through October. Two mules, known as Dick and George, take turns towing the "John Quincy" and park rangers will be aboard the boat to tell of the canal park history and answer questions.

The name, suggested by author-historian Frederick Gutheim, was selected because it was felt the boat deserved a name that would "combine historical and interpretive values."

Although I have devoted space in this column to describing a trip John Quincy Adams made on the Ohio & Erie Canal, during which he passed through Stark County, I did not know that he turned the first spadeful of dirt for the Chesapeake and Ohio 139 years ago. But, according to a recent article in the *Baltimore Sun*, he did just that. It was in keeping with his "strong sponsorship of internal improvements on a national level."

I have seen this area between Georgetown and Seneca, Maryland, and around Great Falls. Canal boat passengers have a treat in store for them. But then so do all those who someday will ride aboard our canal boat as it is towed leisurely up the tree-shaded canal from Lock 4 to Canal Fulton. Each spike being driven into the strongly resisting green, white oak timbers of the canal boat's hull brings that time nearer.

(The information about the "John Quincy Adams" was sent to me by Byrl Neff, successful concert accompanist and former Canton resident, who now resides in Baltimore, Maryland.)

July 30, 1967
A Young Man and Old Canals

There is a young man up Akron way, a student at the University of Akron, who has been doing a tremendous job of compiling the history of Ohio canals. His name is David Lieberth. Dave not only compiles the history himself, but he then works the material into a 30-minute radio program broadcast over the university's radio station, WAUP-FM, which is found at 88.1 on your radio FM dial.

Dave has put a great amount of time and energy into his project and an equal share of his considerable talent. He has found, as have a number of others, that the old canals "grow on you" as you delve into their history.

Last summer Dave and WAUP produced 15 half-hour programs titled "Along the Ohio Canals." Their coverage was extensive but, according to Dave, the programs were unsuitable for statewide distribution because they were too long for commercial stations and "not very entertaining" for anyone other than a canal buff.

But the enterprising young producer worked on and now has a new series of 15-minute programs that contain more music, dramatizations and other portrayals of canal life.

Some of the best of the original master tapes will be included in the new series, such as panel discussions with officers of the Canal Society of Ohio, interviews with well-known canal buffs from throughout the state and music by Buddy Cassull,

Akron folk singer.

Dave and WAUP have an idea and a problem. They hope to press the series of programs on a set of four LP records and give them free of charge to all Ohio radio stations (175) and to all county school systems. But they need funds. They are searching for money to make and distribute the programs.

Being cognizant of the great degree of interest in canal history on the part of pupils in Stark County schools (Stark being a canal county) as it has been revealed to me in many ways since I began to write this column, I think Dave's records would be well received and much appreciated by the school systems. If anyone would like to help solve the financial problem, Dave may be reached at WAUP, the University of Akron, Akron, Ohio.

If the series comes into being and if interest warrants it, Dave and WAUP will produce a long-playing record for general distribution to the Ohio public. The record probably would be distributed through historical societies.

Dave Lieberth and WAUP are to be congratulated for their contribution to the Ohio story.

Sierra Club Visitors

The Sierra Club, with a membership of 34,000, is one of the nation's outstanding conservation organizations. It is particularly well known in the West but it has chapters throughout the nation.

Hiking is one of the major activities of the club. And it was to do just that — hike — that a small group of the Ohio section of the Great Lakes Chapter of the Sierra Club came to Stark County last Sunday. All from Cleveland, the club members spent the afternoon hiking the Ohio & Erie Canal towpath from Crystal Springs to Lock 4 Park. They were conducted on the hike by member Ray Simpson of Canton.

Ray told the visiting hikers, in a running commentary, about the history of the canal and informed them that its towpath in Stark County is an official segment of the Buckeye Trail. He also showed them Stark County's canal boat, under construction in Canal Fulton, and Clyde Gainey's Old Canal Days Museum there. Maps of the hiking area were presented to the walkers prior to the hike, which was concluded with a light lunch at Canal Fulton Village Park.

Word Gets Around

Word of our canal-boat project is getting around the state in many ways. One way is through the Canal Society of Ohio's quarterly magazine, "Towpaths," and the accompanying letter from the society president, Ted Findley of New Philadelphia. The following paragraph is from Ted's most recent letter:

"The Louisville Sportsman's Club is coming right along with the building of a canal boat at Canal Fulton. And the gates at Lock 4 are being rebuilt — so that before too long we will be able to take a trip from Canal Fulton down the old canal, 'locking through' on the way!"

Canal Novel To Read

Rome, New York, was in the news recently as it was the site of a four-day celebration marking the 150th anniversary of the start of the Erie Canal. Shortly after I wrote about it in this column, I received a call from Paul Hauschulz of Canton, who said he had a historical novel entitled *Rome Haul*, which he thought I might like to read and then give to the Old Canal Days Museum at Canal Fulton.

The story is about life along the Erie Canal when that waterway was the lifeline between New York, New England and the West. I got the book and it looks like interesting reading when the snow flies. But that is some time off.

And so is the next "Along the Towpath." For the next four or five Sundays, this column will not appear in *The Repository*. It's vacation time again.

September 10, 1967

Back From Banana Boat Country

It has been a long time and it seems a lot longer since I last sat down to write this column. Frankly, after an exciting three and a half weeks in Costa Rica, it is hard to settle down to writing about things along the towpath.

And as for canal boats — I didn't see a single one. The only boats I saw were banana boats. And I don't mean the big ones that transport bananas from Central America to the United States. I'm talking about the small ones used to bring bananas down the river from the farms to the end of the railroad lines.

There is a kind of similarity at that to the canal era.

In the canal-boat days in Ohio, this was frontier country in every sense of the word. And there was no other satisfactory way to transport crops.

Today, in sections of Costa Rica it still is frontier country in every sense of the word. And where the railroad ends, there is no other satisfactory way to transport the banana crop than by boat. So, although the scenery and the vegetation is vastly different, I couldn't escape the feeling that transportationwise, I was in a period of time not far removed from the canal-boat era.

Meanwhile, while I was goofing off eating bananas and drinking coconut juice, things were going on here at home on the canal-boat front.

The first Tuesday night after my return to Ohio, I drove to Canal Fulton and found a crew busily at work on the canal boat. No dramatic advance had been made, but the steady construction progress was continuing. Most of the hull boards have been cut and are ready for assembling.

My piled-up mail also indicated activity on the canal-boat lecture front. Checks from garden clubs indicated that Mrs. Mary Regula of Navarre was continuing her generous policy of speaking about the canal and then turning her compensation over to the canal-boat fund and that Mrs. Ruth Bender of Canton was following suit.

After hearing Mrs. Regula speak recently, members of the Laurel Ridge Garden Club of North Canton decided that, for their September meeting, they would walk along the towpath "to see at firsthand what she had described."

Meanwhile, Paul Baird, procurement expediter for the canal-boat project, was telling the story of Stark County's canal boat at the State Fair and, at the same time, collecting funds to help build it.

The Ohio Conservation Congress, whose president this year is Dale Jefferson of North Canton, donated space in its booth at the State Fair so the Louisville Sportsman's Club could put up an exhibit featuring the canal-boat project in Stark County.

Much of the display appeared in the exhibits building at Canton's Central Plaza last May. Arranged by Jim Cozy, president of the sportsman's club, the exhibit also contained photographs and materials supplied by Ted Findley of New Philadelphia, president of the Canal Society of Ohio.

Paul reports many people from all sections of the state showed interest in the boat building project and other aspects of the canal and metropolitan park development in Stark County. And a number of them supported the boat project financially by purchasing "Canal Boss" badges.

Have you become a "Canal Boss" yet?

Canal Story on TV

Clyde Gainey of the Stark County Canal Lands Development Advisory Committee and Gale Hartel of Canal Fulton Rotary Club also have been telling the story of the canal-boat project. Actually, they have been telecasting the story. Clyde and Gale were interviewed recently on a Youngstown TV program about the canal boat and the canal redevelopment. They took Clyde's nifty model canal boat and a number of canal days pictures with them. The 15-minute show was in color and, according to Clyde, they have been invited back to keep the Youngstown area viewers abreast of the canal developments in Stark County.

September 17, 1967
When Canal Meets Mountain

The engineering marvels accomplished in the building of America's early canals never cease to amaze those who really under-stand the magnitude of the early canal builders' achievements.

Usually the canal buffs, engineers and others who become interested in the canals are impressed by the precise stonework of the locks, the fact that the entire canal bottom was sealed with a clay lining or the marvelous control of the fall of water over long distances. They consider what was accomplished, realize what crude tools and equipment were used and are more impressed than ever.

Usually one thinks of this construction work as having gone on out in the open fields and countryside with some of it, of course, taking place in wooded areas.

But what do you do with a canal when it comes smack up against a mountain? Do you build a giant trough up over the mountain and haul the boats up and let them down on a series of cables and giant wheels — like a cable car arrangement or a ski lift? Do you go around the mountain?

When they built the Chesapeake and Ohio Canal late in the 18th century, they did neither. The early canal builders dug straight through the mountain, creating a 3,117-foot tunnel, which stands today as a monument to man's determination to overcome physical obstacles that stand in the way of progress.

The hand-cut Paw Paw Tunnel took 14 years of what has been described as "almost subhuman labor" to build. Its construction involved wage riots (yes, they had them back in the 1840s) and loss of life but it was completed and stands today for all to see. It is 24 feet wide and is lined with seven layers of brick. With star drills and mallets, picks and wooden wheelbarrows, some 250 men worked in shifts, boring the tunnel entirely by hand through a ridge of shale almost three quarters of a mile thick.

The men worked on six faces at once. They started, of course, at the north and south portals. Then they put down two shafts from the top of the mountain 360 feet above. At the bottom of each shaft they began to dig in opposite directions, thus creating four more faces and enabling the digging to go on at six places at the same time. But to accomplish this they had to haul the spoil out by buckets and winches — 360 feet to the top.

It was a tremendous task but the tunnel was finished, reducing the barge trip along the Potomac River's Paw Paw bends by five miles. Its usefulness was short-lived, however, and, in 1924, the canal company went under without ever having achieved financial stability. Ultimately the canal became the property of the federal government — all 184.5 miles of it, including the Paw Paw Tunnel.

In the meantime, erosion and age had attacked the tunnel. Moisture seeped through the work shafts into the tunnel's brick liner. The builders had only loosely refilled the shafts with spoil. Freezing and thawing of this water worked so many of the bricks loose that great cavities appeared in the liner as the bricks tumbled into the water of the canal. The water in the tunnel became clouded with mud and catfish took up residence. River birch, spicewood, cattails and pine trees took root in the canal bed at both ends of the tunnel.

This is the way the tunnel looked in June of 1964 when State Sen. Ralph Regula and I walked through it during a three-day inspection of the Chesapeake and Ohio Canal. We wanted to see what the government had done to restore the C&O and we hoped to get some ideas as to what could be done with Stark County's section of the Ohio & Erie.

Today the Paw Paw Tunnel has a new lease on life. But that story must wait for next week's "Along the Towpath."

Enjoyed Canal Hike

One of the latest groups to find a hike along Stark County's rewatered section of the Ohio & Erie Canal enjoyable is the C.R. Weaver family of Wooster. Mr. Weaver, a statistician at the Ohio Agricultural Research and Development Center in Wooster, called me from Massillon to inquire as to the best place to hike the towpath. He had wanted to hike the Buckeye Trail and learned from friends that the canal towpath in Stark County is an official section of the Buckeye Trail. Accompanied by members of his family and friends, he hiked from Crystal Springs to Canal Fulton. According to a card I received from

him, they had a delightful time. He said the trip kindled an interest in the history of the canal and he feels it "certainly merits more publicity concerning its existence."

September 24, 1967
Canal Literature Growing

Part of the last paragraph of last week's "Along the Towpath" becomes the first in this week's column: "It certainly merits more publicity concerning its existence." Judging from this week's mail, I would say the canal definitely is getting more publicity.

Two publications deserve special comment.

The September issue of "Echoes," a publication of the Ohio Historical Society, features a picture of Stark County's canal boat and an article telling of the activity associated with the boat and the park development. The article congratulates the county commissioners for acquiring the canal lands and names Stark County organizations and individuals active in the canal-boat project on a volunteer basis.

The other publication is "The Canawler," a new four-page tabloid published by

The Exchange Bank Company of Canal Fulton. Edward Harriman, president of the bank, wrote in the first issue: "It is our intention, as a public service, to help restore this gallant story so this generation and future generations to come will remember the local historical places and events that have helped to give us this great nation."

The initial issue, which includes 14 photographs, is well done and contains much information for all who are interested in the canal and the role it played in the development of Ohio. "The Canawler" is a welcome addition to canal literature.

The Paw Paw Tunnel

Taking up where we left off on the story of the Chesapeake and Ohio Canal's Paw Paw tunnel renovation, it must be pointed out that there is one basic difference between that project and the ongoing attempts to refurbish our own Ohio & Erie Canal in Stark County — namely money.

Whereas the limited accomplishments achieved under the guidance of the Stark County Canal Lands Development Advisory board are the result, almost completely, of volunteer labor and contributions of organizations and individuals, the C&O tunnel project had federal funds to draw upon.

In 1961 President Eisenhower proclaimed the C&O a significant relic of early America and designated it as a national monument. This brought it under the protective cloak of the National Park Service.

Restoration started in July of 1966 and I have not seen the tunnel since then, but the plans called for expenditure of at least $306,000. By October of that year, the pumps had sucked some 90,000 gallons of water from the tunnel. Bulldozers invaded the tunnel and shoved out tons of mud, weeds, bricks, coal carried by the canal boats, and a few snakes and catfish. Bricks carefully matched with the originals were worked in the cavities in the tunnel lining by masons. The weakened portions of the towpath and its retaining wall were torn out and replaced.

Even the rub rails on both sides of the tunnel, which protected the boats from hitting the tunnel walls, were remade and installed. More than 5,000 feet of them, at a cost of $12 a foot, were replaced. Some 615 wrought iron posts, which hold the guardrail, were sandblasted, each one requiring half an hour of labor.

According to plans, the tunnel, cleaned and restored, was to have been opened by the middle of October 1966 and was to remain open until December, when it was to be sealed to prevent seepage-freezing and renewed deterioration.

This past April it was to have been unsealed and reopened. More work was scheduled for April by the park service. Contracts were to be let for repointing all the bricks and the stones of the portals and wing walls. More sections of the towpath were to be resurfaced and interpretive exhibits were to be placed at the tunnel and at Lock 66.

A new road, properly marked, was to be cut from Route 51, which passes the tunnel just across the river from Paw Paw, West Virginia. The restorers found the guardrail within the tunnel worn smooth by the slipping and burning of the tow-ropes. It will be left that way. The depressions and the initials that were carved in it through the years can be felt and, in some places, seen. They, too, will be left that way.

Plans also call for the banks of the canal to be made park-like at some places, with picnic tables and perhaps bridle and bicycle trails.

Much of what has been done to restore the Chesapeake and Ohio Canal also can be done with our own Ohio & Erie. Some it has been done and more has been started — the one major difference is the availability of state and federal funds.

If Stark County residents approve the tax levy for the metropolitan park system, the canal, as one phase of the proposed park system, would become eligible for state and federal funds. This could really break loose the logjam of pent-up ideas, proposals and plans, which are frustrated by the lack of money.

This column will not appear while the writer is on assignment in South America. He should be back "along the towpath" about the middle of October.

169

October 22, 1967
Fun for 'Boatorists'

It's a little late this year to go canal cruising. But — while the snowflakes fall outside and the hearth logs snap and crackle inside — one can make plans for next year.

And anyway, our Ohio & Erie Canal hardly is ready yet for anything more than canoe or pontoon boat cruising. By next summer though, Stark County's authentic 60-foot canal freighter should be ready to take passengers south from Canal Fulton to (and through) Lock 4.

Even so, to do any serious canal cruising at the present, one must look east — preferably to the Erie Canal in New York State. This mighty canal, which served as a model for our own Ohio & Erie, outlasted its Ohio counterpart as a going waterway and today is still very much in operation.

But, increasingly, its traffic is made up of sleek powerboats operated by pleasure boaters.

Whereas, more than a century ago, pioneers to the Ohio country came to the wilderness from the Atlantic seaboard via the Erie Canal, today the down-East boating enthusiasts come to Lake Erie joyriding and vacationing.

Proof of the developing interest in canal cruising is the fact that marinas are springing up along the canal just like motels along a new highway.

In the old days, the best time the packets could make was about 4 miles an hour. Today, the power-packed super cruisers and yachts are permitted to go 6 miles an hour in land cuts and up to 10 miles an hour in lakes and rivers that make up a part of the canal system.

This leisurely speed, although twice as fast as the original canal watercraft traveled, still gives the modern "boatorists" something of the feel of early canal travel.

As for locking through the locks, today's canal explorers again can experience much the same sensations as early travelers — while they are being lifted or lowered as much as 35 to 40 feet.

Today's locks and the Erie Canal are larger than they were originally. Some of the locks now require between 4½ and 5 million gallons of water to lock a boat through.

There is roughly 350 miles of canal, lake and river between the end of the Erie Canal at Buffalo and its junction with the Hudson River north of Albany. Some 35 locks must be traversed and 245 bridges passed under in that distance.

Originally there were 83 locks on the Erie Canal.

There are branch canals that can be explored along the way, such as the Oswego Canal, which goes north to Lake Ontario, the Black Rock Canal off the Niagara River and the Cayuga-Seneca Canals in the Finger Lakes area.

And sometimes canal travelers find an attractive canalside park where they can tie up at night.

So whether it be by canoe, cruiser or sailboat, there is adventure to be had — canal cruising on the Erie Canal.

Trail Coordinator

At a recent meeting of the executive committee of the Buckeye Trail Association in Columbus, it was announced that Robert Paton of Worthington has been appointed state trail coordinator for the division of parks and recreation of the Ohio Department of Natural Resources.

Bob Paton is treasurer of the Buckeye Trail Association and is keenly interested in the development of the trail throughout the state. He sees the Buckeye Trail as the backbone of a network of trails throughout Ohio and his duties as working with local groups to interest them in planning and building a section of the Buckeye Trail in their home areas.

He plans to do this by giving talks, showing slides and planning and holding work-session hikes.

State and federal representatives at the Columbus meeting offered their cooperation in establishing and maintaining the trail on lands under their supervision.

It was brought out at the meeting that Stark County is an area in which much interest has been aroused for extending the present segment of the Buckeye Trail, which coincides with the Ohio & Erie Canal towpath between Crystal Springs and Canal Fulton.

Organization of trail clearing and marking sessions was seen as the immediate need in Stark County.

October 29, 1967

Girl Scouts Scout the Canal

When one writes week after week, month after month and year after year about canals, it is easy to forget how exciting that first introduction to the canal can be — especially for the young.

Sometimes, it takes a letter like the one I received last week to remind me. The letter was from Mrs. Larry Struttmann of Canton, one of three adults who assist Mrs. Frank Mark, leader of Girl Scout Troop 472 at St. Michael's School. The Scouts and their leaders recently took a boat trip to Lock 4 on the Ohio & Erie Canal and, according to Mrs. Struttmann, enjoyed it very much. Following are excerpts from her letter:

"Feeling like true 'canawlers' because of the nippy, damp air and the story of early canal days being told to them," the Scouts rode a pontoon boat down the Ohio & Erie Canal from Canal Fulton to Lock 4 Park. The trip fulfilled one of the requirements for earning a "My Community Badge" — that of visiting a historical place in the local area.

"Capt. Arnold Bland and First Mate William Knight wove a story of days when the canal was bustling with activity as we glided down the smooth water."

The girls thought it interesting that the old canal boats had a mule stable in the center of the boat to house a "fresh mule." As they moved slowly down the canal, the Scouts saw muskrat houses, a wasp nest, numerous bright red cardinals, tall elm trees and "lovely fall foliage along the towpath."

"Shep," the pretty brown collie that meets every boat as it approaches the lock, didn't fail the Girl Scouts. He jumped into the water, barked and ran alongside the canal until the boat was out of sight on its return trip.

"Hearing about the rivalry between the canawlers and the coal miners made history come to life for the girls. They saw the McLaughlin dry dock where boats were repaired, the wide spot in the canal where boats had to wait their turn to go through the lock, the old swimming hole and a pine woods where deer are seen.

"The girls almost resented the coming of the railroads, which started the decline of canal transportation. The hull of the authentic canal freighter now being built made the Scouts feel that, in the near future, they may be able to ride a real canal boat."

Visiting Clyde Gainey's Old Canal Days Museum after the boat ride helped the girls to understand what the old canal boats really looked like and to visualize the people who operated and rode and worked on them.

Canalside Luncheon

Fall, lovely colorful season of the year that it is, was at its best last Sunday afternoon. Many northeast Ohioans drove out into the hills to admire and revel in nature's leaf-painting artistry. Some chose the Ohio & Erie Canal and its towpath in Stark County as a close-at-hand, easy-to-get-to place to contemplate the sheer beauty of the fall landscapes.

Members of Louisville Sportsman's Club were among the latter as were some of the members of Division 3 of the Ohio Conservation Congress. The latter were guests of the sportsmen and their wives at a covered-dish luncheon in Canal Fulton's village park.

The conservationists also were shown the sportsmen's current conservation project — the 60-foot canal freighter being constructed just across the canal from the park pavilion.

Then, members of both groups were treated to 1¼-mile pontoon boat rides down the canal to Lock 4 Park and back. The rides were through the courtesy of the Canal Fulton Rotary Club and Peter Neidert of Canal Fulton.

Arriving at Lock 4, the canal travelers disembarked and toured the county's small but pretty park. There they saw numerous improvement projects under way, including the patching and painting of the lock and the rebuilding of the wooden gates.

Viewing the improvements wrought by Paul Marks, foreman in charge of canal reconstruction, with a minimum of funds, it was easy for the group to see what could be accomplished in the area with the county, state and federal funds, which would become available for park development if the metropolitan parks levy wins favor with the voters.

November 5, 1967
Canal Progress Hinges on Issue 5

This month, Along the Towpath will begin its fourth year. During the last three years, much has been accomplished in reconstructing and renovating the Ohio & Erie Canal in Stark County. And yet, to those who have been bringing new life to the old canal, it seems little enough. Seeing the great potential of the canal, its towpath and environs for a historical, educational and recreational park makes them eager to develop that potential to its fullest.

That's why these volunteers, who have given of themselves, their time and their money to redevelop the canal and initiate canal-oriented projects, are waiting with bated breath for the decision of the voters on the proposed metropolitan parks levy. Passage would bring state and federal funds on a matching basis to Stark County. It also would enable the planners to carry out their many exciting ideas for a canal parkway.

Speaking of planners, Constantinos Doxiadis, noted international urban planner, attended a conference at Kent State University last week and, talking of the plight of the American city, said we must begin comprehensive planning immediately and implement the plans quickly. The noted planner says the second megalopolis in the United States is now forming, extending from Milwaukee and Chicago through Akron and Cleveland to Pittsburgh.

"We have entered the final phase of the (urban) crisis," Mr. Doxiadis said. "We have decay of the transportation network, contamination of the water, pollution of the air and disappearance of green under asphalt to make space for parking. In the next 10 years the urban population will grow 50 percent and it will double by the end of this century. We can't wait. The time is NOW!"

If the voters of Stark County believe what Mr. Doxiadis is saying, they have an opportunity Tuesday to do something about it at the ballot box. By voting for Issue 5 to provide funds for the development and operation of the Stark County Metropolitan Park District, they will be taking a very positive step here at the southern edge of the No. 2 megalopolis, to preserve greenery and enable our local planners to move against a comparable urban crisis, which could add Stark County to the megalopolis.

One needs only to look about to see the housing developments springing up everywhere throughout the county. One of the most recent, just getting under way, is just north of Canal Fulton, not far from the developing megalopolis at Akron.

It rates special mention in this column for several reasons. The tract, which in-

cludes Lake Lucern, has been written about numerous times in this column. Local planners and others interested in the development of the canal had hoped the lake and its surrounding land could be bought by the county or state and used as a part of the metropolitan park system, perhaps as a wildlife refuge.

One of the plans called for diverting the lake's overflow, which now empties into the Tuscarawas River, into the canal so that the section of the canal extending north to Summit County could be rewatered more easily. That section now is dry and heavily overgrown with trees and brush.

However, the new owner of the lake, Robert Kaiser of Canton, owner of Kaiser Homes, Inc., seems willing to divert the overflow into the canal if it can be worked out satisfactorily to all concerned.

In preparation for the residential development, the lake is being drained so stumps and trees can be cleaned out. Mr. Kaiser plans to raise the lake about 6 feet above its previous level and divert all overflow into the canal. His willingness to do this augurs well for future development of the northern section of the canal if money becomes available. Passage of the parks levy could make that money available.

November 12, 1967
Canal Fulton Has Visitor

Is a renaissance of the canal era possible — in part?

Could modern-day replicas of the old freighters and packets again ply the waters of refilled canals in many states east of the Mississippi — towed authentically by mules or horses (but this time only for fun and education)?

Could inns, restaurants and taverns, restored or reconstructed, appear again along the canals?

Could museums be established at canalside in key locations — to tie together the great story of the canal era and make it comprehensible, inspiring and entertaining to Americans young and old?

Could maps of this new Canal Land America be printed and made available to the nation's tourists?

There are people who believe all these things can be and should be done.

Frank B. Thomson, director of the Canal Museum in Syracuse, New York, and secretary of the Old Erie Canal Park Study Committee appointed in 1965 by Gov. Nelson Rockefeller, more than likely is one of them.

Realizing that some of these things already have been or are being done in a number of states and that groups of "canawlers" in various sections of the eastern half of the nation began independently to restore and develop the canals in their respective areas, Director Thomson is thinking some interesting thoughts and following them up with plans.

This was revealed during his recent visit to the Canal Fulton area. I did not have the pleasure of meeting Mr. Thomson but several of the leading canal enthusiasts in Canal Fulton did and they report their visit was mutually enjoyable and rewarding. Clyde Gainey, Ed Harriman and Gale Hartel showed the New Yorker canal development activities in the Canal Fulton area and then listened with interest as he told of plans for the Erie Canal and accomplishments to date.

I asked Gale Hartel to write about the meeting with Director Thomson. The rest of this column will be devoted to his report:

"It is apparent that Mr. Thomson is a dedicated 'canawler.' He has visited here before and, having heard of our efforts, returned to see what progress we have made. Somehow it was heartening to talk of our problems and how slowly we seem to be moving ahead only to find that others have many of the same difficulties and are concerned about progress or what seems to be lack of progress.

"While we look forward to the coming of a museum, his crying need is for a canal park. We mutually agreed that there is merit in moving ahead slowly so that the mistakes made are small and correctable.

"We discussed the mutual problems of financing, organization, volunteer workers,

173

work programs and other canal restoration projects throughout the eastern United States. Such problems might lead one to the conclusion that there is benefit to be gained through closer ties between the various widespread groups associated with canal restoration.

"Frank Thomson has the answer to this in that he is proposing a symposium in the spring of 1968 at Syracuse, NY, to which canal people from Indiana, Illinois, Ohio, New York, Pennsylvania, Washington and other areas would be invited.

"Present thinking is for a Thursday through Sunday schedule where papers could be presented and restoration experiences traded during discussion periods. We assured him that we are enthusiastically behind such an idea where all could gain from the experiences of others.

"We concluded our talks with a tour of Clyde's Old Canal Days Museum, the canal boat construction site and Lock 4 Park. Mr. Thomson was enthusiastic about what we have accomplished on a shoestring and told us that he felt we have moved farther ahead in many respects than any of the other canal restoration projects he has seen.

"Incidentally, he said he knows of a contract let to a boat firm in Maine to build two authentic canal barges and the price per boat is $80,000."

(Stark County's boat is being built by volunteer labor and with unsolicited donations of money.)

Mr. Hartel concludes his report with the following statement: "The perseverance of the people we're associated with in our canal endeavors will certainly make our dreams come true."

November 19, 1967
Season Slows Canal Activities

Did you happen to read "Through a Century in *Repository* Files" November 11? Since it was Armistice Day (commemorat-ing the end of World War I in 1918), one would expect to see reference made to the holiday (now called Veterans Day). The writer of the column did that. In the section "40 Years Ago," he told about the downtown parade and the dedication of the new $130,000 armory on Shroyer Avenue SW.

But in the section "100 Years Ago," he had to find some other subject, as November 11, 1867, considerably predated the signing of the armistice. The following indicates what was considered news 100 years ago:

"With the approaching winter, navigation on the Ohio Canal would soon come to a halt. Boat traffic on the canal would be resumed in the spring and boat owners were feverishly trying to move all passengers and freight before frigid weather closed the locks."

Today, canal activity of a different sort also is coming to a halt with the approach of winter. The sounds of hammer and saw no longer are heard at the "shipyard" in Canal Fulton, where the county's canal boat is being built. A huge (90 foot by 28 foot) plastic cover is on hand, ready to encase the boat in its cocoon for the winter.

The cover was donated by Boyd G. Heminger Inc. of Canton, builders. It is due to contributions such as this, along with the volunteer labor, that much of the progress has been made in the restoration of the canal and associated projects.

Down at Lock 4 Park, activity has just about come to a halt also. One project, stopped by the weather when about 90 percent completed, is the patch-cementing and painting of the concrete lock. Some $300 worth of a special cement was used in the work, accomplished while most of the water was kept out of the lock by cofferdams.

Another major project halted temporarily is the rebuilding of the lock gates. The gates had rotted to the point that there was danger of losing the pattern. This would have made replacing them largely a matter of guesswork.

But Paul Marks, foreman in charge of canal reconstruction, acted in the nick of time to save the pattern. All four gates were lifted out of the lock last spring by the county engineer's men and equipment. Since then the two smaller gates have been rebuilt of white oak and given three coats of preservative. They probably won't be returned to the lock until next spring.

All the white oak for the gates was donated. Paul Baird, Peter Neidert and foreman Marks canvassed the countryside in search of good white oak trees and then hauled them to the sawmill for cutting.

Paul Marks then rigged up an old cemetery tent in which he worked, building the new set of locks from scratch. As there is no electricity at the lock, he borrowed an old generator, which produced enough electricity to light the tent and operate his personal power tools. The gates are so large (Paul estimated the smaller ones weigh three tons each and the larger pair five tons apiece) that 50 penny spikes (about 6 inches long) were used to nail them together.

After the gates are placed in the lock, all new sweep arms will be built and attached.

One of the major problems confronting the canal foreman as he sought to replace the old gates was the seeming unavailability of a lathe big enough to turn the four large wooden hinges of the gates. Without the hinges, the gate project wouldn't get off the ground.

Then Robert W. Raper, president of Akron Extruders, a division of Samco Inc., appeared on the scene and said he had a lathe at his plant at Canal Fulton that was big enough to do the job. He said he would donate the labor and use of the machine. The hinges require special machining as three sides of the big timbers are flat and one side is rounded. Two hinges and two doors have been completed.

If Paul can get some permanent electricity at the park, he will go ahead with building the two larger doors when the weather permits.

I wonder if *The Repository* of 2067 will publish an item telling how in 1967 residents of the county were trying to restore the old Ohio & Erie Canal and build a canal boat like those in use 200 years ago.

November 26, 1967
Towpath Action in Tuscarawas

It certainly isn't spring but new life is stirring along the old canal down in Tuscarawas County.

Perhaps it is too early to be optimistic about reconstruction developments there, in view of seeming indifference to calls for action in the past, but certain things happening there are encouraging.

Organization and organizations probably constitute the difference.

For many years Ted Findley of New Philadelphia, president of the Canal Society of Ohio, lectured, showed slides, wrote articles and worked in many ways to persuade Tuscarawas County residents and officials to preserve the many vestiges of the canal era within the county.

More recently Ray Crumbley, managing editor of the *New Philadelphia Daily Times*, took up the cause. He also spoke about the intrinsic value of the canal lands to the county and wrote stories proposing action to save and restore the canal where possible.

State Sen. Ralph Regula of Navarre, co-chairman of the Stark County Canal Lands Development Advisory Committee, went to New Philadelphia to speak and explain how Stark County had moved ahead in its canal restoration program.

Ralph Romig of Tuscarawas, Claymont schoolteacher and a columnist for the *Uhrichsville Chronicle*, visited the Canal Fulton area and used his column to encourage interest in the canal, its educational and historical values and its reconstructions.

Tuscarawas County commissioners and other interested persons were invited to meet with the Stark canal advisory committee for more back grounding. They came to Canton and were offered help by the Stark committee. For it was recognized by everyone that Tuscarawas County had far more canal lands, locks and other remnants of the canal days to preserve than did Stark County.

But nothing came of it. Highway proj-

175

ects claimed some of the locks, long stretches of the canal were destroyed for highways or filled in for other reasons and more sections of it were sold outright to private individuals.

These areas are gone forever.

But much worth saving remains and it looks like two organizations — the Tuscarawas County Historical Association and the Ohio Outdoor Historical Drama Association — are going to do something about it.

Henry Spring of Uhrichsville, president of the county historical group, told the association's membership that the county commissioners have expressed their support of plans to restore the locks of the Ohio & Erie in the Bolivar-Zoar area. The commissioners will endeavor to get title to the canal lands from the state, he said.

The group, visualizing the area as an "alluring tourist attraction," plans to rebuild some of the locks in that area.

Plans also are under way to build a canal boat similar to the one being constructed at Canal Fulton so "visitors will have an opportunity to journey down the canal and return to the days of yesteryear." A fund for that purpose has been started.

Ted Findley and Ray Crumbley have joined the historical society, which now has more than 200 members and is shooting for 2,000. About 60 persons, mostly members of the society, recently toured the canal in the Bolivar-Zoar area to "look things over" with an eye toward reconstruction possibilities.

I asked Ray what he thought about the recent upsurge of interest in canal restoration in Tuscarawas County.

"We've taken heart again," he replied.

I asked Ted the same question and his answer was:

"I think the picture looks good now since we have local organizations pushing for it. I feel optimistic about it now, particularly the section between Zoar and Bolivar, where Locks 7, 8, 9 and 10 are."

Among the rebuilding ideas visualized as possible projects by the historical association is the reconstruction of Ft. Laurens, located on the canal at Bolivar.

A county museum is another project being considered. All of the projects are pointed toward making Tuscarawas County "the No. 1 tourist attraction in the state."

Mrs. M. Paul Redinger of Dover, president of the historical drama group working hand in hand with the historical association, reports progress on several projects. Drawing on the wealth of history in the Zoar, Schoenbrunn and Gnadenhutten areas, the drama group plans to create and produce an outdoor drama similar to those that have proved so popular in several other states.

It seems to me that some of the fascinating history of the old Ohio & Erie Canal might be ideal for inclusion in such a drama.

If the canal plans for Tuscarawas County are realized, they should blend nicely with developments in Stark County and be neatly linked together by the Buckeye Trail, which is expected to follow the towpath much of the way through the two counties.

The Bolivar-Zoar area of the canal is the northernmost section within Tuscarawas County and consequently the closest to Stark County.

If and when the southern half of Stark County's section of the canal is restored, the linkage would be natural and would create a two-county park strip that could be enjoyed by the residents of both counties.

December 3, 1967

Hiking, Biking and Overnighting

Every so often one of the nation's big newspapers does a feature article about one of our historic eastern canals. The most recent to come to my attention occupied the entire front page of the Sunday *New York Times* travel section. The headline read: Retracing the Towpath Along the Old C&O. Seven photographs and a map helped to tell the story.

The story, in a nutshell, had to do with the writer, who described himself as middle-aged, and a woman companion who rode bicycles from Cumberland, Maryland, to Washington, 184.5 miles along the towpath of the Chesapeake and Ohio Canal.

It was particularly interesting to me because several years ago, when interest in restoring the Ohio & Erie Canal in Stark County first was springing up, State Sen. Ralph Regula and I, with members of our families, drove that 184.5 miles and stopped at many places along the way to inspect the canal and its historical and recreational features. We talked of bicycling the distance sometime in the future.

In the meantime, an increasing number of hikers and cyclists have been using and enjoying the C&O towpath.

Along the 120-mile leg between Cumberland and Harpers Ferry, West Virginia, a series of "Hiker-Biker Overnighters" has been established at 10-mile intervals. The overnighters are constructed very simply, serving primarily as rest stops. There is no shelter but the facilities do include a hand-operated water pump, an outhouse, small fireplace and garbage container. And the area immediately around these facilities is cleared. Signs tell how far it is to the next hiker-biker.

At the Cumberland end of the towpath, the grown-over canal bed, like much of the Ohio & Erie in Stark County, is obscured. But the author of the *Times* article and his companion were directed to it and began their challenging journey. The writer, whose bicycling had been limited to an hour or two at a time on the streets of Manhattan, found himself scheduled to pump more than 30 miles a day for six days. He and his companion rented lightweight bikes in Washington, and shipped them, along with 30 pounds of clothing, camping gear and themselves by train to Cumberland.

They found the first mile of the canal had been filled in by highway construction, just as many areas of the Ohio & Erie have been. But from then on the towpath was passable.

The writer comments about the quiet and beauty of towpath travel, observing: "Most of the time we had the towpath completely to our ourselves. During the six days, the only others we met who were 'doing' the canal were a group of hiking Boy Scouts and a young man on a bicycle."

Local residents, out to enjoy a walk along the towpath, would stop and talk with the travelers and wish them well.

The two cyclists also took in the historical attractions like the battlefield at Antie-tam, where one of the bloodiest battles of the Civil War was fought, and Harpers Fer-ry, where John Brown staged his raid. They found crowds of tourists at both places. But no one else had arrived on bicycles.

At Seneca, Maryland, 22 miles out of Washington, they began the last leg of their trip along the almost fully restored and rewatered canal. They passed day campers on a canoe trip and a group of bicyclists out for a short spin on this well-cared-for section of the towpath.

The *New York Times* article made the trip sound interesting and like fun.

One of these days a similar trip conceivably could be made along remaining sections of the Ohio & Erie Canal, via its towpath, and the steadily developing Buckeye Trail. Hiker-biker overnighters, canoe liveries, bike rental agencies and hostels all could be established to make canal and towpath travel more enjoyable.

There is great potential for development of this type in Cuyahoga, Summit, Stark and Tuscarawas counties particularly. Historical sites and communities and museums would add to the interest of hike-bike travel along the Ohio & Erie towpath.

The Chesapeake and Ohio Canal has it now. The Ohio & Erie could have it — tomorrow.

December 10, 1967
Blue Blazes To Mark Buckeye Trail

One of the many interesting aspects of the canal restoration and developing project is the shift in emphasis from time to time on the various canal-oriented activities.

Throughout the four seasons, one activity after another is spotlighted. With fishing, canoeing and canal-boat building

more or less over until spring, the emphasis seems to be shifting to hiking, riding and biking.

This was focused sharply last week by the visit to Stark County of Ralph Ramey, recreation supervisor for the division of parks and recreation of the Ohio Department of Natural Resources, and Robert Paton, trail coordinator for the Buckeye Trail.

The two men from Columbus met with the Stark County Canal Lands Development Advisory Committee and talked hiking and biking among other things.

Both were enthusiastic about the progress being made in extending the Buckeye Trail and the cooperation they are receiving as they meet with individuals and organizations in the various counties of the state. Some 120 miles of the trail are completed and in use, including the scenic section from Tar Hollow State Park in Ross and Hocking counties to Burr Oak State Park in Athens and Morgan counties.

The section from Cincinnati to Rocky Fork State Park in Highland County will be completed and marked soon, according to Bob Paton. The Cleveland Metropolitan Park board has indicated it will cooperate with the trail builders in Cuyahoga County. And Muskingum Conservancy District officials have promised cooperation in Tuscarawas County, Bob reports.

After being assured of the cooperation of the canal lands development advisory committee in Stark County, subject to the commissioners' approval, he said:

"We have commitments which will take us from Cincinnati, with only one small gap, to the north edge of Stark County. We

hope, by next April, to put out a new state map showing the Buckeye Trail. Later we hope to have sectional maps available at a minimum cost for families and others who want to hike the trail."

The trail — going over the hills and through the valleys — is expected to measure 500 miles when completed.

A special "Buckeye Trail Blue" paint has been developed to mark the trail. "We want people to use the Buckeye Trail without any fear of getting lost. The blue blazes will let them know they are on the trail," Bob explains.

Commenting on the beauty of the terrain, he said:

"We are taking people through pretty country — through historical country."

Ralph, nodding his head in agreement, said:

"We want people to enjoy seeing things along the way, not just getting there. We are planning loop trails off the main trail, maybe with a salmon-colored blaze, which will take hikers to points of special historic or scenic interest."

Al Zaleski, president of Tri-County Trail Association, who was present at the meeting, announced that the trail riders are willing to clear and blaze the rest of the Buckeye Trail through Stark County.

Ralph was equally enthusiastic about the bikeways through the Wonderful World of Ohio the state is developing.

The first one is "a bicycle tour through Amish Country" in Ashtabula, Geauga and Trumbull counties. The bikeway is clearly marked with green and white "bike route" signs bearing a picture of a bicycle. An information folder includes a map showing the bikeway route and listing points of interest and special events. The points of interest include Punderson State Park, a maple sugar operation at Burton, the Geauga County Museum, an Amish harness shop, school, pallet factory and blacksmith shop, a 19th century trestle bridge and a covered bridge, old mill, bank, inn, historic Windsor Mills Church, cheese factory, waterworks and goat farm.

The second bikeway, in preparation in Fairfield County, will be through "Covered Bridge Country." The third route will be the bikeway in "Old Mill Country."

The fourth bikeway very well may be located in Stark County. Some 25 to 30 miles long, Ralph says it is being thought of in terms of the bikeway through "Canal Country." Dayton has its "Kettering Bikeway," Canton has a 1½-mile bikeway in its park system, the state of Wisconsin has Wisconsin Bikeways and now there is reason to believe Stark County will have its Canal Country bikeway.

When the blue blazes of the Buckeye Trail, the green and white bikeway signs and possibly some Boy Scout trail markers (if the Scouts make the towpath trail an official one) appear on the towpath, it will be hard to recognize it as the same overgrown, partially impassable path it was a few short years ago. And think of the healthy, wholesome fun and enjoyment it will provide for all who travel it.

December 17, 1967
Students 'Find' Canal

More and more voices are being heard — telling the canal story. And more and more reports and papers are being written — about the canal era. Students, from the elementary pupil to the university undergraduate, are discovering and being fascinated by the old waterways.

Among those who wrote to me recently seeking information for the preparation of a "canal paper" was Mark Westgerdes, a junior at Brunnerdale Seminary. Mark, who is making a report for his history class, sought information on Ohio's canals and maps showing their routes.

Rebecca Loader, a junior at Newcomerstown High School, wanted the same kind of information. She is preparing a term paper on the canals pointed toward answering a specific question. The title of her paper is "Ohio's Canals: Were They Worth It?" Rebecca set out to find out whether the canals were worth all the time, effort and money they cost. She reports that everywhere she went for help, she found "people ready and willing to help in any way that they could."

I wonder what Rebecca's conclusion will be.

Then Carl Ashley, a junior at Ohio State University, dropped in with his tape recorder. Carl, who was readying an oral report on the canals, is a student in the university's school of journalism.

One of the youngest "canal scholars" I have heard of is 10-year-old Richard Regula, a fifth-grade pupil at Navarre Elementary School. Richard is doing a special report on canal history, complete with pictures. I hope to see Richard's report when it is finished, for I have seen his interest in the canal being developed during the last four years.

Richard is the son of two of the most popular speakers on the canal in Stark County, State Sen. Ralph Regula and his wife, Mary. As a result he has had far more contact with the canals of America than most fifth-grade pupils.

Not only does Richard ride over the filled-in bed of the Ohio and Erie Canal, past a former canal tavern, each day on his way to and from school, but he has accompanied his father and mother on hikes along the towpaths of the Ohio & Erie and on inspection tours of the Chesapeake and Ohio Canal in Maryland and the Whitewater Canal in Indiana.

Among the voices recently added to those telling the canal story is that of Tom Metzger, who also came to know the canal at an early age. When he was 3 and slightly older, he used to look out the window of his great-grandfather's house on the canal in Massillon and watch the canal boats go by. His great-grandfather was William Chapman who lived on Canal Street in 1903, at which time the boats were still in use. Canal Street today is First Street W in downtown Massillon.

In his work as an abstractor through the years, Tom has unearthed some interesting information about the canal. The old records revealed various legal disputes and troubles over the canal lands in and near Massillon and Navarre during the past century. Tom combines his memories of the canal with the information and anecdotes he has collected from his work in his talk entitled "History of Navarre and the Ohio Canal."

Still another voice that has joined the "canal speakers" is that of a man who is no stranger to this column — Clyde Gainey of Canal Fulton, member of the Stark County Canal Lands Development Advisory Committee and owner-curator of the Old Canal Days Museum in Canal Fulton. Clyde recently was scheduled to speak to the history classes at Northwest High School — about the canal that long ago brought Ohio pioneers within view of the present site of the school.

Because of these speakers and students, the canal is becoming known to more and more people. It is appreciated more today, and hope for a new existence for the canal in this decade, as an historical, educational and recreational parkway, grows even brighter.

December 24, 1967
Found — Bailer From the 'Nailer'

It sure doesn't look like much. Sort of long and skinny — and rather tinny. You might even say primitive. But it did the job and it is a "rare thing" today. It is on display at the Old Canal Days Museum in Canal Fulton.

"It" is a canal-boat bilge pump, which, according to curator Clyde Gainey, was part of the original equipment of the canal boat "Nailer," owned and operated by George Myers of Canal Fulton. The "Nailer" was one of the last canal boats to go into Cleveland from this division of the Ohio &

Erie Canal.

Shortly after the decision was made to build an authentic canal boat in Stark County more than a year ago, the search began for a bilge pump. The pumps, although not very pretty, were essential equipment on the old vessels. But no one could find an authentic pump that had been used on a canal boat. Not even a good description or picture of one was turned up.

Then one day, Arnold Blank of Canal Fulton heard about the search. Arnold "just happened" to have one of the rare pieces of equipment, which he generously presented to the museum, along with an account tracing its history back to the "Nailer."

It seems that Arnold was a boyhood pal of Roy Myers, son of George Myers who owned the "Nailer." Both of the boys loved boats. When the "Nailer" was decommissioned, Roy gave the pump to Arnold, who used it on his 23-foot pleasure boat, which was docked on Turkeyfoot Lake. That was in 1910.

The pump, Arnold recalls, was about 9 feet long. But, as he did not need such a long pump to remove excess water from his smaller boat, he cut about 4 feet off.

Later, Arnold sold his boat and the pump stood in a corner of his boathouse for years, then disappeared. For 15 years Arnold had no idea what happened to it. One day, while cleaning out the boathouse, he fished up the old bilge pump while using a garden rake to retrieve some old tires, which had been used as dock bumpers but had fallen into the water and ended up in the mud on the lake bottom. Arnold figured some youngster had thrown it into the lake. Being in the water, it was preserved. Otherwise, it probably would have been thrown away or destroyed long ago.

While the "Nailer's" bilge pump has been added to Clyde Gainey's remarkable display at the Old Canal Days Museum, it will serve admirably as a model for a comparable pump for Stark County's canal freighter now under construction.

About the same time, Clyde came into possession of an old paint grinder or pulverizer, which was part of the original equipment used on the state repair boat operated by John Moore of Canal Fulton. Clyde says he was told that the state canal boat maintained and repaired the Ohio & Erie from Barberton to Navarre.

The heavy metal grinder was used aboard the boat to grind colored paint pigments into powder, which was mixed with oil and turpentine by the boat's crew and used to "keep up" canal installations.

When the state boat reached the end of its service days and was destroyed, one of the pieces of equipment salvaged was the grinder. John Moore's son-in-law, Dave McGee, and his brother, Frank McGee, helped salvage the boat. So the grinder was stored in their paint and repair shop on West Cherry Street in Canal Fulton. One day Clyde got a telephone call from Jim McGee, son of Frank, who said he could have the paint grinder for the museum.

Because of the generosity of Arnold Blank and Jim McGee, countless Americans will have a better picture of the canal boats when they visit Clyde Gainey's Old Canal Days Museum.

December 31, 1967
Tunnel Under the Golden Triangle

The vastness of the canal systems of early America continues to amaze me. How such an extensive network of commercial waterways could exist and function, be so instrumental in the development of our great nation and then be almost forgotten is difficult to understand.

And yet when some vestige of one of the old canals is unearthed today, it brings forth comments of amazement, almost of incredulity — like something as old as the pyramids had been discovered instead of remnants of an era that began less than 200 years ago.

The most recent instance of this to come to my attention was a feature story published in the editorial section of the *Pittsburgh Press* earlier this month. Two photographs and an artist's drawing embellished the story.

The writer used a lot of imagery to convey to the reader the "would you believe?" nature of the recent discovery of the "legendary" Pennsylvania Canal tunnel in downtown Pittsburgh. An excavation crew at the site of the new U.S. Steel Building on Grant Street came on the mouth of the 810-foot tunnel after tearing away 28 feet of earth.

In 1829, when it was opened to traffic, the tunnel, like the Chesapeake and Ohio's 3,118-foot tunnel near Paw Paw, West Virginia, was considered a marvel. But for more than 100 years it had been buried in the Steel City's Golden Triangle — and forgotten.

Everywhere and every time a lock, tunnel or aqueduct of one of the old canals is brought to the attention of 20th century engineers, they have plaudits for the early canal builders.

Richard Corry and Hy Perlman of a New York construction firm are no exceptions. When they saw the workmanship of the stone masons who built the tunnel, they remarked: "Those sandstone blocks — 12"x18"x30" — were set beautifully. Judged by modern standards it may not seem so great but it was really something to build a canal tunnel about 18 feet wide and 14 feet high. It was a fine job — pity it has to go. But that's life."

The engineers indicated that for more than 25 years the canal and tunnel linked Pittsburgh with the rest of America. Although it is contrary to some opinions, the two engineers believe the canal tunnel was underneath the Pennsylvania Railroad tunnel where the two tunnels crisscrossed underground.

The canal tunnel (for those who know Pittsburgh) ran through Grant's Hill to Sukes Run. Because of it, Pittsburgh's trade swelled greatly. Millions of tons of cargo were transported each year faster and cheaper than ever before.

Cold and dry spells spelled trouble for the canal, however, and it had to be shut down from two weeks to two months each winter and often for an equal period each summer.

The Pennsylvania Canal ran between Pittsburgh and Philadelphia and provided

Lock No. 40 on the northern leg of the Ohio & Erie Canal is visible in the distance in this view looking south on the towpath in Cuyahoga County.

Canal Society of Ohio

a speedy (for those days) trip for travelers. It usually required 10 days to three weeks to make the journey across the state.

The Pennsylvania Canal's history parallels that of most of the other canals in that it was unable to compete with the "iron horse" and finally was sold, in 1857, to the Pennsylvania Railroad.

An 1830 map of Pittsburgh shows the canal paralleled the north side of the Allegheny River and then crossed the Allegheny via an aqueduct across Pittsburgh along the east side of Grant Street to what then was Seventh Street.

It entered the tunnel at a point then known as Strawberry Alley. The tunnel route generally followed Tunnel Street. The canal became an open canal again south of Grant's Hill and finally passed through four locks and entered the Monongahela River.

But today it lies buried beneath a great city, its monument the modern metal and brick buildings that create the Golden Triangle's 20th century skyline.

Those who read this column are indebted, along with me, to John Stoner, an elementary teacher in the Jackson Local School District, for bringing the *Pittsburgh Press'* historical feature to my attention.

It has provided still another chapter in the lengthening narrative of early America along the towpath.

Book Five·1968

January 7, 1968
A Look Back From 1968

In this first column of 1968, let's do a switch. Let's look backward instead of forward and see what was accomplished and what wasn't, with respect to canal reconstruction plans.

The headline on the "Towpath" column January 1, 1967, read "Canal Plans for the New Year." It contained statements from some of the persons most directly involved in planning the development of the canal lands in Stark County.

For example, State Sen. Ralph Regula, cochairman of the Stark County Canal Lands Development Advisory Committee, foresaw increased use of the canal in 1967. This did occur.

He hoped the gates at Lock 4 Park could be repaired or replaced. The lock was repaired and painted and two of the four gates were replaced with new gates but not installed.

One of the goals the senator stressed was the desirability of establishing a metropolitan park district. This was achieved but the failure of the metropolitan park levy to win support of the voters was a major disappointment of 1967.

The hope that the rewatered section of the canal could be extended south toward Massillon was not realized nor was an official Boy Scout Trail established on the towpath in 1967.

But planning for development of the Buckeye Trail along the towpath in Stark County was advanced with the senator taking an active role in the programming.

William Keen, cochairman of the canal lands committee, who was mayor of Massillon a year ago but who now is the county's first administrator, looked toward the further development of the 1,200-foot park north of Massillon on the filled-in section of the canal. No progress was achieved on this project.

Mr. Keen also hoped that additional property between the canal and the Tuscarawas River could be acquired but several factors, including lack of funds, prevented this.

Cochairman Keen was hopeful the state would purchase Lake Lucern north of Canal Fulton so it could be used as a state park and a source of additional water for the canal. The lake was purchased in 1967 but not by the state. So it will not become a state park. The possibility that it can be used as a source of additional water for the canal still exists, however.

Gervis Brady, director of the Stark County Historical Center, hoped to see the Stark County Historical Society's canalside museum under way during 1967. Although planning progress has been made, ground has not yet been broken for the museum.

Another objective in 1967 was that the general development plan, as it applies to the canal, would be completed by the Stark County Regional Planning Commission. At year's end it was 35 percent completed. The new goal is completion by the end of 1968.

There was hope too, that the county's canal boat could be built and launched during 1967. It was not. But more progress was made on it than on any other canal-oriented project during 1967.

At the beginning of the year there was little manpower and little money to build the boat. Then the Louisville Sportsman's Club, headed by Jim Cozy, volunteered to build the boat. By the time winter arrived, the hull framework was completed. Roy K. Preece, construction boss for the boat, and Carroll M. Gantz, design supervisor, have finalized their designs and blueprints and expectations are that the boat will be launched this summer.

Going into 1968, it looks as though development of the canal towpath through Stark County as part of Ohio's Buckeye

Trail and construction of the authentic canal freighter are the two projects most obviously progressing.

Behind the scenes, efforts to get the metropolitan park system started and to build a canalside museum hold promise. Young 1968 could be bigger, canal-wise, than 1967.

January 14, 1968
Movie To Include Canal Scenes

Today's episode in the continuing story of the redevelopment of the Ohio & Erie Canal in Stark County starts with a jaguar hunt in Brazil.

And it ends with plans to make a movie — a 90-minute, 16mm color film — about Ohio. Seven to 10 minutes of the film will feature canal scenes taken throughout the year, showing activity on the canal or along the towpath during all four seasons. There will be 50 or 60 scenes showing hikers, boaters, fishermen enjoying the canal, bird life on and near the towpath, construction of the canal boat at Canal Fulton, activity at Lock 4 Park and other places of historical interest.

How does this tie in with a jaguar hunt in Brazil? Very easily. Don Campbell, the jaguar hunter, is making the movie. While hunting the big cats Don also took some motion pictures. Now he seldom uses a gun, preferring to "shoot" with his camera. Making and showing his pictures became an avocation for Don.

Then he decided to put a film together about Ohio, based on the knowledge that everyone can't go hunting jaguars in Brazil, but most can travel and enjoy many interesting places in Ohio — if they know about them. His movie will show opportunities for recreation existing in the state, scenic panoramas, conservation projects, pollution problems and other aspects of the Ohio scene.

While searching for historical material about the state, Don came on an old postcard that showed three canal freighters in the canal somewhere near Navarre. It is one of the better canal-scene postal cards ever printed. Don plans to use the card scene in his movie as the introductory view to the section on canals. When the movie is completed, he will use the film as part of a presentation to civic and fraternal groups, thus spreading the canal story ever further.

All those healthy, hearty people who like to hike in the winter wonderland, take note: The division of parks and recreation of the Ohio Department of Natural Resources and the Buckeye Trail Association will sponsor the third annual Hocking Hills Winter Hike Saturday. The hike, along the beautiful Hocking Hills section of the Buckeye Trail, will get under way at Old Man's Cave and end five miles later at Ash Cave. There will be a break at lovely Cedar Falls, which usually is a cascade of white ice at this time of year.

More than a dozen qualified hike leaders will be present to lead the groups along the cliff and creekside-trail and through the hemlock-lined gorges. Melvin Rebholz, chief of the parks and recreation division, said a new section of woodland trail will be followed for the first time on this trip.

Warm clothing, good footgear, a sack lunch and plenty of color film — that's all you need to have a wonderful time in one of the most scenic sections of the state.

Readers may recall that I participated in the hike last year and wrote about the experience the following week. An estimated 600 persons from throughout the state and some from other states made the hike last year. There were young hikers and senior citizens on the trail. Leo Armstrong, at 81, and Grandma Emma Gatewood, at 79, were the oldest hikers and made the trip in fine style. So if you like to hike and you like the winter season, head for Logan in Hocking County Saturday. You'll find a lot of folks like yourself there.

January 21, 1968
Navarre Eyes Canal Park

Navarre, unlike Canal Fulton, no longer has a rewatered section of the Ohio & Erie

Canal flowing through it. Neither does it have a well-preserved lock nearby such as the one at Lock 4 Park. Navarre's Lock exists today only on picture postcards. And most of the canal bed within the village has been filled in. But the town fathers have plans to utilize the remaining canal lands in a way that will benefit all the residents of the community.

Some time ago, they asked the Stark County Regional Planning Commission to prepare a playground design for the canal lands and conduct a parks need survey for the village.

Early this month, the planning commission completed its work and submitted a report. It was found that, with one exception, all the parks and playgrounds were in or just outside the eastern half of the village. Only the Golden Age Fishing Pond, a spring-fed pond in the bed of the old canal, is in the western half of the town.

But the survey shows there are two areas at the western edge of the village which are "possibly suited for park development." One is the Ohio and Erie Canal lands owned by the village and located to the rear of lots facing on Canal St. on the north and Ohio St. on the south. The second is a 16-acre tract west of Wilmont Rd. and south of Canal St., which adjoins the canal lands.

The commission submitted a design for a canal-lands park and an alternative for a recreational center that would incorporate the canal lands, new village hall, a roadside park and extensive playground development.

What Navarre will do with respect to the planning commission's recommendations remains to be seen. But it almost certainly will be something that will make the old canal lands more attractive and possibly link it compatibly with the canal segment of the Stark Metropolitan Park District of the future.

Action in Tuscarawas

News from Tuscarawas County indicates that action to acquire four to five miles of the canal lands southeast of Bolivar is, or soon will be, under way by the county.

At the same time, more canal land in the county is being sold to private individuals.

Nearly an acre of the old Ohio & Erie lands were sold for $656. The land is in Goshen Township, which includes New Philadelphia.

County Engineer Charles R. Young said land descriptions will be prepared soon so the county may obtain the land for public use. The land is available from the state without cost.

The land sought extends south from Bolivar to the junction of Routes 8 and 212 and contains four canal locks. Cleaned up, the area would be very scenic.

Present at a recent meeting to discuss which lands were available were Mr. Young, Deputy Engineer Dean Davidson, the county commissioners, Walter Begland, land manager of the Muskingum Watershed Conservancy District, Henry Spring, president of the Tuscarawas County Historical Association, and Ted Findley, president of the Canal Society of Ohio.

January 28, 1968
Buckeye Trail Report

Bob Paton of Worthington, Buckeye Trail coordinator, is really making trail — not in the fields and woods and not on the towpath but on paper — on the maps. He was in Stark County again last week, this time with Harry Wilkie, who came from Cincinnati to help make the Buckeye Trail Association inspection of the proposed trail through Stark County.

The Ohio & Erie Canal Towpath from Crystal Springs to Canal Fulton was designated a part of the Buckeye Trail in 1966 but now the trail association wants to approve the route throughout the entire county so it can be cleared and blazed.

Stark County is fortunate in having ownership of the canal lands. Thus the trailmakers can follow the canal towpath through the county with relative ease, without the necessity of obtaining rights-of-way, easements or agreements with individual landowners to cross their properties.

Only in a few places is it necessary to deviate from the towpath. Massillon and Navarre are the two major areas where other routes must be utilized. It was to check on the proposed trail in general and these non-towpath links specifically that Bob Paton and Harry Wilkie came to Stark County.

As officers of the trail association, State Sen. Ralph Regula of Navarre and this columnist were charged with laying out the proposed route throughout Stark County. Working with Al Zaleski, president of the Tri-County Trail Association, whose horsemen will clear and blaze the trail when given the go-ahead, we charted the proposed route.

Almost immediately, Bob and Harry were here "to look over" the planned route. Sen. Regula took them on a tour of the southern part of the towpath and I showed them the northern half.

Action on the Stark County section of the trail is expected at the February meeting of the Buckeye Trail Association executive committee in Columbus.

If the green light is flashed, Al Zaleski and his trail riders will pitch in to make trail during the winter so the Stark section of the Buckeye Trail will be ready for blazing in the spring — from Summit County to Tuscarawas County.

Park Use Is Big

In attempting to analyze the voters' rejection of the levy to provide funds for operating Stark County's Metropolitan Park District, many causes have been advanced. Possibly, some residents felt the county park system would not be used much since all of the major cities and many of the villages within the county have parks of their own.

But this would not be the case, if one can judge from the experience of Cleveland.

Cleveland has many parks within its borders. Yet this does not prevent millions of Clevelanders from enjoying the Cleveland Metropolitan Parks' "Emerald Necklace," a string of parks that ring the city outside its limits.

During the last three years, annual park attendance has averaged 13,845,500. A breakdown of the 1967 attendance by park, follows: Huntington, 576,000; Rocky River, 6,620,000; Big Creek, 306,000; Hinckley, 1,560,000; Brecksville, 531,000; Bedford, 861,000; South Chagrin, 825,000; North Chagrin, 1,680,000; Euclid Creek, 635,000; Bradley Woods, 159,000.

Granted, Cleveland has a much larger population than Stark County. Still, these figures are impressive. They seemingly indicate people would use and benefit from Stark County's Metropolitan Park District — if there were funds to breathe life into it.

February 4, 1968

Purchase Spells Progress

One of the most encouraging recent developments associated with the canal restoration program in Stark County was made public at the annual meeting of the Stark County Historical Society. The announcement that the society had purchased nearly an acre of land adjoining Lock 4 Park came as very good news.

The property fronts on Erie Ave. and adjoins the park just south of the entrance. Strategically located, the property could be used for a number of purposes.

Dr. R. K. Ramsayer, president of the historical society, expressed appreciation to the Stark County Foundation for the grant that made the purchase possible.

Gervis Brady, historical center director, expressing satisfaction with the purchase, said efforts are under way to acquire additional land near the park.

Advanced planning calls for construction of a canalside museum near the lock. Restoration of the lock and replacement of its gates is continuing. The lock is expected to be operational by the time the canal freighter being constructed by the Louisville Sportsman's Club and Canal Fulton residents is completed, hopefully this summer.

With development of the Buckeye Trail

advancing steadily, (it will pass through the park and within sight of the museum), scenic little Lock 4 Park stands to become one of the most interesting historical-educational-recreational locations in Stark County.

Death of a 'Canawler'

With the passing of Charles A. Croft, 86, of Barberton, still another of the few remaining human links with the canal era has been broken.

Mr. Croft, as a young man, was one of the "canawlers" who hauled coal from the Chillings Coal Mine near Dover to the Akron Paper Mill. It usually took two days to make the 45-mile trip with two horses and a mule pulling the slow-moving freighters. Mr. Croft, who was born in Bolivar in Tuscarawas County, recalled that, at times, the canal boats carried as much as 70 tons of coal.

I regret that I did not get to know Mr. Croft before his death. I would have enjoyed talking with him about the canal, for he must have made many trips up and down Stark County's section of the Ohio & Erie Canal.

The 'Asphalt Canal'

Ever hear of an asphalt canal? They have one in Mexico. At least that's what they call it. Actually, it is a highway that spans the historic Isthmus of Tehuantepec in southern Mexico. Known as Highway 185, it runs from the Atlantic to the Pacific in this area, which has been considered for a water canal. Travelers on the asphalt highway generally make it coast to coast in four hours, enjoying dramatic scenery on the way.

One of the many bizarre schemes to provide access from one ocean to the other would have constructed a triple-track railroad there — not for trains but to haul oceangoing vessels. If this "vision," proposed in the late 1800s, had come to pass, they might have called it the "Iron Horse Canal."

More realistic plans for a sea-level canal across the isthmus have been shelved for the present due to the prohibitive cost. If such a canal is made, it ought to be a pretty one. It would wind through sweet-scented citrus groves and it wouldn't freeze over in the winter.

In the meantime, if you want to travel across the Isthums of Tehuantepec, you will have to rely on Mexico's "Asphalt Canal."

February 11, 1968
Are We Seeing a New Canal Era?

Historians of the future may look back on these days and designate the 1960s as the "new canal era" — a least in the Ohio counties traversed by the old Ohio & Erie Canal.

I'm joking, of course. But seriously, the historians may very well make note of the widespread restoration and recreational utilization of the long-dead waterway in the last half of this decade.

It is interesting and surprising to note how restoration programs have come into being in several counties at almost the same time and are developing concurrently in much the same way.

I recently told how Tuscarawas County, after a slow start, seems to be moving ahead with plans to restore and develop a section of the canal between Zoar and Bolivar. The potential there is great and the plans are tremendous and many-faceted.

Similarly, in Coshocton County, a real opportunity exists for the development of recreational areas that are canal centered and historically oriented.

The citizens of the city of Coshocton are being asked to help raise $100,000 in a campaign designed to "give them one of the finest recreational facilities" in the state. With Uncle Sam chipping in, they expect to have $166,000 to complete their "open spaces" program. Donations from business, industry and individual citizens are being sought.

The idea for Coshocton's Lake Park recreational areas began in 1958 when Thomas B. Leech, then mayor of Coshocton, had the foresight to obtain the canal lands from the state for the city. This included all the canal lands from the south border of Roscoe to the Keene Township line, all cottage sites on the Lake Park towpath and the three canal basins, Roscoe, Middle and Mudport.

The first step to be taken now probably will be the modification of the master plan, with assistance from Ohio State University and the state park board.

The city's weekly newspaper *The Commentator* writes:

"The master plan would encompass a diverse development to include virgin forests on the hillsides, beautiful parks and picnic areas, nature trails, playgrounds, canoeing and boating docks along the river, camping, baseball, fishing, swimming, ice skating, and historic sites and markings. What the committee feels will be a great tourist attraction is planned with the dredging of the canal and restoration of the towpath between Lower Basin and Mudport Basin to the north. A canal excursion boat could be run on the canal between these areas. The area, as envisioned, could be of statewide interest with the historic sites of Indian settlements, the canal, and Colonel Henry Bouquet's camp preserved and marked."

The area also has the unique and well-preserved canal triple lock as one of its most interesting features.

Stark, Tuscarawas, Coshocton — each county has its own special history to preserve and relate. Each has its own brand of scenery to display and perpetuate. Each is a canal county and each may have a canal boat to heighten interest in the canal parks.

If all of this comes to pass, maybe it could be designated the nouveau canal era after all.

Manry To Sail Canal

I haven't read anything since before Christmas about Robert Manry, daring skipper of the *Tinkerbelle*. At that time, the indomitable conqueror of the Atlantic Ocean and his family were at a marina in Sarasota, Fla.

They were living aboard their 27-foot yawl, *Curlew*, looking forward to spending Christmas in the Bahamas. After that they planned to visit the island of San Salvador, where another daring conqueror of the Atlantic stepped ashore in 1492. That would be Christopher Columbus.

Then their itinerary called for a bit of canal sailing.

The Manrys (Capt. Bob and his wife Virginia, daughter Robin, 16, and son, Douglas, 13) left Cleveland in August. They sailed through the Great Lakes to Chicago, down the Illinois River to the Mississippi and on to New Orleans. Then they sailed around the Gulf of Mexico to Key West and on to the Bahamas.

Their return trip will take them up the intercoastal waterway, which is much like a canal in some sections, to New York. They will pass the skyscrapers of Manhattan and go on up the Hudson River to the eastern terminus of the Erie Canal.

Then the family will sail across the state of New York on the canal to Buffalo. From there it is just a short voyage across a little bit of Lake Erie to Cleveland and home.

The Manrys have had a number of adventures during their voyage and Capt. Bob is writing a book about it. No doubt it will have a chapter or part of one on their canal experiences.

February 18, 1968
Tree Expert Prescribes for Canal

The Canal Fulton Rotary Club and the new Canal Fulton Junior Chamber of Commerce held their first joint meeting recently and out of it came the hope that their combined efforts will stimulate interest in and support of the canal development projects.

Speaker was Oliver D. Diller, curator of the Secrest Arboretum at the Ohio Agricultural Research and Development Center at Wooster. His topic was "Trees for Shade and for Beauty," slanted especially to apply to the replanting of trees along the Ohio & Erie Canal towpath in the village.

Prior to the meeting, Mr. Diller and

Gale Hartel, chairman of the Rotary Club's canal-project committee, spent several hours inspecting the types and condition of the trees along the towpath.

Because some sound trees will have to be cut, along with the dead ones, if the canal boat now being constructed is to be towed by a team walking the towpath, Mr. Hartel's committee wants to replace them. The new trees, however, would be planted on the side of the towpath away from the canal, and, in time, would grow to overhang the canal, adding natural beauty to the old waterway.

In his talk, Mr. Diller said he believed the canal area could be made a place of beauty with the proper arrangement of good trees. He advised against planting cheap or short-lived trees. He explained that the proper choice of shade trees is essential, not only from the standpoint of aesthetics but with regard to maintenance costs over time.

The arboretum curator said the canal area already has many varieties of trees. Some of those he identified include: honey locust, cottonwood, black walnut, white ash, shingle oak and soft maple. He suggested planting flowering dogwood for added color.

She'll Write of Canal

A Canton resident soon may be instrumental in helping to spread the story of the canal, its history, folklore, restoration and future development throughout the state via the magazine, "Valley Views," a slick-paper quarterly published at Solon and distributed statewide.

Marian Clover has been asked by the magazine's editor to write a story about the Ohio & Erie Canal, paying special atten-

tion to these aspects. Mrs. Clover hoped to base her story on a trip down the canal by pontoon boat with a troop of girl scouts. But her deadline is prior to the spring launching date of the pontoon boats. So she may base the story on a family canoe cruise down the old waterway.

Mrs. Clover also intends to write about the construction of the canal boat and the plans for a museum at Lock 4.

February 25, 1968
Trailblazers Trim Towpath

I can't be sure, for I wasn't there, but the action going on last Sunday along the towpath of the Ohio & Erie Canal in southern Stark County most probably was reminiscent of comparable activity in this area 150 to 175 years ago.

It was mighty cold but that didn't deter 18 members of the Tri-County Trail Association (17 men and one woman) from clearing trail from the Tuscarawas River north to Riverland Rd. roughly three miles. Using axes, saws, hatchets, machetes, the trail association members cut the trees, standing and fallen, from the towpath and trimmed the brush back so a hiker or horseman now can traverse the trail without difficulty.

It may have been in much the same way that the pioneer Ohioans opened up wagon trails to and through Stark County. The modern trailblazers didn't have to contend with Indians however.

Al Zaleski, president of the trail association, was enthusiastic about the progress of the group.

"Everyone pitched in and worked," he said, "and the one female member of the path-clearing crew did her share with a pair of pruning shears."

With obvious pride in his organization, Al announced that the women members had volunteered to paint all the official blue blazes of the Buckeye Trail on the trees and otherwise mark the trail after the men finish clearing it. They plan to make stencils to achieve uniform marking.

Al said the group plans to continue clearing the towpath next Sunday – from the Riverland Rd. crossing of the canal north to Navarre. After that they will take a look at what needs to be done in the way of clearing and marking between Navarre and Massillon.

Another day the volunteer horsemen will head south beyond the Tuscarawas River toward Bolivar. They will cut trail down the middle of the dry canal bed for a way and then return to the towpath.

As I keep saying — volunteers, they're wonderful!

Thinking Spring

A cold, blustery, wintry night in February is a good time to stay indoors where it is warm and think about plans for spring. And that's just what a group of men interested in getting Stark County's canal boat completed and in the water did one night last week.

There were nine of us present at one of the most informal and pleasant meetings I have attended in a long time.

The canal-oriented bull session was held at the home of Roy K. Preece, construction boss for the canal boat, who resides east of Canal Fulton. Also present were:

Jim Cozy, project overseer and president of Louisville Sportsman's Club, which is building the boat; Carroll M. Gantz, head of the industrial design section of Hoover Co., who is making the design drawings of the boat; Paul Baird, president of Notnac Mfg. Co. of Canton and procurement expeditor for the canal-boat project; Clyde Gainey, member of the Stark County Canal Lands Development Advisory Committee and owner-curator of the Old Canal Days Museum.

Edward Harriman, president of The Exchange Bank Co. of Canal Fulton and representative of the village Rotary Club; Richard Weigand, representative of the new Canal Fulton Junior Chamber of Commerce; Peter Neidert of Neidert and Sons farm machinery and lawn equipment service, whose assistance and equipment have been invaluable in the boat building project, and this columnist.

Plans were discussed, new drawings were studied and ideas were exchanged. Meanwhile, enthusiasm built up to push the project steadily on toward launching day.

May 3, it will be just a year since the posts were set for the boat's keel. Since then it is estimated some 1,120 volunteer hours have gone into work on the boat.

Come May 3, many of the plans made at last week's meeting should be translated into solid three-dimensional form as the canal boat becomes ever more believable.

BRAVO! Alliance Scouts

Regardless of who is building it, the Stark County's canal boat technically will belong to everybody in the county.

Numerous individuals and groups from various parts of the county have and are helping with the project.

One of the latest to help is Boy Scout Troop 104 of Alliance. The Scouts and a number of their adult committeemen plan to take their saws and axes to Canal Fulton March 9 and cut down dead trees along the towpath between Lock 4 Park and Canal Fulton. The Scouts will also remove the dead wood from the towpath.

Three members of the Canal Fulton Jaycees will act in a liaison capacity and the Rotary Club will serve refreshments to the Scouts.

The troop camped at Lock 4 Park last summer and hiked the towpath. Apparently they enjoyed their stay there, for they asked what they could do to help in the canal restoration project. Their contribution is important, for the canal boat could not be towed from the towpath if the trees were not removed.

A Guest Commentary

The column this week will not be about the canal and its towpath. Rather, it will be concerned with the canal's sickly neighbor, the pallid, polluted Tuscarawas River. The once-healthy, clear-water stream, which many older readers will recall from their youth, has been seriously "ill," due to poisoning, for years. As the Ohio & Erie Canal is rewatered and its adjacent lands improved, the river looks even worse by comparison. And its course closely parallels the canal all the way through Stark County.

D.L. Hoagland, a Massillon postman, has written about the change in the river through the years. He prefaces his article, entitled *With Our Backs to the River*, with these words:

"Fresh sources of water are rapidly being destroyed. I believe that the fight against pollution must begin at home. If proof is needed, the front seat of my canoe is open to you. From it you can see the Tuscarawas at its worst. This canoe has also traveled the clean waters of the North, where a refreshing drink of water can be yours merely by dipping a cup over the side. I know that we can never return to that pure state but it is possible to return our rivers to a livable medium. The benefits from such a return are inestimable."

With Our Backs to the River

By D. L. Hoagland

Flowing silently and serenely through the rolling farmlands of western Stark County, the Tuscarawas carries its cross of industrial waste and poorly processed sewage southward to its junction with the Muskingum River.

The Tuscarawas, named for a once proud Indian tribe, a tribe driven to the north by the advance of civilization, bears little resemblance to its former self. Once it was the home of trout, when its waters still held the chill of spring waters protected by the deep shade of uncut forests, and

later it abounded in bass and other warm water fish. Along its banks traveled the fauna of the early days, bear, deer, beaver, mink, muskrat and other small but vital animal life. Indians followed its course, hunting, trapping and fishing, never altering the river's role as a benefactor of life.

As the population grew in this valley, strange things began to happen to the river. Forested hills, which once held rainfall, were cleared; streams of mud and soil spilled into the river, carried by the heavy rains, which ran unchecked down the slopes. Mud and sand clogged the gills of trout and scoured the great spawning beds. Riffles and rapids filled and became mud flats. The stream shallowed and slowed.

Though sluggish and silt-laden, the river still supported wildlife. Coarse fish such as carp and catfish, able to survive in muddy water, provided food for predators and sport for those who loved to spend hours by the streamside in search of quiet and beauty. Great migrating flocks of waterfowl rested on its waters on the long trips to the South in the fall and again in the spring on their way to the nesting grounds of the North.

Then came the sprawling industries. Great factories were built in the valley. Products for the increasing population rolled from the mills and production lines. But a by-product of these necessities was being deposited quietly and stealthily in the river. That by-product was poison. Fish began to die and float bloated belly-up. Great banks of them rotted on the sandbars. Waterfowl, which landed in the oily and acid eddies of the stream, died because they were unable to rise from its waters and could not feed on its poisoned vegetation.

This sad picture confronts us today. The status of a river can be determined easily. Slip a canoe onto the foul currents of the Tuscarawas at the southern boundary of Summit County and make the five or six-hour run to Navarre. You will not see one dwelling that faces the river. We literally have turned our backs to the river. As long as we continue to do so, the Tuscarawas will be nothing more than a lengthy cesspool.

Contrast this steam with others to the

north and south of us. They are the setting of many and varied summer cottages and campsites. Those rivers ring with the laughter of swimmers and boaters and yield relaxation and sport to many. The Tuscarawas again could be a source of pleasure to those in the valley.

Hundreds of summer cabin sites in beautiful woodland settings await only the cleaning of the waters. Landowners along the river would prosper from lot sales. Building material sales would rise and tradesmen in the area would be kept busy building for the ever-increasing army of outdoor pleasure seekers. Additional real estate taxes would roll into city and county coffers.

Canoes and other craft would ply the river's currents. Smallmouth bass again would thrive, molested only by the spinning and fly rods of hopeful anglers.

We can have industry and clean waters also. Do we want a clean river or an open sewer flowing through our countryside? It is up to us.

March 10, 1968
Columbus Once Was a Busy Port

Can you visualize Columbus — Ohio's landlocked capital city — as a busy port?

"Well hardly," you might respond. "Columbus isn't even close to a navigable body of water. Why even the old Ohio & Erie Canal was nearly 12 miles away from the city."

And you would be right. Nevertheless, Columbus once was a port to which boats brought a great variety of Eastern goods at lower prices than had been thought possible. Columbus became a port as the result of a major engineering project, the linking of the city with the canal by means of an 11-mile lateral canal.

Bill Arter, writing in the *Columbus Dispatch Magazine* about this fascinating chapter in the city's history, indicated the reaction of the residents to the completion of the lateral canal when he titled his

vignette *Welcome Waterway.*

Mr. Arter graciously granted permission to reprint his drawing, which accompanies this column, and to quote from his article. In drawing the picture, he worked from an old (about 1880) photo that shows a canal scene, the site of which can be identified today. The drawing shows a packet (passenger boat) in the foreground and a freighter, the two principal types of boats in use on the canal.

Mr. Arter observes that "to a young girl who lived along the canal, the packets seemed like fairy palaces. They were painted white and the windows had green shutters and scarlet curtains. Travelers who had been bruised black and blue riding in bouncing stagecoaches found the smooth gliding ride in a packet a real delight."

Digging of the "Columbus Lateral" was begun April 30, 1827, with a big celebration. Specifications were standard — 40 feet wide at the top and 26 at the bottom, with water 4 feet deep. Locks were constructed four miles south of Columbus and at Lockbourne, where the lateral joined the Ohio & Erie. Just above the point where boats arrived in Columbus a huge guard lock was built through which boats could enter the Scioto River. The river was made "slack" by a dam.

Thus the whole riverfront, up to Broad St., became a dock area, solidly lined with wharves and warehouses. When the first canal boats arrived in the city in September of 1831, all Columbus turned out to joyfully welcome them. It was a great day. Columbus had become a port.

Old Mill To Be Razed

Still another Stark County link with the canal era is scheduled for oblivion. That's the old gristmill building at Navarre, which stood between the Tuscarawas River and the Ohio & Erie Canal for about a century. It's still standing beside Route 21 as you head south out of Navarre. But not for long, according to William C. Evans, owner and operator of the Farmer Supply Company there. The building will be sold "piecemeal" or burned, he said.

Mr. Evans and Wilmer D. Swope of Leetonia, whose hobby is collecting old

mill lore, were helpful in providing information about the old Navarre mill.

They believe the building was erected in 1834, the same year James Duncan laid out the village of Navarre. This would make the mill 134 years old and place its construction in the heyday of the canal period. Mr. Duncan also built a sawmill, which burned down, and several dwellings.

The histories indicate quite a wheat business was done at Navarre and that there was much speculation in wheat before the local merchants failed financially in 1837.

Originally, the mill was water-powered; the big wheel being in the basement of the building. Canal water came from a large millpond back of the building in which canal boats could be turned around. There was a $25-a-year charge for the water to operate the mill. In the fall, when the water was low, the mill could not be operated. And so it first was changed to a steam operation and later to electric.

During World War I, a lot of flour was milled there for shipping to Holland, according to Mr. Evans. He said old records show farmers hauled wheat into the mill from as far away as Sandyville, and he presumes a lot of it was shipped out aboard canal boats.

At one time, the mill was a cooperative and another time it was owned by the Garver Brothers of Strasburg. Since the 1930s it has been used exclusively as a feed mill. Mr. Evans purchased it in 1936. About 30 years ago a millwright from Akron bought the big band wheel that distributed the power from the waterwheel.

March 17, 1968
Scouts' Good Turn Helps Towpath

A number of Boy Scouts from Alliance went all out to do their good deeds for the day. In fact, they spent the whole day doing one big collective deed. Armed with handsaws, hatchets, axes and a power saw, the Scouts cut down trees along the Ohio & Erie Canal towpath in Canal Fulton — trees that had to go if Stark County's canal boat is to be towed from the village down to Lock 4.

Twelve seemed to be the number of the day. There were 12 Boy Scouts and 12 men from Alliance on the job and, by working all day, they took out 12 pretty big trees.

In addition to the Scouts from Troop 104, under Scoutmaster William Mathys, and Troop 54, under Scoutmaster Tom Skelding, there were three or four Scouts from Troop 921 at St. Jacob's Lutheran Church in Jackson Township, three or four Canal Fulton Rotarians and about 12 members of the village's new Junior Chamber of Commerce in the work crew.

Starting at the village park, the towpath trimmers worked their way south for about 1,000 feet to the old dry dock, felling the trees and removing them from the towpath as they went. Richard Vogelman, chairman of the Rotary canal committee, was in charge of the project. Another Rotarian, Arnold Blank, was probably the most popular man on the scene. He served refreshments. Edward Harriman, president of the Exchange Bank at Canal Fulton and vice president of the Rotary Club, said of the Scouts' work, "They did a real good job. They gave it the gung-ho."

An Uphill Canal

You haven't heard everything yet — unless you have heard of the uphill canal. I'm not joking.

The French did it. At least they made a working model of a canal in which the water is forced to flow uphill. The model was unveiled near the city of Lyons in December. If the idea works as well as the designers hope, a full-scale uphill slope may become a key segment of the long-dreamed-of canal from the North Sea to the Mediterranean. The experimental water slope is 200 yards long, about a tenth the size the actual slope would be. It has a grade of 2.8 percent.

The *New York Times*, which reported the unveiling in a story from Paris, suggests the water slope, which was developed by French government engineers, is a possible alternative to the conventional lock and to hauling barges and canal boats uphill in tanks mounted on rollers.

When one or more canal boats or barges approach the slope at its lower end, a tractor mounted alongside swings a mobile wall into place behind the barges. The wall, lined with rubber rollers, fills the cross section of the canal. Meanwhile, a gate at the top keeps canal water from spilling down the slope.

The tractor then climbs the slope at 5 miles an hour, "pushing a wedge of water up the hill with the barges floating in it." When the upper level is reached, the gate is opened and the barges and canal boats move on. Then other boats, headed downstream, move in and are taken down the slope.

Engineers have taken canal boats through mountains via tunnels and they have taken them across rivers via aqueducts. Now they are going to take them uphill on an incline. What will they do with them next?

French Canals Beckon 'Explorers'

What quite possibly is the world's most exciting canal-travel adventure awaits the waterway explorer in France.

With 5,000 miles of rivers and canals — reaching from Dunkirk on the North Sea to near Marseille on the Mediterranean and from the Atlantic Ocean to the Bay of Biscay — beckoning, France must be a veritable dreamland for canal-travel enthusiasts.

Except for the more luxurious powerboats and launches that are in vogue today, canal travel in France in 1968 must approximate canal travel in Ohio more than a century ago. The numerous navigable canals wind through orchards and quiet fields, flow through rugged gorges, pass impressive chateaux and skirt the quays of cities and villages that travelers seldom discover.

If the Ohio & Erie Canal was still intact and navigable, those who traveled it would see a picturesque part of the Midwest that the average traveler misses.

So it is in France. The many canals provide a delightful way to explore some of the most beautiful sections of the country that are almost unknown to those who go there hoping to "see" France.

The canals usually are clear and clean, although the rivers are not. Both, as a rule, have plenty of fish in them.

The frequent locks provide for the tourist an opportunity to see more of the countryside, for he can get off his boat and explore the land nearby while the boat is being raised or lowered in the lock. If the larder of his boat's galley is low, he probably can bargain with the lockkeeper for eggs as most of them raise chickens. If he is still hungry, the canal traveler can stop at any of the numerous villages along the waterways and shop for cheeses, fresh bread and vegetables.

If he would rather eat out, he can find good food at inexpensive country restaurants. Then, in the evening, he can relax at some tiny bistro.

Robert Deardorff, writing in the *New York Times* from Paris, describes this "lazy, do-it-yourself travel in an unknown France" as the kind that invites adventure. The canal boatman, he says, "floats along tranquilly," living off the land and taking his pleasure as he finds it.

He recommends, as one trip, travel on the Nivernais Canal, one of the most picturesque in France. The canal-going traveler can sail past two ancient and beautiful towns, Clemecy and Auxerre, on his way to Fontainebleau.

If he heads southeast through the Canal du Bourgogne, he will arrive in due time at Tanlay, which has a grand chateau, and Dijon, the capital of Burgundy and a gastronomic center.

Sailing through the forested land in the Yonne Valley and pastures in the Loire Valley, the canal traveler will see many intriguing churches and abbeys.

The rolling fields of Provence, which Van Gogh painted, offer the water tourist views of the ruins of Roman walls and baths, a temple and a well-preserved amphitheatre.

Farther upstream, he will see fortifications built by the Popes during their exile from 1378 to 1417. A medieval cathedral and many other ancient buildings are nearby.

The French make it easy to charter a cabin cruiser with four to six bunks on a weekly basis. A booklet supplied gives all the necessary information relative to navigation, refueling points and places of interest along the route selected by the canal traveler.

The photographs that accompany Mr. Deardorff's article whet the appetite for canal travel the French way. It saddens one to think that Ohioans lacked the foresight to preserve their canals the way the French did. What use they would get from the legions of boat-loving Americans.

Information for this and previous columns pertaining to travel "along the towpath" in various nations of the world was provided by Dorothy Ott, Repository librarian.

March 31, 1968
Canal-Boat Renaissance Building

Five years ago, the thought of one honest-to-goodness canal boat operating on the Ohio & Erie Canal — in this decade — probably would have been greeted with derision.

Today, the way people are talking and planning and, yes, building, we are liable to have a fleet of picturesque old vessels plying rewatered sections of the canal between Zoar in Tuscarawas County and Peninsula in Summit County.

At the moment, Stark County has the lead in the boat-building race. Construction on the oak hull of its canal freighter is well advanced and it should be coming out of its winter cocoon in April so that work can be resumed.

Meanwhile, there is talk of building a boat in Tuscarawas County.

And now comes word that a report prepared by an Akron consulting firm for the Ohio Department of Natural Resources recommends old-fashioned canal-boat rides as a key feature of a proposed 29-mile green park strip in the scenic Cuyahoga River Valley between Akron and Cleveland.

The study reportedly will call for an estimated $10 million for the acquisition of land, cleaning of the river, and development of recreational facilities.

The canal boats would transport tourists between Blossom Music Center in Summit County's Northampton Township, the summer home of the Cleveland Orchestra, and Deep Lock Quarry south of Peninsula, a distance of three miles. The plan calls for the creation of a lake at Johnnycake Lock, where the canal separates from the river near Peninsula.

The report says hiking trails, nature study areas, picnic sites, ski slopes and fishing areas can be developed throughout the rugged valley.

The project would cover the valley from the Cleveland suburb of Valley View to the area near the Botzum sewage treatment plant in Northampton Township.

More than half of the 4-mile-wide valley floor is publicly owned. And it is suggested that the rest must be. The study indicates the valley must be preserved as an open space so it may serve an estimated four million Ohioans by 1970.

The head of the consulting firm believes the Akron and Cleveland metropolitan park districts should carry out the development plans, as the two districts already own or administer much of the land in the valley.

The study was a cooperative project. Among the groups that assisted are the Tri-County Planning Commission, the Cuyahoga County Planning Commission, Peninsula Valley Heritage Association, the park districts and local governments.

Described as the last major underdeveloped area between Cleveland and Akron, the valley has problems that must be overcome if it is to be developed into a recreation region. Some of these are flooding, pollution, sludge, silt, debris and objectionable plant growth in the river. Hopefully, the water between Akron and Cleveland will be made clean enough for fish to live and grow in.

Several years ago, this column suggested a parkway, which would generally follow the canal, should be created by the state of Ohio between Cleveland and Tuscarawas or Coshocton counties. Ohio did not do it but it looks as though the parkway is coming into being, piece by piece and park by park. The federal, state and local governments and park districts are all helping. We may get to the moon before the parkway is a reality but, like the moon, such a canal-river parkway is not as far away as it once was.

April 7, 1968

Tuscarawas Is Beauty-Minded

Tuscarawas is out to beautify itself and canal restoration and beautification is a major part of the program. In fact, the county's plan to beautify itself has been detailed in a 25-page report and submitted to Ohio State University in the hope it might win a $500 Sears Roebuck Foundation grant.

A more attractive county is the goal of an enthusiastic committee that met to determine the directions in which the program would move. Sixty organizations were represented when the group met to organize in February. The sponsoring organizations are the county's homemakers extension council, extension advisory council and cooperative extension service.

The beautification report had this to say about the Ohio & Erie Canal:

"The 40 miles of the Ohio Canal and locks, which run from Stark County through Tuscarawas to Coshocton County, have grown up in weeds and trees, and have been used as a trash dump but for one small roadside park. Some of the land has been sold or destroyed. Lock No. 20 was destroyed by the new interstate highway and others will be destroyed if they are not claimed and restored."

Improvement in four areas — historical sites, highways, farms and homes and strip mine reclamation — has been proposed. The 4-H clubs plan to plant 15,000 trees and work on dump sites, Boy Scouts will be asked to clean up the canals as some troops have done in Stark County and garden clubs will beautify with flowers and trees.

"This work should have been started a long time ago, but here, at last, is a beginning," Henry Spring, president of the Tuscarawas County Historical Association, said at the committee's meeting.

And William Lebold, county extension advisory committee chairman, declared, "We've got to keep at it."

If they do, things will be looking up for Tuscarawas County in general and the old canal in particular.

Canal Field Trip

Travel on the towpath of the Ohio & Erie Canal between Crystal Springs and Canal Fulton is not at its best yet but the educational tours have begun.

The first to come to my attention was the field trip for 86 pupils in the seventh-grade Ohio history class and eighth-grade

American history class at Beach City School.

Led by teachers Richard Tormasi and Don Nichols, the pupils hiked 3½ miles along the towpath from Crystal Springs to Lock 4 Park south of Canal Fulton. The pupils, who had been studying about the canal in both classes, suggested the trip themselves.

As a special feature, they heard state Sen. Ralph Regula of Navarre speak on the construction of the canal and its importance to Stark County and Ohio. They also were bussed to Canal Fulton, where they saw the hull of the canal boat being constructed in the village.

It certainly was an excellent way to culminate their studies about an important era in Ohio's history and one they are not apt to forget.

April 14, 1968
Second Issue of Canawler Printed

Readers of "Along the Towpath" who have developed an interest in the Ohio & Erie Canal, its history, its impact on the growth of Ohio, its demise and its current restoration will be interested to know that the second issue of *The Canawler* has been published at Canal Fulton.

The Canawler is jam-packed with canal history, old photographs and stories. This issue even includes an advertisement about the third annual Canal Days Exposition scheduled in Canal Fulton July 12-13.

The celebration, sponsored by the village's volunteer firemen and Rotary club, promises to be "bigger and better than ever." Among the exposition activities to look forward to are "games, rides, boat races, a beauty contest and pontoon-boat rides on the canal."

The pontoon boats will be in operation long before the exposition. Gale Hartel, chairman of the Rotary's canal-lands committee, has announced that the boat's summer schedule will begin Sunday, May 26, in conjunction with a kick-off pancake breakfast. The boat will operate Sundays and holidays on a regular schedule and on Saturdays by charter only.

To further advertise Canal Fulton, its canal heritage and the current restoration project, the Exchange Bank Co. there will stamp every letter it mails out with a canal-boat design in its cancellation die hub.

Edward Harriman, bank president, hopes other postage machine users will give the Ohio & Erie Canal restoration project a plug in the same way so there will be knowledge of Stark County's canal project throughout the United States and Canada.

The canal-boat design, which appears with this column, was drawn by Carroll M. Gantz of North Canton, head of the industrial design section of the Hoover Co. Further use of the design in the form of decals and seals is being considered.

The current issue of *The Canawler* features on its front page a picture of the late W. J. McLaughlin, who built the model of the canal boat St. Helena, which now is a permanent exhibit at the Stark County Historical Center in Canton. Mr. McLaughlin is standing beside his model of the freighter that is the prototype for the authentic canal boat under construction in Canal Fulton.

Boat Work Planned

Jim Cozy, president of the Louisville Sportsman's Club, which is building the canal boat for the county, has announced the summer construction schedule. Plans are to start work April 30, the first Tuesday night after the time change. It is hoped the planking can be started May 15. Then by July 13, with luck, Jim says the completed hull can be turned over and flopped onto the water. The launching would thus coincide with the final day of the Canal Days Exposition.

Come early September, the deck cabins should be erected and under roof so finish work inside the cabins could go on into cold weather.

To speed construction, Jim says much of it will be "farmed out" in sections to carpenter volunteers. Working from keyed blueprints, the boatbuilders should be able to put the pieces together without difficulty when they all are assembled. As of now,

197

part of the boat is to be fashioned in Louisville, part in Canal Fulton and part in North Canton.

It won't be long until the sound of hammer and saw is heard again at the "boatyard" along the canal in Canal Fulton.

May 5, 1968

New Towpath Trail Section Blazed

Hiking the towpath of the Ohio & Erie Canal can be enjoyable in any season but certainly spring is one of the nicer times to stroll along the historical path.

This spring, for the first time in many years, all who enjoy this healthful activity can hike down the towpath from Navarre to where Route 212 crosses the Tusc-arawas River northwest of Bolivar. This section of the towpath was cleaned of brush and fallen trees by members of the Tri-County Trail Association. The final cleanup with rakes and sickles was accomplished last weekend by members of the 4-H Mustangers.

According to Al Zaleski, advisor to 4-H club members, the towpath is "a nice walk right now." In addition to tidying up the path, Al and his energetic 4-H'ers put up a number of metallic blue blazes, which officially mark the towpath as part of the Buckeye Trail. Al says now is the time to hike this section before the weeds grow up because it will be difficult to keep the trail cleared since there is no present arrangement for maintenance.

Hikers may get on the new section near the Alfred Nickles Bakery parking lot at Navarre or at Route 212 where it crosses the Tuscarawas River. There are no provisions for parking at either place at present.

Speaking of the Buckeye Trail, the trail association's newsletter, which arrived last week, announced the group's ninth annual meeting will be June 15-16 in Marietta.

In conjunction with the meeting, there will be hikes for the membership, including one through Hemlock Hollow and the Sandstone Grindstone area. The hikers will continue to the Rocky Mountain sandstone cliff where rock climbing in Washington County began in 1959. As a special attraction, there will be several rock-climbing groups on the cliffs.

In addition to the towpath section of the Buckeye Trail in Stark County, the trail from the outskirts of Cincinnati to Rocky Fork State Park is being marked with blue blazes.

The new route between lovely Cedar Falls and Ash Cave in Hocking County has been approved and also is to be blazed. By early summer, it is expected that the section from Scioto Trail State Forest south of Chillicothe to Burr Oak State Park in Athens County will be marked.

The trail gap between Rocky Fork and Scioto Trail Forest is under study by a Pike County committee. When the gap is closed, hikers will be able to walk from the Ohio River at Cincinnati almost to the Muskingum River without a break in the trail — a distance of almost 200 miles.

A group down Maryland way heard some good news recently after hiking along the towpath of the Chesapeake and Ohio Canal in Maryland's Frederick County. The 850 hikers were led, incidentally, by one of the nation's best-known hikers, U.S. Supreme Court Associate Justice William O. Douglas, and his wife. The good news, revealed at a dinner following the hike, was that a private organization, the Nature Conservancy, has agreed to underwrite costs of land acquisition of up to 1,000 acres along the 180-mile canal. The hike was intended to draw attention to the need for preservation of the Chesapeake and Ohio.

Viva Chechacos!

The big boat got a big boost recently from the Chechaco Garden Club, in the form of an unexpected check. The "Chechacos" had helped out before. They were one of the first organizations to support the canal-boat project. But this time they really extended themselves and generously contributed a check for $100 to the canal-boat fund.

The "Chechacos," as well as others interested in the progress of the canal boat, will be glad to know that work on the 60-foot freighter is under way again. At a meeting of the key personnel involved in the project last week in Canal Fulton, further plans were made to speed construction. Week by week, this progress should become ever more obvious at the "boatyard" by the canal in downtown Canal Fulton.

May 26, 1968
Canal Figures in Park Plans

While Stark County's Metropolitan Park District is like a newborn foal struggling to get on its feet, the neighboring Akron and Cleveland metropolitan park districts are galloping ahead with expansion plans.

When the voters rejected the levy, which would have breathed life into the Stark park district, they figuratively sprayed a sealant over it, restricting its growth. All of its considerable potential remains, but approval of a levy at some future date will be necessary to put the district on its financial feet.

Meanwhile, big things are proposed for the two park districts to the north.

The Ohio Department of Natural Resources released a study report last week that recommends creation of a 20-mile-long park in the Cuyahoga River valley at a cost of more than $15 million. The giant park would be owned by and under the control of the Cleveland and Akron metropolitan park districts.

State-owned lands, including the Ohio & Erie Canal and its towpath within the suggested park area, would be turned over to the two park districts.

Some 40,000 acres in a 4-mile-wide strip would be contained in the big park. Private or commercial development would be banned so as to preserve the area's scenic beauty, according to the state report.

Robert Teater, assistant director of the Ohio Department of Natural Resources, says the report's major function at present is to focus all local, state and federal programming for the area.

The report's recommendations, according to Mr. Teater, "provide direction for the preservation and proper development of the valley to include scenic open spaces, recreational facilities, historical sites and rehabilitation of the Cuyahoga River."

Some private capital has been invested in the area in developments that are in keeping with the proposed recreational plans. One is the 2,450-acre Towpath Village, a proposed new town development that would be a cultured arts and music center. Blossom Music Center, the summer home of the Cleveland Orchestra, and a 40-acre nature tract operated by Kent State University would be included in the area.

Planned public recreational features would include hiking, camping, fishing, nature trails and bridle paths.

The development involving the canal is of particular interest to this columnist as such a canal-associated project was suggested in this column several years ago.

But it was not until a Cleveland congressman carried the ball that any noticeable progress was made. He prevailed upon Secretary of the Interior Stewart Udall to visit the area. At that time, State Sen. Ralph Regula of Navarre spoke to Mr. Udall, urging him to consider extending the Cuyahoga Valley program south to include Stark County, where the canal restoration project was under way under the jurisdiction of the county commissioners and the direction of the Stark County Canal Lands Development Advisory Committee.

The idea of linking the three counties, and perhaps including Tuscarawas County later, is still sound and more reasonable now than ever.

If the voters of Stark County will just approve a small levy for operation of the Stark Metropolitan Park District, it would become eligible for matching funds from the federal government through the state.

The need for funds is the current roadblock to advancing the plans in Summit and Cuyahoga counties also. But once local subdivisions provide funds, they will unlock the gates to a truly exciting park development in northeastern Ohio.

Stark County, through its metropolitan park district, should be a part of it.

Shipbuilder May Visit Canal Fulton

This writer has met and worked with a lot of interesting people since suggesting in this column March 7, 1965 that Stark County ought to have a canal boat on its rewatered section of the Ohio & Erie Canal.

Now that construction of an authentic canal freighter is well along, I have learned of another interesting personality in the boatbuilding field and am looking forward to meeting him. Already he has donated some knowledge that has resulted in important changes in the construction of our canal boat.

James B. Richardson, a 61-year-old master boatbuilder from Lloyds, Maryland, is following the traditions of his Chesapeake Bay ancestors dating back to colonial times. The first Richardson boatyard was set up in the vicinity of Baltimore prior to its becoming a city. Today, Mr. Richardson has his own small boatyard on the family farm near Cambridge, Maryland.

So skilled is Mr. Richardson that he has received commissions for special restoration work for the Smithsonian Institution in Washington. Among the "jobs" he did for the institution was to restore two old Northwest Indian log canoes brought from Vancouver, British Columbia. One was 60 feet long (the length of Stark County's canal boat) and 11 feet wide and had been hewn from a single cedar log.

Another commission from the Smithsonian was to salvage a Revolutionary gunboat sunk in 1776 on Lake Champlain while in action against a British fleet. Mr. Richardson's crew built cribbing and a form-fitting crate to protect the historic vessel during its trip to Washington.

Mr. Richardson also builds sailing ships of the type that plied the waters of Chesapeake Bay 100 to 150 years ago, the period that saw the greatest canal-boat activity in Ohio.

His contact with Canton was made last year when he finished building a 43-foot sailboat for William Embley of North Canton. Recently, Mr. Embley told the Maryland shipbuilder about the canal boat being built at Canal Fulton and was given in return some useful construction recommendations, which are being followed by the men supervising the work on the local canal freighter.

The veteran boatbuilder strongly endorsed use of the "green" white oak lumber for the planking on the freighter and recommended exact boiling times for the planks, which must be bent to fit the curved sections of the prow and stern.

Planking of the hull was to have gotten under way Saturday. Additional manpower provided by Canal Fulton organizations was to help the regular volunteer crews in order to get the boat in the water as scheduled July 13.

Mr. Richardson also has advised the canal-boat construction bosses regarding caulking of the hull, shaping of the planks, and other important techniques. He expressed such an interest in the canal boat that he has offered to serve as a troubleshooter via telephone if quick advice is needed or possibly visit Stark County.

In his capacity of consultant to the Smithsonian, Mr. Richardson has constructed many scale models of authentic historical vessels. He currently is working on a replica of a launch used by William Penn.

Many meetings have been held during recent months by the men responsible for constructing the canal boat, and construction has moved ahead to the point that it now will be obvious to canalside superintendents.

With an "ace in the hole" like the Maryland shipbuilder, the construction bosses and volunteer crews can move ahead with new confidence.

Boat-building Skull Session

There was an awful lot of "building" going on Wednesday night in a room at the Harleigh Inn in North Canton. A great deal of progress was made but it was all in the minds of the men gathered there for a skull session.

The construction would take place later — at Canal Fulton, where Stark County's canal boat is rapidly taking shape. But the boat-building know-how that was dispensed and the lessons learned during the skull session were invaluable.

Key figures in the technical marine talk were Jim Cozy, president of Louisville Sportsman's Club and canal-boat project overseer; Roy Preece of near Canal Fulton, construction boss; Carroll Gantz of North Canton, who made the detailed designs of the boat from a model of a canal freighter, and Edward Harriman, president of the Exchange Bank Co. of Canal Fulton and active promoter of the canal restoration project.

James B. Richardson of near Cambridge, Maryland, master boatbuilder, had spent the day at the canalside boatyard advising and assisting in the first steps of planking the freighter's hull. Tall and tanned, the master craftsman from the Chesapeake Bay fielded every question thrown at him for nearly two hours as the local boatbuilders probed his experience for answers to their specific and immediate problems.

The conversation went something like this:

Q. "Would you put the bottom on first?"

A. "Yes, put the bottom on first and then wrap the side around the bottom."

Q. "Would this complicate maintenance?"

A. "No, it is not unique on the Bay to build them that way."

Q. "About preservatives, do you paint the inside of your planks?"

His answer was lost as the conversation quickly turned to the exterior of the planks and this comment from Mr. Richardson:

"Even though she's going to be here in the canal, she's going to catch some marine growth... and she'll take on several tons of weight (water absorption into the wood every year for five or six years). Properly cared for though, I think she ought to last 50 years. 'Properly cared for' are the key words."

Other typical comments by the veteran boatbuilder went like this:

"Each one (plank) will fasten to the timberhead as you come along."

"I would prebend that piece."

"It might be a good idea put a bolt or two in there."

"If she were mine, I would ..."

"We spray all our pine..."

A number of changes in construction plans were made during the course of the evening, some very important ones. And it became apparent the hoped-for launching date of July 13 would have to be pushed back.

Asked for his estimate of a probable launch date, Mr. Richardson said, "With the enthusiasm I see around here, I think you'll be able to roll her in probably in about six weeks. But you'll have to hold your present enthusiasm."

After the important questions had been asked and answered, I asked what he thought of the job a bunch of Ohio landlubbers had done so far.

"Well, I'm very pleased with what you have done," he replied. "I can't see anything wrong. It all looks like good straightforward work. I'm amazed, however, that you all would take on this much of a boat as your first venture. You know, this is rather an ambitious undertaking. But I think it is terrific."

"Do you think it will be seaworthy," I inquired.

"I think so," was his response.

The maker of sleek custom-made sailboats admitted he was curious to see the anything-but-sleek canal freighter when he heard about it. Now he wants to come back and ride on it when it is finished, as he has never been on a boat pulled by a mule.

This led to the final question of the evening:

"What area of sail will it require to move it if we can't get a mule?"

Laughs all around.

July 21, 1968

Building Buckeye Trail

Hikers, be patient. One of these days you actually may be able to hike from the metropolitan parks that make up the

201

"Emerald Necklace" that adorns the "neck" of Greater Cleveland all the way to Bolivar and Zoar in Tuscarawas County. And much of the way you will be able to walk on the towpath of the Ohio & Erie Canal. Many miles of the canal will be filled with water and look much as it did more than a century ago.

When this comes to pass, the builders of Ohio's Buckeye Trail will have had a major role in bringing it about. The hiking trail from Cincinnati to Cleveland has been taking shape rapidly under the direction of Robert Paton of Columbus, trail director. And actually, hikers who are impatient to walk the trail can do so on many stretches throughout the state that already are blazed.

One of the last areas along the trail route to be developed is the Summit County section. The canal and towpath in Cuyahoga County are in fine condition as is a small section in Stark County.

Plans call for improving the towpath (the official Buckeye Trail in Stark County) and other areas of the canal lands in Stark but lack of funds has prevented this so far. Voters will have the opportunity to make this possible by approving the Metropolitan Park District levy on the November ballot.

Difficult terrain problems plus differing opinions have delayed development of the Summit section of the trail, which will tie the Cuyahoga and Stark sections together.

But Sunday and Monday of this past week much was accomplished and it looks now as though there may be two sections of the Buckeye Trail in Summit County, one following the canal northward and the other heading northeastward from one reservoir to another.

The hikers on this latter section conceivably could reach the network of trails in the northeastern United States when a linkup of the trail systems is completed.

Readers of this column will be particularly pleased that the canal restoration and beautification in Summit County may be speeded up because of the trail development.

Director Paton and John Bay of the Ohio Legislative Service Commission staff, both of Columbus; State Sen. Ralph Regula of Navarre and this columnist, plus representatives of both the Akron and Cleveland hiking clubs and Al Zaleski of East Sparta, president of the Tri-County Trail Association, inspected the proposed northeast trail route Sunday.

Some of us, aided by Paul S. Marks of Canton checked out the canal route the next day.

The canal route north of Akron is not so much of a problem and, when completed, would feature some lovely stretches of rewatered canal and many points of historic and contemporary interest.

Some land must be acquired but John Daily, director of the Akron Metropolitan Park District, with whom we met, indicated a definite interest in the canal route and a willingness to cooperate in making that section of the trail through Summit County interesting.

The southern section of the canal trail in Summit County would extend from just below Clinton northward past several locks (presently dry) and through an industrial area that would not be so much scenic as educational and different, to say the least. Some problems would have to be overcome in the construction of this part of the trail but none seemingly insurmountable.

The main problem bothering all of us was how to get around the city of Akron. The canal and towpath have been eradicated in the city.

Finally, Sen. Regula came up with an idea that appealed to the group: "Why not go through the city on the sidewalks as close to the original canal route as feasible?"

The senator explained that the sight of hikers walking through the city and the blaze marks and Buckeye Trail signs might arouse the interest of the citizens and cause them to explore the trail that ultimately would lead them out into the country and, hopefully, cause many of them to become hikers and users of the Buckeye Trail in other parts of the state.

His plan would make the most of a difficult situation by giving the trail wide exposure within the heart of the rubber capital of the world.

Director Paton, who met with other interested persons and groups in Akron, said the Akron park system officials are willing to cooperate on the project and have some ideas as how best to route the trail through the city.

Those of us who were trailbuilding for two days — often driving along at 60 miles an hour from point to point and from conference to meeting, studying maps and evaluating alternative routes — were a far cry from the pioneers who hacked their way through the Ohio countryside to build trails. But it was interesting, somewhat exciting and we all hope beneficial for untold numbers of today's and tomorrow's Americans.

September 29, 1968

Stamp Club To Honor Canal

When you are away on vacation, work has a way of piling up. So it is with news about the canal and towpath-related activities. So many things have been going on that it has taken me a while, following my vacation, to catch up on them. But I have pretty well sorted them out now and will pass some news along to those of you who may have wondered about the status of the various activities.

The mail this week brought notice from the Stark County Stamp Club that it plans to honor the Ohio & Erie Canal in Stark County at "Starpex 68," the club's eighth annual stamp exhibition and bourse October 12-13. The free public event will be at the Sachsenheim Club and will feature "philatelic exhibits, special attractions, United States post office and special cachet and cancellation." The special envelopes bearing the canal-boat cachet can be purchased at the exhibition.

Down Coshocton Way

Canal buffs who haven't heard much about Ted Findley of New Philadelphia will be glad to know that the president of the Canal Society of Ohio is on his feet again after a long illness. One of the first places

Ted visited after he became mobile again was Canal Fulton — to see how the canal boat is progressing. He also got to Coshocton for a "doings" in conjunction with the restoration of the canal and the canal town of Roscoe. He reports the work is progressing nicely.

Among the speakers at the Coshocton program were State Sen. Ralph Regula of Navarre and his wife, Mary. Sen. Regula told of the engineering that went into the construction of the canal and how it was built. Then Mrs. Regula spoke of the "romance" of the canal and how the people lived in those days when the canal was so important. The senator followed up with plans for the future development of the canal lands in the various counties before allowing his wife to get in the last words. Color slides helped to enliven their presentation.

Their talks were so well received that a Coshocton resident mailed the canal-boat construction fund a check for $100. The generous gift not only is inspiring to those who are building the boat but it is indicative of the interest the project has for Ohioans beyond Stark County's borders.

Canal Canoeists

Over in the western part of the state, two 20-year-old canoeists pushed off from Cincinnati recently for a 154-mile trip through history — via canal. Marvin Brenneman and Danny Harpster, both of Delphos, attempted to navigate the old Miami and Erie Canal to Delphos, their hometown, as part of its "Old Fashioned Canal Days" celebration.

The trip by aluminum canoe included

river and highway detours in areas where the abandoned canal had been filled. The boaters hoped to travel 22 miles a day. In the absence of any further report, we can only hope they made it — and in time for the celebration.

Joint Canal Tour

Canal buffs may be interested in the Pennsylvania Canal Society's tour with the Canal Society of Ohio October 18-20. The joint meeting and tour will be hosted by the Pennsylvania society and the headquarters will be at the Holiday Inn in Johnstown. Activities scheduled include a ride on the world's steepest inclined plane, caravan trip to downtown Johnstown to see canal dioramas in the Cambria Free Library, views of various sites along the old Pennsylvania Canal, a tour of the Conemaugh Dam and a look at the world's tallest smokestacks located on the site of the Pennsylvania Canal.

October 27, 1968
New Hope Visited at Last

Sometime after "Along the Towpath" appeared in the *Repository* for the first time in November of 1964, a major part of one column was devoted to the Delaware Canal and the canal town of New Hope in Pennsylvania's Bucks County.

I had never visited New Hope but I'd heard of it and read a little about it. What I heard — to anyone interested in canals — sounded fascinating.

Several times later, I again wrote of New Hope in "Along the Towpath" and printed a picture of one of the launch-type, mule-pulled canal boats they operate there for the public, from May through October.

I determined to visit New Hope someday, for I felt certain it would have much to offer that could benefit the Stark County Canal Lands Development Advisory Committee in its efforts to develop Stark County's section of the Ohio & Erie Canal and our canal communities along similar lines. But it was not until this past summer that I was able to make the trip, while on vacation.

New Hope is a captivating little town, which quite exceeded my expectations. It is an atmosphere town and its many little stores are enchanting.

Its commercialism, to date, has been well-guided and flamboyant elements are at a minimum. It has an abundance of historical sites and buildings that have been artfully developed to blend in and through the community most effectively. The place is a natural setting for the many antique shops in the area.

Particularly appealing to canal buffs are the scenic restaurants, which feature patios where diners can overlook the canal and its towpath. They will delight, too, in the tiny library, which is housed in a log cabin that served as a tollhouse for the canal boats and the ferries that crossed the nearby Delaware River.

The huge central hand-cut beam and the old fireplace in the cabin will make the history buff's mouth drool. When one looks at the inn dating back to the 1700s, it is not too difficult to believe that it was just a short distance away that Washington crossed the Delaware.

Canal Fulton and Navarre cannot duplicate New Hope, for neither community has as much "history" still standing. But both towns could do much to emulate the Pennsylvania community by preserving and restoring what they do have in relation to their canal history.

Canal Fulton has a head start and perhaps greater potential but Navarre has some canal-era buildings and towpath extending north and south of its limits. If a section of the canal south of the village can be rewatered, the development possibilities will be greatly enhanced.

Canal Fulton has made considerable progress but more, much more, can be accomplished. It would be a thought-provoking trip for the businessmen and civic leaders of that community if they could go to New Hope to see for themselves what a transformation could be accomplished in their hometown.

One resident of Canal Fulton, the chairman of the Rotary Club's canal committee, did go to New Hope. Now, Gale Hartel and his wife, Lois, operate the Warehaus, a specialty store in an old canal warehouse on the village's Canal St. The store's canal-and-history-oriented merchandise are the stuff of which New Hope is made, on which it has been nourished.

In some ways, Stark County will be able to surpass New Hope. Our canal boat will be historically correct and far superior to the New Hope Barges. Our museum at canalside at Lock 4 Park should be superior in a number of ways, and Lock 4, when the gates are restored, will be a classic.

If only the voters will approve the metropolitan park levy November 5, Stark County will be able to fashion a canal lands strip-park for the enjoyment of its own people that will be of a quality that others might wish to emulate.

Interest in Canal Fulton and its varied canal associations continues to grow. Clyde Gainey, owner-operator of the Old Canal Days Museum in the heart of the village, reports nearly 3,000 persons visited the tiny museum this past summer. These included visitors from 16 other states and three foreign countries. Many of those who visited the museum, individually or in groups, also went for a ride on the canal via the Rotary Club's pontoon boats or hiked along the canal enjoying the scenery.

Next summer, those who register at the museum will receive brochures designed by Mr. Gainey, which will give them a mini-view of Canal Fulton in drawing, pictures and text.

The route of the canal through the village will be shown in bold lines. Points of interest will include the loading dock, site where the canal boat is being constructed, Lock 4, site of the proposed new museum, the library, the present museum and the Canal Fulton Summer Arena.

The exterior of the brochure will feature a revised version of the village's sesquicentennial seal, which has been altered to show a view (inset) of the Old Canal Days Museum.

Slowly but relentlessly Stark County's canal story is being discovered and told again and again to an ever-widening audience.

Buckeye Trail Update

Once again, active work on the Ohio & Erie Canal restoration projects and allied activities has been slowed by the arrival of colder weather. But planning goes on, meetings are held, talks about the canal are given, letters are written, and, whenever possible, more work is done.

This is particularly true for the Buckeye Trail. Under the direction of Robert Paton of Worthington, Buckeye Trail Coordinator with the Ohio Department of Natural Resources, the trail is being put together link by link. In Stark County, of course, the trail follows the canal towpath wherever it exists and never strays far from the route of the canal.

During August, members of the Tri-County Trail Association continued their clearing of the towpath trail between State Route 212 near Bolivar in Tuscarawas County and the village of Navarre.

Harry V. Jones, president of the trail riders, said his volunteers cleared an 8-foot-wide trail, pushing over dead trees and anything else in their way. Their major weapon in this offensive was a bulldozer donated and operated without charge by Gust Malavite, owner of Malavite Excavating Co. and a member of the riding group.

In opening this section of the Buckeye Trail, the horsemen are making it possible for hikers to enjoy one of the prettiest sections of the towpath and canal in Stark County. They plan to continue their work during the winter months.

Meanwhile progress is being made in establishing the trail route in Summit County, which has been one of the most difficult sections in which to plot a trail.

Mr. Paton reports that here too, the Buckeye Trail will follow, as far as possible, the canal lands. This would enable it to tie onto the Cuyahoga County section of the canal that has been preserved intact to the southern edge of Cleveland.

Director Paton reports Mayor Roy Gottwald of Clinton has said the village would permit use of the canal lands under its jurisdiction (by lease) for the trail.

In Barberton, James E. Fearon, director

of that city's parks and recreation department, revealed that the canal lands through Barberton eventually will be part of the city's park program and that he is interested in having the Buckeye Trail traverse the city by way of the park system.

The board of park commissioners has authorized the park director to investigate the acquisition of property along the canal. Director Fearon told the commissioners that the towpath and land between the Tuscarawas River and the canal has great potential recreational uses. Talking in terms of a strip park, he declared that small boats and canoes could be used on the canal through most of the city.

In Akron, several officials expressed interest in the proposal to route the Buckeye Trail through that municipality. Future plans for Akron parks include the development of canal lands where the canal has not been obliterated and the Buckeye Trail will be included in this planning. The Akron planners visualize a route for the trail that will utilize to the best extent possible, the canal, historic features, city parks, and other features. Cooperation of the Akron Historical Society also has been assured.

Ultimately, according to John R. Daily, secretary of the Akron Metropolitan Park Board, the Buckeye Trail's route northward from Akron will traverse canal lands where they are included in the metropolitan parks. Connecting areas between the parks now are being sought by the park board from the Ohio Department of Public Works. When these are obtained, they also will be available for the Buckeye Trail.

Summit County residents have already been enjoying hikes along part of the old towpath. Earlier this year one of the weekly nature walks conducted by the Metropolitan Park District was a conducted tour along Deep Lock Quarry Metropolitan Park in Boston Township.

Director Paton also reports some other news that may eventually benefit the Buckeye Trail.

Before Congress adjourned it passed the national trails hiking bill. Included in this bill was authorization to study 14 trail systems for possible inclusion in the national trails system. One of these is the

The St. Helena II, of Canal Fulton, was the first reproduction canal boat built on the northern portion of the Ohio & Erie Canal. Construction began in 1969.
Canal Society of Ohio

North Country Trail, which is scheduled to cross Ohio, presumably using the Buckeye Trail as its Ohio segment.

If the North Country Trail becomes a reality, certain federal funds will be available for its development. Certainly we can speculate that some of these funds could be used in developing the Ohio section.

At least, as the Buckeye Trail planners go into the winter season, they can add some hoping to their planning and dream bigger dreams as they envision a trail that will have, if not something recreational for everybody, at least a lot of recreation to offer many.

Book Six · 1969

January 12, 1969
Boat Building in a 'Greenhouse'

I was talking with a fellow the other day who passed on a little philosophy couched in words that couldn't have been more appropriate for the moment. We were right side up on top of a 60-foot-long boat that was upside down.

Tony Patz of Port Clinton on Lake Erie was busy plying the trade he had just retired from after 39 years "in the business." I was watching and trying to learn something. The boat on which we were standing was Stark County's canal boat, which continues to take shape slowly but steadily.

Tony Patz and Lawrence Johannsen, also from Port Clinton, are retired boatbuilders who spent last week performing a vital task in the construction of the canal freighter - caulking the seams (spaces between the hull planks) of the boat.

Tony's philosophy - he was talking about life as he carefully and skillfully tamped a long rope of oakum into the seams to make it watertight - was this: "It's a short rope that doesn't have some kinks in it."

It has been that way with the canal boat. It has been a long time in the building, the first work getting under way in June of 1966. And there have been some kinks along the way. They had to be unraveled, like the caulker's oakum, before work could proceed. And they have been.

Considerable progress has been made during the past month. It had to be to get the hull ready for the caulkers who were available only for one week.

Before winter set in, a large framework was constructed around the boat, which was covered with heavy plastic, donated through the efforts of the Bliss Co. This provided a shelter that could be heated, making it relatively comfortable for working in below-freezing temperatures.

Although most of the hull had been built with volunteer help, it became obvious that full-time workers would be required to get it ready by the caulkers' deadline.

As a result, building contractor Richard Mohler of North Canton and his apprentice, David Wahl, were employed. Their work has been of excellent quality and the canal boat has taken shape to the point that it truly looks like a boat.

Financial donations made it possible to employ Mr. Mohler and Mr. Wahl. More contributions and volunteers will be needed if

they are to push the boat ahead to the point that it can meet the projected launching date in April. If both are forthcoming, prospects for completing the boat will be greatly enhanced.

Although they never worked on a canal boat before, boatbuilders Patz and Johannsen speak optimistically about the big freighter they are helping to make "seaworthy."

Tony Patz said, "I think it will work out nice. I don't want her to sink either."

Lawrence Johannsen nodded in agreement.

"We've put out quite a few boats," he said reassuringly, while driving the cotton caulking rope tightly into the open seams of Stark County's biggest boat.

January 19, 1969

Skimming the Canal on Skates

Remember those Currier and Ives-type Christmas cards? The ones showing colorfully garbed skaters gliding over the ice of a millpond or frozen country stream?

An artist might have duplicated those scenes Sunday at a number of places along the Ohio & Erie Canal between Canal Fulton and Crystal Springs. At numerous spots, young skaters swept or shoveled the snow from the ice to make their individual arenas and moved up and down the canal on their flashing steel blades.

Red-cheeked and bright-eyed, the skaters all seemed to be enjoying themselves. I know, for I was there.

Starting at the northern end of the rewatered section of the canal just north of Canal Fulton, my three companions and I traveled the frozen canal some five miles to Crystal Springs. Most of the way zigzag lines in the snow told us that someone had been there before us. Only in one of the more remote areas did we pioneer where no skater had preceded us.

My companions were State Sen. Ralph Regula of Navarre, with whom I had both hiked and canoed this same stretch of the canal; his son Richard, and nephew, Tim Regula.

We found that work to improve the towpath during the winter is under way, in that many of the dead trees along the towpath have been cut. The trees fall onto the ice where they can be cut into small sections. In other seasons of the year, when the ice coating on the canal has disappeared, removing the trees is much more difficult.

The younger generation won the 5-mile "race" but the senator and I came in a respectable third and fourth. And we all thoroughly enjoyed our winter trip on the canal.

By coincidence, so did Terry K. Woods of Canton and his wife, who told me about it in this letter (edited for space):

"Nowadays, when a person thinks of canals, if one thinks of them at all, it is usually in terms of warm weather recreation. Even the so-called "canal buff" or "canal nut" as I classify myself, will seldom go tramping along the back roads and through the swamps of Ohio in search of an overgrown towpath or moss-covered lock unless the temperature is quite a bit above freezing. However, every time someone who was present while the canals were still in operation is interviewed, he never fails to mention a facet of canal recreation that many of us are missing — ice skating. "More than one local history of a canal town takes quite a few paragraphs to describe the importance that skating on the canal had upon the winter social life. Don Zutavern of Canton, who lived on a farm between the canal and the Tuscarawas River (where the canal crossed the river by aqueduct into Tuscarawas County) from 1902 to 1913, is emphatic about the pleasure of skating on the canal.

"His most vivid memory of his life along the canal was the time that he... skated from Bolivar to Canal Fulton, a round trip of well over 40 miles. When I commented that 40 miles seemed like a difficult skate for a 10 or 11-year-old boy, he replied that it was a bit difficult as his younger sister, who couldn't skate very well, had accompanied them and that he'd had to push her most of the way to Canal Fulton and all the way back.

"Mr. Zutavern's description of that and other skating trips, the extreme smoothness of the ice, the absence of wind in the low-lying canal and the fact that you could 'go someplace' while skating rather than 'round and round' made me want to try it. The first weekend of the New Year seemed like a good time to go, so last Sunday afternoon my wife and I dug our skates out of the pile of little-used items in the basement and set out for the canal.

"We took old Route 21 out of Massillon and sighted tracks and skaters as soon as we came abreast of the watered section of the canal. There were quite a few people, mostly children, gathered at Crystal Springs, but I was headed for Lock 4 Park. My original intention was to skate from there to Canal Fulton to see the progress on the canal boat.

"A number of people were skating above and below the lock when we arrived. We got into our skates, slid somewhat unsteadily down the bank onto the bypass and then out onto the canal. It was quite an experience. The ice was indeed smooth and the wind practically nonexistent.

"However, my skating ability limited the 'go somewhere' advantage of canal skating. I managed to wobble the few yards from the lock to the basin below Canal Fulton before my legs and ankles decided it would be advisable to drive to the boatyard. The rest of the afternoon was spent on that stretch of canal, never too far from a stump upon which I could lean to rest my legs.

"I did enjoy skating on the canal though and I fully intend to go again and build my leg muscles to the point where I can 'go somewhere.' I heartily recommend canal skating for anyone interested in canals, skating or both.

"Stark County is blessed with a stretch of canal excellently suited for skating. The rewatered section of the Ohio & Erie from Canal Fulton to below Crystal Springs provides more than five miles of fine skating. I have found, as the youngsters of this and many past generations have known all along, that the canal may be enjoyed during any season of the year and winter is one of the best."

May 4, 1969
Towpath Through Tuscarawas

The Tuscarawas River Valley in Tuscarawas County is scenic, historical and very much on the upgrade. Within the past year the upgrading has become more noticeable as an increasing number of individuals and organizations have become interested in restoring vestiges of the valley's history and developing it for recreation and tourism.

In yesteryear, the Ohio & Erie Canal ran the entire length of the valley in proximity to the river. Today efforts are being made to restore sections of the canal that were not destroyed and preserve them for future generations. Work on the towpath of the canal between Bolivar and Zoar, in the northern part of the county, has been under way for some time and the improvement is marked. I hiked the towpath in this area recently and found it in excellent condition for walking. It was a bright, sunny day and the violets and other spring flowers were everywhere in evidence, adding to the enjoyment of hiking the historical path.

Edward W. Richard of Bolivar, chairman of the Tuscarawas County Canal Lands Advisory Committee, reports that since December some six miles of the towpath between Route 8 (about six miles northeast of Dover) near Zoarville to Route 212 at the southeast end of Bolivar have been cleared for hiking and horseback riding. Most of the clearing was accomplished in six days by volunteers, he said. These included advisory committee members, the Bolivar Lions Club, two local chapters of the National Campers and Hikers Association — the Buckeye Bacon Burners and Swiss Wheelers — and Tuscarawas County Boy Scout troops 84, 90, 92, 94 and 99.

Bulldozers and power saws were brought into play to clear a path roughly 8 feet wide. Brush, small trees and most of the poison ivy have been removed. Plans call for spraying the remaining ivy near the towpath. Dead trees were cut and removed and the area around locks 7, 8, 9 and 10 was given special attention. Signs identifying the locks also were placed nearby. Interested groups also have provided and placed birdhouses and trail markers, and offered to affix tree identification markers.

Mr. Richard said the committee is hopeful of renovating a portion of the canal, which links the four locks, for recreational purposes because, he said, "Four historical locks and a good hiking trail adjacent to a better (we hope) Tuscarawas River near historic Zoar and Fort Laurens in this northern part of picturesque Tuscarawas County in an area or prehistoric prominence due to the crossing of the Indian trails deserve to be enhanced by a usable park and renovated canal."

Other programs also are going forward in Tuscarawas County, notably the production of the state's first outdoor historical drama, *Trumpet in the Land,* which will depict the deeply moving story of the Moravian missionaries who attempted in the 1780s to fashion a Christian world of brotherhood among men in the Tuscarawas Valley. The stirring narrative will be presented in the summer of 1970 in an amphitheater to be constructed on a hillside near the restored village of Schoenbrunn. The entire Tuscarawas community is marking the beginning of the village 197 years ago with "David Zeisberger Week." Highlight of the program commemorating missionary Zeisberger's founding will be a parade from New Philadelphia to Schoenbrunn.

Stark County's neighbor to the south is rich in history and scenery. It is an interesting place to visit. By highway, the two counties are linked conveniently — by towpath, interestingly.

June 3, 1969

The Passing of a 'Canawler'

Since this column last appeared, Ohio & Erie Canal buffs and others interested in the preservation of the history of the canal era lost a good friend.

Ted H. Findley of New Philadelphia, past president of the Canal Society of Ohio, passed away Saturday, May 24, after a long illness.

Ted was one of the first persons interested in the canal lore that this writer became acquainted with after my interest was whetted by a 16-mile "exploration" of the old Ohio & Erie canal bed and towpath between Canal Fulton and Navarre in the spring of 1964.

His interest in everything associated with Ohio's canals led him to assemble possibly the largest private collection of canal memorabilia of any citizen of the state.

Ted was generous in sharing his knowledge of our early waterways and worked diligently for many years to stimulate interest in restoring some of the key vestiges of the canal system that somehow managed to survive the march of progress.

Seeing in this column a means of helping his cause through continuous and relatively widespread dissemination of the canal story, he was always eager to help me by providing information from his storehouse of facts or by taking me to see something I was interested in writing about.

When I suggested an authentic canal boat be constructed for use at Canal Fulton and Lock 4 park, Ted was enthusiastic and did what he could to support the project. Although his major efforts were in Tuscarawas County, where, as late as 1966, 12 of the original 14 locks in the county still were in existence, Ted made a number of talks to organizations in Stark County to help stimulate interest here.

He said repeatedly: "We want to get the different service clubs, the historical societies, the Boy Scouts and Girl Scouts, the garden clubs and other civic organizations interested in the canal development to help us make certain restorations."

Several school groups in Stark County heard Ted speak and show his slides. The pupils developed an affection for him and honored him in various ways.

All who knew Ted, including this writer, will miss him and his willingness to share his vast knowledge of the canals. And we will particularly regret that he was denied the opportunity (which he was

greatly anticipating) to ride on Stark County's authentic canal boat, which is scheduled to be afloat this summer.

In the passing of Ted H. Findley, we have stood on the "towpath" and regretfully watched an esteemed canawler "lock through."

July 6, 1969
Splash-In Is at Hand

By this time next week, the long-awaited splash-in day should be over and Stark County's canal-boat hull either should be afloat in the Ohio & Erie Canal at Canal Fulton, as many of us hope, or it will be on the bottom of the canal bed, having sunk, as some nonbelievers have predicted.

I said hull because that is all that will be splashed in. The deck of the authentic freighter and the three cabins —fore, aft and midship — are still to be added. More money, time and effort will be required but the hardest part of the job is done. So splash-in will have been a gala occasion for those of us who have worked for and on the canal boat.

Barring unforeseen circumstances, employees of Henry A. Selinsky Inc., using two large cranes, are to lift the 60-foot freighter from its resting place at the Canal Fulton "boatyard" next Saturday, turn it over and deposit it gently into the waiting waters of the canal.

To the men who built the hull and to those of us who mostly watched and shared in the planning, the "boat", as we refer to it, is a beauty.

A great deal of thought has gone into its design and much loving care has been showered upon it during construction by the Stark County landlubbers who have brought it from an idea to a reality.

It was just over three years ago that the first work got under way with the laying out and cutting of templates for the boat. Changes have been made since then and, in fact, the original plans were abandoned in favor of a different model, a replica of which is on display at the Stark County Historical Center in Canton.

While the boat was under construction by volunteers another project was started — the building of new gates at Lock 4 south of Canal Fulton. This was started in the spring of 1967 and completed within the past month. The refurbished lock, as planned, will await the canal boat's first trip.

The canal-boat hull has been painted a gleaming white above the waterline, in keeping with the color scheme of the model. When the vessel is completed and painted, it should be a showpiece.

For those who gather to watch the big boat hull splash in, do not be disturbed if water flows into it. This is expected and necessary. Not until the white oak timbers have been in the water long enough to swell together against the caulking will the hull be watertight. Portable pumps will be used to keep the water from getting too high when it is first launched.

To repeat, barring the unforeseen, the big splash-in should have occurred before this column appears again.

Though there has to be some apprehension about such an event, since it is a first for all concerned, the committee that has brought the canal boat this far is confident all will go well. In fact, the last matter discussed at the group's most recent meeting was the type of seating to be provided for the paying customers.

March 29, 1970
Report on Canal Boat

To those Stark Countians who haven't been to Canal Fulton recently to see the canal boat, I can report that a great deal of progress is being made. Work has gone on through the winter and the boat that floats impatiently beneath its plastic shelter is a far more impressive craft than it was last fall.

Since the hull was launched last July 26, lumber for decking and framing was obtained and prepared for installation. The hull's interior was treated with preservative and painted. In late November, major carpentry work began and the main deck and gunwales are now in place. The cabins are framed and sheathed, the foredeck, afterdeck and steering deck are completed and the rudder assembly is finished. The catwalks also have been constructed and work is about to begin on canvassing the roofs of the cabins. Final painting is under way, interior finishing of the cabins is proceeding and the canvas awnings are being made.

A blacksmith shop has even been established near Canal Fulton especially for creating some of the iron fittings needed to make the canal boat truly authentic. Several dozen of these fittings have been forged by hand. Wood patterns for the heavy capstan have been completed now are in the foundry being cast.

Despite the progress being made, there is still a need for volunteer labor on Saturdays to help with the painting, caulking and finishing work. Anyone interested in helping to build the boat should contact either Gervis Brady, director of the Stark County Historical Society, Carroll Gantz at the Hoover Company or this columnist.

If there are any skeptics remaining who doubt that the boat will be completed, the fact that mules are being sought to tow the canal boat should help remove their doubts. Several members of the canal branch board of managers of the Stark County Historical Society traveled to Dellroy in Carroll County last Sunday to inspect a team of mules offered for sale by Ralph Gore. And quarters near the canal that would be adequate for "canal-boat mules" were being sought during the week.

No one has yet heard a canal boat horn sounding at Canal Fulton, nor has anyone seen the long-eared silhouette of a span of mules on the towpath of the Ohio & Erie Canal. That is, not since the turn of the century.

But it shouldn't be long now.

Epilogue

A Dream Becomes a Reality

The "splash-in" didn't take place until July 26, 1969, and the *St. Helena II* was still under construction when *Along the Towpath* made its final appearance in the *Canton Repository* on March 29, 1970. But Al Simpson's passion for the canal boat project and the larger one — reinventing the canal — was as strong as it was at the end of that first rain-drenched 16-mile hike.

Simpson's final column, a progress report on the canal boat and one more call for volunteers to complete it, said, in part, "Work has gone on through the winter and the boat that floats impatiently beneath its plastic shelter is a far more impressive craft than it was last fall... If there are any skeptics remaining who doubt that the boat will be completed, the fact that mules are being sought to tow the canal boat should help remove their doubts... No one has yet heard a canal boat horn sounding at Canal Fulton, nor has anyone seen the long-eared silhouette of a span of mules on the towpath of the Ohio & Erie Canal. That is, not since the turn of the century. But it shouldn't be long now."

And it wasn't. The *St. Helena II* plied the Ohio & Erie waters near Canal Fulton until 1988 and was replaced two years later by the *St. Helena III,* a twin built of concrete, which is operated by the Canal Fulton Heritage Society.

Mr. Simpson went to Washington to be U.S. Representative Ralph Regula's press aide in 1975, a year after Congress approved legislation creating the 33,000-acre Cuyahoga Valley National Recreation Area. Regula, who had been elected to his first term in 1972, supported the bill, which was sponsored in the House by John Seiberling of Akron and in the Senate by Howard Metzenbaum of Cleveland. Nearly 30 years later, Regula would sponsor the legislation to make the recreation area a national historic corridor.

Preservation of the canal and towpath received a major boost in 1975 when a National Park Service suitability-feasibility study stated, "As a historic entity, the Ohio & Erie Canal has been judged to have national significance," opening the door to a decade of cooperative efforts among community groups, park agencies and local governments.

In 1986, the North Cuyahoga Valley Corridor was founded in Cleveland to make a connection between that city and the Cuyahoga Valley National Recreation Area. Three years later, the Ohio & Erie Canal Corridor Coalition was founded to preserve, interpret and develop the natural, historical and recreational resources along the canal from Cleveland to Zoar.

Looking back in 2002, Daniel M. Rice, executive director of the Ohio & Erie Canal Corridor Coalition, reviewed what has been accomplished along the towpath since series ended. By 2002, 68 miles of the 101-mile Ohio & Erie Canal Towpath Trail had been completed, more than 45 community organizations and local government agencies were working on the preservation, interpretation and development of the Ohio & Erie Canal National Heritage Corridor and more than $256 million of local, private, state and federal investment has been leveraged for projects associated with the initiative, Rice said.

Other accomplishments included:

Publication in 1993 of the National Park Service's "A Route To Prosperity" study of canal lands in Cuyahoga, Summit, Stark and a portion of Tuscarawas counties. The study recommended National Heritage Area designation by Congress.

Opening in 1993 of 19 miles of the Ohio & Erie Canal Towpath Trail within the park.

Congressional approval in 1996 — after two unsuccessful attempts — of legislation designating the Ohio & Erie Canal National Heritage Corridor. Regula sponsored the measure in the House and spearheaded the bipartisan cooperation required for its passage.

Creation in 1996 of the Ohio & Erie Canal Association to serve as the management entity for the Heritage Corridor. The association represents a merger of the Cleveland-based, Ohio Canal Corridor and the Akron-based Ohio & Erie Canal Corridor Coalition. Secretary of the Interior Bruce Babbitt so-designated the association in a ceremony in Navarre in June of 1997.

Completion in 1999 of the Stark County Trail and Greenway Plan, utilizing the Towpath Trail as the central spine.

Designation by President Clinton in 2000 of the CanalWay Ohio Scenic Byway as a National Scenic Byway. This 110-mile vehicular route parallels the canal from Cleveland to New Philadelphia.

Publication in 2001 of *Towpath Companion: The Traveler's Guide to the Ohio & Erie Canal Towpath Trail.* The book provides detailed information about trailheads, parking, food and lodging locations adjacent to the trail. The first printing, 5,000 copies, sold out in 2002 and another 5,000 copies were printed.

Completion in 2001 of the Summit County Trail & Greenway Plan. Utilizing the Towpath Trail as the spine, more than 500 miles of proposed trail and greenway connections were identified.

Opening in 2001 of the renovated canal-era Mustill Store on the banks of the canal in downtown Akron.

Many of these accomplishments are directly related to the efforts of Simpson and Regula, Rice said, adding, "More important than any of the physical accomplishments is that we now have a generation of citizens who are committed to preserving, interpreting and celebrating the legacy of the Ohio & Erie Canal. Through their involvement... local community partnerships and individuals are practicing the ethic of resource conservation."

This, Rice concluded, is an important enduring legacy of Simpson and Regula, whose collective vision and passion continue today in the hundreds and thousands of community volunteers.

"I'm amazed and delighted with what's going on today," Simpson said in the fall of 2002 during a visit to Northeast Ohio that included a tour of the corridor and a hike on the towpath with Regula. "This is like just seeing a dream becoming a reality because if you read through my columns you'll see where I suggested just what's happening today... He (Regula) visualized a hikeway, a trail from Cleveland to Portsmouth. I went further. I said why don't we push to see if we can have the whole thing restored and have a strip park all the way through? That's what's happening."

Al Simpson (on the right) posed recently for this photograph with Ralph Regula (with hiking staff in hand).
Al Simpson

This on-deck photograph, taken on June 17, 1970, documented the "first ride" on St. Helena II.

Canal Society of Ohio

Index

224

Tuscarawas County Boy Scout Troop 84-209

Tuscarawas County Boy Scout Troop 90-209

Tuscarawas County Boy Scout Troop 92-209

Tuscarawas County Boy Scout Troop 94-209

Tuscarawas County Boy Scout Troop 99-209

Tuscarawas County Canal Lands Advisory Committee 209

Tuscarawas County Chamber of Commerce 19, 21

Tuscarawas County Commissioners 20, 21, 73, 74, 87, 89

Tuscarawas County Historical Association 176, 185, 196

Tuscarawas County Road 102 20

Tuscarawas, Ohio 73, 85, 148

Tuscarawas Indian Trail 120

Tuscarawas River 2, 3, 4, 6, 8, 14, 15, 19, 20, 22, 27, 34, 37, 41, 43, 46, 51, 53, 58, 82, 86, 105, 131, 138, 140, 142, 143, 151, 156, 173, 183, 189, 190, 191, 192, 198, 206, 208, 209, 210

Tuscarawas-Walhonding Valley and Ohio Railroad 160

Tuscora Stamp Club 58

Two Brothers (canal boat) 68

Tyler, President John 92

Udall, Stewart 43, 44, 48, 49, 105, 111, 199

Uhrichsville, Ohio 125, 126, 149

Uhrichsville Chronicle 125, 175

Ulrich, Albert 125

Union Army 80th Ohio Volunteer Infantry 160

Unity School of Christianity 62

University of Akron, The v, 109, 165

University of California 80

"Up Through a Century" 111

Upper Canada Village 45

Urwin, Emmett E. 54

U.S. Bureau of Recreation 88

U.S. Department of Agriculture 99

U.S. Department of Housing and Urban Development 110

U.S. Department of the Interior 89, 94, 110

U.S. Highway 52- 25

U.S. Route 30- 8

U.S. Soil Conservation Service 56

U.S. Steel Building 181

Vail, Lewis 135

Vail, Robert, Jr. 1, 31

Vail Nurseries 28

Valley, Harry 46

Valley Belle (boat) 142

Valley of the Tiger (China) 80

Valley View, Ohio 195

"Valley Views" 189

Van Amburgh Circus 92

Van Dyke, Dr. John M. 68, 108

Vanik, Charles A. 94, 95

Vietnam War 13

Vodrey, William H. 135

Vogelman, Richard 193

Wabash and Erie Canal 83

Wahl, David 207

Walhonding Canal 105, 159, 160

Walker, John W. 110-111

Wallin, Dick 89

Wang (Chinese botanist) 80

Warehous 205

Warren, Ohio 88

Warwick Estate 147

Washington, D.C. 4, 5, 43, 86, 94, 177

Washington, George 22, 92, 118

Washington County 198

Washington Post 43

water pollution 43, 44, 51, 53, 86, 124, 172, 191, 196

Watson, Howard N. 16

Watson Lake 76,

Watts, Connie N. 99

WAUP Radio 110, 165

Wayne County, Ohio 12, 110, 114, 115

Waynesburg, Ohio 37, 38, 146

Waynesburg Lions Club 145

Waynesburg Parent-Teacher Association 145

Waynesburg Rotary Club 145

Waynesburg Village Council 145

Weaver, C.R. 168

Weber, Harry S. 85

Weidner interurban 98

Weigand, Richard 190

Weis, J. Harvey 161

Welcome Waterway 192

Welland Canal 96, 120

Wells, Lester J. 70

West LaFayette, Ohio 46

Western Electric 92

Western Reserve Historical Society 119

Westgerdes, Mark 179

Westinghouse Company 92

White, Dr. Paul Dudley 91

233

234